# *365 Days*
# *of Self Love*

### *Daily Exercises from*
### *Experts Around the World*

**Foreword by Sunny Dawn Johnston**
**Compiled by Kim Richardson**

# Dedication

This book is dedicated to you, the reader. We want you to know we see your commitment to yourself and honor you wherever you are in your journey to fully loving yourself. As we heal and learn to love ourselves, we start to heal the world. Always love yourself first!

# Table of Contents

## FEBRUARY

# APRIL

## MAY

## AUGUST

## SEPTEMBER

## NOVEMBER

## DECEMBER

# Foreword

When Kim Richardson, a longtime friend and colleague, asked me to write the foreward for this book, I agreed immediately. Self-Love has been one of the greatest journeys of my life. One of the hardest and one of the most rewarding. Over the years, my self-love and lack thereof has affected multiple areas of my life ... anything from relationships, self-esteem, finances, spiritual connection, success and most importantly ... my ability to BE with me.

When I was in a loving place with myself, I found myself in healthier relationships, kinder and gentler with myself and others, increased abundance in finances, connection with Spirit through my intuition and spiritual guidance, a sense of success regardless of the external measurements or evidence, and an absolute peace within me just being me.

On the other hand, when I was in the lack, I found the exact opposite. My relationships were unhealthy and without boundaries; I was critical, judgmental, and berating of myself and others; I experienced a lack of money; I felt not good enough in most areas; I was disconnected from Spirit and my natural guidance system and no matter what I did I couldn't stand the silence within me. It was deafening.

Maybe you have felt some of these feelings ... or all of them. Maybe you are dealing with them right now and aren't sure where to turn or what to do to feel better and shift the energy. Well, my friend, you have landed in the right place, with the right book in your hands. This is your sign that you are EXACTLY where you need to be … and I know you have been looking for a sign.

The women that have shared their journeys in this book have been where you are … and came out the other side. Through the stories you will see yourself, identify with the limiting beliefs that have held you back … and most importantly … know the next steps to take to be one step closer to LOVING YOU, completely. *365 Days of Self Love* is an everyday experience. It isn't just when you feel like it. It is an absolute commitment and intention, each and every day. Literally 24/7/365.

You will get to a place of realizing that it isn't enough to just "try" to focus on self-love. It is a MUST! With this new book you have the inspiration, the tools, and the reminder to do the work consistently. Your relationships, self-esteem, finances, spiritual connection, success, and peace are waiting for you to love and embrace yourself.

You, my friend, deserve to experience the LOVE in every moment of every day. I cannot tell you how much your life will change, for the good, when you can love yourself through it all … the good, the not-so-good and the blah in the middle that we all experience at times in life. Your future self will thank you for this investment now.

With Love, Light and Joy for your Self-Love Journey,

*Sunny Dawn Johnston*

Sunny Dawn Johnston is an acclaimed transformational thought leader, changemaker and psychic medium. She is the author of twenty books, including her flagship bestsellers, *Invoking the Archangels* and *The Love Never Ends*, which have become the cornerstones for many of her keynote topics such as intuition, mediumship, and the angelic realm.

Through her courses, private sessions, and live events, Sunny has grown and cultivated a diverse global community. Whether in-person or online, her strong mentorship encourages thousands of students to connect with their heart and the core of their being and guides them to experience life in a newer, more positive light.

Sunny resides in Glendale, Arizona with her loving family and a strong network of friends. A firm believer in work-life balance, she focuses on family, service, hard work, and friendship to encourage harmony in all areas of life.

**Connect with Sunny** at sunnydawnjohnston.com

# Introduction

## Why a book about self-love?

*I*n my personal journey, I have discovered that when a problem in my life arises or things just do not seem right, the answer is always to love yourself more. When I dug deep into the issues I was having and walk the steps backward, I found that I was not loving myself in every capacity. Whether it is setting boundaries, learning how to say no and not feel guilty about it, learning that is it necessary to fill your cup before you fill everyone else's, or just simply learning to be my own best friend. As I worked on healing those areas in my life, practicing self-love became the most important and focused part of my life. As time went on, I continued a daily practice of loving myself everything around me started to change. My relationships were better, everything functioned better, and ultimately, I was much happier and so were the people around me.

There was a time that the negative self-chatter ruled my life, that the societal beliefs were so ingrain in my head that it became debilitating, and I did not recognize it. I was my own worst critic saying things like, *you are so fat, and you are not good enough.* I was slowly killing myself trying to keep up with what I thought the world wanted me to be.

The crazy thing was, I did not even realize how much I was not loving myself. You see, I saw myself as a pretty confidant, go-getter kind of woman. It took a huge tragedy that led me to Sunny Dawn Johnston who walked the healing journey with me, I could not have thought of anyone better to write the foreword for this book and I am honored she said yes! The journey, although it was not an easy one, helped me see the many ways I was not loving myself. I had learned to put on many layers of masks to get through every day and became the best actress there ever was. When I had my awakening so to speak, I was sharing everything I was discovering with my best friend of twenty years and she said to me, "You are the most beautiful and confident person I know, I had no idea you were feeling this way." Even she did not know the *real and vulnerable me*.

The day I started taking those layers of masks off, one by one, it was liberating. I could be one person, my true self and it no longer mattered what anyone thought of me. I felt safe because I had become everything that I needed that I did not have in my life. I became the protector of the little girl inside that had been hurt so badly. No one was going to hurt her again. She was never going to be subjected to anything that made her feel unsafe or uncomfortable.

My mission in life has become to change the world. Changing the world can seem like a big task, however if we heal ourselves and share with one person something we have learned, it gives them permission and the courage to do the same. That is how we change the world, one person at a time and it starts with us.

Practicing self-love is more than self-care like taking a bath or getting a massage. Self-love is digging deeper on an emotional level. We are always learning and growing and leveling up in the game of loving yourself. Although I have come so far, I know there is so much more to learn and grow, and consistency is the key.

I am overjoyed you picked up our beautiful book! This means you are ready to put yourself first and create a daily practice of self-love. This book is filled with easy, practical exercises to help you get centered in self-love. It is meant to be used daily because as I said earlier, consistency is the key. The more you practice it, it will just start to become part of you. You can either chose today's date and do that exercise or you can randomly flip though and whatever page you land on, know that is the perfect exercise for you that day. No matter how you use the book, there is no wrong or right way. Do what feels right to you! The important thing is, you are on a journey of discovery my friend, now sit back and revel in the changes you are about to see within and around yourself.

Much love to you my friend, I am excited for your discoveries ahead!

Love,

*Kim Richardson*

**Kim Richardson** is a Mind, Body, Spirit Practitioner, author, publisher, and graphic designer. Kim has a real love and passion for helping small business owners accomplish their dreams. Through sharing her own personal experiences, she empowers individuals to transform their ideas into reality.

Author of the best-selling book, *High Vibe Eating, a Cookbook for your Mind, Body, and Spirit.*

Publisher and co-author of the *52 Weeks of Gratitude Journal, Kindness Crusader, and 365 Days of Self Love.*

Coauthor of *Living Your Purpose, 365 Days of Angel Prayers, Spiritual Leaders' Top Picks.*

Be sure to visit Kim's website to claim your free gift and connect with her on Facebook.

**Connect with Kim:**
Website: KimRichardson.Kim
Facebook: kimrichardson444

# Meet Charlie

**Charlie Fenimore** is our resident Earth Angel. He spreads love and joy every where he goes. We could not have a book about self-love without including his wisdom sprinkled throughout the book. I hope you feel the loving energy in his messages.

Charlie is a messenger of the spirit who was born with Down syndrome. Since his teens, he has received inspiring messages from the angelic realm. Author of *Happy in Soul—A Very Special Prayer for Peace*, Charlie is a public speaker, a love ambassador with The Love Foundation and an honorary peace minister through the Beloved Community. Charlie and his mother Jannirose share the mission of carrying his hopeful messages to a world that hungers for healing. They reside near Weed, California, close to majestic Mount Shasta.

*"The spirit of love makes anyone of the clouds shine with joy. We can live in smileness today and every day with our brightful loving hearts. Remember, life is wonderful and beautiful and good!"*

**By Charlie Fenimore**

# January 1

## I Am
### By Florence Acosta

*T*hese are two of the most powerful words in any language because the words we say after them shape our lives. The power of *I Am* is constantly at work. If you look in the mirror, *I am fat.* If you don't succeed, *I am a failure.* If you make a mistake, I am stupid. If you lose something, *I am unlucky.* If you are outspoken, *I am too much.* If you compare yourself to others, *I am not enough.* If you deprive yourself of something, I am not worthy.

Many times, we use the power of *I am* against us. We do not realize how it is affecting our future. Words have creative power. With your words, you can create your future for better or worse. The words said after *I am* define who you think you are and what you experience in life. If your self-talk includes negativity, you will be given situations in your life to continuously reinforce those thoughts time after time. Like attracts like. It is important to practice mindfulness, whenever you say the words *I am.* Follow them with positive words describing what you are or what you aspire to be. Your words and your thoughts are the energy you put into the Universe to invite things into your life.

It is up to you to choose what follows *I am.* Don't be against yourself, be on your side. Remember, what follows the words *I am* is on its way to you. I invite you to focus on the positive things in your life and watch your dreams unfold. *I am abundant. I am beautiful. I am brave. I am confident. I am courageous. I am creative. I am enough. I am joyful. I am peaceful. I am worthy. I am loved. I am love. I am grateful for the things that the Universe is planning for me that I do not know about yet.* I invite you to declare your *I am* affirmations daily in a mirror to change the vibration of your life.

# January 2

## Are You a Procrastinator?
## By Debra Moore Ewing

There. I asked. In my mind, I always labeled it as an ineffective behavior pattern. That is until the day my spiritual mentor, Sunny Dawn Johnston, said it is about self-love.

What? Seriously?

I thought a lot about this as it has been a lifelong habit. I remember needing a present for a party I had known about for two weeks. However, I waited until that afternoon, ran to the store to purchase a gift, and wrapped it on the hood of my car before driving to the party! Have you ever done that?

Procrastination creates unnecessary stress in our lives and it is the killer of our hopes and dreams. Whether it is a new diet or exercise regimen we are thinking of starting, going for that goal we always dreamed of, starting a new business venture, or writing that book, why do we sabotage ourselves? What is the fear? I encourage you to go within and find the answer. It is time to get out of your way. It is time to love yourself enough. You *are* enough of a reason to live your happiest and best life! We only have this one life. Time passes quickly. In the blink of an eye, you will find yourself another ten years down the road, so I encourage you to make that list of your dreams and desires. Make an action plan, start checking the actions off and see how it feels deep inside to love … yourself … that … much. If fear is holding you back, fear is nothing more than false events appearing real. The only real fear is not taking action! If you break it down to the *facts* and get the story you have created in your mind out of the way you may end up laughing at yourself! Eliminate the story, focus on the goal, and the path to get there. You *are* worth it! Besides, what have you got to lose?

I believe in living life with no regrets. Procrastination is something I have mastered. In 1987 I took a leave of absence from my job to start writing a book. Thirty-three years later it is not finished. That is why I joined this project. To eliminate my fear, love myself enough, and get out of my way. What do you think? Will you join me?

# January 3

## Your True Colors
## By Ewa Blaszczak

Everybody is unique. And yet there are only four types of operating systems which are hard-wired in our brains. These determine our talents, needs, motivations, predispositions, and habits. We use four colors to distinguish these systems. When we get to know our true color, we can better understand ourselves and thrive.

1. Red is the operating system of a warrior. In the world of warriors, victory counts, as well as everything that is related to victory: goals, rivalry, and strategy. The fuel which provide the reds with energy to thrive include challenges, power, and freedom. Reds! Always have your goals in front of you. You are natural leaders, courageous and determined. But also bring your loving attention to your shadow, which is the tendency to control others, being abrupt, and pushing others too hard.

2. Yellow are inspirers and masters of social skills. Intuition, creativity, and optimism are their talents. Attention is the fuel for the yellows. They bloom when they are seen, when they stand out from the crowd. Remember to create yourself space for self-expression and creativity. Surround yourself with people and shine your light! Be also lovingly mindful of your shadow, which is a chaotic nature, egocentrism or over-promising.

3. Green is the energy of harmony and peace. A typical green is sensitive, obliging, empathetic, and cautious. Security is the rudiment for the happiness of greens. It may come from

a feeling of being needed. It may take form of a thorough planning, preparing contingency plans, or using the baby steps method to achieve goals. Greens! Create yourself a safe space to live. Love your delicate and sensitive nature. Beware of falling into a victim mode. Do not deprecate yourself and mind your tendency to resist changes.

4. Blue are the analyzers and experts. Knowledge, expertise is what matters most for the blues. If have are blue, you may have difficulty loving yourself due to tendency to perfectionism. Don't set your bar so high. You are inquisitive, composed, and a great mentor. Risk management and systemic thinking are your things. In order to thrive, invest in your self-mastery. Choose environments where your expertise is acknowledged and respected.

1. Which of the four colors or operating systems feels like home?

2. Are you providing your operating system with the right fuel to thrive?

3. What is it about your dominant color that you love the most?

# January 4

## Today Do Only the Things That Bring You Joy
## By Bernadette Rodebaugh

During the year 2020, I discovered I had an autoimmune disease. So, while the whole world was worried about COVID-19, I could not afford to be worried about anything because I knew it has been proven scientifically that stress affects one's immune system and mine was already under attack.

I dropped everything and anything that brought me stress. I no longer listened to the news or allowed family members to talk about the virus. I also pulled back from any friends or family that made me feel more tired when I was with them, or after they left, than I was without them. With no guilt or explanation, I canceled all meetings that didn't bring me joy. Maybe they thought I was flaky, but I didn't care because I knew my body was telling me that I needed this time to heal and I should reserve my energy.

These little items gave me extra time to meditate and take walks and do the things that brought me joy to aid in the healing of my body, which ultimately guided me to hear my body and soul telling me what else it needed so that it could heal.

This motto of only doing things I enjoyed every day worked. I am now healed! Since then, I am still selective of who I spend my time with and what items I spend my energy on.

I've realized that my body was talking to me long before the illness appeared. It was telling me whenever I would become easily tired or stressed that those things were not for me and I shouldn't waste one precious moment or day doing things that don't feel good doing because life is short.

Now it's your turn look at your list of things to do for this week.

- Are there any places that you don't look forward to going to?
- Are there any people you're meeting with that make you feel tired?
- Can you delegate anything in your to-do list? For example can you have your groceries delivered or order food in, so you don't have to cook?
- Can you gracefully decline any offers of things to do this week that don't bring you joy or are unimportant to you?
- *Now choose one thing to do this week just for you and your joy!*

# January 5

## I Am Enough
## By Gloria Dawn Kapeller

This statement has taken me my whole life to actually feel it. Being abused from when I was six years old to nineteen years old when I escaped. Yes. I feel I escaped as then I had the nerve to stand up for myself and say no because I no longer lived in the same town as my perpetrators. Standing up for the six-year-old me, took over fifty years, but I faced my abusers in court and even though they were not convicted, I felt that I had my say and stood up for me.

It took a lot of healing work to finally say that I am enough. I was always worried what people would think of me and I have had a hard time saying no. I'm a real people pleaser and doer. This is getting better as I get more mature and know that I only have to please myself and learning to know my limits and limitations. My family is still my priority, but I know that I can only do so much.

I like to think about how we feel when we are enough. Start by writing down three affirmations a day that can help to show you that you are enough.

How do we feel when we are enough? How did the abuse define me as a person? It made me a much stronger person who could deal with the life lessons that as a soul I came here to learn. The abuser tries to keep you feeling small and that you will never amount to anything. The more people share what has happened to them and share their stories, it would make the incidences less. Abuse needs to be brought into the light out of the darkness.

I have begun to share my story in hopes that if it helps even one person share their story and speak about what happened to them or if it helps one child not go through what I did and that it's okay to tell, then I will have made a difference.

Asking the right questions and making someone feel safe is our ultimate responsibility.

# January 6

## Love Is Abundant
## By Courtney Parreira

The frequency of love is abundant if we soften ourselves enough to take notice.

The majestic Spanish sage basking in the sunshine softens to allow the honey bees to drink its nectar. This is love.

The hummingbird, creating stillness from movement, hovers, knowing of the respite and security offered by the branches of the apple tree. This is love.

A child cuddles with his mother in the vulnerable shadows of dawn. This is love.

Soften through breath; soften into love.

Take three cleansing breaths through the heart. One breath is for your spiritual self. One is for your soul self, and one is for your earth self. Set your intention for opening up to love.

*I open myself up to the vibration of love around me.*

Repeat this intention, whether out loud or to yourself, until you feel the vibration of love within and around you.

Now, switch your focus to your surroundings. Where can you find love occurring naturally? Does it hover near you, just as the hummingbird hovers near the branch of the apple tree? Take notice of the love around you. In honor of it, softly smile and acknowledge its presence. This action further activates the vibration of love within you and around you. Complete this activity when there's a pause in your day. Doing so will exponentially increase the amount of love you experience for self, others, and our world.

# January 7

## Free your Needs and Fears
### By Judith Manganiello

*T*he more you need something to change, the more you fear that it will stay the same. When you hold onto your needs and fears, you wind up creating more of them. Releasing the fears and control is the way you can learn the lesson of what you are holding onto that keeps you from self-love. For example, if you feel that you are not *worthy* or *good enough* for love, you will not be able to receive it, whether it is self-love or love from others. You might say, *I want to be loved,* but remember you must feel worthy and deserving of love.

Be aware of the messages that you are sending out. These create vicious cycles that only you are the one that can fix, clear, transform, and release all your beliefs. It is time to release those fears!

What are your needs and fears? Create a list. Then take one at a time and gift or pray it away. Fill the empty space you just released with Divine Radiant Love and Light trust that you have released it! Get into your happiness and no longer look for the fear.

If a feeling or thought pops into your head or heart, gift it away until you get into your happiness again. It should get less intense in its energy each time you release it. Sometimes the first time is enough… It will depend on your trust.

### Releasing Fears or Needs Prayer

*Consciously, I am aware that I have this fear of _____ or this need of _____, and through the gift of my free will, Spirit, which you gave me, I am gifting this over to You.*

*If You want to show me where in my cellular self this is being held, or where it came from, show me in my dreams tonight and give me the wisdom to heal it. From all past, present, future and from the beginning of my existence. Then fill the empty space you just released with Radiant Love and Light.*

*Then trust that you released it.*

# *January 8*

## Perfectly Imperfect
## By Carrie Newsom

So much of our lives is spent making categories. This part of me is good; this part is bad. I am good at taking care of my children, but I eat too many cookies and that is bad. What if we stop categorizing ourselves? What if we eliminate the labels of good and bad? What if every piece of ourselves just *is*? And what if that is okay?

We spend our whole lives putting things in categories. That is just how our brains work. Everything is assigned a negative or positive status. "My eyes are pretty, but my thighs are too chubby." "When I eat broccoli I am being good, when I eat cake I am being bad." Part of being a whole, integrated, happy person is to start unraveling those categories. Of course, healthy eating should involve lots of vegetables and fewer sweets, but broccoli or cake is neither good nor bad. Nothing about my body is either good or bad; it just is. We assign arbitrary value to everything. With those nonsense values can come great self-loathing, shame, sadness.

I have found there is less self-hatred, less self-blame, less disappointment when I remember that everything just is. As humans, we make sense out of our places in the world by assigning values like good and bad, healthy and fattening, pretty and ugly to our bodies, our world. If we take a step back and look at our bodies and lives with a more neutral eye, we dare our hearts to be gentler with our opinions.

When I challenge myself to think in a more matter-of-fact way about things, I do not beat myself up for decisions or my appearance or qualities that I have. Changing my perception of good and bad to a neutral "everything just is" stance has helped me learn to love myself, and my life, more.

Let's focus less on whether things are good or bad, and pay more attention to the fact that everything just *is*. We are perfectly imperfect, made just the way we are supposed to be. And that is very good.

# January 9

## Self-Love from Quantum Energy
## By Charel Morris

*I* love taking my clients into the quantum field. It is a magical way to work! I am introducing quantum energy to deepen your self-love practice. To do this I am bringing the quantum energy to you.

My initial contact with quantum field was in meditation. I was calmly meditating on my purpose in this life. Suddenly, I was sitting on the edge of the universe, hearing a voice telling me that I am here because by living I create energy and my energy expands the universe. And that goes for all living beings.

Now, I do not present this as a scientific discovery, but in my heart, I realized that my being here is sacred. We all provide this sacred energy to create our universe. We are from the source creator, so we are creators. We are one.

Get comfortable. Close your eyes. Take a deep breath. Inhale for a count of six, then exhale for a count of six. Continue this throughout your work.

Let your imagination and your awareness expand around you. Continue breathing and allow it to flow into and out of your heart. Allow yourself to imagine, sense or feel your breath flowing in and out of your heart, moving your love and energy through your heart with each breath.

Notice above you, from the far side of the universe, brilliant, liquid, white light flowing down towards you. Coming closer, it becomes even more radiant, more beautiful, and you are entranced by its presence. As it enters Earth's atmosphere, you know it is for you. It sparkles even more as it comes closer.

It begins to gently wrap around you. You realize your heart energy is blending with this sparkling, liquid, white light energy. You are sensing warmth, love, care, and joy as this quantum energy connects with you. Allow this sacred magical energy to move in, through, and all around you. Welcome in this powerful sacred love that you feel deeply within your heart, your core and your spirit. Be with this for as long as you like. Knowing that this energy – is a sacred experience of self-love coming to you from the pure source.

# January 10

## Celebrating You
## By Grace Redman

*H*ey Hey, Beautiful Soul!

Today I would like to invite you to celebrate you and give yourself a gift! I know you have been working very hard! You have done an incredible job managing it all! It hasn't been easy and there have been times you wanted to throw in the towel and you didn't! You've got up dusted yourself off and kept going. You are a bad ass!

Whether you are juggling a busy work schedule; managing work and family; managing your own workload and the workload of others because the team is shorthanded; if you have been focused, head down in your business, making that forced pivot; or making an effort to keep everything afloat in your home and personal life, you deserve to be applauded!

I know *you are doing so much*! And you have made it in one piece to this new day! *You've got this! We've got this!*

We can be our own worst critic and beat ourselves up for what we believe we should be doing …. Blah. Blah. Blah! You probably know what I am talking about.

I want to tell you that you are *fricking amazing*! Take some time for you today. Give yourself a gift. The gift can be whatever you enjoy and brings you joy. The gift can be a warm salt bath, a play date with your dog, a fun purchase, or dancing naked in your bedroom mirror. It can be whatever your heart desires!

You have been doing, doing, doing, for others and today have some compassion for yourself and do for you!

Yes, that may sound easier said than done and you may not think that now is the right time, but there is no better time than now to take care of you and celebrate all that you have been doing! You are doing your best and I really want to acknowledge that!

You are a role model to all those around you. Today when you celebrate you and gift yourself some tender, loving care, you are setting the example of how taking time for you is an act of self-love.

# January 11

## Your Heart's Core Values: True Reflections of Self-Love
## By Lisa A. Clayton

One of the best ways to activate a higher dimensional frequency of self-love is to know your heart's core values.

Your heart's core values are powerful. They are the embodiment of the heart's intelligence and operating principles that give meaning to life, revive spirit, and create a sense of wellbeing. As we connect with our heart's core values and our actions reflect them, the better life seems to work and flow.

Your heart comes alive when you are aware of your core values and activate them daily. Every time you activate or reflect on a core value in your heart, you are feeding your heart love nutrition and powerful energy.

How do you know your core values? Imagine a spaceship comes to take you away from earth and only leaves your heart as your legacy. What would you want to be "heart-known" for and what would others say of how you lived from your heart which left an imprint on earth?

Take a piece of paper and draw a large heart on it. Inside the heart list your core values. A few examples of my heart core values include love, leadership, truth, essence-connections, compassion and kindness. List at least twelve core values to get started.

Make several copies of your heart and post in places that are visible to you throughout the day…on your bathroom mirror, your refrigerator, your computer screen, dashboard of your car, and include carrying them in your wallet.

Each time you look at your heart's core values and feel appreciation and gratitude, you generate an energy of self-love and powerful feelings of self-worth. Inspirational ideas and creativity that are aligned with your heart's core values flow effortlessly and open doors to new opportunities. Your heart becomes a close friend and guide, tapping into its intuitive intelligence for helping you make wise life choices with trust and confidence.

Knowing your heart's core values and looking at them each day is a simple yet powerful exercise to uplift your heart to a higher consciousness frequency which emulates strong love vibrations to yourself and others. By reflecting with and reviewing your heart values daily, self-love amplifies and expands naturally with ease.

# January 12

## Forgiveness
## By Carolan Dickinson

*W*hen I was beginning my spiritual journey, I found myself unable to move forward at times when I was trying to heal from the past. I discovered that there were places in my soul where healing could not take place because I had not been able to forgive a person or a situation. Most importantly, I found that I had the most trouble trying to forgive myself. One of my very first spiritual teachers, Reverend LaVeta Dilman of Palm Springs, California, taught me this simple and easy forgiveness exercise.

This exercise works great for forgiving anything, including yourself. You can work with any of the archangels at any time, but since we are releasing something when we forgive, I like to work with Archangel Michael. Surround yourself with his energy and say, "Please surround me and be with me, creating sacred space."

Sometimes it is not always easy, or even a good idea, to ask someone for or give forgiveness directly because of the nature of some wounds. This is one of the beauties of this exercise. You don't need to be in their presence, nor do they even need to be physically in the world. You aren't absolving anyone of bad behavior. However, you are changing the energy of that situation to one that can be healed and released. For sure, you will feel lighter and have a spirit of ease as it changes and transforms.

Envision the person, place, or thing and say, "******, from my heart to yours, I forgive you for anything real or perceived you may or may not have done to hurt me from this lifetime or any other."

Repeat this three times.

Then reverse it. "******, from my heart to yours, I ask your forgiveness for anything real or perceived that I may or may not have done to hurt you from this lifetime or any other."

Repeat this three times.

# January 13

## The Masks
## By Kim Richardson

Do you sometimes feel like an actress? Do you have a different personality to suit your situation? You see, for numerous years, I wore many masks; the mother, the teacher, the wife, the coach, the friend, sister … the list goes on and on. In each situation I became who I thought everyone else needed me to be. In doing so, I lost a sense of who I really was. I became the best actress in the world. Not many people knew the *real* me, shoot, I did not even know the real me anymore. Life had taken over, and I was not a priority.

I encourage you to take an inventory of the masks you don. Pull out a journal and make a list of them all. As you list them, think about:

- Who you are when you wear them? Do you like this person you are? Are you being your true authentic self?

- Why do you wear them? Are you looking for their approval in order to be happy? Are you putting on the mask as a way of protection from something? Is there some feeling of fear deep inside?

- What would happen if you took the masks off? Will you lose people in your life? Will you feel vulnerable? Will people not like you anymore? Will you be seen?

As you answer these questions with many more possibly coming up for you, as you journal you can start to peel off the masks one by one. It may have taken you several years to add all the layers of the masks, be patient with yourself as you remove them. You will find there may be some healing to do as you remove each one. Take the time to walk through the healing, experience it, thank it for the lesson it provided, and release it. Then … move onto the next mask.

Once you remove all the masks, get to know yourself, who you are meant to be, and what you want most out of this life. Then, start being your authentic self. The more you practice this and resist putting the mask back on, the easier it becomes. Soon you will not worry about what other people think, and you might even be surprised at how many love *you*, your authentic self even more.

# January 14

## The Very Best Homecoming
## By Jannirose Fenimore

*I* am grateful to share life with a master in the art of living love. Every day, my son Charlie—who is blessed with Down syndrome—shows me how it looks to live fully from the heart. Through the depth of loving kindness he so naturally embodies, I receive poignant lessons in what it means to love myself.

One of the most stunning qualities Charlie possesses is pure, laser-focused presence. Whenever I find myself in the midst of a difficult time, my earth angel is there to love me through it. He has a special way of seeing deeply into my heart and soul as he graces me with his undivided attention. Through his innate compassion and kindness, he assures me I am not alone.

The teachings that are woven so beautifully into Charlie's loving gestures are always breathtaking to behold. I can still remember the pre-Charlie years when self-reflection was far from my awareness. I recall being hesitant to look inward because I was afraid of what I might find. My special boy models the healing value that loving presence brings to those unexplored regions of my sacred self. His natural ability to meet me where I am carries a powerful lesson.

Never one to judge, Charlie has the rare ability to simply witness my process when I need support, and he does so even when tears or anger start to flow. He will sit in blessed silence to honor me as I journey through the sometimes-messy territory of my tender heart. Thanks to my unassuming mentor —whom I suspect is Heaven sent—I have begun showing up for myself.

Perhaps you learned long ago to prioritize the needs of other people and have forgotten to include yourself on the list. My heartfelt prayer is that you might find the courage to turn inward and discover your deepest truths that long to be heard—your hopes, your dreams, your joys and your sorrows.

Just as you attend so mindfully to others, be sure to tune into the small voice within that deserves your loving attention. Throughout each day, drop into the silence of your heart with full presence, and listen without judgment.

The very best kind of homecoming occurs when we return to the miracle of our creation. May we remember to celebrate this priceless gift throughout the days of our lives.

# January 15

## Holy Healing Heartness
## By Charlie Fenimore

*We have a good life to live in light, bringing brightness to our eyes. Angels come to our path and love us so much. Peace will be our world with joyful stars of hopeful. Living joyness about our bright of hearts is the holiness of healing every day.*

# January 16

## Between Heaven And Earth
## By Bonnie Larson

*H*ave you straddled the fence or felt conflicted between religion and spirituality? As a minister I have. Following years of study, my understandings and convictions deepen in my heart, yet somehow I realize one without the other seems incomplete.

Zealous critics, perhaps well intended, only deepen the chasm. With judging, squinting eyes, they utter, "Oh, I see, you're a *social Christian!*"

Could that imply we attend church for social benefit and accolades? It certainly *feels* like criticism. Of course, we know religion is far more than an armchair event. It is a participatory invitation, after all. And yes, there are joyful, social elements.

Lynn Sparrow Christy takes it a step further, "I've heard it said that religion is for those who are afraid to go to hell and spirituality is for those who've been there. Well, *evolutionary spirituality* is for people who've been to both hell and heaven and now know that we have a choice as to which decides the destiny of our world." [1]

Without question, as the Earth hurls 67,000 m.p.h. through space and time, we are in unprecedented territory. The story of humanity unfolds before our very eyes. The good news is, we are privileged to participate—all of us—every day! Is it possible our collective is to evolve from the earthly material human consciousness toward divine cosmic proportion?

Consciously co-creating is the key. During a morning prayerful meditation, I quiet my mind, meeting my creator at my heart center. Feeling deep appreciation, I express heartfelt gratitude, then ask that I may be an expression of our creator. *Make me an instrument of your love, your peace.*

Amazingly, there are no *others*. We are all on the same team, pushing and digging in or fully embracing this transformational opportunity. As Lynn so eloquently describes, "Life continues to evolve toward ever-greater diversity and complexity; and at human consciousness, which continues to grow to ever more expansive reaches and sees an underlying unity of purpose." [2]

Together, we stand at the very precipice of a great awakening! Continually building upon the foundation of wisdom and a greater understanding of the cosmic mysteries is key to my daily self-love.

# January 17

## Disengage from Social Media
## By Giuliana Melo

One big thing I had to learn was to disengage from pages and people that drained my energy. As the world has changed and shifted from in-person meetings to online, more of us are spending more time in social media. This is a blessing and a curse.

As sensitive beings, we absorb so much energy from this medium. It is really imperative to be mindful of where you are putting your energy and what you are consuming. Politics and news are hot topics, and most humans are reactors and tend to be way more vocal hiding behind the keyboard than they would be if in person.

A big part of loving yourself is recognizing where you are putting your energy and only surrounding yourself with positive and uplifting content and creators.

Today, take note of how you feel as you scroll your page. Does it distract you from real life and the people around you? Do you have your phone at the table when you are eating with your family? Today, just be the witness as you become more present to your habits.

Technology is indeed a blessing and we are meant to create a real life and social life balance.

Here's a journal question. Am I spending too much time on social media and not with my family? How is technology affecting my life?

# January 18

## Hobbies
### By Ashlie Bradley

*Y*es! Please! Give yourself this treat. By hobbies, I mean anything that takes you out of the mundane and into presence and/or a creative space. It is such a wonderful, accessible way to be in touch with our inner child, with source energy, and with the now. It's a space to take us out of the masculine, to-do, left-brain, and into our feminine, creative, right-brain. It's a place to be fluid and flow verses being rigid and structured. It's a state of being to pause rather then go, go, go.

I mean look at children and see how inspired they are by their creations. Whether it's sand castles, a Lego towers, or Play-Dough people, they are all in. In these little hobbies of theirs, they become so creative and so present. Innocence and joy is in their sweet expressions. Well, guess what? We are them. All of that creative juice is still within us, too. It's just bottled up waiting to be released! Lost in the day to day of adulting, we've abandoned this sacred part of ourselves.

What lights you up? What makes you feel something? Do you still have dreams? What ignites that pulse of joy you yearn for? Maybe cooking colorful meals. Maybe planting or arranging flowers. Maybe sewing or making fun jewelry. It could be that it has been so long you don't know anymore.

Feel into what attracts you. What gives you even just a nudge of inspiration? Follow that. It could even be the boat next door. Why do you admire it? Is it the thought of being on the water? Maybe you start a hobby in fishing or shell collecting. This is just an example of how you can dig deeper to find a soul spark. With constant spark tending, a wild fire of inspiration and creativity will rise. This is where our hobbies are born. We must cultivate this part of us to live a well-balanced life.

I encourage you to carve out some time today and start feeling into what lights you up. Put your hand on your heart and feel into that space. Breathe, connect to yourself, and let your soul speak.

# January 19

## Get Your Very Own Drum
## By Margaret-Maggie Honnold

*G*ood morning to a new day where you can choose to be happy or not. To love or not. To walk forward with grace and joy or not.

Boy, that choice is such a lesson to learn. It took me years.

I am a seventy-two-year-old widow, who lectured about choices to my children and grandchildren, clients, patients, and friends while I ignored that advice for myself. I marched to the drummers of others and did not listen to my special drum beat or pick up my drum until 2016.

I was visiting my sister in Utah and had the pleasure of meeting "The Drum Lady." During that encounter I learned there was truth to that old phrase about marching to the beat of your own drummer. I learned about vibration and had my vibration raised by drumming. I came home with my handmade drum. Since that time, I have taken more seriously what it means to live a high vibe life. But...

I also struggle with depression. When one is depressed, it is exceedingly difficult to make positive decisions or follow-through when you do. For several years, I did not even dust my drum, let alone enjoy the benefits of its vibration. So, what is the answer when you are so busy with other expectations or so down that you cannot dust your drum? You take little steps and make changes slowly but steadily.

Today, at least for today, embrace your drumbeat by settling in and choosing to listen only to your vibrations. Set small goals that will benefit you alone. Make today a baby step day. Here is today's baby step plan.

First, eat. My grandmother always said, "Have another cream puff, it will make you feel better." It did. It made me fat, too. Do not eat your stress in an unhealthy way today. Have a healthy meal. Eat food that both enhances your energy and feeds your soul.

Second, sit outside in the sun for a while. Embrace the light and warmth. I use a happy light daily while the dark days are here. This will increase your vitamin D level and mood.

Third, pray or meditate about what you are to do next to love yourself more and to care for the person that God would have you become. God has a plan for you, ask Him what it is and, listen to the answer.

# January 20

## Cancel Self-Doubt
## By Marilyn Miller

ancelling self-doubt offers a great opportunity for more self-acceptance, self-confidence and self-love. Learning to love myself without reservation came so much easier once I learned to first talk back to my inner critic and then to banish it. I nick named my inner critic the "self-doubt monster." I pictured it as a green Humpty Dumpty type character about two feet tall. It often tried to talk me out of things I wanted to have or jobs I longed to do. It offered limiting advice aimed at keeping my life small and safe. But in reality, it played the role of a negative cheerleader,. Here's the way I found to override its negativity.

- Imagine your self-doubt monster as a character and give it a cartoon voice. Not your mother's or a negative friend's.

- Write down what your self-doubt monster says to you. Study the list.

- Are these things true? Usually they are not the truth about you.

- Write down empowering statements to counteract the criticism. It says, "You're not smart enough to do that." So you write, "I am as smart as others doing it, so I can do it too if I choose."

- Whenever you catch yourself listening to the self-doubt monster, say, "Thank you for sharing. I'm driving the car. You're a passenger. I can tell you to get out any time I choose."

- Now, you can also send the self-doubt monster on vacation. Pack its bags and give it a one-way ticket to a far distant location.
- Enjoy the following poem I wrote about my own Self Doubt Monster

**"Ode To My Self-Doubt Monster"**
There is a Monster deep inside.
I know him well; he cannot hide.
Just in case I do something right,
He knocks me down in a critical fight.
Someday I'll get the best of him.
It will be my turn to wear a grin.
To stamp him out might be a sin.
To love myself is the way to win!

# January 21

## Unconditional Love
## By Dee Dee Rebitt

*W*hen we give meaning to love especially when its unconditional love, most people will feel extremely uncomfortable I, for one, was that very person, and I am still working on it.

I do not recall this word being tossed around my home growing up as a child. Besides other extenuating circumstances in my life as a child this could be a good reason why. I spent my whole life trying to be people pleasing, but I always felt uncomfortable around people. I had a lot of trust issues that go back to childhood. And I still will back off from a person if I feel off around their presence. It is my radar, I guess, but I have learned not to second guess it.

When I started on this path to healing myself from the inside outwards, I had been giving of myself to everyone all the time in every part of who I was, but not giving to myself. I was the one person whom I needed the most and I was ignoring the signals that love was not shown to myself the one whom desperately needed to be loved.

I had been feeding everyone's soul with my love and I forgot me in the process. I played the martyr even. I always gave of myself no matter what the cost. After going through different avenues of self-healing and reading countless books, I realized that there has got to be something here for *me*.

It was called taking my power back and setting up boundaries, pulling back the reins. No wonder after finally figuring things out for myself, I had no choice. My life had been spiraling out of control and I was burning out. And as soon as I took back my power and stood up for me, things shifted. Not everyone was happy with the new and improved me.

Now, I walk away from those that have no respect of myself or my feelings. I have learned to say no, and to take much needed me-time, filling my own cup first.

# January 22

## I am Creating my Life Through Love
## By Ellen Elizabeth Jones

" *L ove yourself first and everything else falls into line. You really have to love yourself to get anything done in this world.* " *Lucille Ball*
We come to Earth to master self-love. Love is the one thing in this world that will always bring you joy. Joy is the highest expression of love. The purpose of one's life is joy. When you feel as though you are not loved, you may find yourself surrounded by feelings of inadequacy or sadness. Finding love does not necessarily mean a romantic relationship; it can be the love of family, friends, fur babies that can satisfy this human need. When you have love in your life, you can always tap into the feelings and happiness that love expresses. Do you love yourself? Do you show yourself care, empathy, kindness, and understanding? Do you find yourself exciting, interesting, and amazing? This type of self-love comes first. Love yourself and the rest will follow. If you are like most people, you do not love yourself completely yet.

There is only one definition of love that truly matters: the one you define within yourself. To figure this out, you must do the inner work. You have to take a deep dive into who you are and relentlessly pursue yourself with passion.

Consider the love that is present in your life. Love comes in all forms. Your job is to discover what is true for you.

When you learn to love yourself, it becomes easier to attract the love you seek into your life. You begin to set clear boundaries because you know your self-worth, love someone else without losing yourself, make decisions that align with who you are, and achieve emotional maturity.

How do you learn to love yourself? It is a daily practice of choosing yourself. Affirmations are a wonderful to begin claiming yourself as a child of the universe. Anything that follows "I am" becomes your truth. Become disciplined with your thoughts and words. The stories you tell yourself matter. Each day say one thing that your future self will thank you for. Explore and expand experiences that make your heart and soul sing. Choose love whenever and wherever you can. Love is always and all ways a choice. You are beloved.

# January 23

## Create your Life
## By Nancy Meikle-Mousseau

*T*wenty years ago, I bought a roll of wallpaper and applied it to the wall behind my washer and dryer. Continually adding photos of things that made me happy, the feeling I had when I looked at those pictures was how I wanted to *be*. I started adding things of what I wanted to *do* in the future and *have* in my new home. When we finally moved, all my ideas manifested into fruition with ease and grace because they were in my vortex (a place where all my dreams and desires live waiting for the right moment to come true).

Years later, I saw an ad on my Facebook account about a vision board course. I instantly had the knowing I needed to take this course and start teaching it. I have learned over the years to listen to these universal prompts. They never steer me wrong. I have enjoyed coaching participants in vision board workshops for years now and each workshop provides the opportunity for the participants to drop their roles and be guided back to their self, a self they have forgotten. They are guided through meditations, inner work and time to remember what ignites their spark. This is their self care that feeds their soul.

I have created many boards in the past years. As each board's visions have manifested, new goals require my attention. Where intention goes, energy flows. The trick is to get in alignment, concentrate on staying happy and let the universe do the rest. I recommend everyone create a vision board. Science has proven the power of the brain and visualizing. Your brain can be trained to create outcomes you most want. Seeing your vision board everyday affirms your desires, keeping you focused on your outcomes you want to create.

# January 24

## Healing Your Inner Self
## By Melanie Morrison

In every relationship that we have, it is well known that each one takes work. In a romantic relationship, we understand that it is important to communicate, do acts of service, share deep thoughts, and authentic emotion, show affection, be attentive, embrace laughter, silliness, and joy. If relationships begin to drift apart, or it seems that a marriage is failing, we know that we may need to put in extra effort to mend differences, forgive, and grow close again.

Now that we have acknowledged the truth in this, let's apply these concepts to the relationship we have with self. If we find that we are numb, disconnected, addicted, depressed, bored, irritable, uncomfortable in our skin and/or generally unhappy, it is a good indication that it is time to put in a little extra work to mend our heart, forgive ourselves for neglecting our needs, and grow happy within ourselves again.

Take a moment to check in today and really ask what is missing in your daily, weekly, monthly, and yearly routine. Is it laughter? Is it dance or music? Is it creativity? Perhaps it's connecting with your physical body. Perhaps it's being attentive to your thoughts and emotions. Once you have identified at least one thing per day, week, month, and year, take a moment to give yourself forgiveness for not providing these things sooner. You can do this by saying this out loud, to yourself, or writing it in your journal.

"Dear Self, I know that you have been feeling neglected I'm sorry for not giving you the time and attention that I know you need to thrive. I know that you have been doing the best you can. I forgive you for not doing these things sooner. Thank you for giving me signs to make be aware that a change needed to be made. I love you exactly the way you are right now. I am committed to put in extra effort and work to meet more of your needs and care for you deeply and authentically. You deserve love. I love you."

Just for today choose one thing from your list that you will do for yourself. Congratulate yourself, you have taken the first step towards a better relationship with you.

# January 25

## What if I Fail? No. What if I Succeed?
### By Janice Story

*D*o you often find yourself asking, *what if?* Are constant fears or worry-based thoughts running through your mind until they almost drive you crazy? Do you say things like *what if I choke on my interview and don't get the job?*; *what if I can't make it on my own?*; *what if they don't like me?*; *what if something bad happens?*; *what if I fail?*

As if our minds aren't busy enough, we do this and add to the internal chatter, chaos, and stress of everyday life. Sure, some of those things may happen, you might fail, but what if you succeed? We may just be standing in our own way—blocking our successes. How much have you missed out on because those simple two little words kept you from doing something?

Next time you catch yourself in the middle of one of those thoughts, try shifting it into something positive! If you insist on utilizing the words *,what if,* try shifting the energy. Think *Wow! What if I do get this this job and I will have the freedom to change my life?* Or perhaps it will be *what if I do go on this blind date and meet my soulmate that has been waiting just for me?*; *what if I do go on that trip, and make the amazing memories culminating in the experience of a lifetime?*

A huge part of loving yourself is paying attention to exactly where you place your thoughts. If you constantly think about everything that could go wrong, it will! You must create the space within yourself to allow every amazing thing you deserve to come into your life. When you learn to shift your thoughts and your words, it truly starts opening the doors and allows your deepest desires to become reality.

When you wake up every morning, think about the following things and implement them into your daily routine.

- Choose a positive mantra and repeat it throughout the day.
- Be mindful of where you place your thoughts.
- If you notice yourself in a *what if* mind frame, make sure you start focusing on the possibilities of *what could be!*

Don't be so afraid to fail that you neglect to give yourself the chance to succeed!

# January 26

## End Sarcasm
## By Ewa Blaszczak

Sarcasm is the opposite of love and an underestimated vicious poison, which ruins our self-esteem, our relationships, effectiveness of our work teams, creativity, and impacts our immune systems.

If you want to understand what sarcasm is, you should watch any random episode of *Doctor House.* Here is just one of the epic quotes from this series. "Somewhere out there a tree is tirelessly producing oxygen for you. You owe it an apology."

Sarcasm hurts! It makes you feel small, irrelevant and ridiculous. It causes the worst toxin ever—shame. And here is the best part; the most harmful sarcasm is usually the one we feed ourselves with.

Sarcasm is triggered by our reptilian brain, and it is based on the most primitive mode that tells us, "attack in order to survive." In today's world we add humor to cover up the fact that we treat others with contempt and want to hurt them.

Communication expert John Gottman, PhD, proved that there are four main communication toxins which ruin our relationships. These are: blaming, defensiveness, stonewalling, and contempt which includes sarcasm. They have been scientifically proven to be the best predictors of a divorce. And guess what? Sarcasm and other forms of contempt are the most destructive of them all!

Sarcasm is so harmful because it combines hostility and humor. When someone attacks you with hostility, your reptilian brain should fight it. But the humor covering the hostility makes you smile, which triggers physiological reaction overriding the self-defense system. So you get a punch on the face and smile to your aggressor. And then the suppressed emotions erode your immune system. Communication toxins are proven to be predictors of how many infectious illnesses you are going to have in the next four years.

1. Do you use sarcasm to shame yourself? Name some examples.

2. Is the environment you live /work sarcastic?

3. If you use sarcasm, check your intention underpinning the words. Do you want to give a negative feedback or is it just that you feel goofy and playful? End sarcasm. Be true to yourself and use words with kindness.

4. Speak up when someone is overusing the sarcastic language in your presence. When we name sarcasm, we take away its power. Drive the conversation back on constructive tracks, by saying, "I've noticed sarcasm but let us focus on the business issue at hand."

# January 27

## The Release
## By Danielle Fierro

There was a time when I floated through life. My habits and routines were the same from one day to the next. I felt stuck, unfulfilled, and uninspired. The things that previously brought me joy no longer gave me that same feeling of enjoyment. I wasn't quite sure why I felt that way. The only thing I did know was that I wasn't happy. I finally realized that I had done the work to improve myself but many of my habits and the people around me were the same. I was still drinking, going to the bars, had the same "friends," and followed the drama in social media. I didn't feel like I could share my true self with my "friends," so I kept living my old life in my new mindset. I couldn't do it any longer. I had to honor the new season of my life and release that which no longer served me. This was a wonderful form of self-love that truly honored who I was as well as who I was becoming.

We must take an inventory of our whole life as we move from one season of our life to another. Life becomes more difficult if parts of your life are not congruent with your new mindset and outlook. An exercise that can help you through this process is to ask yourself a series of questions.

Here are examples of questions to consider. What do you allow into your life that no longer serves you? What are you listening to/reading/watching that doesn't bring you joy? Who do you have around you that doesn't support you? How does social media make you feel? Who do you have as friends on your social media and how do their posts make you feel? Who do you enjoy spending time with? What keeps you from doing the things that you like to do? What are time suckers? Where are you inviting drama into your life? Why do you need drama (i.e. excitement, boredom, avoidance, etc.)? How do you follow the news and how does it affect you? You can include any other questions that you can think of as well.

The answers to these questions will help direct you to the people, habits, and things that you can release. Releasing is a form of self-love that makes room for things that will bring you joy and allow further growth.

# January 28

## Rolling Hills Of Life
## By JoAnne Eisen

Life can feel like an endless amount of rolling hills with all its ups and downs. You think you have a grip on life only to find yourself off track. You think you are flourishing only to realize you have crashed. You wonder: Where is my owner's manual to this vehicle I choose to drive through this crazy terrain of life with?

You choose to create such magical things in this life's experience bringing you to deeper learning. But, you don't' quite have all the information needed to navigate your way. You might feel you veered off your life path. But have you?

This crazy terrain of what seems to be a peaceful and beautiful landscape of rolling hills magnified is so much more.

Your body, which is the vehicle you were born with, has an internal navigation system. Feelings and emotions are critical components of this system, helping you to stay on track. Please don't dismiss these gifts. Love and trust those parts of yourself. They are tools needed to navigate life's ups and downs, helping your inner being to calm self-doubt, fear, unworthiness, assumptions, and more. These are emotions of limiting beliefs. Distractions that keep you from being the magnificent human you already are. Every day is a new day. Changing your outlook on life gives you the power and ability for incredible new outcomes. Be the observer of your life. Pay very close attention to your words and perspectives. No matter what, learn to love yourself unconditionally, giving yourself a break when needed. Remember, your birthright is to make mistakes. That's the magic of this experience called life.

You are a product of your ancestors, passed down from generation to generation, co-creating life and experiences differently.

How beautiful is that? It may not feel wonderful, but a change of perception frequently solves everything. Start by taking the time to understand you're deeply rooted emotions. They need to be acknowledged. We all have them and are expert magicians in how we wield them to serve us.

We can be afraid of what is under the hood of this vehicle we are driving, and sometimes it can feel scary. Imagine that terrain full of rolling hills. From afar, it is peaceful and calm. That is the truth of who you are as a soul!

# January 29

## Dreaming
## By Delores Garcia

*W*hen was the last time you laid on a grassy hill and watched the clouds morph in and out of shapes that delighted your imagination, dreaming of lands far away? I can remember doing it when I was in grade school in my quiet hometown in Southern Idaho, more than forty years ago! It is long overdue for many of us! In our quest for self-caring activities, dreaming can truly create buoyancy for our soul and add a spring to our step.

When our soul craves the power of creation, dreaming is the gift we have. Dreaming gives our soul the power of creation in addition to the power of freedom, just as when we were sweet, innocent children with our whole lives ahead of us. Our soul still craves that. The first step is to note what your heart and soul desire. Remember, there are no limits on these dreams, just like when we were ten! No limit! And absolute open-ended permission from the abundant Universe to have our heart's desires that are for our highest and greatest good.

The second step is to pick one dream item at a time and list out all of the reasons why you want it. This list will enhance your thoughts about what you actually desire. Remember, there are no limits on this, nor any need to justify what you want! Enjoy the dream! Just let it flow. You are allowed to have your heart's desires from a benevolent Universe. When this list seems complete, proceed to the next step.

The third step is to list reasons why you believe you will have this dream. This list will enhance your belief that your dream will come true. What we truly believe is what we manifest into our experiences. The more deeply we are believe that our dream will be ours, the more the Universe will deliver. This second list will also reveal sources of doubt you may be harboring. Often doubts are a little sneaky as they hide in the dark corners of our minds, whispering discouraging ideas to us. Ask yourself "What do I need to believe for this dream to vibrate at the same level that the dream-come-true vibrates at?" The more you believe with assurance and feel so deeply, the more you will manifest your dreams.

Dream big. Believe hard. Feel deeply. Dream comes true!

# January 30

## Plant a Little Love
## By Amy I. King

*M*y garden is a source of great joy for me. I have focused on it for the past several years. Never one with a green thumb, I had a plant here and there but never had anything that survived very long. I began with a few small plants in the windows. I researched which plants would work best in which windows. I bought the pots, the soil, and the plants. I began to love them daily.

I branched out to potted plants on my patios. I live in a home that backs up to a golf course. There is a patio area on the front and back. Both are now filled with beautiful, healthy plants. On the front patio, there are bougainvillea, plumeria, birds, of paradise, and more. In the spring and summer, the blooms bring so much beautiful color. It satisfies my soul to know that I had a hand in the beauty. In the back, I have roses (a first for me), tons of spider plants, geraniums, and butterfly bush.

I realized that connecting with the earth is one of the most incredible forms of self-love. Choosing the right plants for each section of your garden, the appropriate pots, and planting everything with your own hands in the soil is a source of great pride. Over time, feeding and caring for plants becomes second nature and begins to feed your soul. Caring for something other than yourself is self-love. The care you give comes back to you, always in all ways.

You can start small and get one plant. Choose something that brings a smile to your face. Maybe something that flowers or has beautiful leaves. Focus energy on that plant each day. Plants do not usually need daily watering, but they do love attention daily. Touch the leaves gently, speak kindly to your plant. I know it sounds a little strange but trust me, it is fantastic! You will begin to feel the energy that the plants are giving you. The relationship is symbiotic. You feed and water and love the plant, and the plant, in turn, loves on you with oxygen and beauty. Self-love isn't always solely about us; sometimes, it is all about the connection to something else.

# January 31

## So Simple
### By Mindy Lipton

*M*editate. Breathe. Deep breaths in through the nose. Hold. Now out through the mouth. Try not to do that in reverse. It may not be very pretty.

Oh, but I am pretty. In fact, that is one of my affirmations on my bathroom mirror. I cut it out from an egg carton and it says, "Good Morning Beautiful."

I have Alexa play "I Feel Pretty" from my very favorite musical, *West Side Story*. I dance around my five-hundred-square-foot apartment to "Dance at the Gym." It all raises my joy and vibration for a fabulous day.

Today is a Monday so, of course, I had Alexa play, "Monday, Monday" by the Mamas and the Papas. It's so simple. I love it! I love me.

Loving yourself does take discipline however. I have been diagnosed with depression and I do have mood swings. So when I first get up I put on that music and get the coffee going and I would say that 99 percent of the time it works like a charm. I live in a fifty-five plus community that has given me the nickname, Sunshine. I like my new name.

Practice loving yourself. Tell yourself you are pretty. Listen to a song that raises your joy. Find a new song every day of the week and sing along with it. Practice the simple art of giving yourself joy through song.

# February 1

## Begin Within
## By Jamie Rudolph

*H*ow do you begin your day? Does it begin with a blasting alarm followed by rushing out the door?!

What if you started your morning filled with self-love?

Wellness begins as an inside job. How we care for ourselves on a daily basis greatly impacts our overall wellbeing. Those first morning moments can be a hectic, stressed-out time or an opportunity for mindful moments filled with healthy rituals to nourish our body, mind, and soul.

Begin your day with mindful breathing. Find a comfortable seat near your bed while you slowly breathe in and out—just be. Bring your awareness to your belly then your lungs. Feel your shoulders rise and fall while the breath enters and exits your body. With each breath continue to feel your body expand in all directions. Allow your mind to be at ease. If you have a mantra or positive phrase, this is an excellent time to remind yourself of those positive thoughts or set an intention for your day ahead. Mindful breathing has an impact on your mental and emotional state while helping regulate heart rate and blood pressure along with stress levels. This morning ritual has a lasting influence on your body, mind, and spirit—begin within.

# February 2

## Whispers From the Heart
## By Ann Marie Asp

*C*an you remember the very first time you felt those sensations and gentle nudges from your heart? I look back now upon that special day with such appreciation.

There was a soft stirring that came forth on that special morning as I got ready for school. My entire being became filled with such an overwhelming sense of pure joy and peacefulness. I knew in that moment that my life would be changed forever. The awkward and shy little girl who always wanted to be accepted was taking that first step in revealing to herself the wonder of who she was.

There have been many circumstances from that day and throughout my life that have played an instrumental role in who I have become. Little did I know that the people who played a part in these stories would become my greatest mentors. It is with sincere appreciation that I give thanks to the many teachers that helped pave the way. It was through these difficult, and at times overwhelming situations I began learning to pay attention to those inner callings from my heart. Those callings shared with me that I had all the resources I needed to become the great person I came here to be. Those gentle callings effortlessly sparked the passion inside me. I began to tune in daily and listen to those gentle whispers that flowed so freely from my heart.

I ask you to take time out of your daily routine to listen to the gentle stirrings that are in need of your attention and caring embrace. You can easily start with just a few minutes a day. You will soon begin to feel the awakening of this beautiful vessel that has always been there, but now you will understand the free-flowing whispers it sends to you throughout each day letting you know how special you truly are.

Be open today by making sure to pay close attention to each tiny pulsation. Those pulsations will always keep you aligned with your highest potential. It is in this connection to your heart that will bring forth a wisdom that only you hold the keys. This daily practice will assist in taping into the beautiful gits that are uniquely yours and yours alone. Tune in today and each day going forward, listen to the beauty of the whispers from your heart.

Are you listening?

# February 3

## The Infinite Journey of Self-Love
### By Nanette Gogan-Edwards

*My* personal journey of self-love began with honesty, vulnerability and breaking the cycle of guilt, shame, and silence. Sharing my struggles, flaws, emotions, and triumphs was the beginning of an important and necessary transformation to achieving a greater spiritual awareness. In sharing my story, I realized how many other women had experienced the same challenges and my extremely heavy burden began to lift. This connection gave me confidence and strength and a deep love for others. At that moment I knew I had something to offer! We all need to feel heard, accepted, and not alone in our challenges. Along this infinite journey I've learned to love and accept myself as well as those around me.

What is your story? Have you shared it with others? How did you overcome the most difficult part? Don't be ashamed, do not be afraid of judgement or rejection. Your story is the seed that, when planted, will blossom into new life! Give others the opportunity to heal and to grow into who they are meant to be. Through this transformation you will also grow and blossom!

Self-love begins when you allow yourself to feel the pain of the past. As N.A. Turner says, give it space and "allow yourself to grieve for a moment until you decide you must part ways in search of positivity again. You will learn something from it, you will become stronger and more resilient.".

*"Why Pain and Suffering are Necessary if You Want to Feel Happy"*. N.A. Turner – The Ascent

# *February 4*

## Come Home to Your Love
## By Paula Marie Rennie

What does self-love mean to you?

I remember when I was asked this very question to my surprise I was lost for words. My attention has always been focused on pleasing, supporting, and doing for others. It's where I learned to earn my sense of worth and feel loveable, needed, and wanted.

I'm not too proud to say, many times in my life I've sacrificed my true inner happiness and self-care for others simply because I didn't really know how to love myself or what my needs were. Sound familiar?

When I learned how to come home to myself and place my full attention on me, my life changed for the better in all areas. I felt my soul's true essence and heck, I started to love her! I learned to listen to my insecurities through my feelings and focused on my body's symptoms, which revealed my true needs. I stopped abandoning myself when with others by presencing myself more authentically, confidently and lovingly.

It's your turn! Grab your journal and try this as a daily practice.

- Find a comfortable space to sit or stand quietly. Breathe slowly while observing your body and breath.

- Where is all your energy? What does it feel like? Be aware of your thoughts and notice in your body where is there tension?

- Imagine calling all of your energy home back to you from all places, people, and situations. Draw it down into the centre of your body, down into your hips, feet, and ground it down like roots into the Earth.

- Come home into your heart space and calm your mind by inviting your inner child in to this loving space. Listen to your soul's true yearnings and desires, receive its clarity, strength and wisdom.

- Observe your body and where there's tension ask, "I wonder what I'm feeling?" Let the response come through your senses.

- Now ask this feeling, "I wonder what I need?" Let the response come through your senses.

- Imagine yourself now in the future interacting with others, stand in a posture that keeps your attention also on yourself. Feel your vibrant, powerful energy expanding out into the space as you express yourself openly and confidently. How does this feel?

- In your journal note down your reflections. What other ways can you appreciate your needs more? What support could you receive from others?

# February 5

## Fond Memories
## By Marsha Johnson

*M*any of us have had a relationship that has not turned out to be quite what we wanted or ended the way we thought it would. We may have been wronged, been lied to, or been taken advantage of. If we hold on to that grudge or feeling of discontent when we think of that person, we are really hurting one person and that would be ourselves. When a relationship ends through our hand or other, a hurt can be experienced like no other. Sometimes we are at a crossroads and that person goes one way and we go another.

To help us get past this, we need to remember that there was some good in the relationship at one time. This applies to any relationship, a close personal friend, a work colleague, or even a casual acquaintance. There are good qualities there, but because of our bias in the situation, we just cannot see them.

One way to help us feel better, and thus heal our anger or frustration, is to take a minute or two and journal about that person. Write down some qualities or a situation where that person helped you or others. Now, I know, it may be hard to think of something like that through our anger or discontent, but once you start, other things will follow. Once you do that, spend fifteen minutes thinking of the good in this person. Sit with a picture of this person (or visualize them in your mind's eye), thinking of their good qualities. This mending of your relationship will help you be at peace and not feel anger in your heart. Anger and resentment only hurt the one holding onto it. You will find after a while that when you see them, think of them, or hear their name, you won't feel anger, and maybe a smile will cross your face.

# *February 6*

## Camaraderie
## By Dominique Trier

*P*art of learning to love and appreciate ourselves is learning how to do the same for others. As a little girl, I spent most of my free time in front of the television imitating my favorite singers. When I had moments to myself, which ended up being often, as my sisters were grown and my parents were always working, I would practice my vocals. Because I spent so much time practicing, I ended up having opportunities in my school choir that led me to feel a sense of belonging and confidence. However, not everyone I encountered was fond of my successful choir auditions that led to solos and a place in leadership at school.

In fact, in one instance I remember a new girl at school speaking to my good friend about feeling like she did not like me for some frivolous reason. My friend quickly responded, and told the new girl that I had mentioned I liked her. This new girl did not anticipate the positive response, was taken aback and became quiet. My friend told me about it, and in that moment of juvenile awkwardness, I realized how important it was to root for one another. If I had never mentioned my positive support towards this new girl, and if my friend would have never mentioned our interaction to the new girl, she would have felt unwelcomed. I knew I needed to take this information in a way to encourage a productive environment and speech, instead of giving into adolescent pettiness.

The negative interaction ended by creating a positive one. My friend and I created positive interactions that did not project any insecurities. We projected inclusivity and love with our camaraderie. One of the most self-empowering actions is empowering those around us. This childhood lesson has bled into my work and personal relationships as an adult. One of the best ways to love ourselves includes cultivating positive relationships around us. Helping others grow can help ourselves grow. Camaraderie has not only created networking opportunities, but opportunities for having more esteem and love for myself. We can all ask ourselves, what can I do to create esteem and camaraderie between others and myself? Do my actions empower others and myself? And to give a satisfactory ending to the story, the new girl and I became friends.

# February 7

## Self-Talk
## By Sarah Berkett

Be aware of your monkey mind and self-talk. Notice when your inner critic or negativity comes up. Do not criticize the inner critic. It does not help the self-love part. It just creates more criticism and judgement. Bring in that compassionate parent part of you and say, "Hey inner critic, I know on some level you are trying to protect me but it is not working. This is not the way I want to talk to myself."

You are so hard on yourself without knowing it because it has become a habit to think this way. It is not you, just a part of you.

Set a reminder on your phone that says, "What is my self-talk right now?"

And if it is not empowering, choose not to judge or feed these thoughts, then change directions by choosing another thought—a thought that is uplifting!

# *February 8*

## Hot Mess
## By Selena Urbanovitch

Do you ever feel like you are a hot mess? Like you cannot do anything right? Do you ever just want to scream and throw something? Is it like you woke up on the wrong side of the bed? I hear you; those days are further apart and less frequent since I take these moments as an opportunity to breathe, pause, and look at the moments from a different perspective.

When these moments show up for you, I want you to try these things that have helped me. These tools helped me center and ground myself so that I can be more in the moment.

1. Stop and take three deep breaths-in through the nose and out your mouth, down to your tummy. Be aware of the breath moving in and out of your body. Feel the oxygen course through your lungs and tummy, breathing out of your open mouth! Breathe in peace and breathe out whatever needs to go.

2. When you now look at the problems at hand ask, "What is it I wasn't acknowledging? Do I need to walk away from it?" If the answer is yes, then take a break and go back to it later.

3. Third thing is to let go of what you cannot control. Take time out for you whether it is, stopping and have a cup of coffee or tea or maybe lay down for a nap. Try to honour what your body needs at that time.

We sometimes need to forgive ourselves of all the pressures we put on our daily lives and know that sometimes we just need to honour ourselves knowing we are worth it. It isn't selfish to say *no* or *sorry*

*I am unable to do this right now.* I always find that when the universe is trying to show us something, we sometimes try to ignore it. I find that they keep putting things in the way until I listen. Hence feeling like a hot mess and things going sideways for me is the universe saying, *slow down and take a break.* We are not here to be unhappy; we are here to live the best version of ourselves. So, take a deep breath and know you are so loved and you are worthy of an abundance of peace. Love lights the way when you allow it to do so!

# *February 9*

## Forgiveness Hawaiian Style
## By Stephanie Fontaine

*I* do not know about you, but there have been plenty of things that I have needed to let go of and have forgiveness for in my lifetime. Depending on where we are in our healing journey, forgiveness can be a tricky thing. Understanding, learning, and accepting that forgiveness is 100 percent about and for *me*, has been a key piece in reaching a new level of self-love and acceptance within.

It was approximately four years ago when I first heard about Ho'oponopono. I was participating in a group class and my mentor brought it up during a lesson one day. I liked the concept, it felt good in my heart but I am not sure how much I understood it or appreciated it at the time.

Ho'oponopono is an ancient Hawaiian practice of forgiveness and reconciliation. The Hawaiian word translates in English simply as "to make right." Ho'o ("to make") and pono ("right"). Basically, you are asking the divinity to clean and clear away any thoughts, beliefs, and programs that are no longer serving you. We want to reach a place of peace within ourselves. When we are at peace within our mind, body, and soul, and our internal environment is clear of all the things we let weigh us down, then we will begin to experience shifts in our external environment.

Ho'oponopono kept coming into my awareness again and again. It's now four years later and I am confident to say I have a much deeper understanding and appreciation for the practice. It has been a consistent part of my routine for the last couple of years and I believe in its healing and freeing power.

Dr. Joe Vitale writes about the ancient Hawaiian practice in a way that really contributed to my deep appreciation and understanding and there are plenty of videos and literature available to assist you in gaining the value and wisdom of this sacred tool. The best part about Ho'oponopono is that it is easy and can be done anywhere at any time.

Here are four simple phrases you say and the order of the phrases is not important. The phrases are as follows: *I love you. I'm sorry. Please forgive me. Thank you.* Repeat them like a mantra, either silently in your head or chant them out loud. Do what feels right in the moment.

I love you. Thank you.

# February 10

## Letting Go of Attachment
## By Susan Hoyle

*H*ave you ever been so attached to an outcome it created stress in your body? Anxiety? Depression? Worry? Did you lose focus in your life? Maybe even created dis-ease in your body? Well, there was a time in my own life that was a regular part of my daily routine. Especially with my kids. If something did not go their way at school, with friends, I would want to jump right in and fix it. After all, I was the ultimate fixer of everyone's problems. Or so I thought.

As I did more work on myself, and the story I made up about myself as a child and especially a mother, I realized. My self-worth was tied to my *fixing* things for others. As a consequence, I was not allowing my kids to follow their own paths in this life. This meant allowing them to make mistakes, allowing them to feel hurt, anger, along with the joy. I suddenly realized if my kids never felt pain or suffering, how would they ever grow into adults, capable of emotional regulation? Wow. What a hard grueling process that was for me.

If any of this resonates with you, I encourage you to pick one area in your life, where you can see you are overstepping or meddling in someone else's journey. Take out your journal and make a list of those you believe you have been doing more *directing* or *fixing* and less compassionate listening. Breathe into this exercise. It can be difficult to see these traits in ourselves; I know it was for me!

As you get your list, and it could be one person, begin to see what this person truly *needs* from you. Do they need answers? Or do they need your *compassionate listening* and understanding? Trust the process of letting go of attachment to the outcome. This brings us into the present moment. Let go of your *expectations* in this situation. Whatever happens, happens. It isn't right or wrong, it just *is*. Just try this for twenty-one days and see what a ripple effect this may have on you and your family.

# *February 11*

## Five Steps to Self-Love (Ernest Holmes)
## By Charel Morris

The first day I learned how to experience Ernest Holmes's five step treatment was the day I knew I had found my spiritual home. After a few hours of practicing this type of prayer we were asked if anyone wanted to volunteer to pray for others in our church the next morning. Out of nowhere, my hand was in the air! I have never regrated that day or that presence within me that raised my hand.

Forty years later when reviewing my toolbox of skills on self-love, this five step treatment came to the front.

After decades of exploration, Ernest Holms presented the golden threads that he distilled in from his study of religious teachings. This he named the five-step treatment. It is a practice, one that each person can scientifically prove. One that will improve your life.

Approach this with an open heart and a sense of being connected to something in the universe – out there. If you are still not sure, the way I was that day, simply reach out with your heart and intentions and give it a try. You have nothing to lose and so very much to gain.

It's a simple process we called **R • U • R • T • R** – Once you get the simple statements and it connects with you, start expanding it with your own words. You can do that by trusting your intuition and your heart.

- **R**ecognize – God is one. The infinite is one.
- **U**nify – And I am one with all that is.

- **R**ealize – I know that I am one with love. I deserve to love and care for myself. I feel that love surrounds me at all time. I am filled with love and love for myself.
- **T**hanks – I give thanks and gratitude to God, the infinite, the one that is all.
- **R**elease – Knowing that the power is not in me, I release this to the one, the infinite, to God and know that it is already done in the mind of the universe. And so it is. So I let it be. Amen. Thank you. Peace.

When you are comfortable with these basic statements then begin to use your own wording and thoughts. And through this five step treatment speak to the universe and call in what you want to manifest or experience in your practice of self-love.

# February 12

## Word Dump
## By Symone Desirae

*H*ave you ever had one of those moments where your brain feels like it's in overdrive due to obsessive thoughts? You know the ones, thoughts where you worry too much about something or think about a situation and try to play it out in your mind. Next time take a note of how your body reacts when these thoughts are on repeat like a broken record. Do you feel stressed? Tired? Out of control? Does this pattern of over-thinking keep you awake at night?

Back when I was taking an education course, I was worried about how I was going to pay for it. I would constantly fret over if I had enough money for my other bills along with this course. Did I have enough for my rent? My insurance? It was a constant replay of these thoughts and my mind would spiral out of control. My body would become tense. I was stressed, not sleeping, and I was in constant worry mode.

I began what would be known as the word dump. I would write what was on my mind, and how it made me feel. It soon began to be what felt like a hundred different things running through my mind were in actuality three things on paper. The broken record replaying over and over again made the list of worries in my mind larger and more problematic than they actually where. I was shocked the very first time I ever did a mind dump on paper and saw just how small the problem actually was compared to what I had thought it was going to be.

Take a moment to write down at least one thing on your mind that is worrying you. Reflect on how your mental list compares to your physical written out list. Every time I get in my head about something I close my eyes and take three big deep breathes in and out. This helps me to clear my headspace from overthinking or worrying too much.

# February 13

## To Give is to Receive
## By Tabitha Weigel

When we think of self-love, we tend to think of the self. We look to the individual routines and practices that promote self-exploration, self-healing, self-awareness and self-growth. The theme is clearly the focus on self. Yet, I am here today to remind you of the beauty and the blessings gained when we give our self—our time, our energy, our material—*to others.*

To be generous and give from the heart is to share your light, your joy, and your spirit in a way that raises the energetic vibrations of the world and (you guessed it) of self. It's to give from a genuine space and to give without the expectation for something in return. It's to simply give with ease. This act of love and abundance is pure, straightforward and almost instinctual. With such generosity of self, you are calling in an abundance of love and prosperity. An energetic cycle is created, a cycle of giving and receiving. The more we give, the more we receive.

Besides wanting to obviously create this beautiful cycle of giving and receiving, there are other more immediate benefits. Think of a time when you were generous with yourself in some form. You hugged a stranger, cooked a meal for a struggling friend, donated what you could to a charity of your choice, or volunteered your time and energy in some way. Think of how you felt after such act. Proud, warm and fuzzy, generous, with purpose, glowing and capable are a few words that come to my mind. Your soul and heart are flooded with high vibrations and gratitude. There's a gratitude to be in the position to help, gratitude for the blessings within your life, and gratitude for the exchange of such genuine and humble energy. Your heart chakra explodes with love; love for others and love of self! It's a win - win for everyone involved!

So take time today to share that brilliant light of yours. Stay true to you and keep it simple. No "I shoulds" are involved. Act from your heart and let it lead you to whom or where you are needed. Trust that even the smallest of gifts can make a world of an impact, for both you and those touched by your act of love.

# February 14

## Radical Acceptance
## By Talia Renzo

ach and every one of us has a story to tell. At some point in our stories, we faced a challenge. Sometimes the challenge wasn't an exterior conflict, or another person, it was just ourself. Have you ever been your own biggest battle? Have you ever felt like the only thing getting in your way of your happiness is yourself?

In my own story, I have been my own biggest obstacle. I struggle with mental illness. The tasks that seem the easiest for others are sometimes the hardest for me. Sometimes I have more hard days than easy days. For example, in the mornings if I have to brush my teeth, take a shower, and do my hair, sometimes I have a panic attack because it becomes too overwhelming. I am incapable of achieving these routines in order. When I think I am ready, I have to try again. This happens with many different situations, several times a week.

I radically accept that I have a condition that can limit my ability to be as proactive as anyone else. But I love myself through it all. I love myself through the panic attacks. I love myself through the trauma. I love myself through the physical pain. I radically accept myself, because I am allowed to be who I am. I learned to love myself, my mind, and my body through forgiveness, grace, and radical acceptance. This is a daily practice, and yes, it is exhausting, but incredibly rewarding because I'm reminded every day that I have another day to live my life.

Just the other day, I was driving home, incredibly overwhelmed. It was like I received a nudge from the universe. My racing thoughts came to a halt, and I heard in my heart, "God wouldn't put you through all of this, if he did not think you were strong enough to survive."

I must remind myself daily through positive affirmations. "I forgive myself. I am capable of loving myself and others. I am unconditional love."

I hope that my story touches your heart, just as doing this project touched mine. If you struggle with mental illness, please know that you are not alone. Love yourself and celebrate who you are, even if it's just during this moment as you're reading this beautiful book.

# February 15

## Mermaid Mantras
## By Tonia Browne

*What I say to myself matters, so I speak kindly.*

Mermaid mantras, which I created specifically for the gentle soul, are a fun way of describing affirmations. These mantras send vibrational messages to the universe. They are written or spoken in the present tense and are uplifting and empowering. They can be hugely beneficial because they rehearse a sentiment you hope to achieve and distract you from a behavior or feeling you want to change.

We are often unaware of how negative our self-talk can be. Instead of inspiring us into positive action, we scare ourselves into non-action. Instead of seeing signs that support our flow, we cling to things that drag us down. Noticing our own internal conversations is important. Interjecting with a mermaid mantra sets a positive vibe and can help cast away thoughts and emotions, empowering us and leading us into a more positive place.

When you catch yourself being negative, restore the balance with the opposite. If you feel uncomfortable with the mismatch between what you are saying and what you feel, use the words *I am willing* if it feels more authentic. For example say, *I am willing to see things from a positive perspective.* This can support the vibrational match you seek.

Mantras are a powerful healing tool and taking time to create your own demonstrates an act of self-love. When I notice my own negative self-talk and feel my vibration sink, I give myself a mermaid mantra as I would give a float to a non-swimmer. It helps me remember that I can see things differently and therefore experience things differently—not in the future, but right now. Here are some examples. Have fun designing your own.

*Miracles happen for me out of the blue.*

*I ride the waves of my life with grace and joy.*

*I am comfortable with my own shine.*

# February 16

## Creative Balance of the Five Elements
## By Virginia Adams

Balance, we all know we need it, but how do we obtain balance in a chaotic world? Just the thought of having to find balance may overwhelm some. Throughout the pages of this book, you will find my tidbits of creativity to support you in a quest to return to balance using self-love and the five elements of Chinese medicine.

The five elements are wood, fire, earth, metal, and water. Each element can be found in nature, and aspects of their energy are found within our essence. Playfully balancing these aspects with the use of our creative mind can be fun and rejuvenating. In Chinese medicine, each element represents an emotion.

Let's take a pause and remember that all emotions are good. Let me repeat that all feelings are beneficial and useful for our balance and growth. When we embrace this fact and lovingly approach our emotions, we begin to find balance. Denying, running, or covering emotions creates dis-ease within our physical, mental, emotional, and spiritual bodies or knocks us out of alignment. Sit with that idea for a moment.

What is alignment and to what are we aligning? We are created with, and in the likeness of, Source energy; this is our womb of balance. The truth is that we never fall out of balance or alignment; we never lose our connection to Source, though it may feel like it. There are many circumstances or life events that would veil our alignment and have us feeling out of balance. Our task is to remember our source, and within that recollection, we return to balance. Ahhh, we just created a little space for us to continue our exploration of the elements.

These are the five elements, the emotions attached to each, and the possibility for realignment.

- Wood – Anger – Germination
- Fire – Joy – Growth
- Earth – Worry – Transformation
- Metal – Grief – Reaping
- Water – Fear – Storing

Take a few moments today and play with these words depicting the elements. Write them down, journal, make a chart, draw/paint a picture, or collect a few objects to represent them. How does each of these elements make you feel as you read and explore them? Do you like one more than another? Do the emotions attached to some make you feel more resistant to their energy? There are no right or wrong answers; curiosity and playfulness are key in your exploration. Remember your source; you are creative energy.

# February 17

## Give Yourself Permission
## By Crystal Cockerham

As children we are trained to ask permission for practically everything. Heck, in elementary school you very likely played the game, Mother, may I? As adolescents, you still needed and were expected to ask permission to do practically everything that wasn't part of your expectations: go to school, do your home-work, do your chores, etc. Then, around your senior year in high school or the time you jolt off to college, you suddenly find that you are expected to just do and be in charge of everything.

All of this asking permission trained you to live up to the expectations of others and not to deviate from the norm around you. For some of us, there comes a point where their own independence and drive to succeed takes over the need for approval from others. For others, this point is hard won, if it shows up at all, due to various unhealthy childhood reasons or perhaps unhealthy co-dependent relationships or even because of too much ingrained responsibility.

Living to fill the expectations of others and not feeling fulfilled or propelled by passion is not being in love with yourself because you aren't being the version of you that you incarnated in this body to be.

If you feel there's no time in the day for *you* to unwind, read a book, attend a yoga class, or even think through something for yourself, it's time to give yourself permission to do so.

It is time to give yourself permission to step outside the day to day and break from routine.

- If normally you wake up and go to the coffee pot before showering, try doing the opposite.

- If you take the kids to school, go to the grocery store, and then go home and clean, switch it up.
- Do as many things differently as you possibly can and give yourself permission to be frazzled, discombobulated, even a few minutes late for something.

It is these moments when you are outside your routine that you are able to see what no longer serves you and the you that you are becoming. Give yourself permission to change it up. Give yourself permission to explore new paths, hobbies, careers.

Give yourself permission to change, to be a newer version of you. One that you are in love with. One that you continue to explore and grow with.

# February 18

## Self-Love is Staying in the Now
### By Vonnie L. Hawkins, LCSW

*I* discovered my healer's journey in early 2014 when I first sought to heal myself. For nearly three decades as an adult, I overvalued my mind and earned my living as a critical thinker, a rational, cognitive-influenced, problem-solving paralegal professional. All solutions came as the result of piercing, logical analysis because emotions were not to be trusted. Spock was my favorite *Star Trek* character!

After finishing a tough first year as an independent nonprofit consultant with seventy-hour work weeks, a long drought of work left me in a state of financial crisis. My greatest fear of working independently was finally being realized. I had gotten busy and failed to pipeline enough contracts to survive. I had no money coming in, no contracts, and was falling behind on my bills.

But from this dark time came the most transformational gift. After years of "trying" to meditate with no success at creating a sustained practice, I had exhausted all of the logical, cognitive ways to remove myself from the difficulty. Through a series of synchronicities, I realized the answer must lie in a realm unavailable to my logical, rational, conscious mind— meditation.

I came across *First You Sigh*, which I finished in just a few days. I began to engage in toning meditations during sessions with Beth Johnson which she recorded. Beth's work includes leading the listener through series of resonant oh, oooh, ah sounds that are pointed to stuck areas in different parts of the body. Through this practice, I began to re-establish the long missing connection between myself and my physical body. This form of unusual meditation as an introduction to the journey led to meditating longer and more often, strengthening the mind-body connection.

From this work, I took back initiative in my life. I began to eat healthier, meditate daily, and feel more joyful. Feeling better and being present in the now, I began offering to volunteer to help non-profits write grants. Work soon flowed and as I checked in to my path through meditation each morning and focused on the now, the worry about the future fell away and opportunities came once again. By investing in self-love through self-care, the doors to pursuing my dreams re-opened.

How do you reconnect with now? How could you strengthen your practice?

# *February 19*

## Sweet and Pretty
## By Tanya Thompson

*I*magine a little girl or boy under your care. Talk to yourself as if you are talking to that little child. The innocent child that is doing their best, but might spill a little milk, may color outside the lines, and make other mistakes. You're not meant to be perfect or judged against any other person.

A life coach asked me to list every negative thing I thought or believed about myself and then beside each of those statements, she had me reframe my statements as if I were talking to a little girl in second grade. What would I say to her? Reframing negative self-talk into a forgiving and loving language will change your life.

In a really high-pitched voice, with a squeal of excitement, my older sister would say to me, "You're so sweet and so pretty. I just love you to death."

She did this every time she greeted me, from when I was a baby to now, some forty something years later. When I find myself down the rabbit hole of negative self-talk, this is what I replay in my head to get me back to the reality that we're all kind, beautiful, and worthy of love and belonging.

# February 20

## Self-Forgiveness is Self-Love
### By Talia Renzo

*W*hen we are the hardest on ourselves, is when we need to be the most forgiving to ourselves.

"I am not worthy of this."

"Why do I deserve this?"

"I am not good enough."

"I am not pretty enough."

"I am not skinny enough."

These are just a few of the infinite examples of our inner critic and ego that puts roadblocks in the way of our journey to self-love. These examples hydroplane us off course and make it harder for us to get back on track.

The best thing you can ever do for yourself is change your negative thoughts and perceptions. Change how you would negatively view yourself. Take the ugliness of your feelings and paint them into something passionately beautiful.

"I am worthy of this."

"I am deserving of this."

"I am good enough."

"I am beautiful inside and out."

Make these positive affirmations part of your daily life through every part of your day, and I promise, you will make changes within yourself that you didn't think were possible. The way that you view yourself can reverse your low self-esteem, depression, mood, and your confidence.

Even if the negative perceptions of yourself, did not come from your own mind, and came from the opinion of some else, you must remember that how YOU see yourself is more important than what anyone can think or say about you.

After years of emotional and even physical bullying in school, I had to forgive those who hurt me, and I had to forgive myself. I had to step out of the person that those bullies created me into. I had to step into the person that I wanted to be. I needed to find my own voice and decide who I wanted to be. I was no longer going to be chained to the names that people gave me. I was going to reinvent myself, and love myself for all that I am and all that I am yet to be.

So please, put your hand on your heart, close your eyes, take a deep breath and love and celebrate yourself. You have a purpose here. No matter what anyone says, your purpose is not to live in pain, hurt, and suffering. By reading this book, you are one step closer to finding your purpose.

# February 21

## Mission Possible
## By Sheryl Goodwin Magiera

*I* have been on a self-discovery mission uncovering the person I left behind once I became a mother, even though it was a role I gladly accepted. However, in the process I stopped paying attention to what I wanted and dreamed of and focused on everyone else, making sure their needs were met before any of mine. Isn't that what moms do?

After many years, one day I instantly realized that I hardly recognized the woman staring back at me in the mirror, and I knew it was time to start considering my needs. I loved taking care of my family but desperately needed to take care of my desires as well. I was not sure what that would look like, but I was worth the effort.

I started discovering little things I used to love and new ones as well. I went back to school and finished my degree, I started traveling without my family but with girlfriends. I had previously let friendships fade away for soccer games, volleyball matches, birthday parties and volunteering; the list goes on and on. It was not out of spite, just out of family necessity.

The older my children became, the more independent they were and so was I. They needed me less and I needed me more. I discovered how much I missed me and it propelled me forward little by little. I get better at doing things for myself each year—not only with self-care, but more importantly with love and soul-care. I'm papering my the inside as much as the outside and discovering who I was meant to be.

Things I have learned along the way:

Change your story.

Become the person you wanted to be.

Celebrate your life.

Little shifts make big changes.

Live beyond the dream.

Use your gifts to impact others.

Be kind to yourself.

My journey is far from over as I get excited about uncovering and discovering more of me. If you struggle like I did, start small; find one thing you love, and do something just for you. The dream will become a reality if you let it in. Nothing is impossible, rather just the opposite, the mission is possible.

# February 22

## Create Your Own Self-Love Wisdom Book
## By Paula Obeid

*I*nspirational quotes provide us with a blast of wisdom to get our energies focused on our goals. Reading quotes on self-love offers us a boost of inspiration needed to remind us of our truth.

Many people love inspirational quotes. I know this to be true since they are posted all over social media. Rumi is one of America's bestselling poet and I know this to be true since he is endlessly quoted on Instagram.

Although I love social media, I would like to share an old school practice; create your own self-love wisdom book.

The wisdom book will be your private project where you can use your creativity to contain all your wisdom on self-love. It will be a book which is a blend of inspirational quotes, pictures and all things that delight you! It will be a collaged, visual representation that reminds you that *you are love!* I recommend that you create your self-love wisdom book in a mindful way. Be sure to delight in the process of finding the perfect quotations that touch your heart or even create your own inspirational quotes!

As everything on the self-love journey, there is no wrong way to create your wisdom book. The goal of this practice is not to create a perfect book but create a perfect expression of self-love for yourself. Your book is a personal self-love inspirational boost needed to remind you of your perfection. Just follow your heart as you bring together a collection of quotes, words, and pictures that are significant and remind you to love yourself unconditionally. You can also use the book as a meditative tool to focus on self-love and compassion.

If you would rather have something to hang on a wall to focus on during your meditation, you may prefer to do a collage on a self-love square. In this case use a square piece of cardstock. Remember to incorporate quotes, words, and images that bring you joy and have a self-love significance. In both the wisdom book and the self-love square, you are welcome to write affirmations or prayers. Use your creativity to create a specific focus on self-love.

On returning to social media, look for Rumi self-love quotes for a blast of wisdom.

"Your task is not to seek for love, but merely to seek and find all the barriers within yourself that you have built against it."- Rumi

# February 23

## Just Breathe
## By Denise Kirkconnell

As I have journeyed through my life in turbulent and happy times, becoming aware of my breathing has been instrumental in helping to calm down and maintain my energy. I realized long ago I would hold my breathe when I was stressed. At some point I realized that when I did this, it only made the situation worse by causing anxiety and other intolerable side effects.

Back when yoga was becoming popular was the first time I heard the saying, "Don't hold your breath." I was amazed at how just hearing that would set into motion the next few chapters of my life of practicing breathe work. It has calmed me down in some of life's most challenging moments. It is something we are already doing naturally. I strongly recommend learning how to control it so it works for your best and highest good.

So I began with the most basic of breathing techniques, which was to breathe in through my nose for four counts and release through the mouth for four counts. Repeat this several times at a slow and easy pace until you feel a shift in your body's energy. It can take a few times of doing this to understand and experience its full benefit. Give it some time. You can begin to slow down the triggers of anxiety and other things when we pay attention to our breathing.

I challenge you to try this short visualization while working with breath work any time of day. Breathe in the beauty of your life. Breathe out anything that no longer serves your highest and best good. Open your heart to the natural serene being that lies within you. All is well. You are loved. And so it is.

# February 24

## Weaving Sacred Geometry
## By Marie Martin

The patterns that show up in your life come from within and are old friends learned at a young age. Like unseen lines foraged from your heart to be broadcast into every area of your life, the habits and thoughts touch patterns spine out in a complex web. Each layer of this web is formed with steps that will lead you down a journey.

I wish that all your journeys be joyous for you, but with life being much as it is at some point, you are likely to face difficulty. It is in those times of difficulty; you will find out what your patterns are made of.

The patterns in your life can lead you to contentment or discontentment. For example, you may have heard the expression that people are likely to marry someone like their parent. For many of us, this is fine, but what if your parent was abusive?

Is it possible to break the chains of unhealthy and harmful patterns, even those we are not aware of? The answer is an enthusiastic yes! For the better part of the last fifteen years, I have been delving into my own life and restructuring my patterns. Here is what you will need to get started.

Restructuring or reforming patterns starts with paying attention to when you feel the worst. Sweetheart, you cannot backburner or bury whatever in your world is making you unhappy. You need to lean in and learn why does it keep showing up? There is a trigger consciously or unconsciously happening through your actions that makes the unfortunate outcome come back and around into your life.

When you work with unhappy or negative feelings, you can find the trigger to your pattern. Once you know what that pattern trigger is, you can go about changing it. It may take time, but imperfect action is your best friend here. When you work to modify an existing pattern, you have to retrain part of your brain to work in a new way, a better way, a way where it is possible to shift your current self into your ideal self. I will leave you with this thought. The patterns you weave in your life are a living form of sacred geometry, a picture you chose to weave. What kind of image will you make?

# February 25

## Your True Essence
## By Nancy Toffanin

We are all essence! We are created by energy, aura, and life force. It's what makes us all unique. To fall in love with someone's essence truly creates expansion within us! It helps us see our own essence and unearths all the protective layers we created.

Experiencing higher heart connections, falling in love with someone's essence, and being deeply connected with someone spiritually helped me truly love myself. By accepting the way we are, not trying to change one another, you are making your heart expand and learn unconditional love.

Sometimes we look at someone's external being; we label them and put x's besides their name. If we saw behind all the wounds and traumas, and loved their energy so much we'd often create a new box for them. Having experienced magnetic connection on an energetic level, I felt so calm in these people's presences and electrified.

Falling in love with someone's essence helped to open my gateway to self-love.

When we are in flow in a relationship, loving someone unconditionally and accepting him with no judgment, it teaches us to see someone's true essence. In creating a new box with this person, it helped me to love myself and expand my heart. The biggest lesson I learned was that that my heart was so expansive that I can deeply love more than one person.

It also opened me up to a deeper love with someone else creating a connection on all levels.

Choosing to see the true essence of each other helps us to become the best version of ourselves. In order to grow and maintain this, we need to support each other in becoming the best versions in our relationships. When we get caught up in the physical world, we don't feel someone's energy. In accepting each other completely, all the judgment falls away. We can be free to expand, grow, and transform. When we live from our true essence, it strips away all barriers we put up. It helps us become authentic. If our story over-rules our essence, that makes it hard on us. There are many layers to self-love and those include working through fears, not putting labels on anything, having boundaries, being true to ourselves, and remembering that all have value.

Self-reflection

1. How do you shape shift in your relationships?
2. Do you put your perception of people into boxes?

# *February 26*

## Your Hands Are All You "Knead"
## By Salli Sebastian Walker

*W*ould you like to learn how to give a massage to your loved ones? Once you learn the basic steps and techniques of a good Swedish massage, you will be well on your way to sharing this beautiful art form with others. As a licensed massage therapist for thirty years, I hope this guide to Swedish massage resonates for you.

Let's start with twenty-five reasons why you and others can reap the benefits of a massage. According to the American Massage Therapy Association, they are:

1. Relieves stress,
2. Relieves postoperative pain,
3. Reduces anxiety,
4. Manages low-back pain,
5. Helps fibromyalgia pain,
6. Reduces muscle tension,
7. Enhances exercise performance,
8. Relieves tension headaches,
9. Helps you sleep better,
10. Eases symptoms of depression,
11. Improves cardiovascular health,
12. Reduces pain of osteoarthritis,
13. Decreases stress in cancer patients,
14. Improves balance in older adults,

15. Decreases rheumatoid arthritis pain,
16. Tempers effects of dementia,
17. Promotes relaxation,
18. Lowers blood pressure,
19. Decreases symptoms of carpal tunnel syndrome,
20. Helps chronic neck pain,
21. Lowers joint replacement pain,
22. Increases range of motion,
23. Decreases migraine frequency,
24. Improves quality of life in hospice care,
25. Reduces chemotherapy-related nausea.

Choose a lotion or oil such as almond for a luxurious experience. You may use your hands, forearms, or elbows. Here are some techniques.

- Effluerage: long sweeping strokes that can alternate between firm and light pressure and applied with the palm of the hand or fingertips.
- Petrissage: kneading and squeezing the muscles of the body to achieve deep penetration.
- Tapping or tapotement: consists of rhythmic motion that utilizes the fists or the sides of the hands.
- Friction: seeks to create heat to the tissue. The palms of the hands can be rubbed together or the hands can vigorously rub the skin.
- Vibration or shaking: helps loosen the tissue by using a back-and-forth motion with the fingertips or the heels of the hands.

The gift of touch is like no other. Your family, your friends, and you are sure to benefit from these techniques.

# February 27

## Energy Tune-Up
## By Sarah Berkett

The following is an activator of sorts that another one of my mentors had me do a few years ago. I still do it to this very day and it keeps me accountable for myself. Get a picture of yourself from when you were six or younger and look at it every day. Put it in your purse or have it on your work desk or night table. When you catch yourself being critical of yourself, this is who you are criticizing. Your younger self at that time knew you were loveable exactly the way you were and did have any insecurities. This little girl still lives inside of you. If you can connect with her eyes in that picture, you drop right from your head and into your heart. This is one of the fastest tools that moves you from self-criticism into self-compassion and self-love.

When we are in this place of self-love, we are more likely to have kinder thoughts and be courageous in addressing the things we do not really want to face. Acknowledging and validating our inner child can bring healing and much transformation.

# February 28

## On the Glow
## By Ashlie Bradley

In the fast-paced, on-the-go world we live in today, an on-the-glow morning routine is necessary to maintain balance. Starting your day centered is crucial for setting up a day of internal success. Without it, being swept into the daily rat race becomes normal. We might even forget to take one conscious breathe. Over time, this way of being becomes mechanical, leading to a loss of connection. All you need is twenty to thirty minutes of mindful practice to assist in this loving shift. I have listed below a handful of effective bits to start your day with. Find what works for your authentic self.

- Stretch
- Meditate (in bed if you like)
- Brisk walk
- Ten long conscious breathes
- Drink 16 ounces of water
- Fifty squats
- Name twenty things you are grateful for
- Read a positive book with your coffee
- Dance to a favorite song
- Appreciate nature
- Journal a few intentions for the day
- Speak affirmations in the mirror
- Pray
- Smile

These steps can make a cosmic difference in the vibration you operate from each day.

And that makes a difference to your universe as a whole. Morning routine is one of the most loving gifts we can give to ourselves. The magic of high vibrational living is always available, it just begins with tapping in. So let's get the morning party started, it's time to glow up!

# February 29

## I See
## By Lisa Seyring

*W*hat is your perception? Have you ever wondered about this? What is it that you're actually seeing with regard to your life experiences? Is yours the only perspective? Have you ever had the experience where you pivot your perception just a bit and a whole new understanding of a situation or of yourself appears? It's like magic! A whole new world opens up.

I love perception. Inviting in another perspective has truly helped me change the trajectory of how I experience myself. I once scolded myself for being so quiet. I then shifted my perspective and asked, "What does being quiet allow me to do?"

To my delight and surprise, I realized that being quiet allowed me to be an excellent listener and that I actually listened with my whole being, and not just my ears. It completely changed my narrative. This shift in perception invited me to move from the constriction I felt in judgment to the openness of love and acceptance. I widened my lens to seek deeper understanding of myself and also situations. I endeavored to see from a different perspective. I shifted my lens to come from the field of love.

The following exercise was an immense help because it taught me what it felt like to shift my perception. I needed assistance getting out of my own way and to practice seeing from other angles. May the following exercise help you to experience shifting your perception at will, as it did me.

1. Select a table or coffee table that you can easily move around so you can observe from four differing angles.

2. Collect five different items of varying sizes and colors and put them in a tight arrangement in the center of the table.

3. Sit in each of the four positions and describe out loud in detail what you see. Allow yourself to travel around the table.

Each angle will provide you with a different perspective of the arrangement. Nothing changes with the arrangement, only your perspective of the arrangement changes. The position of your perspective changes everything! Now, apply this to life. What new information can you glean by making a shift in your sight? Loving the self is an inside job. Become familiar with your inner dialogue and know there is room to shift your perspective to invite more love into the equation.

# March 1

## Move Your Body 30
## By Debra Moore Ewing

One of my spiritual teachers, Sunny Dawn Johnston, has created a movement called *Move Your Body 30*. It is catchy, only thirty minutes, and the results set your tone for the day not to mention if you do it first thing, you are done! No excuses, just thirty minutes, and you, my friend, are worth it!

I have always exercised at a gym. However, during the recent pandemic that hit our world, gyms were closed. I am embarrassed to say I had no idea how good it felt to be out in nature even just in my subdivision! It forced me to leave the confines of my home to get my thirty minutes in. Even my husband got on the bandwagon and while he has now returned to work, he gets up earlier and walks every morning.

Look at it as setting the tone to receive your energy for the day and to get your endorphins going. Starting your morning energetically releases dopamine and is pivotal in helping to kick-start your day!

I am smiling as I write this. I have never taken the time to just enjoy nature in my neighborhood and surrounding area. I saw people on horseback and met others walking their dogs. I noticed a new insect that I had never seen and after posting a picture on Facebook found out it is one to steer clear of! Apparently, its sting is extremely painful! I enjoyed watching the sunrise over the mountains and the tops of saguaros where sometimes a bird was perched soaking up the rays. I even made note of a cacti seedling and will be anxious to watch it grow. I always thought I would have to drive my car someplace to experience nature, but in all honesty, it is as easy as walking out your front door!

Are you sitting on the couch reading this right now? Are you thinking, "Okay. I will start tomorrow?" Seriously? Come on! I encourage you to get up, grab a coat, mittens, and hat if you need one, go outside and start walking! Even if it is only fifteen minutes. Just get started. Please do it now for *you* because *you* are worth it! You will be amazed at how much better you feel! Trust me. I promise! If I can do it, I know you can, too!

# *March 2*

## Your Heart Connection. Your Self-Love Connection.
## By Lisa A. Clayton

*T*he more you connect with your heart; the more self-love will be generated. Connecting with your heart is as simple as a few deep and slow breaths into your heart area. Asking the mind to focus upon breathing into the heart gives it a "job to do," helping eliminate thoughts running rampant. Focusing upon heart breathing for two to three minutes calms your nervous system and brings your heart and mind into coherent states of working together.

Once you establish this connection, visualize everything you are grateful for, appreciate, and love in your life. This starts a powerful love wave flowing in your heart. Activate the feelings of appreciation and gratitude as you breathe into your heart. Your heart is pumping up for self-love.

Next, feel deep appreciation and gratitude for being alive in this present moment on this amazing planet and having this moment of opportunity to connect fully with your heart. Feel deep gratitude for your heart never missing a beat to keep you alive. As you continue to breathe slowly into your heart, thank your heart for its magnificent job on the physical, emotional, mental and spiritual levels.

Now, activate feelings of love, care, and appreciation for yourself. Keep breathing slow and deeply in your heart as you activate these feelings. Visualize the space between your heart chambers, the heart's sacred space. Breathe directly into your heart's sacred space with love, care and appreciation.

Now, visualize roots growing with an anchor securing the feelings of love, care, and appreciation into your heart's sacred space. They are securing stability and inner strength for you to access when the ego starts to ruminate negative thoughts or initiates self-sabotage talk. You can access your heart's sacred space with a few deep breaths and trust that love, care, and appreciation are there as strong, anchored roots.

Next practice radiating like the sun's rays. Radiate pure love beaming from your heart's sacred space to every cell of your body. Inhale slowly into your heart's sacred space and exhale by radiating golden light-rays throughout your body. You are filling each cell up energetically with super charged love light. Keep this synchronized breathing going for at least five minutes.

You have just taken a self-love bath energetically with the power of your heart leading the way by radiating love, care, and appreciation for your unique and beautiful essence being.

# March 3

## Tiny Dancer
## By Ann Marie Asp

From the moment I could walk, and throughout my adult life, dance has always held a special place in my heart. As a child I would spend countless hours creating magical and free-flowing movements from my body, bringing to life the tiny dancer within me. It was while creating these mesmerizing movements and passion-filled dance routines that an inner flame began to grow. It was that flame that touched something deep within my calling heart.

This new discovery allowed me to bring forth a passion that I had kept hidden for so many reasons. Self-expression did not come easily for me, especially in front of my peers. I trust many of you have faced this fear at some time in your childhood and adult lives. By learning to tune in to this amazing gift, I began to look at myself with a newfound love and appreciation of how special I really was. Once we learn to tap into the unique wisdom and style that is only ours to open, it is there we find the answers to our true calling and purpose.

Take time out of your day today and connect with the tiny dancer within you. Let go of all inhibitions and expectations. Bring forth that creative free spirit that wants to be seen and heard. It is through this awakening within each one of us that we are then provided the opportunity to channel our energies into a more joyful and fulfilling life.

So, what are you waiting for?

Today is the start of bringing to life that amazing dancer within you. Turn on your favorite music, you know the songs where you just can't stop moving once you get started. The songs that take you to that magical place. Put on your favorite t-shirt and leggings. Grab those glitter dance sneakers.

Slowly tune into that place of your own individual creativity. Within there lies the wonder of the amazing you. Open yourself to this new transformation. It is now your time to shine! No room for fear or worry.

Remember the quote you've got to dance as if no one is watching. You will begin to feel an appreciation for those beautiful gifts that are yours alone. Give thanks to that tiny dancer for the joy and inner peace she has blessed you with today and every day moving forward. Take a bow, you deserve it!

# March 4

## Let Mother Earth Love You:
## Finding Love in All the Right Places!
## By Charel Morris

Most of us have experienced the concept of grounding. Simply you imagine a cord moving from the base of your spine and into Mother Earth. This is usually done before a meditation or visualization. It may feel nice and easy. Maybe you don't feel anything at all. Either way is fine. There are many facets to consider when using your grounding cord and many reasons to use your unique cord. The results are both powerful and positive.

First exercise. To begin with, I want you to imagine that you are sending a cord from the bottom of each foot. As they emerge, they blend together into one cord. Move this cord into our Mother Earth. It doesn't matter if you are standing barefoot in the wilderness or you are on the forty-fourth floor of your office building in downtown Manhattan. Your intention and your imagination know exactly how to move your grounding cord into the Earth. Sense, see or imagine your cord easily and effortlessly moving towards the center of our Earth. As it moves, shift your awareness and your intention to moving love down through this cord. Let love pour from your heart and your whole body down to through your grounding cord. Allow your awareness to experience this happening.

You are sending love, your most precious and powerful energy, from your heart down into our Mother Earth. As your grounding cord reaches the center of our Earth your love pours out and begins to spread and flow into our precious mother. As she receives your gift, you become aware that a high-flying love vibration from the heart of the Earth that is moving back into you. This infinite love, that is pulsing through your body, moves into every corner of your soul releasing tension, sorrow, separation and pain. This rush of pure love pours back into you is lovingly igniting every cell in your body.

Allow this exchange to continue. Pour your endless love into our Mother Earth. You are filled with gratitude for this magnificent gift from our mother. Accept her gift and allow in all the healing that she provides. Now move into your practice of self-love mixing in the love that Mother Earth has offered you.

# March 5

## Dare to Dream – The Rainbow Connection
## By Bonnie Larson

*W*hy do we dream? Lovers and dreamers share their magical outlooks and the promise of finding deep and satisfying joy. Something within each of us searches for a spiritual or physical connection to that which we most desire.

Through the liberal arts, we are inspired to reach a little higher, dream a little bigger, wish a little harder, and to believe. Musical arrangements speak loudly as instruments drive home the point at our very hearts. There is a reason for that soft, fuzzy feeling. It's human design, desiring to experience the deeper meanings of life.

Rainbows temporarily reflect vibrations of light under just the right conditions. Violet, the color of light, a shorter wavelength, bends more readily. Red, the vibration of passion, yields more slowly, surrendering to the possibilities of fulfillment. It's so personal, depending upon our point of view.

Isn't that like a dream? To realize our deepest desire, to find our true love, we must first believe. Looking not only within but also beyond ourselves. Sometimes as far as the stars and the heavens. The morning star, Venus, the first to rise, illuminates the sky until the sun rises. She shines most brightly, the goddess of love, beauty, and desire. *Look what it's done so far.*

The sweet-sounding voice calls softly, inviting our dreams. The promise of gratification if we dare to dream. Self-love's expression not to be ignored. True happiness usually involves others. The rainbow connection begs the question: What's on the other side? Some choose to believe—*in lovers, the dreamers, and me.*

# March 6

## Starting Over
## By Gloria Dawn Kapeller

How many times have we had to start over in our lives? From failed relationships, heartbreak, separation, abandonment, death, we all have had to start over at some point. What sets us apart is how we handle and deal with what life hands us. Either we rise above and deal with it or it gets the best of us.

I like to look at it as lessons that we as souls have come to learn and what is the messages or growth that our souls have wanted to take away from these life experiences. I believe that there is always a silver lining in what we experience. If life hands you lemons? Make lemonade.

An exercise that I like to do for self love is to journal. Write down your thoughts, feelings, acknowledge them and then burn it if you need too. Release and don't let it fester. Release it and you will feel better. We are often taught to bury our feelings, keep our emotions bottled up and just keep going. My belief now is that we need to deal with our emotions and let them go. Can you give yourself even five minutes a day to writing down in a journal what you need to say, how you are feeling, both the good and bad, no judgement? Practice makes perfect, so for the next thirty days can you make the promise to yourself to sit down for five minutes and write down your feelings? This will definitely lead to more time and before you know it ten, even thirty minutes will have gone by. I started this way and before I knew it, I was writing more than that. We all can take five minutes to improve our lives.

# March 7

## Beautiful Dreamer
## By Jannirose Fenimore

*L*ong ago, I had a dream so riveting that it changed my life. This breathtaking vision came at a time when I was striving to live my purpose. In those days, I had already begun my journey of self-realization—so I understood about the parts of ourselves that can be shrouded from our awareness. But I would soon learn on a personal level how profoundly these unknown aspects affect our wellness in mind, body, and spirit.

And even though I share life with an earth angel—my son Charlie whose innocent lessons in loving are ever present—I had not yet uncovered the parts of me that cried so desperately for the depth of love and attention that he so naturally reflects.

But back to my dream…

In the first scene, I was holding an infant that could have been my twin with her black hair, brown eyes, and peach-colored skin. She was absolutely perfect—a vibrant, healthy girl. As the picture faded, I saw myself spread in many directions on my personal quest to serve humanity.

In the second scene, the baby seemed quieter. This was so subtle that I thought I might have imagined it, so I was not too concerned. Again, the vision closed with an image of me immersed in my activities of selfless service.

In the third scene, my sweet daughter looked pale and listless. I noticed these changes but did not seem particularly worried as I kept pace with my busy schedule as a teaching healer.

It was the final scene of this dream that rocks my world even today. I remember the disbelief I felt when I found my sweet baby girl lying so still in her crib. In that heart-wrenching moment, I cried to the heavens in anguish, "My God, what happened?"

The answer I heard so clearly shook me to the core. "You forgot to feed the baby."

In an instant, I understood the meaning of this unsettling message. I was so focused on my calling that I ignored the cries of my soul, and a part of me was dying because of it. To this day, I have not lost sight of the profound gift of awakening this dream granted me.

With deepest compassion, I will ask you one important question. Is there an aspect of your precious self that you have forgotten to feed?

# March 8

## Hopeful Shining Courage
## By Charlie Fenimore

*L*ove is about living the light that makes our hearts shine like the sun. We need joy from spiritness for our minds and courage to be hopeful. We can heal from hurting with our joyful brightness of loving, and life will change.

# March 9

## I Led Three Lives
## By Marilyn Miller

*D*o you ever fantasize about glamorous careers, careers you feel you could never achieve? I certainly did. As a teenager, I saw myself as a ballerina living in New York City. But since I'm five feet nine inches tall with irregular toes not suited for toe shoes, I gave up that fantasy. I have also admired famous authors, movie directors and Pulitzer Prize-winning journalists, never aspiring to be like any of them.

Over the years, I've discovered fantasies help me recognize heartfelt dreams. As a young person, I dreamed of being in spiritual service, but I saw few opportunities, as women could not be ministers at that time in my denomination. Native Americans tell us that our cherished goals often begin with a fantasy. Take a moment. Fantasize about what you would do if you could do anything regardless of talent, training or experience. One of my fantasies was to have an international career with homes in the United States and Europe. What fantasies do have you have?

- Draw a large triangle on an eight-by-eleven piece of paper. Outside each of the three corners of the triangle, write one of your fantasy career choices. (Remember, you need no talent, training or experience to choose it.)

- Inside each corner.write what attracts you to that career. It could be travel, service, wealth, fame.

- After writing what benefits attract you to each fantasy, see if the benefits you seek show any similarity to the others you have listed. For example, do you prefer working at home? Do you want to help people?

- What does your heart long to do?
- Write those similarities in the center of your triangle and study what experiences you are looking for.
- As you study what attracts you to each career choice, you may find the experience you are seeking.

Regardless of the actual career, you may discover that some benefits you like can be achieved in many careers. Once I did this exercise, and I put opera singer as one of my choices. I can sing a little, but I have never wanted to study opera. However, just voicing that fantasy led me to begin writing song lyrics with a friend who writes music. Our songs have been published, and I have even received royalties. Happy fantasizing!

# *March 10*

## Activities of Daily Living
## By Margaret-Maggie Honnold

*A*ctivities of daily living are basic developmental tasks that are often used as mile markers to judge physical growth. Developmental tasks change at different life stages and build a foundation for moving on in the aging process. I was flabbergasted when I discovered, at sixty-five, the concept of developmental tasks continued into old age. It made me look at myself very closely and oftentimes, it was painful. But the result is worth the effort.

Learning self-love at seventy-two, what am I thinking? Well, as an adopted child who spent a lifetime at the bottom of the self-love pile because of life circumstances, I can guide you into many ways how not to do it. For example, like a lot of women, I put everyone but myself first because that was what my mother, and my mother's mother, and her mother did, and I needed to prove I was good enough. You proved that you were good enough by putting yourself last. Interesting, isn't it?

Today, focus on activities that remove judgment in your mind and heart. Pick one or two to which you can say "so what," and then forget.

Aging is a good example of society's unreasonable expectations. Here are a few of the things that are old lady self-care activities that help to cope with the aging changes.

Permit yourself to wear your readers to fasten your bra.

A good pair of merino wool socks worn to bed at night facilitate better sleep.

Embrace the dog drool from your bloodhound who gives fabulous snuggles. Dogs do not care if you are cleaned up and dressed up, or have make-up on your face. Although, it is a good self-love practice to bathe more than twice a month.

Self-love is not a group project. Incorporate your inner hermit into your planning sessions.

Say thank you and do not bat an eye when your housekeeper offers to buy you leak-proof panties.

Learn to love a nap. No one copes well when tired and a good night's sleep is often elusive as we age. Turn off your inner voice even if it takes a little help to do so.

Stop looking so closely at what you feel are your shortcomings. Often it is hard to believe we are lovable because we know our flaws and failures even if the world does not.

Make today a "believe you are worth it day."

# March 11

## Find Your Joy
## By Janice Story

*I* often hear some of my clients, along with other people in general, say that their life no longer seems to have any meaning or purpose. They feel stuck, unsure of the next direction they want to take. Everyone appears to be so caught up in the everyday chaos that has taken over the control panel of their thoughts that they tend to almost be functioning on autopilot. I think we've all been there at least a few times.

I begin asking them questions like "What makes you happy? What brings you joy? What do you really like to do?"

I've been amazed lately from people responding with "I have no clue."

Everyone has become so busy they've forgotten about the little joyful things in life that make them happy or maybe they really don't know what happiness or joy feel like.

When we start bringing more happiness and joy into our lives, it changes everything around us. Our personal relationships grow stronger as our own moods shift and we begin spreading joy to others, creating an amazing ripple effect. We become physically, emotionally, mentally, and spiritually happier.

The difficult part is the how. How do you reach this happiness and find your joy? While it is not a snap your fingers and everything will change overnight rapid fix, there are practices you can begin if you want to create some positive changes in your life. Here are a few ideas and suggestions to help you get started.

- Compile a list of at least twenty-five things that you like to do (even if it is eating an ice cream cone or your favorite candy bar. Those little things that make you smile.) Be sure to include a variety of things on your list and enough items that you can easily pick one to do no matter how much time you have.

- Make at least three copies of your list.
- Keep one copy in your wallet or purse, one by your bed, and one wherever else you tend to spend a lot of time.

If you've had a rough day, pull your list out, pick one item, and treat yourself.

# March 12

## Looking in the Mirror
## By Karen Cowperthwaite

Self-love is something that needs to be practiced every day. It is the unconditional belief that you are worthy of your own love without having to achieve or be accepted.

How do you start to love yourself? One of the earliest spiritual teachers I was introduced to that strengthened my self-esteem and self-confidence was Louise Hay. For six months I met with a group of women every other Sunday afternoon to study her book, *You Can Heal Your Life*. In it, she presents a tool called mirror work. As the name suggests, by looking into the mirror you begin to talk to yourself with love and kindness. When your day has been easy, you look into your eyes and tell yourself "That was an amazing day!" When challenges are faced and disappointment weighs you down, you speak to yourself with care and concern, letting that part of you know it will get better.

When I first began, it was difficult to stare into the eyes that were looking back at me. But the longer I stayed there, the easier it became to have compassion for the beautiful soul on the other side of my reflection. It can be a split-second connection or a several minute soul stare that evokes a feeling of oneness. Each passing of a mirror is an opportunity to stop and greet yourself with a "Hi, beautiful," or a "You look marvelous." For moments when you have more time, an affirmation can be said with love for your true nature. We can express lovingly the amazing gift that we are and accept ourselves unconditionally. At any given moment, we can choose to be a vessel for love or we can choose to be a vessel for fear. Louise would say, "Let's begin right now in this moment to choose love. It's the most powerful healing force there is."

Begin with a thirty-day commitment to make the smallest change in the way you talk to yourself and the way you look into your eyes. Encourage yourself for the small changes you make. Every act of self-care demonstrates your belief in your worth as a spiritual being. You came here for a purpose and self-love is a moment-by-moment decision. Allow the simple gesture of a wink, nod, or whispered "I love you" the next time you look into the mirror.

# March 13

## Is Your Outer World Affecting Your Inner World
## By Bernadette Rodebaugh

When I turned twelve, I found out that I had a hereditary illness. If I removed a particular organ and then took medication the rest of my life to take the place of the organ, then I would be fine. This life-changing event made me hyper aware and anxious of my body and my health. I became a hypochondriac overnight.

After counseling I learned many things but one of the things that change my life the most was "what we think about we bring about." I found as I stopped focusing on the negative or fear of illness, I simply didn't have health issues anymore.

So, when Covid-19 became a preoccupation of our world, I was not consumed with it and did not allow information on the news to overly affect my daily activities. This was a *huge milestone* in my life because nineteen years earlier this was not true!

This is even more interesting because my husband is overly obsessed with the news. It's kind of like a hobby for him.

When I noticed my husband's interest in the news was affecting my peace of mind, I told him, "I know this information is very important and interesting to you, but I have already been educated on this information and now choose not to focus on it! So this means if you want to watch the news while we eat dinner etc., I will go into our bedroom and eat my dinner or whatever until the news is over. This is no problem to me because I know it's important to you."

He said, "Okay, I understand."

So now, I gracefully leave the room every time he has the news on, and we're both happy during that thirty minutes.

Now I ask you to do some soul searching in your own life and ask yourself in what areas in your life do you need to create healthier boundaries so that you can be happier mentally, physically, or spiritually? Take out your journal and write down those situations. I suggest short bullet points; there is no need for long drawn-out scenarios or to dig up deep emotions with these topics. When you're done writing down these bullet points, write down *positive* boundaries for the future to handle these situations.

# March 14

## The Negative Voices
## By Danielle Fierro

There are so many times that your mind is bombarded with negative thoughts. It sounds like voices or chatter in your head. It feels as if your feet get stuck in the mud, preventing you from growing. You may hear it as self-doubt, comparison, criticism, judgment, or scarcity. All of which are fear based. You don't have to allow fear to control your thoughts and actions. You can take back your power and diminish the control that the negative voices have on your life.

The first step is to be aware of how often the negative chatter enters your mind. Awareness is key in determining how often that happens, what form it takes, and what it's about.

An exercise you can do to gather this information is to keep a small notebook with you for three days. On the first day, make a tick mark in the notebook every time you have a negative thought. Just this simple count could be surprising. On the next day, make the tick mark and write down the form in which the negative thought presented itself (i.e. comparison, scarcity, judgment, criticism, etc.). On the final day, do the same as you did on the second day, but also write what the thought was about (i.e. money, career, your appearance, relationship, etc.). Looking back on this information may provide you with the details of the frequency of the negative voices throughout the day, how it most often comes about, and for what reason. Use this information to acknowledge the fear or issue, get to the root of the issue, and find a way to redirect it. Don't be afraid to feel your feelings. That sounds strange but we tend to push away and bury the uncomfortable feelings that we don't want to face. Doing that doesn't get rid of them because they may bubble back up, unconsciously, through the negative voices in our head.

If you look back at the information you collected, you may find that the negative chatter comes up when you are at the brink of your comfort zone. You might be facing growth in an area of your life or wanting to take a risk. Think of the negative voices as an alarm, alerting you to when you are getting close to the edge of your comfort zone. Then you can confidently take the step to expand your comfort zone.

# March 15

## On Being Grateful
## By Nancy Meikle-Mousseau

*F*or many years I have noticed that when I did something for someone else, I enjoyed the feeling that accompanied the act of doing. I was thankful for that feeling. When I added a voice to that thankful feeling, it seemed to set a momentum for things going right for the rest of my day. I was led to seeking the difference between being thankful and being grateful. Being *thankful* is a feeling; being *grateful* is an action. The expression of gratitude is the continuous flow of being thankful.

When I became a student of Reiki, one of the principles I learned was *Just for Today, I will be Grateful*. I was inspired to buy a desk calendar and write on the back of each day's slip of paper what I was grateful for, just for that day. Reflection of contribution, alignment, spoken words, good deeds for me and for others and the little things that end up being the bigger things, all were written down and put in a gratitude jar, with love. At the end of the year, I sat reading each piece of paper and was full of gratitude. I noticed a shift in myself, looking for things and people and ways to be grateful and they appeared to me every day. Each year, I bought a desk calendar with positive words or pictures that provoked a good feeling. I chose a different container to hold my gratitude. As each year passed, my gratitude notes were lovingly wrapped in ribbon and kept in a special box. I created a grateful mindset without even trying. The mindset grows over time, becoming an intrinsic part of my self love practice and has a significant impact on my state of well being.

*The grateful exercise*

Purchase a small desk calendar that is inspiring to you and that has pages you can rip off, as well as a glass jar with lid or box that you like. At the end of your day, reflect and find three to five things that filled you with gratitude. If you are struggling, you can always be grateful for your bed. Start small and by looking for things to be grateful for, you will start a wonderful momentum of self love.

# March 16

## Breathe into Peace
## By Ellen Elizabeth Jones

Our breath is an incredible tool that we can access any time to self-soothe, slow down, become mindful, and create a feeling of calm and safety in our bodies. We do not normally pay attention to our breathing. Deep breathing exercises are a great way to reduce stress. Taking a few moments to concentrate and breathe deeply calms not just the mind but the body. There are many ways to practice deep breathing, all effective. There are countless exercises and strategies that can be helpful. This exercise can help you *breathe into peace.*

1. Find a quiet, safe space where you will not be disturbed for a few minutes. You can set a timer if this is helpful.

2. Close your eyes and take a few full, deep breaths.

3. As you inhale, think about the oxygen that is flooding your body. Visualize golden light traveling through every part and cell of your body, filling you up with effervescent life.

4. If it aligns, imagine this life you are breathing in is full of compassion and warmth for you. With each inhale, imagine this love and comfort being sent into every part and every cell of your body.

5. Each time you exhale, imagine releasing any tension, self-criticism, or resistance. Try not to force your breath out too quickly. Let it flow as you breathe out slowly and naturally.

6. Continue breathing in and out like this for several minutes. If your mind wanders, simply notice it without judgement and then refocus on your breath.

7. Repeating a mantra such as "breathe in gratitude, exhale grace" can be helpful.

8. As you end the meditation, take note of any changes to your mind, body, and emotions. Note whether you feel calm and relaxed or if any tension or resistance is still present.

This exercise is not simply about feeling relaxed. The purpose is to return to your center. The benefit of allowing yourself time to observe without judgment or criticism creates space for greater self-awareness and peace.

# March 17

## What is Self-Care?
## By Carrie Newsom

We often hear about self-care. What exactly does self-care look like? It's an elusive concept for those of us who are givers, who care for others before we focus on ourselves. While the idea is a great one, putting self-care into practice can be difficult. We often don't know where to start. What constitutes taking care of ourselves? On the top on my list are things like a massage, bubble bath, getting my nails done, but I often cannot find time for those things or don't want to spend the money on them because they don't seem like a priority. I circle back to the feeling that I don't know how to take care of myself. This leads to feelings of shame. As a parent, wife, educated woman, why don't I know how to take care of myself? Why is this part of me broken?

I've realized that self-care doesn't have to mean spending time and money on extravagant luxuries, although that is fun! Self-care is about celebrating that I am alive. It's about becoming aware that I matter; I am important; I am enough. It's about knowing that it's ok for me to rest, to find comfort.

One of the biggest ways we can take care of ourselves is to recognize the feelings we have, and just feel them. Don't worry that your anger is too large. Or that your concern is too deep. Too many women worry that their feelings are too massive, too audacious, to fit into the space they feel they are allotted in life.

There's no such thing as feeling too much feeling! We are allowed to feel everything. Even the most difficult emotions can teach us about which way to move in life, what decisions to make, what is important, how to shift our focus. I encourage you to sit with your feelings and not medicate them away, eat them away, shop them away, or stuff them down. The emotions we feel are our inner guidance, and it is important to listen. Sink deep into your gut and sit with the feelings. Feel all the feels. Know that the difficult emotions will not last forever. Trust that your feelings are a beacon, shining a light on the path ahead.

Just let your heart feel the feels without shoving them down and ignoring them. Take care of yourself by recognizing your feelings and giving yourself space and grace to process those emotions. You are worth it. Celebrate you by shining a light on your feelings.

# March 18

## Take Life Slow and Easy
### By JoAnne Eisen

When I come upon exciting information, I become ravenous to learn all I can as fast as possible. That trait has not served me well throughout my life. You might ask why?

When I was pregnant, I was excited to have my baby and share our lives together. During the last trimester, I was very impatient. You cannot speed birth along. A baby comes when it's ready. I made myself miserable trying to hurry that process!

As I traveled my journey, I was determined to do inner work. To understand the spiritual truths of life. I was extremely impatient, trying to force the process. I was not changing fast enough. This was clearly the judgment of my ego. I went to classes, teachers, and mentors, always searching for that perfect answer, only to find more questions. This was extremely frustrating. I didn't believe I could trust my inner guidance or my connection to the spiritual world. Once again, my impatience didn't allow my processes to unfold naturally. I started to observe the futility of my actions and knew that slow and steady always wins. Your human experience is to trust your inner knowing and love yourself unconditionally, hopefully, at all times.

There is a deep desire to understand life, but you forget to stop, value, accept the wisdom you were born with, and embrace the abilities you already possess. You look outside yourself for the truth and the happiness you desire when happiness has been inside you all the time. No amount of education, seminars, mentorship, or classes will make you feel whole, happier, or more successful. No amount of searching outside of yourself will bring you the joy you desire in life. You were born with it. Stop looking so hard to find the answers that are already within you. You have the best mentors and teachers you could ever need with you at every moment. You entered the best school that ever existed when you were born: the school of life. You are your own best guru if you can trust your soul's guidance.

Explore all aspects of life without hesitation.

Life is to be lived and enjoyed. Please don't rush through it. It will happen as it is meant to happen. All you need is to trust and unconditionally love yourself. You are unconditionally loved at all times in all spaces.

# March 19

## Seasons
### By Florence Acosta

The trees shed their leaves as part of the cycle of renewal in the fall season. In order to grow, we must release something—this a universal principle. We are in a constant process of self-discovery and integrating new information, aspects of ourselves, perceptions and ideas, as we realize that the old patterns or ways of doing things may no longer work.

In the long, cold, dark winter months, we rest. We practice stillness. We go within. We examine the dark and the light of our own experiences and life. We contemplate how to bring change, expansion and growth faster. We explore our dreams in depth for the hope of the new year.

Nature provides the nutrients it needs to create new and abundant foliage in the spring. In fact, it is by releasing the old leaves to the earth in the fall that provides the compost for nourishing the soil—the foundation for new growth and fuel for renewal in the spring. Hanging onto what no longer serves us hinders the ability for new growth and expansion.

In the summer months, we celebrate the sun and the warmth. We celebrate the chirping birds and the trilling toads. We celebrate the full bloom of trees and flowers. We celebrate the fruits of our labor and a vibrant life.

When we let go of what no longer serves us, we realize we must step out into the unknown and into the flow of life, trusting that life will unfold in divine order and timing, trusting that life is happening for us, trusting the process and having faith that we are completely supported by the Universe.

Releasing what no longer serves and calling in our dreams are things that can be practiced frequently in any season. For this exercise, you will need a small piece of paper, a pen, a lighter, and a bowl. I invite you to write out a list of things you want to release on one side. On the other side, I invite you to make a list of things you would like to call in or are dreaming of. In a well ventilated space or outdoors, you may burn your list of things you are calling in and releasing to the Universe. When we release what no longer serves us, we create space for our dreams to grow.

# March 20

## Parenting Ourselves
## By Dominique Trier

*A*s we age and experience new responsibilities, our focus goes beyond ourselves and we face difficulties we could have never anticipated, but taking care of ourselves is nonnegotiable. Sometimes these difficulties seem relentless, like consistent disasters we have seen transpire in the year 2020. In spite of the disasters we see in the world and personal turbulent times, there are expectations of us from work and interpersonal relationships. It can be overwhelming to tackle never-ending tasks.

Because we may not be used to new and challenging experiences, we can feel ill-equipped, or a lack of support. During the thick of it, there can be a lot of negative self-talk since negative situations can breed negative thoughts. Through all of the pessimistic and cynical thoughts, we need to remember that these thoughts are not what we would relay to a child going through a hardship. These defeatist thoughts are not what we would have wanted in our developmental years, so why are we emboldening negative situations? It is easy to let situations take a hold of us and be in a default mode of spiraling, but how would we parent ourselves? How would we uplift, cheer up, or support others, and why aren't we practicing that for ourselves? We pour ourselves empty at times to make sure others are full of energy, but what about our energy? Protecting our inner monologue and making sure we care for ourselves leads to inevitable self care and love. Ask yourself the following when you need extra care.

- How would I parent myself?

Maybe answering this question will lead you to applying to a new job, staying home, writing down plans of action, going on a vacation, practicing a new language, or lighting a candle. We are deserving of gentle and constructive actions. Maybe we weren't given certain things like attentiveness or grace in our childhoods, but these things that were absent no longer have to be. Whatever those missing things are, we are capable of giving them to ourselves, and we will feel love because that is the action we are taking.

# March 21

## Surrounded by Gold
## By Amy I. King

Have you ever found yourself in a rut? Things were going fine in my life, but I was missing something. I felt like I was on a hamster wheel. I had buried several close family members and it had left me depleted. I needed something new in my life. I had felt a calling to travel to Hawaii alone. I had been there many times, always with others. This time, I knew I needed to go solo. A very intuitive girlfriend told me that I would meet a man surrounded by gold. That sounded amazing to me! I planned my trip and was on my way. Landing in Hawaii, I was both excited and nervous. I spent the rest of the day getting groceries and relaxing at the condo. On the second day, I ventured to the north part of the island.

There, I met a man. He had long, jet black hair, a goatee, and a smile that crinkled the sides of his eyes and lit up my life! When our hands connected, it felt as though I was meeting someone who I had known forever. He introduced himself, and we talked for a while. We exchanged numbers with plans to meet up later. We spent the rest of my trip together when he wasn't working. He took me to waterfalls, out to dinner, and we explored. He took me to places that weren't heavily populated with tourists. It was the best trip of my life, and being with him brought me back to me. I had lost myself in all of the loss I had experienced. Sometimes self-care is doing what isn't typical to get a different result.

I had been to Hawaii numerous times, and every time, I knew that there was something there for me. Something or someone that I needed to experience. I found him, and he was integral to my healing.

If you are feeling the pull to go somewhere or do something, do it! Life's regrets should only be the things we haven't done. Make those reservations, get that plane ticket, go to that concert. Life is short, and the little nudges are the universe telling you there is something for you.

It's worth mentioning that the name of the man I met was Aurelio. It is the Spanish word for "Golden."

# March 22

## Elemental Heart Frequencies
## By Courtney Parreira

*P*art of self-love is awakening to our hearts and honoring them. Just as we differ from each other in appearances and abilities, our heart frequencies differ, too.

There are four unique heart frequencies, one of which we carry. The frequency reconnects us to nature, ourselves, and each other. The heart frequencies are water, air, fire, and earth. Regardless of which we identify with, our heart frequency speaks to our truest ways of relating to the world around us. Awareness of our elemental heart frequencies attunes us to the ways in which we show and receive love, and it promotes our value and self-worth.

**Water Heart Traits:** Strong emotion. Deep inner connection. Fluid. Tendency to take shape of the structure around you. Expands in open space. Tests and rests upon boundaries.

**Optimal state:** Active emotional introspection.

**Air Heart Traits:** Five bodily senses oriented. Uncontainable. Moves past boundaries and reworks pathways. Unwavering motion. Shifting. Changing. Constant. Dizzying; Goal/solution oriented.

**Optimal state:** Active synthesis of ideas.

**Fire Heart Traits:** Passionate. Intensely enthusiastic. Easily ignited by people or actions. From zero to sixty in the blink of an eye. Warm intensity. Active yearnings. Active body. Roar.

**Optimal state:** Purposeful kinesthetic activity.

**Earth Heart Traits:** Strong and immovable. Quiet. Reserved. Needs time to process. Takes time to move or activate. Methodical. Grounded. Slow and robust movement that builds. Foundational. Needing rest.

**Optimal state:** Resting intuitive introspection.

Which frequency most resonates with you?

How can you use this knowledge to honor your brave and unique heart?

# March 23

## Who to Trust
### By Judith Manganiello

*G*rowing up, I saw everyone's Light as who they could be, not who they were choosing to be. As a result, I was bit by someone every day. I did not even get angry or mad; I just got sad. Unfortunately, this just felt normal to me until I learned to love myself.

Once I mastered the art of self-love, my whole life started changing. I received this prayer while helping someone in a session. It wound up helping us both. It is funny that I do not have the best memory except when I channel a prayer. Then I remember it forever. Learning to listen to Spirit and trusting your intuition is the ultimate form of self-love and preservation. Once you state the prayer, start tuning into the signs Spirit sends you.

*Spirit, I want to know when a snake is a snake is a snake. Spirit, I want to know*

*when a person, a place, or a thing is going to bite me. I am paying attention.*

*I want a punch in my solar plexus (which is your gut), or a big red flag waving in*

*front of my eyes. Keep waving and keep punching with grace and ease until I get it.*

Since I said the prayer, when I meet people, I will usually get the punch if something is not right. If I chose to ignore it, I have gotten bit. I have learned the hard way to no longer ignore it.

One night after I was finished working at my store, my wonderful husband made dinner as always. He is a wonderful cook. I was in a hurry to get home and was speeding. Suddenly, I got this red wash in front of my eyes. I slowed down because I thought my eyes were bleeding. I never realized it was my red flag. The fourth red flag was a police officer with a radar gun aiming right at my car. I did not get the ticket because I received the message and slowed down. When I told my husband the story, he said that he works with that officer and he would have given even his own mother a ticket. I was incredibly grateful that I paid attention to the red flag before it was too late. I do not speed anymore no matter how hungry I am. lol!

# March 24

## What You Focus On, You will Find
## By Stephanie Fontaine

*H*ave you ever noticed when you get a new car or see a car that you love, it seems like you begin to see that same type of vehicle almost every time you are on the road? This is an example of how to understand the principle behind the practice of *What you focus on, you will find*. Where you focus your attention plays a very big role in what you attract into your life. The universe responds to what you focus on and it delivers what you ask for without any criticism or judgement. Often our *asks* of the universe are not even conscious requests for things. Our thoughts and beliefs are powerful, activating the law of attraction and are said to be the ways in which we manifest our reality. There are a plethora of books that speak to the universal law of attraction, if you are interested in learning more.

In 2006 I was introduced to the book, *The Secret*. This was where I first began to understand and grasp the concept of this Universal Law. Like I mentioned earlier, the universe will not judge you, so it is important to be mindful of your thoughts, beliefs, and what you ask for.

Fast forward to 2018, my mother passed away in February and then her cousin passed away in May. They were extremely close and were like sisters, two peas in a pod. The day after I learned of the passing of my mom's favourite cousin, I saw two paper hearts on the ground in separate places. For me, it was a message from them that they were together again. After that experience I began seeing hearts everywhere. I created a challenge on my social media page, encouraging my friends and followers to be on the lookout for hearts and to share on my page any that they found. The heart pictures started streaming in.

I encourage you to do the *Find a heart challenge*. Invite more love into your life, perhaps even sharing this challenge with those whom you love. Every time you find a heart, give gratitude for the love you are receiving, record it in picture form or perhaps journal about it. Choose what works best for you in tracking the love you are receiving by finding these hearts. You will be surprised just how much love is out there.

Happy Heart Hunting.

# March 25

## People Pleasing
## By Symone Desirae

Are you someone who is always saying yes to others? Do you feel like you're being pulled in all directions or even burnt out? Does responding with the word no bring nervousness, anxiety, or discomfort to you?

Replying with no to someone can feel stigmatizing or confrontational. Many people feel the need to over explain themselves to avoid this notion. But the responses of "not at this time" or "no, thank you" are sufficient answers and you, may need to get comfortable with the uncomfortable. Know that there isn't a necessity to have an explanation to come after a refusal.

There are many polite ways to say no to someone. Some can be as simple as "Thank you for thinking of me, but at this time I'm going to say no." Or even "I would love to, however I can't make it."

These are some easy ways to respond. You don't have to go into further details as to why. Take a moment to reflect on areas in your life that you can start to say no. As you begin to do this, you will find how effortless it is to politely decline and allow more time in the day for yourself.

# March 26

## Sacred Healing Bath
## By Melanie Morrison

Our first encounter with love began in the womb. As we floated in the watery solution, we felt comfortable and safe. When life becomes hectic and I seek renewal and comfort, I always return to the water. Water, with its promise to cleanse, heal, and renew, gives me the refuge I need.

The first step to creating a healing bath practice is to set the scene. Cleaning up the surroundings, create boundaries for this time and set the intention that this bath time experience is to be your personal home spa retreat. You can light a candle, gather your favorite bath salts, oils, or stones, pick a flower, and/or play your favorite light tune.

Once the water is running, the experience has begun. Hold your hands over the water and set an intention for this healing bath. You can say out loud or to yourself, " I infuse this water with love and healing. May this water wrap me in love as it cleanses me within my soul and also the outer parts of me. I embrace flow within my life and embrace positive change."

Once you are in the bath, take time to feel your body relax. Notice your feet. Can you touch them? If you can, do a light self-massage on your feet and calves. Take a moment to thank them for all their hard work. Thank them for holding you, balancing you, and supporting you, day after day. Sink back into the water. Close your eyes. What do you, hear, see, smell, and feel?

With your eyes closed, hover your hand slightly above your body, starting at the bottom and working your way up to the top. As you breath in, pull in the love surrounding you. As you breathe out, send love through your hands and into your body. Notice how each area feels. Do certain areas need more love and attention? Do some areas feel vibrant while others feel empty? Send each area the love and attention it needs.

Allow yourself some time to feel the emotions that come up throughout this process. Give thanks for this time in the healing waters of Earth's womb. As you rise, feel the dirt, grime, and all that was fall away. Watch the dirty water drain as you let go and embrace the future, fresh and clean, inside and out.

# March 27

## Faith and Trust
## By Giuliana Melo

All you need is faith the size of a mustard seed
1 Mathew 17:20

*I* have always had faith in God, universal consciousness, angels, guides, and goddesses. Faith is encouragement and comfort in the unseen. It comes before a prayer is answered.

Trust is confidence, assurance, and belief that we are being guided. I have had to learn to trust the process of life, trust myself, trust God, guides, angels, and the humans that God sends me.

We are meant to trust that God has a plan even when we don't understand it.

We tap into faith and trust by tapping into our own intuition which is the voice of the divine within us that always guides us on the right path.

The different ways we tap into our intuition are through our senses, feeling, seeing, knowing, hearing, and tasting.

Some signs that we are being guided are numbers, feathers, songs, smells, animal signs,.

What are you noticing? Do you have faith in something bigger than us? Do you trust that the Universe has your back?

Here is a prayer that I want to share with you.

"Prayer to The Divine"

Dear Father in Heaven,

With and from your infinite love for us,

You have created blessed angels from heaven to be our guides

During this earthly journey.

Thank you for this blessing. We love and appreciate you for this aid.

Please may we feel, see, hear, and know their help during this life.

Help us stay in the light of heaven.

Please watch over all of your children.

For this we pray

Amen!

# March 28

## Ikigai – Your Reason to Live
## By Ewa Blaszczak

*I* *kigai* is a Japanese concept referring to the purposeful life. *Iki* means to live and *gai* stands for a reason. *Ikigai* is the reason for being alive. The studies conducted on the Japanese island of Okinawa, which is known for a high number of centenarians, prove that Ikigai increases the longevity of the population of the island. When people know why they get out of bed every morning, their life has more meaning. This in turn reduces stress, anxiety, prevents cancer and cardiovascular diseases. Identifying your personal *Ikigai* and living it can boost the level of neurotransmitters such as dopamine contributing to feelings of pleasure and satisfaction as part of the reward system. Yet another study conducted in Japan showed that centenarians who lead a purposeful life have an increased level of DHEA, a vitality hormone. DHEA is known for restoring telomeres in human's DNA thus prolonging the expected life span.

There are more benefits to finding your personal Ikigai. Your brain needs to know the 'why' of what you do every day, for the 'why' refers to values. The language of values triggers feelings and appeals to the limbic brain – the part of the brain responsible for engagement, determination, trust, passion and loyalty.

In order to discover your *Ikigai* you need to find answers the following four questions:

1. What are the things that you love doing?
2. What are you good at – list your talents and skills.
3. What the world needs?
4. What could you be paid for?

The place where the four above-mentioned areas overlap is where you find your *Ikigai*.

Remember that crafting your *Ikigai* is a process. Be patient with yourself. Take small steps. Maybe you begin with identifying things you both love and are good at. This is where your passion can be born. Maybe you can figure out things which you love and which the world needs. This is your mission. And perhaps you are able to identify what the world needs and how you can make money providing for these needs – this is your vocation. You can also start with finding your purpose by choosing a profession which will be right for you because it matches what you are good at with what you can be paid for.

# March 29

## Inner Child
## By Kim Richardson

There are many things you needed that you may not have received as a child. There may have been things that have happened to you when you did not feel protected and loved. Today, I encourage you to check in with your inner child.

Sit in a quiet space with a journal. Imagine you have a little girl or boy living in your heart space. Now, imagine you enter the house and see this little girl or boy sitting in the middle of the room with an empty chair next to them. You have seat in the chair next to them and start having a conversation.

In your conversation with this child, ask them how they are feeling and what they are missing in their life? Take some time to journal these thoughts. If you find them feeling sad, lonely, neglected, or abused, dig a little deeper to find out why. Continue to journal your conversation.

Review and take an inventory of what you journaled about. It is time for you to provide everything the child has been missing. This child may not have had everything they needed, but you can give it to them now. If the child has not felt protected, protect them with setting appropriate boundaries. If the child has not felt good enough or devalued, take a moment to realize the self-chatter that happens. Do you say to yourself, *"I am not good enough?"* Do you say other negative things and often beat yourself up as in *"I am not pretty enough, or I am fat?"*

What would you say or do if your own child came to you with these feelings? You would encourage them; you would tell them they are crazy to think the way they are. It's time to speak to yourself/your inner child with the same unconditional loving voice you would your own child.

I check in with my inner child daily. If she is not happy, I do something that will bring her joy. When I catch myself with any negative chatter, I stop to realize that I am hurting her. If I need to make a decision about something, I check in with her to make sure she feels safe, loved, and protected before I move in any direction.

Are you ready to be and provide everything that you/inner child needs?

# March 30

## Laughter
## By Delores Garcia

As I took my walk this morning, I asked my soul what she needed today. Perhaps the morning walk was a self-care activity, but I really desired to know what my soul truly yearned for. That is the deepest, most empowering strategy for self-care: Ask your soul what she needs today.

This morning, she quickly and easily told me she needed laughter. I smiled. She was right. I immediately thought of my best friend and how she and I laugh the best together and we know it. I think she is hilarious. And she thinks I am too. We are free to be hilarious together. I dressed up in an inflatable dinosaur costume for her fifty-fifth birthday, singing "Happy Birthday" and skipping down her street. The videos are priceless! I don't know who else I would do that for!

As they say, laughter is the best medicine. We are designed to laugh and play and have fun, even when we are adults. Perhaps, especially when we are adults. It is a shame in our society that fun and laughter are deemed childish and thus restricted to just the little children. We must stop missing out on the goodness of life. It is our birthright. Laughter relaxes the whole body while boosting immunity. It triggers endorphins while strengthening the heart physically and emotionally.

Who is your favorite person to laugh with? Or perhaps your favorite funny movie or YouTube video? Have you ever heard those recordings of kids laughing? It is contagious! Perhaps a book of jokes? A game night or comedy club with fun friends? Have you tried a laughter yoga class? Today, purposefully seek to smile and laugh and play. Today is the day to enjoy yourself! It is the most self-caring, responsible thing to do!

# March 31

## I Am More Than Enough For Me
### By Dee Dee Rebitt

*D*uring my marriage and divorce, I did a whole lot of work on my internal and emotional issues. Between raising our two daughters, looking after the home, and earning a living while being a stay-at-home mom, I spent a better part of my marriage tending to everyone else. I forgot the one most important person in this equation. ME!

I became focused on everyone else but me. I literally turned off my emotions, my needs, my focus. Life became damn overwhelming at times, especially last few years before I filed for divorce. I started to emotionally disconnect, I started to use food again to stifle my emotions in all I felt, emotionally shutting myself down. I became bitter and sad inside. The disappointment I was feeling left me deeply gutted.

My life and my marriage had failed, and I took everything to heart. I lost what I thought was my only chance of forever happiness. I had reached my dark night of the soul and spent many days and nights on my hands and knees in tears. No one was there to catch me when I fell. I had never felt more alone than during these times.

Finally, through several conversations with a few close friends, I decided I needed to take my power back. Book after book, course after course, I started to see things in a different light. Communication became the key to finding where I finally felt like me and even today, I feel it with healing, ease and grace. It helped to change my mindset and saying no to a few people, including family. I took charge of my own life and set up boundaries, not listening to people's negative talk. I was finally brave enough to approach what were contributors to my marriage breaking down. I finally had absolutely no fear of my own voice or the decisions I made for me. I had finally taken back my power, becoming more than just a mom, but a businesswoman, and mentor. Standing up for myself gave me my voice and others were looking up to me and were watching me. I found me in healing. And realized that I am enough.

# *April 1*

## Forgive Your Way to Freedom and Joy
## By Grace Redman

Some may perceive forgiveness as a weakness when in reality it requires tremendous strength and courage. It isn't all about just forgive and forget. It requires you run through a gamut of emotions such as sadness, grief, anger, disbelief, and lots of 'why me's?'

Honor your feelings. Acknowledge you were wronged. Once we honor our feelings of pain and accept the situation, we pave the way to letting go and forgiving. And when we accept, we begin to free ourselves from the bondage.

Forgiveness is a process and there are some situations that may take you years to let go of and forgive and that's okay. Forgiveness is all about you and not the other person. You don't even ever have to talk to the other person again to forgive. If forgiving the other person feels too challenging, start with forgiving yourself for giving your power away to the situation. They say resentment and anger towards a person is like drinking poison and waiting for the other person to die.

Ajahn Chah, one of Thailand's most famous meditation teachers said:

*"If you let go a little, you will have a little happiness. If you let go a lot, you will have a lot of happiness. If you let go completely, you will be free."*

A benefit of forgiveness is self-growth and expansion. You'll also start to develop compassion for yourself. During this process you'll forgive and have compassion for those that have hurt you. Another amazing benefit is the joy that comes with accepting and loving yourself again. As you become more joyful, you will attract positive people and situations into your life.

To help yourself with forgiveness and letting go, grab a pen and notebook and sit quietly in a comfortable place. First close your eyes and repeat to yourself several times: *I release and let go of all resentments, anger, and sadness.*

Just the intention of letting go begins the process of forgiveness. Then write a letter to the person that hurt you and go at it! Write whatever you are feeling. Let all the anger out on the paper.

Next it is time to burn the letter. As you burn the letter, imagine the person inside a bubble of white light and gently blow the bubble away and repeat the phrase: *I choose peace of mind, freedom, and joy.*

# April 2

## She's Sleeping
## By Mindy Lipton

*I* would often have to say that about my mom, "Yes, she's sleeping."

My mom was a private duty nurse who slept throughout the day. Sometimes we would go shopping if I woke her at a set time. Often times she would sleep right through my attempts to awaken her. She worked so hard. Seven nights a week sometimes. My dad was in the picture, but I might as well have had just a picture. I mean, I loved him and he loved me, but we never had much to talk about. He owned and worked in a gas station in the wrong part of town. I just never had much to say about tires or gasoline.

I guess you could describe me as a brat. I wasn't easy. I had expectations and I just set myself up for disappointment. My teenage years were even worse—raging hormones until I got pregnant and gave the baby up for adoption because we both knew we were too young.

I tried college, but it wasn't for me. My major was secretarial science. I was the lead in the college play, "How To Succeed In Business Without Really Trying," and that put my idea of college out the window. I wanted the stage.

My relationship never really improved with my parents until I decided to get my own apartment. I was out on my own for two months when my mom was diagnosed with pancreatic cancer. Even these days everyone knows that is pretty much a death sentence. I was going to lose my mother. She was only fifty-two and I was only twenty-two. The following year my dad had a stroke. He went to a rehabilitation center had another stroke and died in his sleep joining my mother on the other side.

Self-love came naturally, forcefully; it came on strong. I could stay in the same city where everyone knows your name. Drive the main avenue where the cemetery is in plain view.

The dark cloud would take place over my head and I knew depression was closing in on me. It was time to make a decision.

I decided to follow my dream and move across the country to Los Angeles, California. I packed up my car and drove across this beautiful country of ours. I was twenty-five years of age. Determination steered me in the right direction. For me.

Practice finding your dream. What are you determined to do with your life? Write it out. Think of the past times when your determination pulled you through.

# *April 3*

## Not My Responsibility
## By Susan Hoyle

*I* will never forget that moment when I realized, I was being pulled into discussions and arguments for the sole purpose of fixing them for someone. Growing up, I was always uncomfortable with conflict of any kind, hated disagreements, couldn't stand to have someone not like me. Pretty sure most of you can relate! So it was no surprise as a wife and mother that I felt this uncontrollable *need* to do whatever I could to make these disagreements stop! As a recovering rescuer, this moment changed my life.

First I gained awareness around exactly what my responsibility was. This was the hardest to shift when it came to my kids. I had taught them to call for me each time they had a disagreement. I would come and assist them in working through it. Which sounds good, but I was not *allowing them* the process of figuring out how to work through it. Once I had this awareness, I knew I needed to do better.

Through this new awareness, I came across one sentence that would allow my children to learn from these disagreements, instead of having me solve them. So the next time one of my kids called me at the office to repeat a disagreement they had with their sibling, I would listen compassionately until they finished their story then I said, very empathetically, *"What does any of this have to do with me?"*

Another life changing moment.

The first time I said this sentence there was dead silence on the other end of the phone. But after I began using this sentence, our lives truly changed.

If you are struggling, feeling run down emotionally, I would encourage you to take a look at what may be draining you in your relationships. Take out a piece of paper and write at the top: *Not My Responsibility*: and make a list of all the things you are getting involved in that has nothing to do with you. This can be at home or work. Things they are capable of doing on their own. Choose a sentence that works for you and memorize it. When you are in a situation where someone else is leaning on you to *fix it*, then simply and compassionately state your sentence. Believe me, this allows us to hold on to more of our own energy and not have it drained from our body.

# April 4

## Mirror Mirror
## By Marsha Johnson

*M*irror, mirror on the wall. We have all heard that phrase. Who is the fairest of them all? When you look in the mirror, who and what do you see? Is the mirror your friend or foe?

Ever since I can remember, I would get up in the morning, look at myself in the mirror and give myself a big smile and say, "Hi, good morning," and then have a little conversation with myself.

I decided to take a survey amongst family and friends to see if anyone else did the same. To my surprise I found out that most people do not start their day like this and it had never crossed their minds. To take this further, many said they actually try to avoid the mirror as much as possible.

Oftentimes, when we look in the mirror, we find faults like I'm too fat, too skinny, my nose is too big, my smile isn't right, and would you just look at my hair! On the other hand, when we see others, we often compliment them in some aspect and say that they're handsome, beautiful, have a nice outfit. The list goes on. We find it easy to find the goodness in others, but not in ourselves.

I would challenge you to start off each day by greeting yourself in the mirror with a cheerful "good morning" and a smile. Do this first thing for a week, and as you get comfortable, continue to do that throughout the day. Each time you pass a mirror, maybe wave, but definitely give yourself a smile, and find something nice to say to yourself. Say something like "hey, nice hair day, nice dinner you made. And finally at night try "wow, you made it through the day!" You will notice as time goes on, it will be easier to find something nice you see in yourself. It all starts with a "good morning" from your favorite person … you!

One way to up your game on this exercise is this: If you find yourself thinking one negative thought about yourself, you must then think of three positives to override that one negative thought. For instance if you think, "How could I let XYZ take advantage of me?" Then think, "Three things, I am a loving and trusting person; I look for the good in all people; I have learned my lesson, and I won't let that happen again."

# *April 5*

## Heart Healing Remedies
## By Ann Marie Asp

*M*any of us go through life hoping to find that one magical remedy. The one that would be the answer to our needs. I can remember while growing up that when things happened the first thought was always to call the doctor. They would know what was best to take care of my discomfort. You always somehow felt better after the visit especially when you were sent you home with their special remedies. My biggest frustration was that the symptoms would return before I knew it. All I wanted was to just feel better.

I would later find out that my answers had always been stirring within me. During a training session by a friend, who is one of the greatest mentors in my life, I was introduced to Heart Math. It is a unique system that offers validated scientific techniques to tap into our own inner healing by connecting to our hearts. I had now found my extraordinary remedy.

Here is a special exercise from the that system that I would like to share with you. It has become a favorite practice of mine to use daily. It is called the Inner-ease technique

Find a comfortable position where you can either sit or lie down.

**First Step:** Close your eyes and place your hand on your heart. This begins to release a chemical within the body called oxytocin which is also known as the love hormone.

**Second Step:** This is referred to as heart focus breathing. Imagine you are breathing in and out through your heart. Breathe in for six counts and then out for six counts, always exhaling more deeply than inhaling. Keep this practice going until your breathing feels calm and natural. This can take extra time, especially when first starting out. Do not rush through this step.

**Third Step:** Keep your focus on breathing through the heart. On each inhale imagine breathing in the feelings of ease, love, and compassion. Exhale normally. Repeat a second time. On the third inhale, feel yourself drawing in these beautiful remedies through your heart. On the last exhale, slowly take your hand away from your heart and softly open your eyes. Pay attention to how your body feels in this very moment compared to when you first began the exercise.

Take the time to anchor and maintain these feelings throughout your day.

Your heart will always thank you!!!

# April 6

## Morning Rituals
## By Jamie Rudolph

As the sun rises, begin your day with a ritual. Shift and empower your day and begin the moments after you wake. The morning can have an impactful and long-lasting effect throughout your day—begin it by shifting your mind and body into ease.

There are some wonderful, healthy techniques and ways to begin your morning ritual. Begin your day with breath work. It only needs to be a few minutes and it's a beautiful way to set your intentions for the day. Next, there are several ayurvedic practices to promote a healthy body by removing toxins. Tongue scraping is one such way to remove any toxins which have accumulated while sleeping. It is believed the tongue shows a reflection of the condition and health of your internal body. Following teeth brushing and tongue scraping, use an ayurvedic oral wash containing oil and herbs. Oil pulling is also a helpful way to pull and expel toxins out of the body.

As you continue to move through your morning ritual, skin brush before showering. Why is this important? Skin brushing is a technique which helps to stimulate and move lymphatic fluid throughout your body. It is recommended to use a natural brush with soft bristle made specifically for your skin. Begin with light, short strokes always moving from the outer extremities towards your heart. Skin brushing also has the benefit of a light exfoliation and helps to promote a healthy glow. Continue to support your morning body detoxification, with a hot-cold shower. Alternating between the two temperatures helps to improve circulation, stimulates the immune system, and reduces inflammation and pain while giving your skin a radiant glow.

Following these supportive body detoxifications techniques, finish your morning ritual with a cup of warm lemon water. Lemon is an astringent fruit with alkalizing benefits and it helps remove excess mucus from the body while supporting our liver detoxification process. As you sip on this warming, healthy beverage, be thankful for whatever the day has to offer. Be thankful for your body and all your good health.

A morning ritual is a beautiful way to begin your day. Whatever way you begin your morning, make sure it enriches and supports your body, mind, and spirit.

# *April 7*

## Joy
### By Debra Moore Ewing

*L*ife is not perfect. We make it what it is. We are accountable. I am not giving you lip service. At sixty-six I have had
my trials and tribulations like many. Seventeen years ago, I survived breast cancer. I honestly thought I had played the "C' card
and I was immune to walking that path again. It all changed in
2017 when a rare incurable cancer came knocking on my door.
Thankfully, my undeniable faith is what got me through and
continues to this day. Unfortunately, the chemo depletes my cells
of the feel-good hormone serotonin, which causes tumors in
my body. You do not realize how hormones affect you until you
no longer have them. Therefore, every morning before I rise, I
think about the things in my life that bring me joy and then I feel
grateful. Just making this conscious shift in my morning routine
sets the tone for my day. This is a beautiful planet we live on and
while your life may not be perfect, I know there must be things
that you are joyful for. Do not allow depression or the *woe is me
to creep in*. Sure, it is okay to be on your 'pity pot' sometimes, but
please do not stay there!

Will you do something for me? I want you to take a deep breath
and hold it. Now exhale between your lips slow and steady. Go
ahead. Do it again. That feels good, right? Do you realize many
people do not have that luxury? They may have asthma, COPD,
or emphysema and they cannot breathe deeply like you just did
even with an oxygen machine. Your breath is your life force. It can
give you energy or bring you peace at any time you choose. And
if by chance you are managing one of those diseases you must be

grateful that there is equipment to assist you so you can find joy spending time with those you love.

We are here for such a short time before we go home. You do not have to look far to see there is always somebody in a worse situation. We truly have so much to be grateful for! So please do your best every day to find some level of joy. You truly will feel better. I promise!

# April 8

## Be Confident Knowing your True Essence
### By Paula Marie Rennie

*D*o you know yourself and truly what matters to you? Well, it's time you did, precious soul. As a medium, I communicate with souls who have passed on from this Earth through feeling and sensing their unique essence. I'm always inspired, meeting so many different personalities who share heart-warming stories about their relationships, special memories, and life challenges. Too often, I receive messages from these souls of past-life regrets because they didn't know how to love themselves and be who they truly are.

We all have unique strengths and talents that are gifts to this world. There's nobody like you that has the same purpose or desire to grow as your soul does on this Earth. Knowing your strengths and talents, as well as honouring your weaknesses, is vital to your growth and this becomes your superpower. With practice, you'll start to value, trust, and appreciate how much you contribute to others' lives, by being your perfectly imperfect self anywhere and with anyone.

Get comfy with your journal and center in your heart space. Let your souls essence qualities flow to you from the below reflections. If you're not sure of any qualities, ask people you can trust who know you well.

- What are five strengths and talents you have that come naturally to you? What's your passions? What gives you joy? Breathe each of these in and feel them ignite your body's energy.

- List five people that inspire you and why? For each person write down what qualities and values they have that resonate deeply with your soul. Imagine igniting the energy of each of these qualities into every cell of your body. What do you feel and look like now? What new ways can you commit to showing up being an expression of these qualities?

- What are five weaknesses you know you have? Be honest with yourself. What don't you like about your weaknesses? What support do they need to grow?

- Close your eyes and visualize all the ways your strengths and talents can serve you and others even more. Let your strengths hold your weaknesses tenderly and notice how your self-acceptance and confidence starts to grow. Feel the power and wisdom of your true essence expand out around you as you confidently and joyfully express your true self in all your interactions.

# April 9

## Wise Time Use
## By Marilyn Miller

*I* spent so many years living with the stress of incompletion before I learned how to use time. We all have the same twenty-four hours in every day. There is no way to manage expanding that, but we can learn to use time more wisely. I used to jump from project to project never really being complete with items on my to-do list. But I learned to value my time using a method that helped so much. The first step is to limit your daily "to do" list.

- Write down only six things you want to accomplish each day.
- Write your list the night before or first thing in the morning.
- Number each item one through six in the order of its importance.
- Finish item number one before moving on to your second item and so on.

By NOT going on to item two until you have finished item one, you can finish what is most important by the end of each day. If you have only completed one or two items, you have done what needed to be done with the highest priority. If you finish your entire list, you can always add more items.

Now, that you know how to prioritize your "to do" list, here's another time use secret. Use short breaks to maximize your productivity. An old industrial psychology study done in the early twentieth century reveals how men who were moving loads of pig iron increased their productivity. Observers saw that if the workers rested for five minutes between each load of pig iron they carried in wheelbarrows, they could increase their productivity four times instead of carrying load after load without breaks.

- After you finish each item on your list, take a short break of five to ten minutes.
- Do some breathing exercises, stand up, stretch, drink water, or eat a snack.

# April 10

## Learning to Love Yourself Through Other's Suffering
### By Nanette Gogan-Edwards

For the past ten years, I have had the pleasure of meeting and working side by side with incredible people. I've been blessed with the ability to transfer several times and expand my skills within my company. I've been at my current location for almost three years and have developed some wonderful relationships with coworkers.

Recently, a fellow crew member suffered a cardiac episode and passed away within hours. His spirit was magnetic and sincere. I often think of our conversations about our senior dogs and our shared love of Colorado and wildlife. He was a person of great integrity and simplicity, both of which I admired tremendously,

I was in the store when he collapsed and did my best to keep the customers distracted while other co-workers assisted him. Occasionally, I would look up out of concern to check on him. His face was bright red and he had sweat streaming down his cheeks onto his neck. He was struggling to breathe and began vomiting. My heart hurt for him as he continued to struggle while waiting for medical help to arrive. Unfortunately, they were unable to save him and he died shortly after arriving at the hospital.

For several days after, I could not help but be almost consumed by the events of that day. Realizing how much he loved his job and knowing he had others surrounding him rather than dying alone at home brought things into a different perspective for me.

Working during the pandemic of 2020 as an "essential worker" has brought many personal challenges my way. Every day has been a struggle to remain optimistic and steadfast. Some days I've wanted to walk out and never return! But having known this wonderful man and having the pleasure of working side by side with him brings me to a new level of love for self and for others.

Take care of yourself physically, emotionally, mentally, and spiritually. Because, in the end, they all come together and leave a legacy; a lasting impression on those you have touched throughout your life.

# April 11

## Liking to Loving You
## By Selena Urbanovitch

For so long I didn't even like myself. I was easily swayed to join in negative conversations which always made space for negative self talk. I was so used to gossiping and talking trash about people I didn't even fully know. It was this seemingly endless cycle that I didn't know how to break free of. At times, I didn't even think it was my fault that I got sucked into these moments. I never did like myself after the conversations. I didn't know that I was part of the problem. I was so jealous of those people I was gossiping about.

Mirror work was one of the hardest lessons that I knew I needed to learn. I needed to see where the hurt was and try to heal it. The saying "hurt people hurt people," resonated so much with me. So how do we change this negative to a positive?

~Take a step back and ask yourself, "How did that make me feel? Do I like how this made me feel? And does this need to change?"

~Once you acknowledge the hurt parts of yourself, the more the universe shows you how you can change. When you are open to change, change happens.

~Now look in the mirror and start saying, "I like you; you are a good person; you now know better so you will do better." They say it takes twenty-one days to form a habit, and this is a beautiful habit to form.

~If you can form a habit every morning looking at yourself then and work from "I like you" to "I love you!" your negatives will turn into positives! If this is hard, that is okay. Healing takes time, and you are worth it!

What I found transitioning from liking myself to loving myself is that I had boundaries. If I was saying nice things to me, then I would say nice things about others. I found that liking myself through all of my lessons made space for me to love me! I now know that life is all about love, that love heals, and love sent out comes back three-fold. And love changes the world!

# *April 12*

## Water and Healing
## By Tabitha Weigel

*M*y connection to water has always existed. As a child I remember floating in water for what felt like hours at a time. I would daydream, reflect and simply be. My love of water was genuine and pure, my joy bubbling, and heart simply full. As I grew into adulthood, I forgot this simple, yet crucial, way of just being and enjoying the peace that is water. It wasn't until I began my journey of self-healing and self-love that I rediscovered the importance of connecting with water when trying to refocus my energy in a way that serves my heart and purpose.

Water is cleansing, holds energy, and has memory. It is life. It is healing. The physical and emotional benefits of creating some form of self-care routine centered around the fluidity of water is magical. It's magical to allow the water to hold, nourish, and cleanse your body, your spirit, and emotional mind. Water is an emotional stimulant and the ruling element of the sacral chakra, the chakra of sexuality, change, emotions, and desire. Embracing and honoring water in a way that calls to you helps balance your sacral chakra, and therefore your overall emotional mindset.

I invite you to take some time today to incorporate water within your self-care routine as well as send love to your sacral chakra, energizing your emotional mindset and re-centering your focus as a healthy and loving self. Take a bath. Soak in a hot tub. Take a few extra minutes in the shower. Keep it as simple as you would like or turn it up a notch and set your space with music, candles, stones, essential oils, salts, and scrubs …. whatever speaks to you! Then, while in water, take some slow and deep cleansing breaths. Holding your hands below your belly button, envision vibrant and free-flowing shades of orange. Allow yourself to feel your body, your energy, and needs. Then repeat a few affirmations such as "my emotions are free flowing and balanced; I honor this sacred body in which my soul resides; I enjoy pleasure in all areas of my life; I am a lovable and desirable being."

Let these affirmations travel throughout you. Feel, believe, and accept them. Give gratitude for water's nurturing qualities. Let it soothe your physical, emotional, and sensual body while cleansing your energy and re-centering your focus and presence.

# April 13

## Grace
### By Ashlie Bradley

*T*his is a very important piece in the self-love puzzle. All too often we become our own harshest judges. We hear that voice (the ego) which says, you can't, you are not worthy, give up etc. The voice criticizes us for not doing what we "should" be doing. The voice that plays our "mistakes" over and over, condemning us constantly. Well, guess what? It's time to take *should* and *mistake* out of our vocabularies. There is only what is and lessons. The more we believe that voice, the louder it becomes, and deeper down the self-deprecating rabbit hole we go. Let us break free from that now, and embody the perfectly whole, being of light and love we are.

A tactic I picked up along the way is naming and giving an accent to the voice. For example, my voice's name is Henry and he has a British accent. The name and accent make it light and airy for me. So now, when he tries to start his stuff, I can pause before a spin out starts. I can laugh and tell Henry to go take a nap! And so he does.

A great friend of mine once told me, "You have got to give yourself grace."

This is truly one of the most loving things we can do for ourselves. Look at you here now, reading this book, seeking self-love. Look how amazing you are. You already have the awareness, so it's just implementing it into your life.

Repeat after me. "I am a magical being full of radiance, love, oceans, and stars. I am perfect and whole as I am."

Only Henry can tell you different—if you allow it. Give yourself a giant hug every day. Look in the mirror every morning and witness the brilliance you are. Over time you will believe this as truth. You have the keys, unlock the gates, and let the love flood in. You are a miracle. Believe it. Believe it. Believe it.

# April 14

## My Mermaid's Menu
## By Tonia Browne

*When I discover what I unconsciously choose, I can consciously choose what I want.*

Sensitive souls are prone to having sensitive guts and consequently can experience challenges in their digestive systems. It is easy to understand why if you believe the gut is the intuitive center of our being.

It was an act of self-love when I decided to discover which foods agreed with me and actioning this knowledge with healthy food choices. I created a list of positive foods, which I call my mermaid's menu, for fun. The result—more energy and a feel-good factor.

Many of our daily habits determine the quality of our experiences and realizing this can help us to sustain wise choices. Choices are not all or nothing, right or wrong; rather, they are one decision after another. With each day there is a chance to choose again. It is the consistency of healthy choices made from informed decisions that change lives, while negative self-talk and judgement depletes resilience. My journey to better health was not a direct route; I took the long way round. I still take detours, but I am more conscious of what I am doing or what I have done and when I veer off my healthy path, I have the choice to find my way back to it again.

If you suffer from gut issues, a good way forward is to discover which foods nourish you and which foods take a toll on your general wellbeing. It may take time and a lot of trial and error to determine what suits your biochemistry, but it is worth the effort. Once you discover what nourishes you, it can be easier to create a new habit rather than focusing on giving up an old one. For instance, if you want to reduce your sugar intake, introduce healthier foods you enjoy rather than merely eliminating the ones that contain the sugar. Over time you find yourself eating healthier foods and your cravings for sugar reduced.

## Consider:

- What is my mermaid menu? How will I decide the items on it?
- What healthy foods can I introduce today that will improve my energy levels?
- What healthy snacks can I prepare in advance ready for my moments of need?

# April 15

## Mirror, Mirror
## By Stephanie Fontaine

*I* am sure the title, "Mirror, Mirror," brings to mind a famous childhood movie for many of us. You may also remember that the mirror was used in a way that was not in the highest good for all. You may be wondering how this "Mirror, Mirror" concept fits into a practice of having more self-love. Mirror work is probably one of the toughest self-love exercises that I have done. To look yourself in the eye, in the mirror, can sometimes be a daunting task all on its own. To look yourself in the eye and say kind, compassionate, and loving things to yourself may at first, feel too overwhelming, uncomfortable, and impossible to do. However, it is totally worth stepping outside of your comfort zone and may be a huge contribution in your journey to having more self-love.

I began my mirror work about ten years ago. I started this practice by simply writing positive affirmations on the mirror with a washable magic marker. They were always there to give me a gentle reminder that I was worthy and enough. They were basic at first. I wrote things like: *Smile, you are beautiful. You are worthy. You are enough.* Over time and with gained confidence, I have incorporated a set of "I AM" statements to replace my third-person affirmations of the past. These "I AM" statements help to keep me focused, creative, and positive—at least most of the time. They remind me that "I AM" a fierce warrior. Now I practice saying these "I AM" statements to myself in the mirror:

- I AM fearless.
- I AM inspired.

- I AM emotionally balanced.
- I AM radiant.
- I AM confident.
- I AM empowered.
- I AM fierce.
- I AM love.

The key is to start with what feels comfortable. Write something you truly believe, then every day change it up. Work towards shifting and changing the limiting beliefs you have about yourself. The goal is to get to a point where you can look yourself in the eyes and without hesitation say those positive affirmations. Ultimately, the goal is to be so full of love and confidence that you can easily look yourself in the eyes and say, "I AM love," and know you mean it.

# *April 16*

## Creative Balance of Wood
## By Virginia Adams

*D*epression is repressed anger. Once upon a time, reading those words made me angry. I remember thinking, *I am not angry; I am sad.* Boy, did I have a lot to learn? Somewhere along the way in my childhood and early adult years, I was programmed to think that it was better to be silent than to express anger. I became very clever at circumventing the feeling and expression of anger. I didn't realize I was doing this; it was a hidden protective mechanism with the underlying purpose of keeping me safe. As the years passed and I no longer needed to protect myself from other people's intense anger, I still fell silent to my emotional upheavals. My children, spouse, and employees knew that I was seething with rage when I became very, very quiet. It took years for me to honor, embrace, and love the angry me. Today, I find creative, productive, and loving manners of expressing my anger. Yes, anger can be loving!

Wood means anger and germination. Let's play with the element of wood and see what we can germinate in our quest for self-care and self-love. Sometimes we do not know that we are holding onto anger in our physical and energetic bodies, or on the other hand, we might be acutely aware that we are angry. In either case, the following exercise is perfect.

Go out into nature and find a big, supportive tree to sit with and rest your back against. (If you are unable to go outside due to climate or physical restrictions, imagine this in your mind's eye while holding onto something made of wood.) Now, close your eyes and imagine that the tree and its roots have you in the most comforting embrace. Feel your feels. What do you notice coming up? Allow it to flow. Tell the tree all of your trials and tribulations; do not deny any thoughts; all are welcome. Do you need to scream? A silent scream with intense force can be a cleansing experience. Sit there in the energy of wood until you are purged and surrounded by a deep sense of peace.

Now take a moment and plant a few energetic seeds of creation near the base of the tree's trunk. What has your anger held you back from doing? Allow the released energy of anger to germinate a new way of expressing your creativity.

# April 17

## Letting Go of Beliefs that No Longer Serve You
## By Vonnie L. Hawkins, LCSW

*I*'ve always been a workaholic. My parents taught that being lazy was the ultimate "sin" so I started working at age thirteen as the hostess in a Shoney's restaurant. My parents loved me. They meant well. But they were also products of their parents' programming, and those parents grew up in the Depression and gave them these values.

I received a lot of praise from my family for working hard. This reinforcement from my family put me in a constant state of hustling for worthiness and in pursuit of the never-achievable perfection. As an adult this meant taking twenty-four hours a semester in college, working seventy-hour work weeks as an entrepreneur or working three and four jobs at the same time, and never feeling like I hit the mark, that I had done enough to be worthy of unconditional love. All this busy-ness never gave me the sense of achievement I needed nor the relief of redemption for my perceived faults and failures as an imperfect human being.

After a recent, intense meditation retreat, I set my clear intention to release all activities from my life that had the energy of "hustling for worthiness." I set an intention to bring flow and ease to my life, and more FUN! I wrote this on my whiteboard in my office to focus my daily intention.

I told my friends and family until they were tired of hearing me say, "I'm releasing all activities that feel like hustling for worthiness."

After a few months, I began to feel the good feeling of true accomplishment that comes from living a balanced, joyful life of ease and flow and purpose, filled with activities that made me truly happy. I consciously released what didn't bring joy, no matter how lucrative, and I continued what did, no matter how "frivolous."

What are the stories you tell yourself that get in the way of you setting aside time to nurture and love yourself? Write them down. Then with a bold black marker, cross them out completely and say aloud, "I delete and transform these beliefs that no longer serve me across all time, dimension, and space."

Write and say aloud, "I choose a life of _____" and fill it with your choices—joy, ease, flow, fun, laughter, creativity, etc.

Release what no longer serves you and consciously invite the qualities you desire into your life.

# *April 18*

## Journeying Inwards
## By Yumie Zein

How well do you know yourself? What does *knowing yourself* even mean? How do you know that you are living the life you want? Are the decisions you are making the ones you really want to make? Or are they mere reflections of the expectations of society? Do you love yourself? What does loving yourself look like?

Those were a few of the many questions I had on my journey towards healing and understanding what it truly meant to be authentic. The problem was no one had those answers. Sometimes I wished I could walk up to someone and just ask them to tell me who I was.

"Tell me please, anything, anything at all. Surely you know something or are at least somewhat less clueless than I am."

When it became apparent that no one had the answer to those questions, even those who thought they did and felt the need to push their own answers on everyone else around them, I began the process of journeying inwards towards myself. Yes, that may sound somewhat deep and intangible, but as a budding explorer of my own world, I began to play around with that concept.

I would begin with one question in meditation.

"Who am I?"

The answers would begin to flood in from my mental mind. I am a woman, a mother, a daughter, a lover, a human …. The list went on. The more times I sat with this question and allowed the labels to be stripped off me, the clearer it was that these labels were human-made descriptions meant to give me a better understanding of the way this world works. But that really is all they are. They are not a definition of who I am but a description of who I am. And who I really am is the experiencer of these descriptions.

Then it dawned on me, I am the experience of *being alive*. Through that lens, labels, decisions, situations, relationships and life itself takes on a completely different perception. Through that lens I can answer any and all questions. Through that lens I am not bound by any external constructs. Through that lens I am free to *be* and to love every moment of this experience.

# *April 19*

## This Little Light of Mine
## By Sheryl Goodwin Magiera

One day, I found myself singing in the shower; a song that popped into my head that I probably had not heard or sung in a long while. Out of nowhere I was belting out, "This Little Light of Mine." As I was singing, I wondered why that particular song came forward. All day long, I randomly found myself singing and repeating the lyrics. After reflecting, I determined it must have been either my higher self, reminding me of my purpose or I was meant to share the message through my writing that someone was meant to hear.

I am reaching out to you as a reminder of all the wonderful qualities and gifts you possess that are waiting to be shared with the world. What are the gifts that come natural and easy for you? What do friends, family, and even acquaintances say you are good at doing? What have you always loved to do? Take yourself back to childhood and remember. Remember what brought you joy then and what brings you joy now?

When I was discovering my unique gifts, I reflected on my childhood and remembered how much I loved to write, specifically poetry. I remembered that as an adult I loved writing in school. It began small and I started again by writing a weekly blog post, which led to being part of this project. I am hoping to show my heart so you can connect with it.

What are your dreams? Even if they feel unreachable, what small steps can you take toward the end goal? How can you bring the joy into your life in a different way? Tap into those beautiful and unique gifts and see what happens. Then share them with the world and those around you. Keep repeating, "This little light of mine ... I'm gonna let it shine," and let your heart shine through.

What are you waiting for? The world is ready to receive the light dancing within your soul.

*This little light of mine* by: Harry Dixon Loes

This little light of mine

I'm gonna let it shine

This little light of mine

I'm gonna let it shine

This little light of mine

I'm gonna let it shine

Let it shine, let it shine, let it shine

# April 20

## Forgiveness
## By Gloria Dawn Kapeller

*I* 've always had to really work on forgiveness. First, I had to forgive myself. I always felt that I must have done something wrong. I also felt that the abuse happened to me because I was adopted and not part of the family. I heard all my life" our children" then they would say 'Gloria and Susan." We were not part of the family-always on the outside looking in, at least this was how I was made to feel.

I had to forgive myself first and know that none of this was my fault, or that I asked for it. I had to forgive those that hurt me and also look at it this way. You choose before you arrive what lessons you are wanting to experience as a soul. It was explained to me that we have soul contracts and soul families. It was said that my abusers would be willing to be the abusers, and as a soul family you could look at it that they full filled the contract and in so doing it did it out of love.

When explained that way to me, it didn't make it right on any level(in my mind), but in a way it did make sense that they helped with the lesson that my soul wanted to experience. I was able to let go of the anger and resentment that I had carried with me all my life. Actually, after I left home at the age of nineteen, I never did go home alone again. I always had someone with me for protection, either friends, later my sons, and then my husband Jon.

When you look at a soul contract, you can see the silver lining in every situation even if it really is a tough lesson. I have a saying "What the hell was I thinking?" but that is my sense of humor coming through.

When I did some counselling, one of the things that I was asked to do was write a letter. In that letter was all the anger, feelings of betrayal. I was writing down everything I was feeling on paper and then instead of sending it, I burned it, releasing me from all those emotions. No one else had to read what I wrote but the simple act of writing and burning helped me so much. The only one I was hurting by holding onto those emotions was me, but by releasing it I was able to start the healing process. This is a practise that I use on a regular basis.

# April 21

## Boundaries
## By Kim Richardson

For so much of my life I was not setting boundaries, or I would try to set them and would find myself allowing my boundaries to be broken. People would walk all over me, I often felt like a doormat.

The reality is you teach people how to treat you by what you allow. If you continue to allow to others to treat you in an unkind or disrespectful way, they will continue to do so. It is possible to stand up in your truth in a loving way. You can simply say, *this is not acceptable to me, this does not feel respectful, I do not feel comfortable with this,* or *that does not work for me.*

Those that love you and are meant to be in your life will rise to the occasion, however there may be many that seem to disappear. Remember, people come into your life for a reason, a season, or a lifetime. Some are simply here to be a mirror for us to look inward and discover areas that may still need some healing or growth. If people do not stay in your life because of your boundaries, then they are not meant to be there.

When you can get to a space where you feel confident enough to establish and hold your boundaries you become a great teacher for others as well. It gives others permission to do the same.

Take an inventory of the areas of your life and/or the people in your life where you may need to establish boundaries and practice using your voice to lovingly set and hold your boundaries.

# *April 22*

## I Dare You
## By Sheryl Goodwin Magiera

*I* believe everyone was put on this earth with special gifts and talents that no one else can duplicate, making each of us one-of-a-kind. Some may recognize this at an early age, while others lag far behind. For me, you guessed it, I was a lagger. Looking back, I think it was because I doubted I had anything to share that was more special than the next person. What I did not realize until much later is that we all possess something wonderful. I believe many search for the answer to the burning question "What was I put here to do?"

Does that sound familiar? If so, welcome to the club, and if not, you were blessed with recognizing your gifts and give yourself a loud and proud AMEN! I hope you are using those unique qualities to make a difference in the world (whether they are in a big or small way, they are needed), but if you are still wondering, let's get to work.

For me it's about stepping into the light. What I mean by that is daring to use my gifts, and having the courage to let them shine. It would be a shame to waste what I have to offer for fear of putting myself out there, failure, or being vulnerable. It is my responsibility to uncover and use my gifts to make the world a better place.

I invite you to start tapping into your internal wisdom and guidance. Trust me, it is in your heart, you just need to carefully excavate it. It starts with baby steps and listening with your heart and soul. What are the things that come easy and bring you joy? What did you love to do as a child? What makes you so happy you can't imagine not doing? Start making a list and let yourself feel and ask the question "What if?"

What if, you let go and trusted your heart? What if you had nothing to lose?

Come with me, challenge yourself in finding your gifts, then step into your light. The world needs what only you can provide; it is your gift to the universe. I dare you not to waste what resides in your heart. Seek your truth, uncover your gold, dare to dream what if. Then shine bright, my darling.

# April 23

## Heal My Heart With My Own Love
### By Denise Kirkconnell

When we get to a place of knowing and accepting ourselves as the imperfect beautiful beings we are, that is true love. We have accomplished healing our hearts with our own love.

With all the heartbreak life brings, learning to love and heal ourselves is a gift no one else can give us. So how do we get here and more importantly how do we stay here?

Nourish yourself with love in every way. Eat healthier. Get out in nature. Take a blissful bubbly bath. Get your hair done. Get a facial or give yourself a facial. Meditate, Do some art. Just do things that fill you up and bring you joy.

When we engage in things that bring us joy, we are loving ourselves in the most basic but impactful way. Part of healing from the inside is stopping the negative chatter that can take over our lives. Stop it as soon as it starts. It is very difficult to catch yourself at first, but I promise it will not be long before you are naturally redirecting your thoughts.

When a negative thought comes, replace it with three positive thoughts. If you have a mantra or positive affirmation, you can use that to replace negative thoughts. This helps to shift our mind from the negative to a positive. The following is a positive affirmation that you can sing to yourself.

"Letting go, letting go, I am letting go, And I heal my heart with my own love."

# *April 24*

## Comfortable in My Own Skin
## By Karen Cowperthwaite

*M*y instinct to hide my body and cover up began to surface when I was ten years old. There was a feeling that my body was shameful, and it was something I could not trust. I remember thinking that my body did not look like everyone else's small bodies. There was a constant comparison game playing in my head. My body versus another girl's body and my body always lost.

I believed I was bigger and perhaps that was true when I compared myself to some of the girls I zeroed in on. I was blind to the fact that there were plenty of other girls my age whose size and shape were very similar. This narrow lens with which I saw myself set in motion the belief that my body needed to be fixed.

Like me, many women have a long-standing history of weight loss attempts. We both laugh and cry reciting the laundry list of weight loss programs, diet restrictions, exercise equipment and quick solutions that we have invested both time and money into.

After forty years of shaming myself for many successful attempts with eventual regain cycle, I just let go. I stopped waking up each morning with judgment of my stomach's size. I quit holding myself back due to how I thought I looked in my clothes. I stopped the beatdown and started thinking about what my body does for me. I realized that my body needed me to listen and to love it.

I made the decision that I could treat my body like it was something to be ashamed of or I could create a new belief that it is healthy, beautiful, and in a constant state of change. All of the energy I used to disparage my body shifted into using my energy to care and love it. When unkind thoughts came up, I would say,

"I am a work in-progress; this is temporary. I choose to love myself even more."

What can you say to yourself when your thoughts about your body turn critical? What will you decide to believe about you? Could you decide to be kind, caring, supportive, and loving? Make a decision and complete this statement for yourself, "I want to be a person who . . ." Fill in the blank throughout the day. You begin the process of creating the future you by making her your focused intention.

# April 25

## Law of Attraction and Self-Love
## By Paula Obeid

The law of attraction is mostly about how you feel. When we truly love and accept ourselves, we hold the key to manifestation. Perhaps a better way to explain "law of attraction" is rename it "law of you." We create what we feel. When we truly love ourselves and feel worthy of receiving our hearts desires, the universe must deliver! Imagine through the power of law of attraction what we could create if we genuinely loved ourselves!! Self-love will influence your feelings and beliefs. Our conscious and subconscious beliefs about how you value yourself is the energy communicated to the universe. Our beliefs on our worthiness is the energy of what we allow to manifest in our lives. Neuroscience has shown that our subconscious brain controls most of our behavior, emotions, and beliefs.

Self-love affirmations and other exercises aid in raising feelings of self-worth imprinted on the subconscious mind. Consistent action developing more self-love can reprogram your subconscious mind allowing the "law of you" to go into effect! We need to treat ourselves lovingly, so it is important to start taking small actions that nurture self-love. The small actions are a way to "fake it till we make it." The actions are demonstrating acts of self-love that lead to energetic shifts.

A practice that is helpful while you cultivate self-love is to write down a list of things you like about yourself. Journal about one hundred ways that *you are amazing*!! This list is for you only, so write everything that you are proud about, the physical, or emotional traits you admire, wonderful memories, or just things you are grateful about. Next read your list in the morning when you wake up and another time right before you go to bed. For a greater impact, read it out loud in front of someone or in front of the mirror. After you complete reading your list, meditate for a few moments imagining what it would feel like if you loved yourself. What would you allow into your life?

If you are serious about getting the "law of you" to work, then self-love is important. When we have a true knowing that we are worthy, it sets the ultimate foundation for manifestation. Self-love is not supposed to be something that we have to earn. You are the most important person in your world!

# April 26

## Sacred Space
## By Crystal Cockerham

One of the most loving acts you can do for yourself is dedicate time & space for yourself that is sacred, & then make it a practice.

It is in this sacred space that you gain the clearest access to the true essence of who you are, of who you were born to be. It is here through your intuitive senses in this sacred space where you can ask for & receive guidance by learning to speak the language of your spirit & soul, which I refer to as your Spirit Speak. You will also:

- Open the doors to knowing yourself like you've never known yourself before—giving you the space to develop the single most important relationship, your inner relationship with your entire being.

- Gain a strong foundation to build from throughout your day by starting the day off in alignment, centered in your being. This improves your overall mood & mindset.

- Help your mind stay clearer for better focus—not just for projects, but it also readies you for whatever pops up. This helps you react & respond with more calmness & clarity.

- Strengthen & trust your intuitive nature. You will be able to gain fresh perspectives that will propel you forward in the decision making & change-implementing process because you will be sure-footed & rooted in your truth.

So how do you create sacred space & develop a daily practice?

1. The first thing to do in order to create sacred space for yourself is GIVE YOURSELF PERMISSION to take time for yourself.

2. Then, COMMIT TO YOURSELF by SCHEDULING THE TIME. Why start with these seemingly simple no-brainers? Because if you don't, you'll never actually experience sacred space. How many times have you said to yourself you want to start "x" & then it never gets started?

3. Now all that is left is to DO IT. Hold yourself accountable, and DO IT. Allow it to become the healthy habit it is meant to be.

Must-haves for your sacred space include undisturbed space & time; a clear, powerful intention; a safe physical space to *be* in; your focused energy & presence. This energy isn't a to-do list item. It is a soul-quenching practice that is vital to your wholeness, happiness, & life fulfillment. Perhaps you might want to add a journal/sketchbook, divination tools, a book, candle/incense/essential oils, crystals, etc.

Sacred Space Have-Nots include anyone else but you, interruptions & distractions (put your electronic devices on airplane mode or do not disturb), & negative, limiting self-talk.

# April 27

## The Human Instrument
## By Salli Sebastian Walker

*D*oes your brain ever run through information that you wish you could share with others? I have studied the human body for over forty years crossing paths with many fun facts. Here is just one nugget I discovered along the way. May this tool unleash the musical rainbow in you.

Our bodies are energy that respond to our every thought. When life gets tough, it can be difficult to find joy in the present moment. The chakras are seven primary energy centers that can be opened. Think of them like the strings of a musical instrument. When one string becomes tight or slack, then everything is out of harmony. Your body is similar. So, when it is in tune, harmony and resonance are restored. Below is the tool you will need as we explore further:

- Crown chakra/top of head: Color is violet. Musical keynote is B, vowel sound (Ohm).
- Third eye chakra /center of forehead: Color is indigo. Musical keynote is A, vowel sound (Ee).
- Throat chakra/throat area: Color is blue. Musical keynote is G, vowel sound (Eh).
- Heart chakra/center of chest: Color is green. Musical keynote is F, vowel sound (Ah).
- Solar plexus chakra/above naval and below chest: Color is yellow. Musical keynote is E, vowel sound (O/top).
- Sacral chakra/between naval and genitals: Color is orange. Musical keynote is D, vowel sound (O/home).

- Root chakra/base of spine: Color is red. Musical keynote is C, vowel sound (U/ooh).

Sit comfortably, back straight, and have the chart in front of you. Please close your eyes and breathe deeply and slowly for a few minutes. Now open your eyes briefly as you check the color on the chart and its location on your body. You can use a pitch pipe app from your phone as you play the note associated with that center. Continue working your focus as you move up the body, stopping on each center. After reaching the top or crown center, come back down and think of yourself anchoring to the earth. Breathe in and out again.

With time you will develop an increased sensitivity to the subtle energies within your body. Have fun with color and music and play around. Make up a song using positive affirmations as your inspiration. For help do an internet search for "Popcorn" by Hot Butter.

# April 28

## Confidence And Freedom
## By Marie Martin

There was a point in my life that fear choked me. I was prevented from moving forward in most areas of my life. I thought that if I moved out of my comfort zone, the area of which I was the most familiar, then something devastating would happen. Every day I felt more and more stifled and did not understand why. But the truth was, I was slowly killing myself by not living. One day I spoke to a man halfway across the country. After some time we fell in love over the phone. Crazy, I know, but I wanted to meet him so badly that I got up the courage to drive to Washington D.C. He is now my husband.

What that experience taught me is that you have to act. When you act you learn how capable you are. When you have yourself to lean on, and you trust your ability to make decisions, this leads to a woman's most valuable trait, confidence.

Confidence, for me, is the ability to trust that I can handle the circumstances that I am placed in. I will have the know-how or ability to negotiate my way through events. In that place of waiting, I would never get the opportunity to learn to rely on myself. I would never have the chance to learn what I liked or who I was.

Does part of this feel familiar? If so, maybe you are keeping yourself too safe! Is there a way you could let out your inner rebel from time to time? Or is there something in your life that is worth enough for you to step outside your comfort zone to achieve it? If confidence is learning to rely on yourself, is there a way that you could take one small step at a time? Is there a way to take those steps where you still have a safety net if you need one?

In the future when you think back on those scary times, the ones in which you do step outside your comfort zone will be the ones you will think about when you approach the next obstacle. They are your little indexes of proof that you do what you put your focus on. Any action, even the smallest kind, is still growing and can lead to a world that is lived in confidently.

# April 29

## Dissolving Etheric Cords
## By Carolan Dickinson

*E*theric Cords are energetic, transparent ropes that connect you to a person, place, or thing that create an unhealthy attachment. They can then manifest as unforgiveness, trauma, and emotional or physical conflict. When we are consciously doing any healing work as we are here, we are promoting or cultivating self-love. It is an act of self-love to heal. It is generous of spirit and gracious to your own soul, and you are so worth it!

Dissolving etheric cords is essentially releasing and healing from past hurts and experiences (including past lives) that left an imbalance in your spirit. Sometimes these imbalances create an etheric cord that attaches to people places and things. Some people can see them, others sense them, and you can even feel them as a tug on your chakra or energy body. By doing this, you are releasing the old and creating beautiful new space in which to grow and flow!

1. Envision Archangel Michael, sending clear white energy from your crown to your feet and ask him to dissolve all etheric cords totally and completely from this lifetime or any other. See, with your mind's eye or inner sight, all those etheric cords dissolving. Look again to see if there are any remaining knots of cords on the inside (They can be stubborn sometimes.), and then untie the knot and the let it fall away once and for all.

2. Ask Archangel, Raphael, to heal any all places those etheric cords touched from this lifetime or any others. See and feel his emerald green energy filling up your entire being and surrounding you with his energy.

3. You can also ask the Archangel, Chamuel, to fill you with rose pink energy to fill you completely with unconditional love. Then say to yourself, "I love and accept myself, exactly as I am." Ask him, "Please fill my heart space front and back with rose pink energy healing all emotional wounds from this lifetime or any other."

# April 30

## Receiving
## By Lisa Seyring

*I* have a big well of love to give to others. What is also true is the well of love I give to myself can run a little dry. I had somehow learned to focus all my attention outward on others and not at all on myself. What I came to understand is that I did not know how to give to myself because I did not have a practice of receiving. I was marching through life without pausing to receive. When my eyes were opened to this lack of awareness, I began to take notice and initiated a receivership revival. If a compliment came my way, I allowed myself to fully receive and savor it by simply saying thank you. If I read a thank-you note, I fully allowed myself to receive the words. When I drank a cup of tea, I allowed myself to receive fully its aroma and flavor.

These little steps helped me to build into a greater receivership. I discovered that if I listened inwardly, I could actually receive messages from inside my being, from inside my heart. I taught myself to pause and listen.

This is one act of love I gave myself that has helped me to establish a receiving relationship with myself. I encourage you to practice receivership. Receive the following excerpt with the intent to feel the vibration of the words and to create beautiful imagery in your mind.

This is what love had to say to me when I listened to my heart.

"Love grows like the vines of a plant, sprouting and lengthening. I want you to see me! No, I want you to feel me. You want to put me in form, yet I am formless. I am a sensation, yet before that I am a vibration. I am elements of warmth and joy. Deeply compassionate am I. You may think me pink, but I am so much more; rich emerald green, arresting azure blue.

"I evoke a response in you. So beautiful are you.

"Can you remember the trust you had in me? Can you remember our partnership? Loving you always, in all ways, I invite you in. I invite you to remember the space of grace, that space of which you are already a part. You know me. You feel me. Meld into me."

# May 1

## Souls of Wonderness
## By Jannirose Fenimore

One of the things I have learned from my earth angel is that there are no small wonders in life. To Charlie, everything that touches his wide-open heart is cause for quiet celebration—even the things many of us would see as ordinary.

I first noticed this when he started pre-kindergarten. Every day when I arrived to drive him home, he would react as if my presence was the most glorious gift he could possibly imagine. And all through his school years and even today, my little guy seems pleasantly surprised that I have shown up once more to meet him.

Charlie's unbridled enthusiasm for everyday happenings extends to routine activities of daily living such as breakfast, lunch and dinner. He eats the exact same lunch every single day by choice and still gets excited when his plate is set before him.

It is a sweet blessing to watch the way my son celebrates the little events in his life with sheer delight—like he never once considered that something so wonderful would happen. To him, this is *"wonderness"* at its very best, and he shows me throughout each day just how to live it.

I have learned from Charlie to find the richness and beauty in what I might otherwise view as mundane. This reminds me of my Alaskan years during which I loved to explore the tundra. I would come upon a tiny plant flowering in all its glory and marvel at the miracle of such a minute lifeform poking through the mostly-barren landscape.

*Wonderness.* For me, having this place of grace as my life's center has transformed my world in more ways than I can express. It is an exercise that involves slowing down, letting go and opening myself to truly see with laser-like depth.

Today, I invite you to embrace your own sense of wonder. If it has been a while since you last experienced it, have no fear—you are probably just out of practice. Start small!

There are countless opportunities throughout each day to exercise your wonder muscles. The only prerequisite is to step back from the demands of the day and allow yourself to fully observe. Where you focus is not important.

Just allow the magic to be revealed from moment to moment, and watch as the *wonderness* of childhood long forgotten brings you new life.

# May 2

## Wonderful Living Joy
## By Charlie Fenimore

*L*oving life around our human heartness is the soul of wonderness. Peace with holy happiness makes our kindful living free. Bright smiles inside our hearts brings lightness to our spirits of love in the shining stars of heaven's joy.

# May 3

## Grieving and Self-Love
### By Margaret-Maggie Honnold

Talking of self-love would not be complete without speaking a little about grief. Grief can block everything positive in one's life. It opens the doors to doubt, fear, crazy decisions, and all sorts of things that do not benefit you. I speak from experience.

My husband of thirty years was my stability. He was my best cheerleader, strongest supporter, lover, partner, and best friend. When he died seven years ago, I thought I would die too. I looked for comfort everywhere but within myself. And of course, did not find it. Serial dating, eating, drinking, shopping, trading cars (that was an expensive one, I traded four times in as many years), and yes, traveling. It was not long until my money was dwindling along with my self-esteem. Grief will give your self-talk a whole crazy dialogue resulting in a diminishing of your self-love.

So, it is a new day. What does one do without reading dozens of books, taking grief classes, or just sitting and vegetating? Realize that it is hard to love yourself when grieving. Grief is universal—young and old experience it, so tell yourself that is it okay. You are not broken; you are grieving.

The physical and mental are connected. Taking care of the physical often helps the mental. Love yourself a little bit each day while you go through the darkness of grief. Not crazy stuff like I did …. Well, maybe a few. But positive things will help with getting stronger. Here are some examples.

First. Get your regular doctor visits and have the yearly screenings recommended.

Second. Find a good diet that makes you feel treated and food that maybe you are the only one who enjoys and enjoy it.

Third. Reference the love verses in the Bible. Read them until you believe them. It is sometimes difficult to believe we are loveable because we know our failures and flaws, even if the world does not. Do not let grief steer you wrong today.

Fourth. Remember there is nothing wrong with counseling or medications to help through a bad time.

Fifth. Today, let your self-talk tell you that it does get easier. Remember what Anne Lamott said. "Grief is like a broken leg, you never get over it completely, but you can learn to walk with a limp."

# May 4

## The Golden Key
### By Judith Manganiello

*I* had no idea I was the one keeping myself trapped in my limited beliefs. I just thought that all my hurts, pain, and suffering I was experiencing was just the way it was. After all, some were living a much harder life than mine. I believed it was just the way life is down here until I received a message from Spirit that I created all my suffering because of my free will choice.

I said, "God, why would You give us free will choice? Look at all the bad choices that we created." But in that very moment I received a wonderful, downloaded message directly from God.

God said, *now, this is your Golden Key to unlock and free everything trapped inside your soul from every lifetime. If it bugs you, it is yours that you allowed and created.*

Then I take my Golden Key, unlock what bothered me, gift it over to my Light for clearing, transformation, and integration from all lifetimes. Then I get happy again until I receive a new message, then I gift that. I keep gifting every thought or feeling that is coming forward to be healed.

In the beginning of the Golden Key journey, I spent a lot of time gifting, but I am happy to say it was time well spent. There is truly little in life that presses my buttons. That is how I know they have finally been healed.

Realize the power you have and use your own Golden Key to unlock all the things you have trapped inside for so long. Release them, rip open the present and find your gift!

# May 5

## Flow With The River
## By JoAnne Eisen

*C*an you imagine a life that feels like floating down a calm river freely? Not fighting the currents or the paths it may take you. When you float through life, it brings peace, freedom, and clarity to what you truly desire. You are choosing the most loving thing for you, which ultimately brings forth the highest good. When life flows with such ease, your human nature needs to find roadblocks to put in your path—causing you to feel the need to turn your boat upstream and paddle as hard and fast as possible. It triggers your attachments to old stories, and you hold on to them as tightly as you can. Your mind yells at you, "I need control back!" You feel you need to push and pull and make things happen! The urgency to take control of your life overcomes you.

Controlling your environment is a learned behavior. I embraced it most of my life until it didn't work any longer. As life crumbled, self-love and acceptance began to take center stage. I remembered that I am in partnership with spirit.

Understanding my emotional attachments and their influence on my decisions changed my life. Attachments create emotional bonds to things or outcomes. Emotional attachments come from insecurities that affect your life. Your need to control something is based on your emotional attachment to its outcome. Its root is fears and justifying them. We believe we are right, but what are the results? Don't be clouded by your attachments to the outcome you think you want. The most self-loving practice is to be loving and patient with yourself. Be the observer of your life. Looking at the overall picture for your highest good, disconnecting from all emotional attachments.

When feeling justified to an outcome, it can feel like paddling your boat as hard as you can up a river. Pay attention to deep-rooted old beliefs, and don't miss the bigger picture. You are perfect and knowing. You desire to be loved, heard, and respected.

It's incredible how we know this is the truth but quickly feel we need to continue paddling upstream.

Release attachments to old beliefs and free yourself to be open to all possibilities. Surrender to the power within you to flow down the river with ease and grace. So many opportunities will await you, and options you never thought possible will appear.

# May 6

## Mentors
## By Nancy Meikle-Mousseau

"First thing in the morning, find a particle of something to appreciate and hold your attention on it for seventeen seconds." Abraham Hicks is someone who holds truth for me. There are many others and by being in their light, they keep me uplifted instead of going down the rabbit hole, where my body does not feel good and other thoughts join the momentum. Just like a snowball going down the hill, when it reaches the end, you are wrapped up so tight, left to feel suffocated with your thoughts or to feel enveloped and cocooned by your thoughts. There is always choice.

So how do you find those others, those mentors, those of the light to shine for you?

By holding this book, you are on your path to light. The authors in this book offer you exercises to guide you to love yourself and feel good. You will resonate with many and I bet they also offer more than the exercises written in this book. Perhaps they have podcasts, webinars, songs, and books of wisdom. Spend time with uplifting people and you will soon find your momentum will be only that of the light. If you catch a negative thought, a fear, an anger, a disconnect, flip it immediately to a song you love, a quote from one of your new mentors and remember the seventeen second rule and you will be on your way back to feeling hopeful, enlightened, and full of joy.

# May 7

## Loving All of Me
## By Janice Story

Growing up, I never really knew who I was,. That's because I was always trying so hard to be like other girls, wanting to wear the same clothes they had, changing my hair to match theirs, etc., just to feel like I fit in with them. I didn't have many friends, and it seemed that no matter how hard I tried to fit in and get others to like me, it just didn't seem to work.

I often wondered, "What I had done wrong? What was wrong with me?"

My self-esteem lowered and I didn't feel worthy. I felt different than others not knowing why.

Later in life, I worked so hard to take care of others instead of myself that I became a master at people pleasing. I was always focused on keeping things peaceful even if it meant sacrificing my own happiness and joy. It seemed like I was always trying to prove myself. I had gotten so lost in trying to become someone I wasn't that I never gave myself an opportunity to discover my own true authentic self.

I have diligently spent the last ten years reflecting on the simple-yet-not so simple question, "Who am I?" I still may not have answers to that question, but in the process of doing the work and through my own self realizations, I have learned to love and accept myself just as I am. Sure, I still get stuck in those self-sabotaging thoughts every once in a while, but I don't stay there for long!

I have learned to love my self unconditionally without judgment. I no longer try to hide behind a mask pretending to be someone that I am not. I am free to be who I am and the person that I was meant to become. I still enjoy helping others and being of service to them, but now I know how important it is to take care of myself first.

I have learned to embrace my flaws and imperfections and I have become more compassionate and understanding with myself. I allow myself to move thorough negative thoughts with grace and ease and then refocus and reconnect. I am truly honoring myself by loving all of me! What steps are you going to take today to start your own journey of truly loving all of you?

# *May 8*

## Learn to Affirm
## By Marilyn Miller

*L*oving yourself helps you achieve what you want out of life. Affirmations offer an almost magical way of creating your dreams. Using them daily can help you change habits, create more income, find potential partners and realize many other desires. There are many different ways to do affirmations, but here is a way that is direct and simple. The first step is to be very clear what you want. Most folks don't know what they want. So, they often end up without achieving their dreams.

Learning to make clear and bold statements about what we want is the beginning of this process but not the end. When we get too specific about our desires, we can block powerful energy that might assist us. For example, if I say I want a certain job, and I affirm that job is mine now, there may be better jobs more suited to me. So, it is more productive to say, "I affirm that the job for my highest good right now is mine. That job is seeking me even as I am seeking it." In that way, I allow universal energy, God, or my higher power to bring options I have not considered.

Another important step is to be clear what experience you are looking for. When you have your new job, do you want to feel "happy and excited?" Do you want to feel joyful and grateful? Use this simple sentence to fill in the blanks to attract your desire:

- "I am _____and _____now that I have found the ideal job for me."
- For example: "I am delighted and relieved now that I have found the ideal job for me."

233

This formula also works if you are seeking a new business, home or romantic relationship. A good affirmation would be "I am happy and grateful now that I have found the ideal business partner for me. If you want to increase your income say "I am happy and grateful now that I am earning $_____ a month."

Another super important point: Avoid making a list of everything you want in a job, partner, or house as you may get everything you've listed along with some negatives you do not expect or want. Divine forces support us when we add "this or something better."

# May 9

## Showers
### By Florence Acosta

*A* shower is a tool for self-care, meditation, and energy healing. First, I focus on my feet and feel them connected to the shower floor. Then I feel the water hitting my skin and fall to the ground. I notice how the temperature and the sound of the shower help relax my body, bringing me into the present moment. Now, I connect with my breath by taking three deep breaths in and out of my nose. On the inhale, I take a deep breath in. On the exhale, I open my mouth and sigh it all out.

I visualize the water cleansing all the negative thoughts and energy that I am holding in my energetic field. On each exhale, I release the negative energy and the water washes it down the drain. I visualize the water with flecks of light first touching the top of my head at my crown chakra. The water running over my head reminds me to live with an open mind. Next I visualize the water running over my chest to remind me to live with an open heart.

When I am conscious and mindful of how I treat myself, I am reminded to take care of myself in the simplest of ways.

My shower is a space where I can truly connect with Source and my higher self to receive the messages I am meant to hear. It is a daily ritual that leaves me feeling peaceful, positive and relaxed. Depending on the time I shower, I use this experience to prepare for the magic of the dreams while I sleep or the magic of a new day.

# *May 10*

## Upholding Healthy Boundaries
## By Dominique Trier

*S*etting boundaries is an essential part of self-love and self-care due to our inability to be everything everyone wants us to be. It is simply impossible to please everyone in our lives. One of the most painful times in my life was when my father became diagnosed with stage three cancer. I remember being notified at work that my father only had eight weeks left to live. My heart sank, and I could not fight back tears as I rushed out of my corporate office cubicle.

I later came to the realization that I was the only one around willing to devote as much time as possible to try to do anything I could to help my dad survive. Not only was I juggling a demanding corporate job, but I felt complete liability for whether or not my father survived. During this time, my close friends and family were indispensable to me for support. I knew I could not do it all, and I asked for help. Time went on and with my help my dad was able to beat cancer.

It was a social worker that one day told me that it's okay if I cannot do it all, and this happened after my dad was cleared of cancer. When the social worker told me I did not have to do everything, I couldn't hold it together. It was the first time someone told me to make sure I followed through with other people being helpful and accountable. The social worker told me it was okay to take a step back to make sure I was okay. Others needed to come forward and help, too. They had just as much responsibility as I did.

This was one of the hardest lessons of my life, holding the boundaries I set and to have people give more help in a situation. I needed to make sure I was taking care of myself. Setting boundaries is one thing, but *sticking* with the boundaries is more difficult. I knew in my heart that if I didn't take care of myself, there would not be a me in existence to help at all in the future. I could no longer go on being an afterthought for myself and others. I had to be a priority, too. *I was and am worthy of the care and love I give*. Setting and upholding boundaries is caring and loving ourselves.

# May 11

## Hey Beautiful
## By Sarah Berkett

*I* was speaking with a colleague just the other day and we were talking about self-love, and how many women really do not like themselves much. She was really surprised because it is not often that we tell other women how we feel about this topic. I know because I have coached women and have had many open up to me. They try to like themselves but something causes them to still feel worthless.

Actually, many women do not even realize that they feel this way. Yet, some of their current challenges are due to their self-hatred or disapproval of themselves. So many women do not feel worthy of their own love. Most times, they seek to feel worthy through others and this is where the problems start.

Take time to answer these questions honestly.

Beautiful one, do you feel as if you love yourself? Do you love yourself with the kind of love that you have for a partner, child, or family members? I can remember having so much anger inside of me and when I told my spiritual mentor, she told me that the anger I was holding onto was direct towards myself.

# May 12

## The Art of Self-Care
## By Nancy Toffanin

One of my biggest lessons was that practicing self-care wasn't selfish. A lot of times we can feel guilty when we pamper ourselves and put "us" first. If we constantly put others first, we are sending a message to ourselves that we don't matter. When we pour from an empty cup, we feel exhausted, anxious, and overwhelmed. We can't show up as our best selves. Forming a practice of self-care is the best gift we can give ourselves. Making our *selves* a priority helps us love our *selves*, expands our confidence, and builds self-esteem.

Self-care is about honoring how we feel and even honoring feelings of anger, sadness, hurt, happiness, etc. and exploring those feelings, and accepting them. When we acknowledge where we are at, it helps with our healing and growth. When we do things from the feeling of obligation instead of love and our heart space, it can cause feelings of expectations and resentments. It's important to have healthy boundaries with family and friends.

Self-care fills our cup. When we take care of ourselves, we help teach other to do the same. Consistency is important; it's the key for creating a habit. The action of doing something every day helps us develop a routine and become more disciplined. Making a list of what we love to do and then setting a time in a calendar every day for ourselves is the key.

With self-care it's important to look at all levels. For some people self-care might be doing a variety of things. There are many examples:

1. Physical: exercise, dance, water, healthy food, massage .

2. Emotional: traumas, triggers and pain, self-love, confidence, healthy boundaries, good self-esteem, practicing forgiveness, identifying, feeling and processing feelings, in balance in our giving and receiving.

3. Spiritual: meditate, journal, practicing gratitude stillness, nature, being mindful, releasing, listening to our heart.

4. Intellectual: Reading, TV/media, thoughts and mindfulness, changing negative.

After we do this process, we start becoming the best versions of ourselves and we practice ultimate self-care. Even if we can't practice self-care every day, we can make the choice to do it once a week. It is very empowering to do and expands our self-love.

Self-reflection

Do you make time for self-care?

What do you love doing?

Have you made a self-care list?

Do you honor yourself?

# May 13

## Just Smile
## By Ellen Elizabeth Jones

"We shall never know all the good that a simple smile can do." Mother Teresa

There is incredible power within a smile. A smile conveys feelings of happiness, hope, and positivity to anyone who sees it. When you smile, you are sending a message to those around you that you are accepted, you are welcome, you are seen, and you matter. A smile is a gift for both the giver and the receiver.

Studies show that when you smile, something wonderful happens within your body. You feel happier because your brain sends a rush of feel good messages throughout your body. Our brains release a chemical called endorphins.

These endorphins are strong enough to have the power to lessen symptoms of physical and emotional pain. They can ease anxiety. Endorphins can help our respiration, circulation, and motor functions. They can make you feel happy, and whenever you smile, you release them. Smiling not only lightens and raises your energy, but it also tells those around you that you are actively participating in your life. They see the light in your eyes and smile on your face and will probably smile back in response. Smiling is contagious in the best of ways. You do not even have to be face-to-face. Have you ever been talking to someone on the phone and heard their smile? Smiling puts people at ease. When you are happy and joyous, you will smile a lot, so it only stands to reason that if you are unhappy you can make yourself happy again by smiling. It's not always easy, especially when you are sad, but it works.

Are you willing to try an experiment? All you must do to make someone happy is to smile at them. When you cross paths with another, smile with your eyes, heart, and grin. Make someone's day a little happier. It is a simple truth. Smile at the world and it smiles back. You have the power within you to make the world a kinder and happier place. By smiling at others, the more cheer will spread. It creates a ripple effect. It is a gift that is fee to pass along yet keeps on giving as it moves from one individual to another. Keep smiling, friends!

# May 14

## Say No
## By Kim Richardson

*D*o you find it difficult to say no? I know this was an area that took a lot of work on my part. I felt like I was being selfish if I said no to others. The reality is, when we do not say no, we can become depleted and resentful.

When someone asks me if I can do something, I tell them I will get back to them. I sit with it for a while and ask myself this question, *does it feel uplifting or depleting?* If the answer is uplifting then it is an instant YES, if it feels depleting than the answer is a NO.

It is important to understand that our cup must be full and over-flowing in order to be of service to others. There are many times in my life where my cup was so empty because I never said no. Once I learned of the artform of saying no in a loving way, my cup started to fill up. Once my cup was overflowing, I had the energy to start saying yes again while paying attention that I did not let *my* cup get depleted again.

Learning to say no in a loving way can be quite the artform. I never apologize, I simply just say that I am unable to assist in that moment or that I am not available. I may offer some other outside solutions if they come to mind, however I am strong to stand in my conviction if my cup is depleted.

How is your cup? Are you feeling depleted, full, or overflowing? If you cup is not overflowing, perhaps it is time to look at areas in your life where you could start saying no.

# May 15

## Making Love to Your Body
## By Yumie Zein

*M*aking love is generally a concept associated with a partner, an external factor required to bring forth those overflowing and gushing emotions of love. There are times in life, however, when the presence of a physical partner and a physical connection to create that is not available. Those times in my life were a beautiful opportunity to explore the art of making love to my own body. I began with the notion that since I am the one feeling the emotions of making love through giving and receiving physical and emotional connection to another, then why not be the giver and receiver of that for me?

It was a challenging concept to digest at first because it meant I had to know what actually feels good for me. How do I like to be touched? Where do I like to be touched? What do I like to hear, to smell, to taste, to see or visualize? Those were all things that had been previously dictated by the partner I was connecting intimately with, but in this process of making love to my body, I was free to explore in whatever way I desired.

These intimate journeys that I began to take with myself broadened my understanding of the difference between sensuality and sexuality. Making love to my body can be something as subtle as slowly rubbing lavender or rose oil on myself. Taking the time to feel every touch and glide of my fingers on my own skin. Feeling the pure pleasure of connection and love with myself. Feeling every curve and mark that makes me who I am.

It can then transform into pure orgasmic self-pleasure or it may not. That is a decision that your own body will let you know. The deeper you connect with it, the clearer the messages become. This process not only allows you to understand what it feels like to make love, it also draws a clear line for you as to what it is that you desire to experience with a partner. You then enter a relationship not out of a "need" but more out of a curiosity to explore what it feels like to connect in that way with an external partner.

# May 16

## Sacred Time
## By Susan Hoyle

*I*f I had to choose one *selfcare* routine I adopted years ago that has made the most impact on my life, it would be my sacred time. As a busy wife and mother taking time for myself was never an option. I guess this was part of my upbringing, telling me taking time for myself was "selfish." Which is why it has had such an impact on my own self-care. For me, self-care was the greatest act of self-love I have ever done. It was telling myself that *I matter, I am enough*! Creating my *sacred time* ritual created a sense of worthiness in me for my spiritual journey. I have a purpose here and I am willing to dedicate time to this purpose.

What is sacred time? It is time I set aside each morning and each evening for myself. It is whatever I want it to be on that given day. That was the beauty of this time for me. I got to choose what it is! And I could change it each day! I got myself a beautiful journal, which I referred to as my *Spirit Manager*. I began writing my thoughts, my questions for my Guides and Angels, even learned about *automatic writing*. Whenever I had a bad day, instead of sharing it with people, I would journal and work through the negative experience. I would know it was completed when I could feel grateful for having had the experience and could document what I had learned. My journal time became a time where I could release my thoughts onto paper. I felt such release through this process. I would ask for guidance.

Once I got the journaling down, I learned about meditation. Adding the meditation piece allowed my journaling practice to grow. I would meditate on something that I needed assistance with, then journal after my meditation. WOW! So many answers would come to me in this process. My journaling grew into documenting my journey which will one day be a memoire.

What is your sacred time ritual? If this is a new concept to you maybe you just start with quiet time alone each morning, before the world is awake, and each night. Maybe it's just taking a bath and reading, or listening to an uplifting podcast. That's the beauty. It is whatever you want it to be!

# *May 17*

## Letting Go
## By Denise Kirkconnell

*W*hen I sit and think of the things I want to let go of, I focus on what thoughts are repeating in my head. Sometimes the thought is so obsessive I must take the time to sit with it.

I ask myself ,what has this taught me? Why is it still relevant in my consciousness? What can I do to move the energy? When I get an idea of what is going to work best for that situation, I implement a plan of sacred time to fill the void that often comes with letting things go. Calling on the archangel, Michael ,is my go-to to begin the process. Archangel Uriel and especially the archangel, Raphael, are also very good to call in when needing to let go of people or things.

Ask them to surround you with their shield of protection as you clear a path to freeing yourself from whatever is holding you back from letting this go.

Letting go requires forgiveness in most cases. Forgiveness has been a difficult part of self-love for me when dealing with personal hurts and grief. In order to recover and move on, we must forgive—not for the other person, but more for ourselves not to be controlled by the grief and hurt people impose on us throughout our lives. We also must include forgiving ourselves at times because we are responsible for being that person. We all have had to experience both sides to really understand and grow.

My most effective and favorite letting-go technique is write and burn. Write your sorrows onto paper and write everything that comes to you. Let it all flow out. When you feel you have written all you have, sit with what you wrote. Repeat it if you think that might help.

And then my favorite part—burn. Get yourself a bowl or something safe to burn it in. Before setting it on fire, say some parting words such as "the words I have written here today serve no purpose in my life or being. I now send you off into the universe far away from me. I free you as you free me. And so it is."

# May 18

## Spend Time In Nature
## By Danielle Fierro

$\mathcal{S}$ pending time in nature is a wonderful form of self-care. Best of all, nature is all around. Being in nature allows you to get out of your head and open up to all the life that surrounds you. This especially helps when you have been stuck inside or going through a stressful time. You can enjoy breathing in the fresh air, feeling the warm sunlight on your skin, and seeing the different colors and textures that nature has to offer. You don't have to go anywhere special. Since I work from home, I like to take walks at the park in my neighborhood during my lunch break. It helps me take a mental break, gets my body moving and the energy flowing. I highly recommend taking a lunch break outside, even if you don't work from home. You can easily take a walk around your office building or visit a local park. Afterwards, you come back refreshed and ready to take on the day.

Traveling is another way of seeing the many different forms of nature. You can visit the beach, go camping in a forest, play in the snow, or relax by a lake. Sedona, Arizona is one of my favorite places to travel to. The red rocks and beautiful formations are breathtaking. This is my go to place to visit when I need to get centered.

Typically, you are moving your body when you spend time in nature, which doubles the self-care. You can enjoy the outdoors while you walk, run, hike, bike, or play with your family. The opportunities to gain health benefits are endless.

Spending time in nature is a wonderful way to elevate your mood and decrease stress. There are so many other mental, physical and even spiritual benefits that you can gain by surrounding yourself and connecting with nature.

# May 19

## Mermaid Medicine
## By Tonia Browne

*When I make time for what I enjoy, I enjoy my time.*

Without time to reflect and restore our energy and inner peace, life can take us in directions we don't really want to go. We are often unaware of this until something significant happens to make us stop and take stock. It doesn't have to be like this—so unexpected and such a surprise. If we had slowed down a bit and become more in-tune with our emotions, we could have more consciously navigated our way and have been more proactive rather than reactive. Looking back, we can see that the signs were there, we just didn't take time to notice them.

Diving deep and tuning in may seem too time-consuming in a busy world, but it can save time and heartache later. Being busy may feel better than slowing down and acknowledging that something needs to change for a while, but not for ever. However fast we run, life catches up with us and asks us gently or firmly to slow down—our choice.

Activities to soothe and restore your soul are what I call mermaid medicine. Such activities support a frame of mind that encourages you to go with the flow when that flow is right for you, but to change channels as required. Ensuring a high vibration and taking time to reflect and restore reduces the need to struggle in currents that are not travelling in the direction you want to go in and help you to be more aligned with who you are and who you want to be.

A high vibration is an important frequency to be in. It is here that energy flows. Offering yourself mermaid medicine is giving yourself time to restore. It reduces tension and improves your joie de vivre. It is an act of self-love to offer yourself time out from goal-orientated activities and seemingly endless external demands. When we are in a positive vibration, we are better placed to see the larger picture, draw to us synchronistic events, and enjoy the process of living. We are also more productive.

Try a deep dive and discover what your inner soul yearns to receive. Make a list of what activities you enjoy and then make them happen. For example:

- Soaking in a bath.
- Meditating in the moonlight.
- Swimming in a river, sea, or pool.

# May 20

## Soul Searching
## By Bonnie Larson

*H*ave you wondered why admired people naturally attract others? Just what is the magnetic attraction?

Natural beauty, check. Well dressed, yes. But, there is something more. Charisma. Confidence. We all notice. Entertainers step onto the stage mesmerizing large groups with a broad smile and the sound of their voice. Waves of adoration waft through the air as they enchant me, too. So why are they so captivating?

Soul searching, I believe we'd like to possess these qualities, too. But, there is more to it than emulating somebody else. Many of us, especially women, believe we fall short. Honestly, for many years I wondered why I was unlike everyone else. Self-conscious, I would try to meld in, yet found comfort on my own. My father asked, "Why would you want to be like everyone else?" That is a good question!

As I look within, there are many admirable qualities. Perhaps it's the outward expression. Do we measure ourselves by others? Do we weigh ourselves by a pair of scales? Oops!

Soul searching, I discover the secret! Rather than looking outside of ourselves, it's finding the beauty within. Each of us possesses a special light, a signature, beautiful vibration. It is as unique as our fingerprints. Once we ignite that spark, there's no holding back. Our beauty radiates forward in all directions.

So, what is that spark? Love! Beginning at our heart center, the spark of life exists. It's there waiting for us to build on. Remember the feeling when we realize we are in love? It's similar to looking into the eyes of our brand new child. Weddings. Baptisms. The puppy with deep, trusting, loving eyes. The Passion of Christmas.

These are the feelings. It is a love existing within us, extending far beyond ourselves.

By holding that feeling of love, the spark ignites. Interestingly, the heart and mind communicate. It begins at your heart center. You cannot achieve it by intellect alone, nor think your way into feeling. You must experience the *feeling* of love, then hold that thought.

Your body will resonate with love. The capacity to ignite that spark, love deeply and unconditionally, are the keys to the attractions we desire.

# May 21

## My Secret Admirer
## By Ann Marie Asp

*I*magine that you are someone on the outside looking inside of you. That someone who knows you so well. Listen quietly to the story she wants to share.

I am so proud of the woman that you have become. I have watched your transformation from the shy and reserved young child who was always afraid to express her inner voice to the dynamic, compassionate, and loving woman you are today.

Your journey has been quite an uphill climb with many stops along the way with hidden treasures always showing up when needed. We can all relate to the bumps that have more than once steered us off our true paths. There is gratitude and appreciation that we now feel for those obstacles that had gotten in our way. They have helped us gain the courage and strength to get back on the road to a life that we are all worthy of. It is that road where we rise above all circumstances in life, knowing it will bring us safely home. It is home to a place that lights up our hearts with such joy.

Looking back over those years with a much clearer vision, you now can sense the innate wisdom of the woman you are today. It is a wisdom that spans the test of time. There were many times when you may have asked yourself, "What is my true purpose in this life?" It was during those times that you would seek the answers from me, your best friend and secret admirer.

Pick up your journal today and begin to dialogue with this remarkable person who knows you better than anyone. Take time with the statements below to see and feel the clarity of what is revealed. This is an exercise you can do daily to tap into the many special qualities you have. It will show why anyone that knows you is thankful for your friendship.

I am grateful to you for. . .

You bring joy to my day by . . .

You inspire others by . . .

I am so proud of . . .

What makes you unique is. . .

What I hope for you is . . .

Always remember that it is your inner beauty and light that shines through in all you do.

Sincerely,

Your best friend and secret admirer

# May 22

## Life Patterns
## By Tanya Thompson

There is a pattern to your life. Whether or not you realize it or acknowledge any particular pattern, one exists. A few years ago, I was gifted a wall calendar that represented my life in weeks from birth to age ninety, it was a standard size poster with a block for each week. This calendar, and the research and ideas behind it, stem from an article written by Tim Urban on his *Wait But Why Blog* (waitbutwhy.com) titled "Your Life in Weeks." I immediately started looking up weeks and years of my life, coloring in major events, births, deaths, the beginning and ending of key relationships, the beginning and ending of career choices, major changes in my life, and moves I had made. Patterns began to emerge. It was as if I had been handed a compass that I didn't know existed until now, but it was a compass for my life.

This is a transformative tool and it has allowed me to make better decisions about my life going forward. I now know that if I'm stringing together a slew of 'bad' weeks, of either "no enjoyment or not building something important for my future or others," then I need to make a change.

As Tim so aptly puts it in the article, "…life is forgiving. No matter what happens each week, you get a new fresh box to work with the next week."

Forgive yourself. Let go of the things you carry around that don't serve you any longer and start anew.

# *May 23*

## The Power of Saying No:
## An Overlooked Act of Self-Love
### By Talia Renzo

*A*ll of our pain makes us the same. But we all have pain that hurts to let go of. When we think about self-love, we think of high self-esteem, confidence, inner peace, and bravery. We don't really talk about how self-love can be so much more than that. Sometimes, saying no is a healthy part of self-love.

In my own life story, I had been abused emotionally and physically. I was horribly mistreated and this resulted in years of guilt and shame about who I was. I was conditioned by the abusers in my life that I was not worthy or deserving of being more than they made me feel like I was.

The truth is that someone who loves themselves does not allow that to happen. I had to make some changes in my life. I stood up for myself—something that I was never taught growing up, some-thing they don't teach you in school. Learning to defend yourself is something that the world forces you to do when you're at the point when you've had enough. I began to say no.

I said no to people who hurt me in my past and wanted to con-tinue to hurt me in my future. I rejected the hurtful actions that my abusers had continue to project onto me. It didn't stop there. I even had to say no to myself on several occasions. When I wanted to feel sorry for myself, I said no. When I wanted to stay comfortable in my bed with my thoughts, I fought to get up in the morning. When I wanted to self-harm, I chose to get help. When I wanted to hold onto my pain, I said no and reminded myself that I had to let it go.

These rejections can be identified through a lens of self-love. Had I not given myself the extra nudge that I needed, more pain and trauma could have come resulted from these situations. But I love myself enough to get help when I need it. I love myself enough to stand up for myself. I love myself enough to take care of myself on the days I don't feel like it.

I encourage you all to give yourself an extra nudge of love this week and you will thank yourself later.

# May 24

## Breathing in Love ... Breathing out Gratitude: Everything Old Is New Again!
## By Charel Morris

*M*any ancient, spiritual or energetic practices are popular because they feel good. Meditating, yoga and mindfulness are popular. But now science is proving they do work. Many of our practices are thousands of years old have become science's modern find.

Currently, breathing is trendy. For those of you who have been breathing since birth, congratulations! It does seem obvious as well as silly. Yet, the fact is that most of us don't breathe in a way that supports the  life you desire. Breathing on automatic keeps us alive, but to support a good life we need to breathe consciously at least some of the time.

Conscious Breathing is our best friend. Working on an important project or just feeling stressed? Take a few deep breaths and pay attention to your breathing. Now you are consciously breathing. It will make your world lighter and brighter.

Counted Breathing is magical! Breathe in through your nose for a count of four and hold your breath for the count of seven. Exhale through your mouth for a count of eight. Do this in rounds of three and I promise things will change. Using this technique throughout your day will allow you to breeze through your stress and anxiety.

So here is next level breathing magic. You can engage other areas of your body when you are consciously breathing, and your results will be magnified many times over. When doing conscious breathing just imagine your tongue relaxed on the floor of your mouth. Breathe in for a count of six and out for a count of six. Repeat for five or more times. This combination connects to just the right parts of your nervous system and you will experience well-being in a few moments.

Conscious breathing is fast and effective way to support your practice and experience of self-love.

# May 25

## Loving Your Body Deva
### By Lisa A. Clayton

As our society reinforces body types of certain weight and shapes that are deemed beautiful and desirable, our self-images crumble, and we stop loving ourselves and start unrealistic improvements to fit in. The perfect and beautiful body is exploited and advertised in how to look, feel and be happy. The external polishing, plumping and reduction remedies start weaving stories of mistruth and falsehoods regarding our bodies.

I became swept up in this "perfect image" quagmire of treatments and diets as my weight rocked back and forth from super skinny to pleasantly plump. It was a rollercoaster ride, and it mentally, emotionally, and physically drained me.

Focusing upon the "spirit" of my body is what knocked me off this roller coaster and brought me to a new level of respect and love for my physical vehicle which carries my soul's eternal light and wisdom.

Your body is a nature spirit. It has a higher intelligence in the spirit world that I call the body deva. Your body has three-dimensional density with an intelligent operating system that most nature spirits; including animals, trees, plants, and flowers lack. We allow this intelligent operating system to mask the essence of being a nature spirit.

Once you realize your body deva is a true nature spirit, one connected to you through higher frequencies of unconditional love and light, you learn to stop negative self-body talk. Negative thoughts, emotions, or actions towards your body hurt your body deva. Why would you want to hurt your body deva when it loves you unconditionally and only wants you to love thyself?

Treat and speak to your body deva the same as you would with your angels, spirit guides and creator, with respect and honor. Start by looking in the mirror every morning and seeing the love-light of your magical body deva reflected in your human body.

Ask your body deva what your human body needs. Listen as it guides you to better food, hydration, movement and rest. Thank your body deva for always being with you and giving you guidance. Feel the difference as you view your body as a true nature spirit.

Create new practices to connect with your body deva daily. Affirm often, "I love you, body deva, and appreciate you as nature spirit." The more you connect in this way, the more you can shift unrealistic body images to true self-love for your body.

# May 26

## Light and Power
## By Giuliana Melo

*"This little light of mine, I am going to let it shine,
let it shine, let it shine."*

Today I want to remind you that you are made of light. You are an extremely powerful being. You were made in the image of God and divine power flows to you and through you. Right now, take a moment to put a hand on your heart, put the other hand on your belly. Notice how you feel as you breathe and as you imagine white light entering your body through your crown. You are a being filled with divine power.

Affirm, "I am safe to be powerful!"

Some terms connected with the light are:

**Lighthouse**—Someone filled with light and guides others out of the darkness. They stand there shining for all in no judgement.

**Light holder**—One who holds a lot of light and maintains their own energy.

**Light protector/light warrior**-—Protects the light. Avoids gossip. Uses their intuition to guide them. Doesn't do anything that doesn't feel good. Is the change they want to see in the world. They also spread light across the darkness by helping fight darkness. Defenders of the light. It is also someone who acknowledges their darkness and heals it.

**Light connector**—Those who connect those committed to serving with light.

**Light worker**—Someone dedicated to being in service in the highest light. They are empathic, selfless, compassionate, kind, and hope filled. They are very positive people. They help serve those who need their souls soothed and they help heal mind, body and spirit. They teach truth and love. They see the good in the world. They want to help mankind.

You may recognize yourself by these qualities! Write down what you think you are. Let's do an exercise. Right now, imagine divine, white light all around you. Ask this light to shield and protect you as you go about your day.

You may be asking why is it important to be a lightworker? Some people are mean and send out negative energy. Sometimes we may even be around negative energy in our homes, communities, and the world. Negative energy from others can make us sick. Negative energy can be sent intentionally and we unconsciously absorb it.

It is up to us to clear, protect, maintain, ground, and connect our energy.

How do you take care of your energy?

# May 27

## Channelling my Inner Artistic Child ~ A landscape that Led to More Self-Love
### By Stephanie Fontaine

*I*f you had told me that one day, I would love creating art, specifically through painting, I would have told you that you were wrong. It is interesting how we box ourselves in by buying into certain limiting beliefs.

I was not really an artistic child. Sure, I liked colouring, but to create a sketch or paint from a blank canvas was not at all my thing. In high school I chose music, drama, and photography as my artistic electives. I steered clear of the actual art classes where painting, sketching, and sculpting were involved. It was not until I was in my forties that I discovered I actually loved to paint.

One day, someone asked, "What makes you happy?"

I did not know how to answer. I thought about it and listed off a few things and they were all things that were for or about bringing joy to other people. I could not actually think of a hobby or activity that brought me joy and happiness.

Not long after, I decided to buy a ticket for a paint night event. I was nervous and excited about my new adventure. The painting was of a young girl standing in (what appeared to me to be) a magical forest. Her arms stretched up, reaching for a beautiful glowing light from above. It was whimsical and magical.

The instructions were straight forward and it felt relatively simple at first. Then came the time we needed to paint the girl. She was solid black, like a shadow, so facial details were not an issue. I must have painted her and then covered her over at least three times. I just could not get her *right*.

Finally, I had to surrender and either attempt to paint her or leave her out of the painting all together. I ended up painting her. However, I did not love her. It was not until I posted my painting on my social media that I came to love and appreciate her. A friend mentioned that they could see a face in one corner. I had not intentionally painted that face. Yet it was there alright, looking lovingly down on my little girl, guiding her from above, encouraging her to love herself; and so I did. I encourage you to channel your inner artist.

What can you paint that will bring you more self-love?

# May 28

## Letting Go
## By Debra Moore Ewing

Peace is letting go of the past or the expectation of how you thought things would be. It is also about forgiveness.

When I was younger, if someone did something to me, I would get angry. You probably have experienced that or you may be going through it now. Holding onto resentment is unhealthy. It is like a cancer eating away at every cell of your being and robbing you of the joy you deserve.

Forgiveness is for you. Quite honestly it took me years to get to that point, but what I've learned about forgiveness is it comes more easily if I send that person love. I no longer want them to suffer. I no longer wish them ill will. Instead, I send love and send them on their way.

People come into our life for a reason or a season. If someone has hurt you or let you down, it is easier to look at the facts instead of the story you made up around it. Take a piece of paper and write about it. Get all your anger out on that piece of paper and let it go. There is something cathartic about writing and purging, then lighting a match to the paper and releasing it.

I remember my visit to the Oregon Coast. I went alone and rented a cabin by the water. I walked to the beach with a pad and pen and wrote everything I wanted to release that was negative in my life. I placed the papers in a copper bowl, lit it, and watched the paper as it burned, setting the intention for my life moving forward. Once it was reduced to ash, I released it into the ocean and let the tide take it out to sea.

I was fortunate to have a dear friend and mentor who was eighteen years older than I was. Something she said has helped me through the years. "When someone shows you who they are, believe them." (Wright, 2001). Think about that. When you give up the hope or dream, they would be any different and look at the facts you are forced to look at who they *really* are. You cannot change someone. The only one who can change is *you*. They are who they are. Let them go so you may find peace.

# May 29

## Chitter Chatter
## By Symone Desirae

*D*o you feel yourself standing in your own way? Do you listen to the thoughts and opinions of others? Have you ever felt yourself second guessing your own thoughts and opinions? Have you ever heard yourself saying negative comments and doubting yourself about something you want to get excited about due to what others may think about you?

I can fully relate to you if you said yes to one or all of these questions. I used to always let other people's opinions and thoughts control my decisions in life, which in turn fueled my own inner negative dialogue. I got to a point where I'd had enough of this internal battle. I took back my power slowly and stopped listening to the outside chitter- chatter.

Take a moment to reflect on who you let control or influence your decisions and opinions in your life. Ask yourself, "Do I want this person to have any more say in my choices?"

If the answer is "no," then internally say, "I thank what no longer serves me, and I allow myself to take back the power of making my own decisions."

Take time to practice honoring you. Listen to your own inner dialog. Does this negative talk come from others or your own self-doubt? Little by little, you will begin to trust your gut feelings and cultivate your own decisions that are right for you. The negative self-talk will start to lesson. Not that it won't ever happen, we are still human after all.

You may even begin to notice the outside nay-sayers will slowly dwindle as you start unconsciously or consciously surround yourself with people who are supportive of you and your choices in life.

Know that at any moment you can flip the switch internally when a negative thought arises or when the unwanted chitter-chatter becomes too much. Give yourself positive affirmations and encouragement even when you are feeling discouraged.

# May 30

## Massage Yourself for Just Pennies
### By Salli Sebastian Walker

*H*ow about experimenting with some of my most favorite heart-healing tools that cost just pennies and can be found around your home? These items are used on your body to give gentle relief. The reason that I can safely claim that they work is because for over thirty years I have been a certified, licensed massage therapist, and so I feel it my duty to share with you these fun and often overlooked tools.

If you have any pre-existing conditions, please consult your physician. These ideas expressed here are not a diagnosis or a cure. They are simply an effective way to relieve and release some tight-and-tender areas in your body, safely and effectively. Know that no one but you, can ever have the close connection that you have to your own sensations and discomforts in your body. So please go slowly and take time to search and destroy these trigger-points which are located within the muscles of your body.

> Items needed: *tennis ball and a long sock or nylon, golf ball, rolling pin, water bottle, marbles.*

> Directions: Place one or two *tennis balls* inside a long sock or nylon. If you have a *golf ball*, please place it in the freezer. A wooden *rolling pin* or dowel rod works well. For the *water bottle*, please remove some of the water and place it in your freezer.

> Treatment: The *tennis ball* in the sock or nylon can be thrown over your back. Now, lean up against and wall rub up and down to massage your back.

The *golf ball* can be taken out of the freezer and placed on the floor and under your foot. Gently roll the ball and let the coolness stimulate and increase circulation in tired feet.

The *rolling pin* is an excellent tool to roll your calves and hamstrings out.

The frozen *water bottle* is a great way to soften the back of the neck. Just place it behind your neck, lay down and feel the sensation of lengthening.

Lastly, the *marbles* are a fun way to strengthen the toes and massage them at the same time. Try moving the marbles one at a time with your toes.

I hope you have enjoyed these tips. Feel free to experiment on your own with these self-massage tools.

# *May 31*

## A Healthy Indulgent Grocery Date
## By Melanie Morrison

*S*o many times we hear that we should listen to our body. But how often do we make time to ask our body what it needs? If we don't practice using our body's intuition, how can we expect to access its wisdom? A good way to start using your body intuition is to schedule an indulgent grocery shopping date. This is how it's done.

- Carve out a day and time that you can go grocery shopping completely alone and without distractions.

- Sit in a quiet comfortable place. Close your eyes and bring attention to your toes, then your feet, your ankles, and continue working your way up to your heart. When you get to your heart , allow yourself to feel the love there. Ask your body what it needs and then bring attention to your fingertips, working your way up to the top of your head.

- Notice any sensations. You might feel as though you hear its complaints of certain aches or pains. Thoughts of how you could treat your body might arise. Journal anything that comes up.

- Take a moment to feel gratitude for your body and all the hard work it does. Let go of any feelings of guilt you might have for not treating it better.

- Try to think of all the healthy things that your body enjoys eating. Now ask your body again what it needs.

- Before entering the store, take a moment in your car and just image that you just got dropped off on the planet from a different time. The time before refrigeration and you have only seen limited small amounts of fresh fruit and vegetables in your lifetime.

- Start in the produce section. Take a brief moment to feel your inner connection with your body. Ask it once more, "What do you need?"

- Explore the produce. What catches your eye? What are you drawn to? What items are you curious about? Allow your body to choose what goes in the cart.

- Give yourself freedom to choose outside of your typical items, lists, or meal plans. Indulge. Enjoy!

# June 1

## Living with Purpose
### By Dee Dee Rebitt

$\mathcal{H}$ ealing and letting go has been an exceptionally long journey for me. I always felt different never sure why.

Knowing what I know now, I can completely understand why I felt this way, but back then I never could. I always wanted to find my group, my circle, my tribe. My growing up and into my teen years and adult life, I was still trying to find my group even if it meant me taking some nasty wrong turns in my life. Lots of bad decisions almost destroyed me. They took me down some deep paths and close calls with my journey, where if I had not made some of those moves and changing my ways, I would not be here to share my story or my lessons with anyone.

I literally had to have some things and people wake me up from my dazed-out slumber. I finally reached a point in my world where I found my angel on earth, my saving grace. The life I was choosing to travel was down a slippery slope of self destruction. I literally had dealt with far too much in my life, I was tired of it all. I could not understand what my soul purpose was and why I was still there.

When I met my daughters' father, things changed. I felt complete. I was happy. I was married, had two girls, and had a career from home, but then I was not fitting into someone else's life anymore. After coming to grips with feeling like my world was shattered once again, I bottled up my emotions and built up that wall once more, but also stifled my emotions.

After so many close calls, I realized my purpose and found my tribe and they accepted me and I felt loved for the first time. Now I have people coming to me, wanting to share in my world and be a part of why I am here, I found my calling and find solace on my journey and part of it was in my writing and healing. I have found my purpose here. I finally found my tribe. I am enough.

# June 2

## Harmonious Balance
## By Courtney Parreira

The music rocks us gently,

Remnants of a lullaby whose notes, sweetest in song,

Send us off to slumber.

We're best in slumber as we await what we've become.

The calls are out,

The messages brief,

The crystalline connections taking shape in the underworking's of time.

Remarkably, it has already occurred,

For time is an illusion.

Your happiness is already present.

Your joy is in your palms.

Rest now for it is here.

It breathes because you do.

Return to the natural state of nature, the beauty and awe that reminds you of your beauty and brilliance. It is real. You've always been able to see it; you've always been able to feel it.

The beauty you miss, the beauty you seek, is all around you and it resonates with the innate beauty in us all. The natural world is our world. We are it. Therefore, we are. To love it is to love ourselves.

Nature calms the soul and shows us the way we used to be. Claim your time in nature today and every day. Which part calls to you most? The trees in a local park? The waves crashing along a shore? The expansive night sky? If you cannot physically immerse yourself in your favorite natural environment, do so energetically. Turn inward and imagine yourself surrounded by all the beauty your favorite natural environment has to offer. Gift yourself at least fifteen minutes in nature each day.

# June 3

## What's Your Anxiety Animal?
### By Carrie Newsom

*I*f your anxiety was an animal, what animal would it be? First one that pops in your head. Don't second guess it. Don't change it. Got it? We'll talk more about it in a minute.

When I thought of my anxiety animal, a cheetah was the first thing that popped into my head. I thought, "Aw man. Cheetah? Let's think of a different animal, something better, more dramatic." But nope. You're supposed to just take the first one that comes to mind.

Then I started thinking. Cheetahs are lightning-fast. I envision them running endlessly in the sparse grasslands of blistering Africa. Never stopping. Never finding what they're running towards. Running, no matter how desperate, hungry, sick, or weary they are. I realized that's exactly what it feels like when I'm anxious! My mind races a million miles an hour, jetting through all the scenarios, all the things that could go wrong, all my worries. It's endless, relentless, dry, and desperate, just like a cheetah's pressured journey.

I once heard Robert Holden, a British psychologist who studies happiness, say that anxiety is just a spot that needs a little extra love. When we feel anxious, it's a signal that we need to give that part of ourselves some extra TLC.

Here's what that looks like: I thought about my cheetah. When I get anxious, I feel frantic and fractured mentally and emotionally. I envisioned putting a collar and leash on my cheetah, and when he starts to run like crazy, I gently pull him to my side and he sits beside me calmly. I'm in charge. He'll listen to me. No more insane running. He can still exist; he is a part of me and that's ok. It's ok to have anxiety. But it doesn't need to be in charge and run my life.

I will tell it what to do and when. So I take my cheetah by the leash and tell him to sit.

Sometimes what we consider our greatest faults or weaknesses are actually our most incredible gifts, if we reframe them in a positive way and learn what they can do for us.

This is a wonderful tool for all of us who suffer from anxiety. It helps understand and connect with our anxiety as a concrete entity, and then find ways to love that little spot in ourselves that is fragile and in need of reassurance.

# June 4

## Set Your Sights High
## By Marsha Johnson

When my son, Danny, was in Little League, there were the minors and the majors. Of course everyone wanted to be in the majors, the big leagues, but to Danny's disappointment, he was selected for the minors. He played there the first year, and he learned a lot, practiced, and got better. Soon he was playing to the best of his ability and the coaches in the majors took notice, and they invited him to play on a major league team.

To my surprise, Danny didn't want to go. He was comfortable where he was, most often had a good game, hit homeruns, made the crucial play, and it was easy for him. We had a discussion about it how if he wanted to get better and play to his full potential, he had to push himself out of his comfort zone. It would be tough at the beginning, but after time he'd improve.

Danny decided to go to the majors, and it wasn't easy. Slowly but surely, Danny continued to improve. He was surrounded by a coach and teammates who encouraged each other and cheered each other on. Most importantly, he was proud of himself, that he pushed himself to be the best he could.

So many times in life we are presented with a situation where we can stay where we are and be comfortable in our environment. Things may come easily and we have some success, but if there is a calling, a wanting of something more, maybe it's time to see that you can move up, be better. Take a chance on yourself. Be uncomfortable. Soon that which has felt uncomfortable will begin to feel natural. You don't want to have regrets, should haves, would haves, or could haves.

Read books, hang out with people that you want to learn from. You may feel out of place, but when you have the courage and strength to try, that's when the miracles happen. Love yourself so much to know that you can do and be whatever you want. Your circle of friends and co-workers can hold you back or pull you up, and you in turn can pull others up. Be sure to value yourself, know that you too deserve to be the best that you can be. Find your team in the majors of life.

# June 5

## Mistakes Cultivate Wisdom
## By Grace Redman

We all make mistakes. It's an inevitable part of life. We stay in relationships longer than we should. We allow others to take our power or take advantage of us. We don't speak up when we know we should.

When we make mistakes, many of us judge ourselves harshly, holding ourselves hostage to feelings of guilt. We will do anything we can to distract us from feeling feelings of unworthiness. We hide behind work, shopping, eating, and other addictions to help us cope and feel better.

We often fall into the trap of beating ourselves up over and over for the same mistake. All this does is allow us to relive the pain, fear, and judgement of the past. This causes us an immense amount of stress and fatigue ... and little personal growth.

Beating yourself up over your mistakes will hinder you from experiencing the magical depths of joy and peace. We grow and gain wisdom and experience from our mistakes. Frankly, I don't even like call mistakes *mistakes* .... I prefer to call them mishaps. There is also power in reflecting on what you can do better and committing to doing it differently next time. That's how wisdom and experience is gained. If you keep making the same mistake over and over, that's no longer a mistake. It's a choice and just own it!

The next time you experience a mishap and find yourself going a few rounds with that mean critical inner voice, listen to it like you would listen to a child who just made a mistake. Would you beat up a child for trying to take his/her first steps and then fall? No, you wouldn't. You would be patient, loving, and compassionate.

View that mean voice as your inner child and speak to the voice like you would to your younger self. Speak with love, kindness, and compassion.

Think of a past mistake that you have been ruminating over. What would you tell your younger self about the mistake? What was the lesson you learned from the mistake?

Doing the above exercise will help you gain awareness. By acknowledging the lesson learned from the mishap, you will be able to begin to experience unconditional love for yourself. Our mistakes are necessary. They us help cultivate wisdom and gain experience. They don't define us.

# June 6

## The Art of Doing Nothing
## By Bernadette Rodebaugh

To most people doing nothing means you're either sleeping or meditating, which is often one trying *not* to think while sitting still. I'd like you to consider a *new* do-nothing technique that will also feed your mind, body, and soul. It is really about doing nothing with the outside world while being inside your head as you live life doing everyday things that you're typically on autopilot doing anyways. For instance, eating, walking, cleaning, showering, etc.

The outside stimulation is considered noise or concentration that makes you multitask with actual thinking while doing these typical autopilot things. The radio, TV, phone, conversation, and social media are good examples of this. I have discovered this extra stimulation of consciously thinking during this time gets in the way of your brain unwinding and I have found it can actually solve your problems of anything that's causing stress in your everyday life.

For me this quiet time is when I get the best ideas for books, workshops, or better ways to handle conflict in my personal or professional life. I have learned that if I don't give myself at least five minutes of quiet time here and there throughout the day, I can't fall asleep at night. That's because instead of sleeping my brain is trying to solve those problems. I often hear people refer to this as their "mind is racing" and they can't fall asleep. I believe this is actually because they haven't given their brains time to think *quietly* until they're in bed!

My favorite quiet time is taking a walk because my mind naturally goes to any unresolved issues I'm having and works it out by the time I get back to my house. I often have friends ask me if they can go walking with me and I lovingly tell them no and that it's because this is when God and my soul talk to me. My other favorite time is driving to do errands with no radio on. For some reason it is very meditative for me and I just get downloads of information with the best ideas!

Let's start this miraculous technique for you: Open your journal and write down three self-care times that you can have without any outside stimulation and then do them at least three times this week! Then write down in your journal what ideas come to you during these quiet times.

# June 7

## Paradise Found
## By Mindy Lipton

*F*or over ten years I was a stand-up comedian in San Diego California. Occasionally, I would drive to Hollywood, California to do a gig at the infamous Comedy Store on Sunset Boulevard or the Improv on Melrose Avenue. I remember once when a comic asked me what kind of comedy I did, I answered, "funny." I knew what they meant but I could not resist that answer.

I love everything about comedy. The timing. The control. The stage. Writing material was never difficult for me. My material was all about things that really happened to me. I am single so I would go to online dating and that was a joke right there.

Female Comics of Hawaii asked me to do a show with them in Maui for Valentine's Day. I jumped at the chance and flew to the islands. I decided then that I wanted to move from one paradise, San Diego, California and move to the Hawaiian Islands, a real true paradise. Oh yes, I wanted to find my soulmate in paradise. However, the only souls I found were in shoes. The gigs were fine, but the humidity and mosquitoes took over.

After six months I wanted to return home. Where was home? I felt like Dorothy in the *Wizard of Oz*. There was "No place like home." Originally, home was Connecticut where I grew up. Many years in Los Angeles, Redding, and San Diego, California. But now? After Hawaii, I reside in Sacramento. I often ask myself why. My brother lived here for years, but recently moved to Las Vegas, Nevada where he had hopes that I would move along with him. Now, I am happily retired, overlooking the pool and jacuzzi I longed for on the sands of Waikiki. Sacramento is the City of Trees, so during the fall season, the leaves colors remind me of the East

Coast. I now have a feeling of peace and quiet after all those leaps of faith. Home, home … is where the heart is. A new community of friends taught that to me.

Cultivate joy in your life. Find a comedy routine that makes you laugh. Visualize the home you want to have. Is it filled with laughter? Find a video or a book that brings those belly laughs into reality.

# June 8

## Letting Go Through Forgiveness
## By Nanette Gogan-Edwards

"Although the world is full of suffering, it is also full of the overcoming of it." -Helen Keller

*F*irst, let's define forgiveness. What does it really mean? How do I do it? Webster dictionary defines the word "forgive": "to cease to feel resentment of or claim to requital – to grant relief from payment of". At first glance this all sounds accurate, all fine and dandy, but where we seem to get stuck is in the action of forgiving. It is actually quite easy to say the words "I forgive you" and go about our business but does that change what we hold in our heart about that person or situation? So much so that we never feel the need or desire to carry the baggage from that point forward?

Some time ago I heard a different definition of forgiveness that jumped off the page and grabbed hold of my heart. It was exactly what I needed to understand and to finally let go of all the pain. Forgiveness is "giving up hope that the past could have been different". Wow! What a revelation! First off, the past can never be changed, there is no hope in the past. Secondly, believing that it could have or should have been different brings nothing but shame and guilt into the future. By refusing to forgive others we ultimately take on the burden of other's actions and are not able or willing to forgive ourselves. This, my friends, is the opposite of self-love.

Give yourself the love you deserve by letting go. All the pain and suffering of the past belongs to the universe, so trust the process and give it away! Nature, the Universe, God, has balance and humans do not. Let your higher power relieve you of your heavy burden and accept the joy and comfort it brings.

# June 9

## Making Time
## By Gloria Dawn Kapeller

Sometimes life get so busy between work, family and other responsibilities. I am a person who tends to be unable to say no, so I am often so busy that I take on more than I really should. I am a wife, mother, healthcare worker, author, and a lot more as most of us woman are. I have a very understanding husband, Jon. He has been my rock, stood beside me every step of the way as I worked through the many stages of trying to heal, He came with me to the police station as I made the decision to charge my three 'brothers.' He went to court and heard what had happened to me as a child and teen. I tell him I love him all the time, but I know that I may not always show him that I love him. He has been my rock, my supporter and confidant. Sometimes actions speak louder than words, but words speak as well.

Write a love letter to your significant other, your children. Let them know how you feel. Sometimes you just need to just express emotions with words. Writing a love letter to yourself can help you feel better. Who knows what you need to hear better than you? Wow, this actually just came to me as I was writing this chapter piece, so that must have been meant to be said.

# *June 10*

## Evening Rituals
## By Jamie Rudolph

*E*vening rituals can help quiet the mind and body and prepare you for a restful sleep. Skin care is an important part of your overall wellbeing and should be incorporated into your daily ritual. Our skin is the largest organ of the human body and often the most forgotten. The skin protects us from foreign invaders and outer elements, regulates body temperature, and contains nerves allowing the sensation of touch.

One of my favorite evening practices incorporates skin care and facial gua sha or massage. Gua sha is a Chinese medicine technique used on the face and body to stimulate lymphatic drainage, tone muscles, erase fine lines, and stimulate blood flow. Gua sha tools help to stimulate the skin while calming the nervous system along with many additional holistic benefits. Gua sha tools come in many different styles and can be made with various materials such as gemstones, crystals, or metal. My favorite is rose quartz which is a natural healing stone and promotes self-love.

Begin cleansing with a gentle yet effective cleanser best suited for your skin type and condition. Follow with rose petal water and mist your skin. Roses are a known aphrodisiac and heal the heart. Next, add a few drops of rosehip oil to your fingertips—spread evenly across your forehead, cheeks, chin, and neck. Rosehip oil is high in vitamin C and helps promote collagen formation. Using your gua sha tool, with light pressure, stroke the tool gently against your skin and move from the center of your face, near your nose or mouth, outward.

The intention is to move the lymphatic fluid toward the lymph nodes while relaxing and firming the muscles. Repeat this over the same area several times and move to the next. On the forehead, start from the upper brows and move the gua sha tool to the hair line. Follow the jaw line from the chin and work toward the ears. If you do not have access to a facial tool like gua sha, you can use your fingers and hands to stroke your face in long, upward strokes and still receive the benefits of self-massage. After all areas are completed, gently remove any excess oil left on the skin and follow with your favorite evening serums or skin care products. This is a beautiful way to incorporate self-love into any evening ritual.

# June 11

## Supercharge your Wellbeing with Nature
## By Paula Marie Rennie

*A*s a child I always found my sense of peace and freedom from the burdens of life when I was out in nature. This is where I developed an even greater awareness and appreciation for the universe and how everything is connected.

The universe's wisdom is always sending us direct messages through nature if we pay attention. I always get excited when I see rainbows. They're my sign that all is working out in my life's plans. The archangels also play with my magical side when I'm out on walks. They delight me by placing unusual feathers on my path. This reminds me to listen to my intuition and trust myself. Next time you're out in nature, intentionally let it bring to you the reflections and signs that supercharge your feelings of wellbeing and connection to a greater universal intelligence. There is always guidance and support around you, you just need to ask and pay attention to the many signs with curiosity and wonder.

Try this flower visualization to connect you to what you truly need, and strengthen your senses to know, value and trust yourself.

- Sitting or standing, close your eyes and ground your feet into the Earth. Start to deepen your breath down into your belly and feel centered.

- Become aware of your body and imagine a flower out in front of you that best represents you and your needs at this time.

- Be aware of all your senses, feelings, and thoughts as you observe your flower.

- What's your first overall sense of its desires? Look, smell, feel its petals. Is your flower blooming or closed? What's affecting it? What does it need?

- What does the center of your flower look like? Are your masculine and feminine qualities in balance? What do they need to be balanced?

- What does your stem look like? Is it grounded and strong and rooted into the Earth? Are their any thorns in your side that are draining your energy and nourishment?

- Imagine yourself letting go of all that does not serve you. Draw to you now all that you need to be radiant and blooming.

- Take a moment to feel, sense, see, and know yourself within the essence of your flower's unique beauty. You can come back here anytime to feel whole, clear, and connected to what needs nurturing and inner growth.

# June 12

## Healthy Boundaries
## By Janice Story

*A*fter working twenty-four years in what became for me a very toxic job, I was finally able to leave and retire from the corporate world. I spent the majority of those years working sixty to eighty hours a week and had no boundaries. Not only did I not know that I should have them, I had no clue what that even meant. People would say to me, "You need to put boundaries in place. Quit letting others walk over top of you."

I never realized that I had been allowing this to happen. When I took a moment to look back through my life and my relationships, I could see and understand that I had been doing this for almost my whole life. I always put other people's needs and wants in front of my own. I thought that's what life was about—helping others, keeping them happy, trying hard not to cause problems, tip-toeing around and just keeping quiet in general so everything remained peaceful. Even if it meant sacrificing my own needs and wants.

My behaviors and patterns originated from my own lack of self-worth and low self-esteem. I didn't really know how to take care of me. I found myself becoming more stressed and really felt stuck. Then something magical and wonderful happened when I truly started loving myself. I learned to use healthy boundaries and that it was ok to say "no." Things began to shift when I started loving myself. Others seemed to be respectful of my boundaries, instead of walking over top of me.

As I continued to learn about and utilize boundaries, I discovered that they not only helped me, but they also made the relationships around me thrive. As my own self-esteem and confidence came back, I was learning what self-love really was. When I started taking care of me first, I was able to take care of and assist others in a more beneficial way. I could help them without allowing myself to become trampled on, and I wasn't giving more than I had to give. In the past I had always felt drained and exhausted.

Don't let yourself be consumed by the fear that putting up boundaries will cause those you love to retreat. You might just discover, like I did, that people will actually respect you more.

# June 13

## Eating to Nourish my Body
## By Kim Richardson

*F*or most of my life I was always on some kind of diet, counting calories and looking at the fat content of everything I ate. I would diet then feel deprived and binge eat everything I was not supposed to have, gaining back all the weight I had lost. This was my vicious cycle and the only way I knew how to live.

After attending my first healing retreat, I discovered there was much more going on inside than I had realized. I was discovering how much my past traumas and beliefs were affecting my life in the present. I spent the next few years concentrating on the health of my mind and spirit and walking the very tough roads to healing. I continued to eat the junk food I so loved as it provided me the much-needed comfort .... so, I thought. As I walked this healing journey, something miraculous happened .... I just started to lose weight. I was eating like crap and not exercising, it made no logical sense to me.

As I became so in tune with my body, learning to love it no matter what the scale said, I noticed that even though I was losing weight, I really did not feel good all the time. My mind and soul were feeling amazing. I loved this new found sense of myself; however, my body was screaming at me and it was time to listen. I had headaches, chronic stomach issues, pain, constipation, chronic female infections, high blood pressure, and high cholesterol.

I started to look at labels differently. I skipped past the little chart with all the numbers to read the actual ingredients of everything I ate, which at the time was all processed, boxed, quick and easy meals. I went further to research what those weird ingredients that I could not pronounce, let alone spell, what they actually were and what the effects they were causing in my body. I quickly learned it was these ingredients that were making me sick. I started to eliminate one thing at a time, hurdling over my addiction to these foods. As I evolved my diet to eat as clean (whole, real, non-processed food without chemical preservatives) as possible, I no longer was plagued with the list of health issues I once had.

Take an inventory of the foods you eat. What is one thing you can give up that is no longer serving you?

# June 14

## Be the Change
## By Selena Urbanovitch

Be the change you want to see in the world. I remember hearing this and thinking, "Yeah right. How can I change the world? I am just me!" What I did not realize was that I did have it in me to change my world. I can manifest what I desire. I just have to ask the universe! If you ask the universe for what is for your highest good, the universe listens! I have learned that when the universe knows I am grateful, more comes to me with ease!

Manifesting through gratitude is the most beautiful thing I ever took a chance on. It all started with a gratitude journal. I'd write in it every night before I slept. It started off "I am grateful for this day...." And I would go all the way through a full page of the things that I was grateful for. And I mean it was a full page. It amazed me when I thought of all the things that happened that day, then the next day was even better than the last. Little negatives were turned into positives. And my world started to change! How would you like your world to be? Would you like to be more positive and have more beautiful things happen in your world?

1. Start with a gratitude journal. Get a notebook that calls to you. Set it next to your bed and make a promise to yourself that you will fill this book up with all of your blessings.

2. Manifest what you would like to see in your world. Is it a better job? Let the universe know what you want.... We let the universe know by writing it down.

3. Make a vision board of all you wish to see. Put words and pictures that inspire you to reach for the stars. And put that vision board where you see it everyday!

4. Do something kind for a stranger, you know, like maybe holding the door for someone behind you.

5. Release doubt and fear and bring in peace and love.

When you start to put out there the change you want to see, you can change your world! And when you change your world for the positive, you manifest your dreams! I changed my world one moment at a time and I believe you can change yours!

# *June 15*

## Climbing the Tower
## By Sheryl Goodwin Magiera

*D*o you ever have those days you feel scattered, discombobulated, and out of sorts? Sometimes I feel like that day after day, creating a long line of days that turn into weeks of feeling not quite right. I find when this happens, almost 100 percent guaranteed, I am not listening to my heart, but rather my head has taken it hostage. I hate when that happens. I do not even realize it until I need to rescue my heart from the tower.

Once my heart has been captured, I must undergo self-care and be gentle with myself. I have to put on my armor, gather my swords, and muster the courage from the harsh words of the should haves and would haves I tell myself. We certainly would not say those same words to our loved ones, yet we say it to ourselves so easily. Judgement and doubt can creep in once you allow the chatter to take over. Letting our heart become captive is human, even though we are doing the best we can in the moment, but if we can learn to quiet our mind as soon as we hear the enemy approaching, we can claim victory for our soul.

Because we are human, we allow the heart to become vulnerable to outside forces. So, how do I take back my heart when it has been captured by the enemy? I quiet my mind, meditate, say affirmations of love, practice self-care, and pray. I get out of my head and invite love in, then I climb the tower and reclaim what's mine.

It does not matter how many times my heart's been taken prisoner; I will always rescue it. Because my heart knows me better than anyone else and if I listen, it will provide exactly what I need. It's my true north and always knows what's best. So, listen up, heart, I am climbing the tower and coming for you.

I invite you to practice listening to your heart and ask, "What do I need?" Be still, quiet your mind and listen to your heart. What is it saying? I promise, the more you practice, the easier it will become to rescue your heart from your head. Climb the tower and take back what is yours. You are worth it.

# June 16

## Sexual Release and Empowerment
## By Tabitha Weigel

*A* respected mentor of mine once shared with me that how I show up in my sexual life is a great indicator of how I show up in my day-to-day life. Meaning, am I vocal? Am I confident? Am I secure in my abilities? Do I understand that I am deserving of pleasure? Do I demand pleasure and play? Am I present? Am I open to receive love? These questions all relating to our sense of self and the many social roles we play. Yet there is something particularly powerful when framing these questions around the topic of sexuality, sensuality, and the wild release of energy that is an orgasm.

Yes, I said it! An orgasm, a moment of pure, unedited, energetic release. A body shaking, heart-pounding sensation and connection to our whole being. Our minds are free of thought or worry, and our presence is fully felt, activating and balancing our root, sacral, and heart chakras, allowing emotions to move through our energetic fields with ease. With this release of energy, there is also a built-in appreciation for the body and the pleasure it can create. A pride, joy and sense of empowerment within one's self can begin to develop and so can a confidence and recognition that our bodies and hearts are deserving of love, pleasure, and freedom. To orgasm with a partner or without is to feel sensual, beautiful, and comfortable within one's own skin.

So, you guessed it, treat yourself today to some well-deserved pleasure and play. Give love to your body. Connect with your body. Explore your body. Share your body and share your heart with whoever you love.

Begin to understand what you enjoy, want, and need when seeking sexual pleasure and security—not what you think you *should* want or need. In other words, do not play by the Hollywood script or have unrealistic expectations of self. Instead, embrace a sacred intimacy, finding your voice, demanding your pleasure, and claiming your divine power. Be patient and kind with yourself if this feels odd to you, but do not deny yourself the possibility of such pleasure and fun. Work to honor your body, accepting it and embracing it with love and a sexual empowerment that is bound to spill over into all areas of life.

# June 17

## Creative Balance of Fire
### By Virginia Adams

*J oy to the world, the light has come.* Humans have gathered around the flames of a fire for warmth, community, ceremony, cooking, and s'mores for all time. Who hasn't found themselves drifting into a peaceful, reflective state while gazing at the flames of an open fire or the flame of a candle?

When I think of fire or flames, it brings to mind the idea of alchemy or the burning of old and the transformation to new. What arises from the ash is the phoenix or the essence of the joy of spiritual growth. Today's quest for self-care and self-love is the exploration of the energy of the element of fire.

A trataka is a type of meditation where you keep your eyes open and focused on an object. Trataka can be done with a candle or an open fire where your full attention is focused on the flame or flames. This gazing meditation supports us in increasing concentration, improving memory, spiritual growth, and an increased state of awareness. Because this meditation is done with your eyes open, it is a perfect option for those who have trouble concentrating and containing a wandering mind.

Choose a quiet and darkened space where you will not be disturbed. Remove distractions like phones. I like to put on noise-canceling earmuffs to intensify my focus.

Make sure you are wearing comfortable clothing and that the room is at a comfortable temperature. If it is chilly, a blanket or shawl can help you stay warm as you sit. With the candle placed on a fireproof surface, sit with it at eye level about two feet away. Choose a comfortable position. Just make sure you're sitting up straight.

Stare at the candle and allow it to be the main focus of your mind. Hold your eyes steady even if you feel distracted or bored as you gaze at the candle. Breathe in joy, focusing on the sensation of the light flowing into you with each inhalation. As time passes, the room around you will fade until your only awareness is the flame. Take your time and enjoy!

When your meditation is finished, lie down, and close your eyes for five minutes. Allow yourself to reflect on what has just transpired—allowing your mind and body to come back into full awareness before you continue your day.

The creative energy of fire is one of spiritual growth and joy.

# June 18

## Just Show Up
## By Marie Martin

*I* have a belief about your unique qualities. You know the ones I mean. The ones from when you were young, you may have been teased about. Those ones that got rubbed up against until you felt raw, but in so doing, they strengthened and polished you. At some point, you may have found circumstances or people who appreciated you for how unique you are. Maybe they even helped you to see that your differences are a part of what makes you so special.

That belief I was talking about is that we are created for a need! Someplace in the big world is a job that needs to be done, and the right person will have that unique combination of skills and differences that you possess. You will often hear me abbreviate this belief to simply "You are the right tool for some job." This job is sometimes referred to as a calling.

I also believe that your calling is trying to show itself to you. It is showing up in your life, time, and time again. But how will you recognize it? By answering one simple question. Is this something I want to devote my life too? Your calling is something that brings out the best in you; it is something that you will find worth in, even if other people do not. It is something that touches a deep-down certainty that what you are devoting your time to is right.

So, I ask you what are you drawn to but have put off for the practicality of ordinary life? It is never too late to start down a road that fills you up inside. Age does not matter; gender does not matter; the only thing that matters is you give yourself a chance. Tools and knowledge can be obtained, but the heart that lives inside of you? You only have one.

I truly believe you were put on this planet at this exact time for a reason. There is something out there or someone who needs what you have to offer. You are powerful in your uniqueness, brilliant in your differences. All you must do is show up, and the rest will straighten out along the way.

# *June 19*

## Living From Greatness
## By Delores Garcia

The twenty-fifth verse of the *Tao Te Ching* teaches us "To know the Way, understand the great within yourself." I used to struggle with the idea of self-care. It felt selfish and self-centered. I never felt I had done anything good enough to deserve any such indulgence. This is the egoic mind tricking us into believing that we actually have to *do* something admirable before we deserve to be kind to ourselves. This could not be further from the truth.

When we have the intention to be self-caring, we ask our Inner Being to guide our human actions for our greatest and highest good. Our Inner Being is benevolent and all-knowing as to what we truly *need*. That is what our soul craves. This is what it means to be self-caring. It is not just an action we do for ourselves, but indeed, it is an intention and an identity of being *soul-caring*.

The *Tao Te Ching* teaches that there is a pure, timeless energy within everything, including you! Understand the greatness within! You have an absolute connection to the Infinite. This is what creates the rightful deservedness of you being self-caring: your inherent greatness.

Perhaps today's mantra is "I am consciously aware of my heritage of greatness" or "I come from greatness. I attract greatness. I am greatness." Let it flow through you. With your inherent greatness as the focal point of your attention, only greatness can emerge from you. Wayne Dyer, in *Change Your Thoughts. Change Your Life: Living the Wisdom of the Tao*, suggests a wonderful self-caring activity:

Watch and listen for the critical comments that originate from your own inner dialogue. When such thoughts emerge in your mind, let them tell you what they want. If you allow those not-so-great notions to speak, you'll always discover that what they really want is to feel good. Give them the time they need to trust that there's no payoff for their existence, and they will happily merge into the greatness within you.

The egoic mind thinks it needs to protect you from pain and disappointments as it may have done in the past. "But with continued accepting attention, the feeling will always eventually admit that it [just] wants to feel great." Inquire within today! There is nothing but greatness there!

# June 20

## Simply Be
## By Lisa Seyring

*I* imagined what my deepest, most loving part would have to say to me. This is what I heard.

"Come, sit, rest a spell with me. Yes, it is me, your Higher Self. I have been waiting for you. I have been here all along. The din of life often overrides my voice and my essence. Alas, you are here now. I prepared this beautiful space for us to gather. Can you feel this spaciousness filled with grace? This is the place where we simply *be*. No agenda, no pressure. It is filled with love and light, where you experience a lightness of being as if suspended in air. Yes! This! This grace! You, too, *can* feel. How, you ask? Follow my lead.

"Sitting comfortably, close your eyes for it is the best way to move your attention inward. Allow yourself to be quiet.

"*I know.* The mind can rapid fire its thoughts, concerns, and fears. You can simply be the observer of them. If it is helpful to you, just place them on your mental whiteboard for safe keeping while you meet with me. I have so much love for you. I want all of your attention.

"*I understand.* You are used to activity, always moving. Trust me when I tell you spending time with me will enhance your movement in life tremendously. I want you to experience this space of gracious love with me. That is right; your breathing is slowing beautifully. Can you sense it? The air is still in our gathering space. Feel the calm, clear buoyancy of it. A simple, welcoming bench invites us to sit where I can cradle you in my arms. As we sit together, I gaze upon you with the absolute love of my essence. Can you feel this love? There are no conditions. It is soft, warm and soothing. Let us just be here, in this space of love. The world will wait for you. Allow me to nourish you and give you rest. You get to simply be in this field of love. Simply be in love with yourself."

Allow these words and this imagery to wash over you and through you. Practice receiving the words and feeling the buoyant space of love for as long as you wish. Allow your imagination to bring you deeply into the vibration of the words and rest.

# *June 21*

## Create a Self-Love Acronym
## By Lisa A. Clayton

*H*ave fun in creative and innovative ways to make a self-love acronym as a daily reminder to love your whole, complete, perfect, and beautiful self.

Here is an example of one I use:

**S:** Say "I love you" to myself hourly.

**E:** Eat organic foods.

**L:** Love every inch of my skin, bumps, and wrinkles included.

**F:** Forgive any negative self-talk immediately.

**L:** Laugh out loud four to five times today.

**O:** Obsess with less screen time.

**V:** Vulnerability is truth, remember that.

**E**: Engage in movement hourly; stretch, walk, and dance.

Words hold energy and vibration. Every letter and self-love phrase you write and say uplifts your energy field to more coherent states. Coherent states bring greater resiliency, clarity, and good decision making as well as choices aligned with love.

As you write and say each letter of your self-love acronym daily, imagine that you are illuminating your energy field—both inside with your chakra centers and outside with your heart's electromagnetic waves that feed the field with your self-love.

Light up the world with your self-love acronym like it's a marquee for an anticipated feature film that's "Now Showing." Your soul is waiting for you to shine and love yourself in this way.

You are a bright star of your life show and loving yourself will light up the world and others' worlds in magnificent and magical ways. Shine on!

# June 22

## Be the Director of Your life
## By Ewa Blaszczak

As an intuitive and a spiritual guide I often read Akashic Records for my clients. In a nutshell it is about channeling information from higher realms. When you consult the Akashic Records, you get the guidelines from angels, ascended masters, or your deceased beloved ones.

One of the main advantages of reading the Akashic Records is that you can look at your life from a broader perspective, which is free from judgement, emotions, and earthly limitations.

In today's exercise you will be able to tap into such broader perspective of your life without the necessity to access your Akashic Records.

I would like you to imagine you are a firm director. Sit down and visualize yourself in a movie theatre. You are sitting somewhere in the back row. You feel comfortable and safe. This is the movie about your whole life—past, present and future. This movie is your creation. You are the director. Notice a remote control near you. Press the 'play' button. Your role is to watch the movie and make any necessary corrections. Take your time.

When you watch the movie about your own life:

1. What draws your attention?
2. What do you like about the life of the main character (being you)?
3. What needs to be changed in the script to make the story more beautiful, happy, fulfilling?

4. Make all necessary corrections. You can change the plot. You can change the scenery, etc. You are the director of this movie, after all.

5. Watch yourself in the movie. How would you describe this person? What do you love about him? What is it that this person needs to understand in order to become the best version of himself?

6. Feel free to experiment with the movie. You can try many options of the scenario and check how they unfold in the future.

7. What is the one micro-correction of your movie which you would like to implement in your real life right now? Choose something you have influence on and do it!

# June 23

### Forgiveness
### By Paula Obeid

*I* am human. I make mistakes. I hold onto self-judgement, actually I hold a two-by-four engraved with the word "judgement." I often beat myself up and validate my feelings of unworthiness. I find that I can easily forgive others. However, I am not willing to forgive myself. Yes, you heard that right! I am not willing!

Forgiveness is a choice just like everything else in life. I have found that making peace and moving forward is often easier said than done. Being able to forgive yourself requires self-love and an understanding that you are worthy of forgiveness. A simple perceived mistake weighs me down just as much as what society would consider a mistake like an arrest. I tend to be my own judge and jury finding myself always guilty!

My journey of learning to love myself started with reading Louise Hay's *You Can Heal Your Life*. After reading the book, I made a decision to look at what was holding me back in life. The answer always came back to loving myself! I developed this practice to forgive myself and find the learning opportunity in the experience.

- First, I decided to give myself a stack of monopoly "get out of jail free" cards.
- When I perceive that I made a mistake instead of pulling out the two-by-four, I give myself permission to feel all the emotions. I pay attention to everything triggered in my emotions and physical body.
- I notice when I am self-critical and judging myself harshly. I then say aloud or in my mind, "Hmm, that is interesting!?"

- I try not to dwell on what I did "wrong." I try to focus on what I learned and how it is going to improve my life for the better. I acknowledge the gift in the experience.

- I remind myself that I did the best I could with the knowledge and tools I had at that time. I am receiving the gift of identifying energy patterns that are not allowing me to fully forgive and love myself.

- I remind myself that everything is perfect. There is no right or wrong. I am doing the best I can!

Forgiveness is important for us and the world. World peace starts with each of us finding inner peace. Remember, identify judgments of all type. Identify the judgments that you held against yourself. Forgive that judgment. Love yourself unconditionally.

# June 24

## S.P.R.—Stop, Pause, Respond
### By Susan Hoyle

*S*.P.R.: *stop, pause and respond* is an exercise I learned years ago out of necessity. Yes, necessity. As I continued down my spiritual path and quest for peace in my life, I realized how much energy I was expending going down these paths with friends, family, and even acquaintances. You know the path. When you start having a discussion, but then you can feel yourself getting aggravated, either with yourself or them. But you continue, full steam ahead, with your *reaction* to whatever it was that *triggered* you into reacting. One of the hardest practices I learned was to feel when my body was shifting into *reacting* to something and stop, right there. I have found myself literally stopping mid-sentence, taking a deep breath, breathing in the white light of loving peace, and in doing so was able to move forward by *responding* not *reacting*. Responding actually moves energy to you while reacting takes energy from you.

When this was first explained to me, it was a hard concept to realize how this would affect my energy. But as time went on, I was able to see clearly exactly how much energy I was expending by reacting to something that was meaningless banter with someone. By stopping and giving myself that pause, that moment to just breathe into the conversation, I was able to listen compassionately and move forward with my response. Instead of moving cortisol through my body by reacting and creating stress, I was able to keep my peace and respond with loving grace.

If reacting is something you also struggle with, I would begin with awareness. Just having awareness as to where you are using energy unnecessarily in your day. You could make a list at the end of the day where your energy could be better spent had you used the S.P.R. technique. The more awareness you have around where your energy is leaving your body unnecessarily, leaving you stressed out and exhausted at the end of the day, the more you can shift this with the *power of the pause* into peace. While this is still something I practice each and every day, it is also something I believe has assisted me in living with greater peace daily. Not feeling that pull into the reactionary behaviors I once had. Give it a try.

# June 25

## The Power of Love
## By Nancy Toffanin

*L*ove comes in so many forms! Loving myself with acceptance, nurturing, understanding, and compassion allows me to expand my self-love. In life I realized there are two choices: love or fear. Living a life of choosing love opens us up to passion, creativity, balance, and magic. It creates infinite possibilities.

One of the biggest lessons I learned came from asking myself if I give from ego or a heart space?

When I give from ego, I have expectations and attachment. When I give from my heart, I have no expectations and I am filled with gratitude. Love is surrendering, being fully open, nurturing, and having intimacy.

In order to love someone else, we need to deeply love ourselves. I show myself love by having dead sea salt bath with candles, buying myself flowers, putting myself first, eating healthy, exercising, setting boundaries, and listening to my inner child.

Creating love wasn't easy. I had to forgive people and myself and heal my heart from my past wounds and traumas. In learning what love meant to me and breaking down my heart, I took apart walls that I had put up for protection. Choosing love, self-love, unconditional love, eternal love, all expanded my heart chakra. I had to learn in a relationship what I needed to feel loved: acceptance, consistency, transparency, honesty, trustworthy, passion, and a higher heart connection. I realized I need physical touch, compliments, quality time, and effort.

I understand my value and worth now and what I won't accept anymore.

The biggest gift I got this year was to become fully aware that I could be alone and feel fulfilled on the inside. I truly didn't need anyone. I am able to perceive that I want a relationship, but I don't need one. I used to judge myself on everything: my weight, my looks, my height, etc. In letting go of judgment of myself, I learned to accept myself.

I learned about self-compassion, giving myself a break. The power of love is inside all of us! Choose today to embrace it.

Self-reflection

What does love mean to you?

Have you worked through your fears?

How do you show yourself love?

Do you judge yourself?

Do you want a relationship?

Are you ready for a relationship?

Do you honor where you are at ?

# June 26

## What Would The Best Version Of Me Do?
## By Dominique Trier

*W*aking up in the morning can bring initial thoughts consisting of "I have to get so much done today. I will make a list, drink some coffee, and handle it." or "Why is it morning already? Can I have three more hours of sleep, at least?"

In the prime of my productivity, I chose to have the first train of thought. Sure, I would go through the latter for the first five minutes of being awake, but we can choose who we want to be every single day. We have to set ourselves up for success and imagine the best versions of ourselves and what they would do.

- Would they buy a planner to manage their time more wisely?
- Would they create a sleeping schedule to make sure their mind and body were prepared for the oncoming tasks of the day?
- Would they drink enough water?
- Would they make time during the week to exercise?
- Would they ensure they were consuming the right nutrition to aid health?

I challenge everyone reading this to ask themselves "What would the best version of myself do?" Envisioning who we would like to be and taking a few steps towards that every day is an active choice to love ourselves and create an innate confidence that is not fake, nor easily shaken. Internal validation is worth more than the fleeting external validation we sometimes crave.

# June 27

## Honor Yourself
## By Kim Richardson

We can often get so busy with life and taking care of others that we forget to take a moment to see how special we really are. Look in the mirror, see how beautiful you are inside and out. Ask yourself, *are you putting yourself first?*

Take a day just for you. Forget the daily to-do's or task list or find someone to cover them if you are unable to skip them. Really think about the task. Trust me when I tell you the family will survive without you cooking dinner. They may order pizza or maybe even eat cereal for dinner. Now, they may not be the food choice *you* want them to have, but it is only one night, let it go every now and then.

Take the time for YOU! Do something special that brings you joy and honors *you* and *your soul.* If you are unsure of what to do, time to reflect on that a bit. Do you just need some quite time to go for a walk, read, maybe go for a spa day? Think about how you would honor someone else and do those same things for *you*!

# June 28

## Let Me Call You Sweetheart
## By Karen Cowperthwaite

*W*hen we recognize our self-talk is really unkind, we can still have a hard time getting off the merry-go-round. Our thoughts seem to start spinning and we jump on and allow them to go round-and-round. It is as if our thoughts have a well-worn and rutted path that when activated take us in the same direction.

Our feelings are the most human part of us. They are important indicators of what is going on, especially because our feelings are triggered by the thoughts we think. If you think your feelings are wrong or bad, you will avoid processing them and they become stuck and stuffed down. This is where we can do the most damage. This is when we end up numbing and hurting ourselves through food, alcohol, isolating, online shopping, binge watching, and so forth. These behaviors take us away from the difficult emotions and right into ignoring what we really need.

One of the ways that I create a more loving space for my thoughts and feelings is to call myself "Sweetheart" or "Sweetie." When I'm feeling exhausted, lonely, or unheard, it's such a simple way to shift the energy of my emotions and it allows for my heart to release whatever tension it was holding onto. The care and attention I give myself helps me know my worth and to give myself the time and attention I deserve. Just as I care for others and call them terms of endearment, so do I love and care for myself.

Another way to be mindful of the words you use when thinking or speaking about yourself is to choose to see yourself in a positive light. Notice when you have conversations with others if you speak kindly about yourself. If you tend to be critical or tell stories about when you messed up, replace them with conversations that are more about facts than about judgements. Little by little, you may notice how you were going to begin a conversation and then decide to share a more energizing story that may contradict what you thought you were going to say. You may even want to call yourself sweetheart.

# June 29

## Heal
### By Kim Richardson

*T*here are many things that happen to us in this human experience. We all experience pain in many ways and on many levels. It is important to walk a healing journey no matter how big or small and there is never a timeline as to when the healing is complete.

I think it is necessary to sit in and feel all the emotions. Often, we feel like we *must* go on and act like everything is okay all the time. This is where we put this mask on and become the best actress/actors just to get through the day. If we continue to do this, soon we have so many masks that it becomes difficult to see and honor who *we* are and what *we* need. Things will show up in a negative way throughout your life as long as you hold onto it.

It may feel painful to walk the healing journey, however the ramifications of not walking it now can be so much more if we continue to hold onto it.

Is there something you are holding onto my friend?

Need help in finding ways to walk the journey? I have found the most supportive and productive way to heal from something is to not go it alone.

1. Reach out to those you trust.

2. Find a community of like-minded, supportive people.

3. When you are ready share your story as you never know who it might help.

4. Find resources to help you; books, workshops, events, retreats, support groups, etc.

# June 30

## Mermaid Mindset
## By Tonia Browne

*Today I see beauty in the mundane.*

If you can see what you have and appreciate it, you are in a positive vibration. As a consequence, you attract more things to you through synchronistic events because you are aware of and open to possibilities. As a repercussion, your life flows and you feel good.

How we see life matters. If, for example, we miss a bus and tell ourselves that things never work out for us, we continue to find evidence of this belief throughout our day, and it becomes a self-fulfilling prophecy. We influence our perception, and this becomes our reflection. When we understand this, instead of spiraling further into the mire with negative self-talk, we can take stock and raise our vibration.

If we train ourselves to see the good and flex the gratitude muscle consciously and consistently, then it becomes automatic over time. We see the positives in situations rather than the negatives. There are times when it feels there is little to be grateful for, but by shifting our energy and being grateful, we rediscover the beauty and wonder of everyday situations. When you choose to be purposefully grateful, you see more to be grateful for.

It was an act of self-love when I began to understand this concept and made a commitment to develop a mindset of being aware, open, and grateful. Through such an approach I began to appreciate the fleeting beauty in everyday experiences and my life flowed. I called this my mermaid mindset.

Explore for yourself. Start a gratitude practice. See your life experiences through eyes of appreciation and with a thankful heart. Give credit each day for the things in your life you may take for granted. Train your mind to look for the positives rather than dwell on the negatives. Start a journal or just allocate some time each day to focus on what you are grateful for. For example:

*I am grateful for the sunshine.*

*I am grateful that I can be willing to see things differently.*

*I am grateful for my friends and family.*

# July 1

## Self-Love Unlearning
### By Lisa A. Clayton

All my life, I have been a teacher of heart and leader of higher consciousness living. My mission is to guide humans to unravel their old stories, tap into the power of their hearts, and come home to the true essence of their souls, that of pure love and light.

My wake-up call of untruths and stories we carry within us happened when I became a fourth-grade elementary teacher. As I read each profile of new students coming to my classroom, I became nauseated. Many comments written were judgmental, stereotyped and biased. These children were eight or nine years old and their school records already portrayed stories they were to believe about themselves.

- Not smart enough
- Not good enough
- Not strong enough
- Not loved enough.

On the first day of fourth grade, I invited each child to write everything they were told or taught about their learning abilities, social selves, and physical appearance. Next, they rolled their papers into balls and threw them in the waste can. Their new stories of self-love, self-worth, and possibilities began that very first day.

What untrue story do you tell yourself? What "not enough" echoes bounce around in your head? How often are you thinking of the past and focusing on the should, could, or would haves?

Your old story creates guilt, blame, self-doubt, negative thoughts, and wasted energy. Think about all the ways your story was fed by past experiences or is still being fed by your choices and unhealthy relationships. Every belief about yourself and who you are is learned. And the truth is you are pure love and light with a soul that is perfect, whole, and complete.

The unlearning begins by becoming aware of the old story and the habits that support the story with beliefs about yourself that are untrue. Write them all down and toss them in a trash can, burn them, or bury them. End the untruths and old story!

Setting an unlearning intention statement daily is powerful. When you find yourself saying or feeling "I am not enough," make an intention statement such as "I am love. I am light. I am perfect, whole and complete. I am worthy and wise." This creates a new habit from heart to mind that becomes a healthy self-love habit!

Your soul knows your true essence story and by setting unlearning intentions, your new self-love story becomes your reality.

# July 2

## Energize your Energy Flow
## By Nancy Meikle-Mousseau

*W*hen I began my Reiki journey as a client and subsequently as a student, I had two inspiring Reiki masters who taught me Reiki in their own unique style. Reiki is a Japanese form of stress reduction and relaxation technique to allow the body's natural ability to heal itself.

I was in awe of such an interesting and yet intrinsic way of an alternative health and spiritual practice. It just seemed so natural for us to have this healing capability available to us through our hands.

I met a young lady, later referring to her as one of my earth angels, who asked me to teach her Reiki and I did not hesitate in saying yes. What I love about teaching Reiki is the opportunity to continuously learn and stay current with the concepts and blessings that Reiki provides.

During self-Reiki sessions, as I place my healing hands on my chakras to align them, I am humbled and grateful for this nurturing energy. This is indeed an act of self-love. When we bestow love upon ourselves, it enables us to give in return an act of love for others.

*The exercise*

We are all light and life energy flows through everything. This energy ball can be created by anyone. The only difference is that Reiki practitioners will include Reiki symbols in their ball.

To begin, sit or lie somewhere quietly where you will have no interruptions.

Place your hands in prayer position at your heart. Say any prayer that you resonate with or simply be grateful for this moment you have gifted yourself. Imagine a beautiful warm ball of energy between your hands, and fill that ball with love, kindness, joy, peace, light, happiness, whatever you wish. Feel the energy intensify in the ball that you have created. Now be mindful of your body, starting at your toes and feel where in your body, you need this ball of healing energy. When you decide, take a deep breath and place the ball that you have created, where you feel guided. Feel the warmth and know you have given your love to this area for healing. Remember to thank the universe for this gift of healing.

# July 3

## In Stillness, I Receive
### By Florence Acosta

*B*eing still means quieting our mind, being at peace in our heart and spirit, regardless of what's going on around us. There are times for action, movement, striving and working or being in the hustle. And there are times when we need to be still.

Being still can be hard. We are used to making things happen and being in control. We are used to action, not stillness. Being still requires us to surrender control. What does it mean to be still? Stillness can look like waiting, trusting, listening, patience, pausing, breathing, or resting. Being still allows us to receive.

I believe rest, sleep, and slowing down can help us all wake up to see the truth of ourselves. Stillness is a bridge to rest. Rest is a healing portal to our deepest selves. Rest is self-care. Rest is radical. When your worth has been falsely tied to how much you produce, resting becomes an act of resistance. Rest is a meticulous self-love practice that cannot be ignored. Rest requires vulnerability, receptivity, quiet and stillness. At times, rest reveals my discomfort, yet it's the only way to unlock my awareness and truly know myself.

If I desire my dreams to manifest and flourish, I seek to find balance in both life's inhales and exhales, ups and downs, wins and losses, the masculine and feminine, work, play and rest. If I want to flourish, I seek to remember to stay present to the flow of life and balance this with stillness and rest.

For this exercise, I invite you to sit quietly. Set an alarm for five minutes or more in a quiet place where you will not be interrupted. Connect with your breath. Connect to its rhythm. Now imagine the sound of gentle waves crashing against the shore of a turquoise ocean and focus on nothing but the peace and stillness you feel. If you find your mind wanders, do not be discouraged. Simply visualize yourself placing the thought or thoughts on the water to be washed away into the vast turquoise ocean.

At the end of your five minutes, I invite you to journal on this prompt: What do I receive in stillness?

# July 4

## Guided Meditation infused with Reiki
## By Stephanie Fontaine

*I* can vividly recall my first few experiences with meditation. It was uncomfortable and my mind wandered in a million directions. I was taking a mindful meditation course and we were about two weeks in when it happened; I had a flashback of a traumatic event as a child. I panicked.

This was not relaxing or creating peace at all, I thought. and I bailed on the rest of the classes. Fast forward about six months and I had decided to learn Reiki and I was at a Reiki share. It was close to summer solstice, so we gathered outside in a large circle to meditate. I did not have any flashbacks this time. However, I remember thinking at one point, *Is this ever going to end?* The more I wanted it to end, the harder it became to focus and stay calm. Inside my head I was screaming for it to finish.

I am happy to say I have a completely new appreciation and love for meditation now. I am able to stay present and at peace while meditating. One of the things that has helped me in my practice is to remember not to criticize or judge myself if and when my mind wanders. In those moments that I catch myself thinking of the past or of things I need to do, I simply remind myself to become aware of my breath again. Focusing on my breath brings me back into my body and into the present.

I have come to enjoy the practice of meditation so much that I almost always include it in my bedtime ritual. I light a white candle, say a prayer, and listen to a guided meditation while I give myself Reiki. This is also something that can be done first thing in the morning if that is a better time for you. There is no right or wrong time to practice self-care with meditation. Perhaps if you are new to meditating, it is best to start with a short meditation and over a period of time, increase the length of your practice. There are also many ways in which to practice meditation; there are walking meditations, silent meditations, and guided meditations. Find a way that works best for you and commit to doing it on a consistent basis as a part of your self-love journey.

# July 5

## Speaking Love over Your Body
## By Yumie Zein

*F*or many years, I was in battle with my body. Growing up as a woman in a conservative society meant that anything and everything feminine was not talked about. Instead, it was hidden and perceived as a burden. This beautiful vessel that I had chosen to carry me through this life experience was a vessel filled with much self-judgement, self-hatred and a whole lot of shame and guilt. Being a woman felt like the biggest burden to me. I needed to be as inconspicuous as possible, the more invisible the better.

"Cover your body and shut your mouth" were the highlights of blossoming into womanhood. I found my own way of hiding through comfort eating and putting on layers and layers of weight and then stacking the layers of required fabric on top. I barely spoke. For many years, I genuinely believed that I had nothing important to say; that whatever I said or did is inconsequential in this life; that I had no role to play in the unfolding of my own life, so it was pointless to even try.

Life felt so heavy. It was a struggle to breathe, literally. At some point during my early adulthood, I was put on a ventilator to breathe for me, and you know what? That ventilator malfunctioned in the middle of the night and I had five minutes of zero breath and a near death experience. Even the machine was not able to breathe for me.

That journey brought me to where I am today, a place where speaking love over my body is my favorite ritual. I adore this vessel. All its scars and marks are each such beautiful witnesses to the unfolding of my journey. I frequently sit alone, sometimes naked, sometimes not, sometimes in front of a mirror, sometimes not, whatever the way my body feels like receiving love in that moment. I very slowly connect to my whole body from the top of my head to the tips of my toes and as I slowly travel across each beautiful part, I say out loud to it "I love you." Sometimes I even expand that into a whole sentence like "I love you, my beautiful hair, for being so wild and free." Or I'll say, "I love you, my gorgeous eyes, for being so clear and sparkly."

# July 6

## Scheduling Time For Self-Love
## By Vonnie L. Hawkins, LCSW

*B*usy people with busy lives often organize their tasks by using checklists. Thanks to neurobiology, we know that performing tasks and checking them off a list causes our brain to release dopamine, a neurotransmitter that sends messages between brain cells and plays a part in how we experience pleasure.

We certainly receive pleasure from doing for others. Do you consider acts of self-love just as important in your work? Do you schedule time for acts of self-love? If not, what gets in the way?

I have often heard that our capacity for self-love sets the boundaries for our capacity to love others, but I never understood this until I was an adult. The better we are at loving ourselves, the better we can love others. However, this knowledge is often considered alongside a puritan value that taking care of ourselves is selfish or self-indulgent or we should always come last.

Do you have this belief as well? Many of us do, and we are left with no way to resolve the cognitive dissonance of these two contradicting beliefs. Therefore, to be worthy, some of us always put ourselves last. We sacrifice our bodies, our mental health, our pursuit of hobbies or joy, in constant giving and sacrificing for others until our cup is empty. But as we all know, we cannot give from an empty cup. How loving can we be when we are drained, resentful and unfulfilled? This is why we *must* prioritize investing in our own well-being through acts of self-love. We do not need to justify taking care of ourselves and indulging in self-love because it literally is a gift that increases our capacity to love others!

In your journal, write, "I am worthy and I deserve to feel good!"

List five activities you can do to just feel good that benefit no one else, and schedule them on your calendar. When you do them, spend the time to revel and be present!

Acknowledge that when you feel good, you are the very best version of yourself and your love-light flows to all around you! You are setting an example for your loved ones by practicing loving yourself, feeling worthy of love from yourself and from others, and receiving love from yourself.

# July 7

## Self-Talk and Self-Love Hold Hands
## By Margaret-Maggie Honnold

Self-love and positive self-talk hold hands. They go together, but you need to work on making them do more than just date. What would your priority be if nothing else interfered? Today let us ponder that idea. Learning self-love is not a people project. It is your conversation with yourself. So today, have a talk with yourself while you permit yourself to embrace your inner hermit. This conversation is only yours.

Negative self-talk can be your worst enemy. We often use it to build concerns and fears to such a peak in our minds that common sense cannot find room. This is called catastrophic thinking. Lying in bed at night, one negative thought leads to another and another and soon one little jog in the road has become an earthquake. We look at things going on and build them up until, horrors, we believe our own negative propaganda. Our self-talk has defeated our common sense and trampled on self-love.

Here is a painful childhood example. My mother was a musician and often her students performed for the public. One family were of special importance to her. Their exceptionally talented kids were in every recital and band and I always wanted to be included.

Finally, I asked Mom one day, "Can I do something too in the show?"

She looked at me and said, "What can you do?"

I was six. I could have done whatever she would have helped me learn, just like her students. Instead, I came away with a complex of never being good enough to be a part of anything musical. Yes, I played the piano, sort of, and the flute, and sang in the choir, but

I never felt talented enough. I had a self-conversation about music my entire life that did not benefit my ability to love myself.

What is the self-talk topic you cannot stop that makes it hard to love yourself? Take time as the day begins and ask yourself, "Why do I have this particular conversation?"

Then listen for the answer. By identifying your negative self-talk, you can then start up a conversation telling yourself what is true and take your inner healing to another level. You are loved. You are your own best counselor and negative self-talk can be put on the never date again list.

# *July 8*

## Celebrate Yourself
## By Danielle Fierro

Often, we think about the times that we made mistakes or get upset that we are not further along than we hoped. We forget to celebrate *all* the wonderful things we have accomplished. Focusing on the stuff we don't have or haven't done will not help to achieve our goals.

Celebrating ourselves helps to build the momentum and excitement for what is to come.

One way to do that is through our goals. We create goals all the time, especially at the beginning of each year. When we do that, we can create milestones within each goal, which helps to track our progress. When we hit those milestones, we shouldn't just go onto the next step. Celebrate the accomplishment. Take a moment to look at what has been done and give that deserved acknowledgement.

Celebrating yourself doesn't have to be formal. I recommend you to review your successes on a daily basis. Make it part of your evening ritual. This is a wonderful way to end your day on a positive note. It keeps your perspective in check and reminds you to focus on the good. Also, by doing a review of your day, you can better determine what works and what doesn't work. When you do this, you want to find at least three successes/positive things for each day. They can be big or small accomplishments. They can even be for getting out of bed because, some days, that *is* an accomplishment. If you are brave, tell others what you are celebrating yourself for. It's nice to have support from your friends and family.

Celebrating yourself is not bragging, being full of yourself, or arrogant. We all should celebrate our successes more often. So, give yourself a pat on the back, a spa day, or any other treat for your successes because you deserve it.

# *July 9*

## Be Your Beautiful Self
## By JoAnne Eisen

*Y*ou were born into this world, unsure, unknowing, and ready to take on the challenges it will bring. You also brought with you the blueprints you needed to maneuver through the obstacles ahead of you. Sounds easy, right? Most of us agreed to forget all we knew at birth or not far into life. I often chuckle to myself, "What was I thinking?"

You are here, so now what is next? Start by remembering you are connected to your Soul at all times. You may have forgotten for a period of this life. Some choose to forget who they are all of their human experience. That can make you feel very alone and separated. The truth is, you are always loved unconditionally and worthy in all times and space. You were born with all the wisdom and capabilities of living your life in calm and ease. You are pure love. You are already successful above all measure. The most critical piece to remember is you are here to express your soul's desire, To fully and freely express your life's lessons unencumbered.

Your spirit lives through you, allowing your desire to evolve and practice all aspects of this life, to live and freely express itself. Never make excuses about who you are! Stop avoiding your abilities because of fear. Never care about what others think of you.

I know this sounds easy, but it can be challenging. I hear you and have that same voice talking in my head. Taking on this human form can be complicated and scary at times. Claiming your power can be tricky, but it is your birthright. Way too often, we are afraid to claim it.

Release old stories and beliefs that are ancient records playing from your past. Live in the moment and allow your uniqueness living deep within you to come alive. It is worth it and beautiful. Don't live your life full of fear. It keeps you going in the wrong direction. Live your life from that sacred heart space deep within your heart. Let that heart lead you along your path. It will show you wondrous and beautiful things. It will show you who you genuinely are. You are beautiful, perfect, and unique. Share that with the world; we need more of that. Be on your own unique life mission. You are here to LIVE during this life. Be you!

# July 10

## Clear Out the Clutter
## By Ashlie Bradley

The time has come to create space for fresh, new, revitalizing energy. To make room for this shift a purge is vital! I am talkin' go through *everything*! Below I have listed a few areas where you can begin!

Electronics: Go through the laptop! The phone! The camera! The emails! Delete the numbers you have not used in over a decade. Delete the old text threads that literally have nothing to do with your present-day reality. Delete the pictures that are not serving your highest good keeping them around. Just do it!

Closet area: Okay, you are still holding on to that outfit you *swear* you will end up wearing again. But have you? I think it might be time to say bye-bye! Go through your dressers, your shelves, your hangers, your chests, your shoe bin, etc.! You get the gist. The energy is stiff and needs to move.

Car: We spend a lot of time in our car, you guys. We are going to want that energy to be top notch. Hit up the glovebox, center counsel, and under the seats. Go through the trunk. I am willing to bet there are multiple items that belong in your fresh, new, purged, tidy garage. Just dive in! I promise it will be rewarding.

It is really all about keeping the energy flowing. Releasing old, welcoming new. Stagnant energy tends to bring down our frequency, which generates a whole domino effect. So do yourself a favor and get your purge on! You got this!

# July 11

## Angels on the Earth
## By Jannirose Fenimore

When Charlie was a small boy, he informed me that he is *"an angel on the earth."* He was quick to say that I am, too.

*"And all of us together in this great big human family!"* he added with an impish grin.

Knowing my son as I do, I understood his meaning. He wanted me to know that we are so much more than we might believe.

*"You are Godness!"* he whispered.

Living with one who has never forgotten his origins reminds me of what is true about my own life. It helps me to recognize my preciousness and potential every single day. Charlie holds a crystal-clear mirror in his divine design that shows me who I really am, and over the years, my ability to receive that reflection has become more finely tuned.

It is a sweet exercise in awareness to imagine being graced by an angel in physical form and then to consider that we are all brilliant creations of light crafted by the same loving hand.

If an angel makes its presence known to us in the here and now, how might we respond?

I expect we will embrace the glorious beauty of our heavenly visitor as its rarified energies of peace and harmony wash over us on every level. I am certain we will experience its love and a deep reverence for the treasures this celestial traveler brings us.

I encourage you to consider my son's gentle invitation to reclaim who you are in the deepest, most authentic way. Bless yourself with a few quiet moments throughout your day to settle into the depths of you—past the heavy layers of thought and worry that can take away your peace.

There, you will discover a powerful, pulsing presence in the core of your being. In Charlie's words, *"This is your Godness!"*

As you breathe in the vibrant energy of your essence, you will be refreshed and renewed. Let this pure life force lift you into remembrance that you, too, are *"an angel on the earth."*

Give yourself the gift each day of dipping into this bottomless well of living light and drinking from it deeply. Allow it to nourish and energize you on every level.

This is how we heal the world—as one by one, we awaken. *"All of us together in this great big human family!"*

# July 12

## Let Go of the Past
## By Kim Richardson

The past can weigh us down in many ways consciously and subconsciously. There may be people or situations that have caused so much pain, resulting in harboring anger. We may hold onto the idea that we are owed an apology and we stubbornly sit and wait for it.

If we choose to hold on to or live in the past, constantly bringing it up or thinking about it, it can rob us of our happiness today. There comes a time where you must become everything you need in this world to ensure you feel protected, loved, and safe. Stop waiting for an apology as typically the people that have it in them to hurt us in such ways are just not capable of an apology.

Work on forgiving and letting go, as you do not want to live their anymore. By doing so, you release the power it has over you and take your control back.

I had the hardest time forgiving some unforgivable people/acts that happened to me in my past.. I now give thanks to those experiences for all the lessons it taught me which helped shaped the person I am today. I send love and compassion for those that have hurt me as I have learned that *hurt people hurt people.*

You do not have to forget, you can set the appropriate boundary to ensure you feel safe, but you should let go of those painful pieces of the past ensure it/they no longer hold any power of you.

When you can let go, you make room for all the new wonderful and amazing things waiting for you *now* and in the future.

Is it time to make a list of things to release and start releasing the control they have over you?

# July 13

## Unconditional Truth
## By Courtney Parreira

*Y*ou are not who they said you were.
You are not weird nor are you odd.
You are not too negative.
You are not the last to be chosen.
You are not the only one they can rely on.
You are not embarrassing.
You are not disgusting.
You are not unconventionally pretty.
You are not the reason.
You are not falling apart.
You are not worthless.
You are not weak.
You are not a burden.
You are not too round or too pudgy.
You are not too small where it counts.
You are not alone.
Yes, these experiences have colored your world, but they do not define you; this is not who you are.
You are a brilliant light,
Bright, strong, and true.
They want you to believe in all of their lies, but you know the truth.
It speaks to you in silence of the morning.
It calls to you in nature's stillness.
Yes, you're reminded of the beauty and light that you hold, your truth, your power.
The graceful harmony of love, radiance, and strength:

This is who you are.

Celebrate and honor your amazing self today. Even five minutes of honoring your strength, radiant light, and love does wonders for your soul.

# July 14

## Note to Self: I Am Enough
## By Sheryl Goodwin Magiera

When you think of the phrase, "I am enough," what does that bring up for you? Does it make you feel inspired, uplifted, and joyful? Or does it bring up feelings of doubt, fear, and unworthiness? If the phrase makes you feel happy and worthy, you are 100 percent right. However, if it makes you sad and feel unworthy, then there's work to be done.

In today's reading, I would like you to reflect on two ideas.

- You are imperfectly perfect.
- You are unique.

You are imperfectly perfect. No one else is quite like you! We owe it to ourselves to be true and authentic. It's hard to show our imperfections and vulnerabilities, but they are what connects us as humans. We root for people that show us raw and real life because we relate to them. We all feel vulnerable at times and don't want to show that part of us to anyone because we may think we seem weak, or uninformed and less than, but when we do show our authentic self, a shift happens, and we grow. No one is perfect!

I invite you to jot down in a journal or think about ways in which you are imperfect that give you character and make you … YOU. For example, I can sound very dramatic during situations, and to me I'm just being passionate, but others may see drama. It's things like that which make me … ME. What are some of your beautiful imperfections?

You are unique. I like to refer to it as your only-ness. No one else is like you. We all have something unique to share with the world. They are your super-powers; what makes you … YOU!

Take time to journal your only-ness, then create affirmations. Affirmations are incredibly powerful, both positively and negatively. For the next thirty days, I invite you to an "I am enough" challenge. This is a daily, month-long commitment to owning, recognizing, believing, and celebrating your beautiful "I am" super-powers. Once or more per day, silently or out loud, repeat your "I am" statements of truth. Believe and visualize your statements.

I am examples:

- I am strong.
- I am courageous.
- I am beautiful.
- I am worthy.
- I am caring.
- I am kind.
- I am brave.
- I am unique.
- I am bold.

# July 15

## Passion!
## By Nancy Toffanin

*L*iving a life filled with passion is key to self-love. Passion encompasses loving something so deeply that it ignites our internal fires. Over the years, I have heard people say that they do not know how to find something they are passionate about. Helping people find their passion is rewarding.

If we choose one thing we love and do it every day, it opens the energy for new things we love to show up. Passion helps us to create, connect, and work towards mastery of self-improvement. Passions do not always have to be physical things; they can be about spirituality, becoming the best version of "you," and helping to empower people. Creating a routine every day of self-care, learning, and self-love. These are rare building blocks that help us create a healthy lifestyle.

Helping people find what they are passionate about is meaningful work. It helps energize us, and it gives us willpower to achieve anything we want.

Some of things I am passionate about are teaching, reading cards, meditations, writing, watching sunrises and sunsets, helping empower people, teaching about moon cycles, and being healthy. Passion comes in different forms. One way to create this is from doing something we love. When we lead with our heart, and the feel the energy of the connection, we can find true passion in another person. Passion can also be for learning new things, art, music, yoga, taking a course, health, and fitness.

Another thing I would encourage people to do is to make a list of things they love, then number them. Look at two choices at a time and then pick the one they love the most. Doing this helps narrow down the things we love and helps us see what we are really passionate about. It ignites our soul when do something we feel passionate about, and it creates alchemy, a fuel inside of us to fill us up on a cellular level. The last few years, I decided to say yes to trying new things, exploring new places, and being open to new ideas. If we want to choose a life filled with passion, these concepts will grow and expand.

Self-reflection questions:

What are you passionate about?

Do you do one activity a day that you love?

Are you creative?

What does passion mean to you?

What lights you up?

What do you really want?

# July 16

## HELP
### By Marilyn Miller

The Beatles wrote a hit with their popular song "Help!" If you've ever called nine-one-one, or heard an actor on T.V. do that, you might also hear "Help is on the way!" The truth is help is always available, but I have often failed to take advantage of it. I used to think I was smart enough to handle challenges on my own. But I have changed my mind. Business executives hire coaches, sports stars use trainers, and dancers, actors, and singers take Master Classes from Master Teachers. There are always experts who can help.

This revelation came to me one day at a summer camp. A friend and I had to set up a venue with many small but super heavy tables for an after-hours Coffee House.

I told her, "Go see if you can find some guys to help us, or we'll never get set up on time." A few minutes later, she arrived with four big men, football player types. They set up the room in minutes.

I asked, "How did you find all those strong guys so fast?"

She said, "I just stood outside next to the flag pool and yelled, 'Help, Help!'"

Now I realize asking for help is a sign of strength not weakness, and it helps me realize how truly loved I am. I believe I am always provided for when I need it.

# July 17

## Declutter Your Head
### By Ewa Blaszczak

We live in times of turbulence and rapid transformation. We call it the V.U.C.A. world, which stands for: volatility, uncertainty, complexity, and ambiguity.

How to stay sane in such an environment? How to cultivate love and not fear? We need clarity and sharp minds to help us navigate through the rough sea of constant changes and detours.

Does your mind often feel like a huge party or a concert? A lot is going on, it is extremely noisy, someone is shouting, someone is pushing you, there is a total mess. Perhaps your mind is cluttered with destructive thoughts: "You cannot do it." "Who are you to even try? "It does not make any sense." "You do not deserve it." "You are not enough." "You should quit." With such thoughts in your head, there is no hope for clarity or constructive actions. It is a perfect environment for fear to thrive.

If you want to manage your life better, gain resilience, and act from the place of love I encourage you to declutter your head from time to time.

Take a piece of paper and a pen. Download all your thoughts on the paper. Without editing. Be honest with yourself. Once you are done, look at your thoughts. Ask yourself the following questions:

- Which thoughts are giving me energy and supporting me?
- Which thoughts are draining me from energy?
- Which of the thoughts are based on facts?
- Which of the thoughts are just an illusion or limited believes which are not true?

The next step is mindfulness. Set the piece of paper aside, sit comfortably, and breathe deeply for a moment. Reconnect to your body. Feel the ground under your feet.

Now, the last step. Take another piece of paper and download the thoughts you think at this very moment. Compare your list with the previous list you have made in the first step. What differences do you notice?

This simple exercise helps us to reset our mind. This is why most of you will notice much more clarity in mind and less thoughts to download in the last step of the exercise. Now, with such a clear, decluttered mind, it is going to be a lot easier for you to act from love and not fear!

# *July 18*

## Notes to Self
## By Amy I. King

*L*etters are beautiful tools for self-expression. We often write letters in order to get all of our feelings out there and heard. But have you ever thought about writing a letter to yourself?

At the suggestion of a counselor, I started writing notes to myself about a decade ago. I was going through a particularly challenging time and needed desperately to reconnect with myself and all of my good qualities. The letters started small, with maybe two or three sentences. They started pretty simple with things like "You are a loving person. I like your hair, and you are smart."

As I connected with myself more and more, I became more involved with affirmations such as "You are connected to all things, and all things are connected to you."

You can write it any way you like. I suggest starting your letter with "Dear (your name)." Then talk to yourself about the things you like about yourself. Write them down in that letter.

I write myself a note any time that I feel a bit down. The letter is a mood booster that helps me to see my value as a human being. We live in a world full of great expectations, and we tend to get overwhelmed in those expectations, thus losing ourselves. These letters are an opportunity for you to find your way back to your most authentic self. May your letters bless you. I'm going to leave you with an example of a letter I wrote.

Dear Amy,

You are an incredible friend. You are there for people when they need you. You take the time to listen and give feedback. You are generous with your time and money. You are patient and loving. When someone is in need, you are there to fill that need.

It's wonderful to be there for others, but don't forget to be there for you. Love is something that you are great at giving. Please make sure that you are also on the receiving end.

Yes, you are mastering self-love, but you also must learn to accept the love of others. Yes, this one is a tough one for you. Growing up in a household where one of your parents made you earn love confused you. That's not it! Love is something that you deserve, it is unconditional.

All My Love, Amy

# July 19

## The Fallacy of Innate Confidence
## By Dominique Trier

*H*aving confidence and esteem for oneself can amplify our lives in countless ways. When I was young, I believed some people were gifted with more confidence than others, and I struggled with overanalyzing confidence because I was raised to prioritize humility. Sometimes I believed that confidence seemed egotistical, and I would mistake confidence with arrogance. It seems silly now that I ever thought being confident and showing humility were incompatible traits to illustrate at the same time.

As I grew older, I realized the correlation between becoming skilled at a task, more knowledgeable over a subject, and my confidence in myself. Looking towards others and learning from them was a sure way for me to not only avoid being perceived as arrogant, but to master new skills, such as six-figure sales generation. The only way I accomplished high-level sales generation was by showing my colleagues I wanted to learn from them and that I did not know everything. I showed humility in wanting to learn and I showed confidence in knowing if I listened, I could be great like them, too.

As *Psychology Today* says, "Confidence is not an innate, fixed characteristic. It's an ability that can be acquired and improved over time." So, my challenge for you is to ask yourself the following:

- What am I able to grow knowledge of or increase my skills at?
- How much time am I willing to set aside for this confidence boosting activity?

- What are my long-term goals with this trait?
- What are my reasons for becoming better at this trait? (Remembering the whys will hold you more accountable when you feel less motivated.)

As any new skill goes, it takes time and dedication, and the confidence will subsequently come. A great book that expands on the devotion of time and its correlation to success is Malcolm Gladwell's *Outliers: The Story of Success*. The time we dedicate to building ourselves up and creating confidence will never be a waste.

# July 20

## Go Love Yourself
### By Judith Manganiello

After I fell in love with the best part of myself, I was gifted a Spiritual bookstore for twenty-four years. I was guided which books to bring into the store. The thing I found the strangest was prosperity and relationships were the best-selling books. Everyone wanted help mainly on those two subjects; they were always the first books to sell. Dreams, angels, astrology, numerology, and healing the body were also great sellers. However, the self-love books were still sitting there on the bookshelves.

The strange thing about this whole message is that when I was able to meet and fall in love with the best part of myself-all the things that everyone was searching for in books started to be gifted to me naturally. My relationship with my husband changed for the better. My relationship with everyone changed dramatically for the better. Even with my entire family, the changes were incredible. I now have the best relationship with my husband and family that anyone would be blessed and grateful to have all because of learning to love myself. I am happy to say I started immediately to even have money miracles as I cleared all the things that had been holding me back. Here is a prayer that I have used daily within myself and my clients. Sit in front of the mirror, looking at your own eyes …

### Getting in Touch with Your Spirit or God Self

Say this one time and choose whether you want to say Spirit or God, "Spirit or God, I know You are in there and I am choosing today, here and now this very moment to connect over to YOU once and for all. I am going to continue to say this until we connect."

Say this daily twice a day by pointing at your eyes and say, "I know You are in there. I Love my Spirit self or God self."

If you forget a day saying, "I know you are in there. I love my Spirit self or God self, "then start at the beginning of the prayer. You will do this every day until you meet Your own Inner Light.

# July 21

## Hand on the Heart
## By Kim Richardson

*H*ave you ever felt anxiety, unsure of yourself, a situation, or just plain not sure what to do? My go to secret weapon when I start to feel that way is simple; I put my hand on my heart and go within while quieting my mind asking God/Spirit what is it that I need to know or feel for this situation.

The quieter you get, you will see that you will receive the answers to your questions. They can come clearly as thoughts that just pop into your head or possibly a bit vaguer as you start to notice signs throughout the day, just be sure to keep your eyes and heart open.

I place my hand on my heart in times I am looking for clearer answers and as part of my daily morning mediation/prayer practice. In the mornings, I ask, every day, *how may I serve today?* I believe we are spiritual beings living a human experience and we can tap into our spirit and our higher power, for me that is God. The more I raise my vibration by healing the past, letting go of the anger, and living as joyous as I can, the more I feel in tune to and receive messages from God.

Get to quiet space when you can, place your hand on your heart, take a few deep breaths and just listen. The more you practice the more obvious the messages become.

# July 22

## Journal for Meaning
## By Tanya Thompson

Expressing gratitude in writing is one of the single most effective tools to reset a bad day or year. It is nearly impossible to hold gratitude in your heart and a negative emotion at the same time.

Several years ago, a dear friend introduced me to the intensive journal method developed by Dr. Ira Progoff. Introduced to the public in 1966, this life-changing experience was developed to give an individual personal direction and continuity in life. Workshops are held in person all over the country and online. This method is much more than journal writing, it is a way of life to actively engage in your past and present, with an eye on your future.

One of the most impactful exercises is from the life context portion of the program. You begin my making a list of every person you can recall ever having a positive impact on your life, without regard to how small or large the impact. You simply start from your childhood and make an exhaustive list of every name or person that you can recall up to the present day. If you cannot recall the name, that is okay, simply put the context you remember (e.g., the lady at the café). You will keep this list and continue to add to it for the rest of your life.

Once you have started your list, you begin to have a dialogue with each person in writing and tell them all the ways in which they had a positive impact on your life. One by one, set aside an hour, and write to them as if you were having a dialogue with them. Tell them exactly the behavior that impacted you in a positive manner, how it made you feel, and how you feel about it now. This is not a letter you will ever send them. If you want to write them a letter later, you can certainly do that, but this journal method of writing a dialogue to that person is only for you and your life context.

You complete this exercise for every name on your list and for every name added thereafter.

I'm not one to cry often or easily, but this single exercise makes me shed tears of gratitude. You realize how fortunate you are and the amazing people that have come into your life and provided you enrichment.

# July 23

## The List
## By Tanya Thompson

We all have a running list of things we need to do. I have always thought my to-do list was pretty current, until I met Tonja Weimer. Tonja is a life coach that worked with me after my marriage ended.

After a few sessions, she challenged me to create a list of things that were in my head that needed to get done. I distinctly remember her trying to get me to list 100 items, or as many as I could. Things like the dentist visit I had cancelled and failed to reschedule, the oil change that was neglected, the junk drawer that needed to be organized … and the list went on. My list included big items like the need to update my will and gather my receipts for tax season, and small items like needing to purchase a new mop.

Not one to back down from a challenge, I dug deep to list every little thing I could think of without having any idea what she would have me do with it. I think I was secretly hoping she would have me throw it away and tell me how unimportant these things were. I was wrong.

After she perused my list, she had me pick two days a couple of weeks out to set aside for her.

"Two whole days?" I asked.

Little did I know that over those two days she would drag me through a time boxed exercise of completing everything on the list. Everything. Items either fell into 'get this done now, you have thirty minutes' or 'schedule these three things' to get done in the future.

This exercise is equally the most awful thing and the absolute best thing I have ever done for myself. This may sound trivial, but these nagging little tasks that linger need to get out of the way for the transformative changes that come next. When we clear the way of this type of mind clutter, then we can spend time on the good stuff without any of this day-to-day stuff getting in the way. Make your list, clear your path, and look forward to the open space that is left to create the life you love.

# July 24

## Self-Love Reflection
## By Talia Renzo

When we think of self-love, what do we think of? For me, self-love looks like a hot bubble bath, a face mask, fresh painted nails, and drinking a glass of wine. But that's not always realistic.

Self-love is defined as "regard for one's own well-being and happiness."

I want you to take a deep breath and envision what you think self-love looks like. Does it have a face? Does it have a setting? Does it have a smell? Does it have a taste? Does it have a description, or a sensation?

When you thought about self-love, how did it make you feel? In other words how do you feel now?

Where do you think the shift was when you thought about self-love? I can only imagine it brought you a sense of peace, maybe even gratitude. So, here is my next question. Why don't you feel that way all the time? What is holding you back from feeling that sensation of peace and tranquility?

Your answer might be about work, schedule conflicts, lack of time, or feeling unworthy. You must remember that there are twenty-four hours in a day. There are seven days in a week. At some point within that time frame, you need to make yourself a priority.

Write down seven acts of self-love that you can do over the course of this next week or even month as long as you remember to check in with yourself and complete your goals! After each one I encourage you to journal how it made you feel in that moment and for the remainder of that particular day.

# July 25

## Life Is Better When Laughing
## By Ellen Elizabeth Jones

*H*ave you ever noticed how present children are when they are playing? Have you noticed how involved they are in what they are doing? They run, skip, jump into action. They are carefree of any future problems. Children do not ask permission to be the way adults do. Try to integrate your inner child and outer adult. What if you remember the childlike feelings of wide-eyed excitement, organic appreciation, breaking free, and being full of awe, wonder, curiosity, and enchantment at this miraculous universe?

What can we learn from children?

**Laughter.** The child in you, like all children, loves to laugh, to be around people that who can laugh at themselves and life. Children instinctively know that the more laughter we have in our lives, the better. Children gravitate to those that make them laugh, who can go along with their jokes.

**Imagination**. Children love to dream, to make up stories, and create. You would too if you allowed yourself. Remember how you loved to draw, make up songs, hear stories, make up your own games, and spend endless time in make believe. A rich and vivid imagination is not only great fun, it is also one of the healthiest aspects of your life as a whole.

**Spontaneity**. Children are willing to try anything on a moment's notice. The child inside you desire to be impulsive and adventurous without having to plan every detail. Being spontaneous is the key to childlike behavior. The ability to pivot and explore opportunities as they arise is a gift.

**Acceptance**. When a child comes into this world, it has no thought that the world can or should be any different from what it is. There is innocence and trust that they will have everything they need provided for them. The child inside of you knows how to take things as they come, how to deal most effectively and happily with everything that shows up in their life.

When you have inner peace, you are empowered to embrace anything. Give yourself more childlike peace today by giving yourself permission to be a spontaneous, present, fun-loving child again.

What is one activity that you can do today to create more curiosity, wonder, and play? I find blowing bubbles a wonderful way to experience and express joy! May you find many ways to experience laughter, love, and play, today!

# July 26

## Self-Confidence
## By Sarah Berkett

What exactly is self-confidence? Is it an attitude? Is it a belief? Or a state of being? Self-confidence can be an attitude about your skills and abilities. It means you accept and trust yourself and have a sense of control in your life. You know your own strengths and weakness well and have a positive view of yourself. Self-confidence is also understanding your own judgements and abilities and that you value yourself and feel worthy. Do not worry about what others seem to believe about you. Try the following exercises to boost your self-confidence.

Talking with others is important, so maintain eye contact when you are speaking. Try not to fidget or look away while the conversation continues; this can make you appear distracted or nervous.

Keep track in your journal for at least sixty days, then go back and you will be surprised how much more confident you have become.

# July 27

## Creativity
## By Crystal Cockerham

*A*re you surprised to see creativity as a topic in a self-love book? Creativity helps us to connect with our intuition, our higher self, spirit guides, guardian angels and the divine. Intuition is a gift that we are all born with. It acts as an internal compass to keep us on our true path. Intuition is knowing a thing (or many things) without knowing *how* you know them, and it is felt within your very being.

Life happens. Pain happens. Dependency on others happens. And these are all causes of feeling disconnected from our intuition, denying that it is there or even real at all.

Creativity is the way back to your intuitive senses. Whether you are coloring, baking, cooking, crafting, painting, sketching, decorating, etc., you are engaging with all of your energy centers through your divine connection. This always happens in the *now*, in the *present moment.*

You see, when you are always caught up in your to-do's, have-to's and must-do's, you are not living in the *now.* You become numb to the nudges from spirit, from your higher self, spirit guides, guardian angels and divine source and from your intuition. This stunts your spiritual growth and as a result, keeps you from loving yourself without judgment.

You were born to be loved. You were born to love yourself and to love others. Finding your way back into love with yourself is finding your creative flow and reconnecting with your intuition. You will learn to use your inner compass to lead the way.

Creativity is the means to help you with this. Allow it to become part of your daily practice. There are endless possibilities to find creative flow and play with this innate life force energy. Take a class if you feel you need to, though it isn't a necessity.

Allow yourself to define creativity in a new way. Start a journal with all the projects or recipes you would like to try. And then work your way through it to find what brings you joy. It is there where the flow is. It is there your intuition awaits.

# July 28

## A Check in with the Elements of Nature
### By Melanie Morrison

*D*o you seek more balance, peace, and support in your life? Do you feel as though each day goes by and you go through the movements, but it just feels like everything is spinning? Disconnected from your purpose, unhinged from meaning and drive?

We have these feelings at various points in our life. These times are perfect for doing a check in with the elements of nature.

Along with getting outside more, we can also tap into the amazing resource of balance lent to us though the wisdom of nature. I am sure you have seen the incredible abundance that our planet provides when all of its elements are balanced. When Earth has a perfect balance of fire or sun, air, water, and the earth, everything is sure to flourish. We are the same. This daily check in with the elements can help bring you back into balance. A question to ask yourself is "how am I tending the garden of my soul?"

Now you can take a moment to review some aspects of the elements in your life.

- Fire: passion, anger, energy, creativity, sensuality, dance, romance, movement, and motivation.

- Air: thoughts, loving self-talk, letting go, breath, words, expression, rising above, speaking your truth, and song.

- Water: cleansing, going with the flow, intuition, emotions, and holding space

- Earth: physical body, self-love, physical surroundings, support systems, organization, and foundations.

- Spirit: intention, connection, silence, unconditional love, reverence, unity, sacredness, and integrity.

Once you have reviewed the elements, find a comfortable spot in nature to journal what came up for you and create daily, weekly, monthly, and yearly activities and goals that will help you achieve more balance within the elements. Just like Earth, when nature's elements are balanced, you are abundant!

# July 29

## Daily Practice
## By Giuliana Melo

*M*ake loving yourself a ritual! Put yourself first.

1. Express gratitude and connect to the divine. Say thank you, thank you, thank you.

2. Call in your guardian angels to help support your energy.

3. Set intentions for the day. Energy flows where your attention goes.

4. Breathe in deeply and exhale slowly at least five times and then resume normal breathing. Connect to your breath. That is the breath of life.

5. Ground yourself to Mother Earth. Place feet flat on the floor. Notice your connection to the earth. You can run, jump, hug a tree, smell flowers, or go bare foot in the grass.

6. Smile, smile, smile. Smiles are understood in every language.

7. Forgive yourself for the past. Forgive others too.

8. Worry about nothing. It is said that worrying is like praying for what you do not want.

9. Ask God "How may I be of service?" and be a kind human.

10. Ask God to guide your steps with love, light, joy, peace, and health.

11. Meditate to tune into your intuition which is the divine within you.

12. Pray in a way that feels good to you.

13. Move your body every day.

Having a daily practice is showing the universe that you are taking care of your divinity and the special being that you are. Make sure to create a practice that you love to do.

# July 30

## Back to Basics
## By Symone Desirae

*H*ave you ever felt like your emotions were out of whack? You feel uncomfortable, irritated in your own skin, and not able to stand hearing the people around you breathe, let alone yourself? Sound familiar?

I was there, feeling out of sorts and looking for a sign from the divine universe to help me. I would have emotional melt downs out of nowhere, and then feel back to normal five minutes later. I was eating junk food, processed foods and anything that gave me a quick pick me up, you know 'comfort' food. I was desperate, looking for signs on how to help myself at the time, unaware of how my eating habits had an effect on my body.

I had been given a book by a friend about how the unhealthy eating I was doing had impacted human hormones. This was the sign I was looking for!

I thought "Wow, the answer was there all this time."

From that point on every time I ate something unhealthy, I would ask myself "Does this make me feel good now or in the long term? Does my body benefit from this?"

Slowly, through eating more nutrient dense foods and eliminating the processed foods, I felt my emotions and body start to respond in a positive way. To this day I can say it is a work in progress. So go easy on yourself if you find you are in the same situation that I was in. Journal any emotions that may come up, and ask yourself what is one thing that you can give up or eliminate from your diet? It can be something small like caffeine, dairy, or even sugar. What can your incorporate into your routine that will benefit you? Perhaps adding yoga, deep breathing, or even physical activity into your routine could help.

# July 31

## The Magic Trick
## By Salli Sebastian Walker

*D*o you believe in magic? I know I do. When I was a little girl, magic seemed to be happening everywhere and my heart loved it. I especially loved Santa.

Listen closely, my friend, for I will unveil the answer to one of the best kept secrets of all time. I will attempt to answer how Santa would come into to my home and make gifts appear under the family tree.

There are many great magicians in the world skilled at producing astonishing illusions, but my mother championed them all. This consummate entertainer managed to produce an illusion so magical that I was stumped for years. As you all know Santa Claus delivers presents to children on Christmas morning. For some reason, he would come to my house on Christmas Eve? I knew he did because we would hear his voice and then—Voila! Gifts would appear under the tree.

As promised, I will soon share how this trick worked and then how it all imploded!

At approximately five in the afternoon, a spaghetti dinner deliciously prepared by my mother would be served in the basement of my childhood home. All five family members would be in attendance to experience the spectacle. It would be very difficult to eat for we were all anxiously awaiting Santa's arrival. The family would then hear loud foot stomps! Could it be Santa's voice saying, "HO, HO, HO! Merry Christmas!"

Where was Mom during Santa's stomping? She was missing this all! That's because she was the brave one who would go upstairs to make sure the coast was clear. Seconds later, she would yell down, "The coast is clear!"

When the family went upstairs, sitting under the tree would be beautifully wrapped gifts.

This illusion was perfectly executed for years and years until one Christmas Eve, Santa did not come to the house as we waited in the basement? Mom had to now reveal the truth about Santa. You see, my Santa was just a recorded voice on our reel-to-reel tape-recorder! That fateful cold night in December, my mother accidentally pushed erase on the tape-recorder instead of play. No more Santa!

The innocence of childhood disappears in a flash. Try using your magic touch to make special occasions unique.

# *August 1*

## Loner and Your Dearly Departed
## By Denise Kirkconnell

The fear of being alone is terrifying to most of us at some time. However, being alone has been a constant must-do in my life. It has always been my time to recharge my mind, body, and spirit, to rest, unwind, and practice self-care. Allowing yourself alone time is self-care!

Yet another win!

Being in my own space gives me the opportunity to tune into and look inward to what I am truly seeking. Environment is everything. Lighten everything around you with paint, candles, and art.

Every time you light a candle, set an intention. Mine are usually for peace and harmony. Other times, I set an intention to accomplish a task or self-care intention for that day. There are endless varieties of intentions. Choose whatever is most relevant in the moment.

What we must remind ourselves of is that we are never really alone. Learning to tune into and asking our dearly departed to guide and watch over us and our loved ones is very easy. They are always there. When lighting a candle, you can do much like you would in a church and dedicate the intention to the memory of one or all of your loved ones. Setting the attention and honoring their memory helps bring them closer to us. Having a picture or something sentimental of theirs close by is very powerful tool as well. Whenever you are feeling lonely, remember to call on your dearly departed. They are eager to guide you.

# August 2

## Show Yourself Some Love
### By Jamie Rudolph

*W*hat exactly is self-love? What is self-love to you?

I think of self-love as practices or opportunities to express self-care and appreciation for showing up every day. Most of us are always doing and giving to others, but often neglect or forget ourselves. We put ourselves last on the list or put our care off until tomorrow.

"Oh, I'll go for a walk later … I'm going to start eating healthy next time … I'm going to make an appointment to go get that facial or massage I've been needing for months."

But it is always tomorrow, right? Does it sound familiar?

What if, we put ourselves first and made ourselves a priority? It does not mean we neglect or put aside family, friends, responsibilities, or obligations. What if you *truly* take the time for you and set aside a special "me" time?

Ahhh … (deep exhale). Doesn't it sound wonderful?

Your me time does not have to be anything elaborate or super time consuming. It can simply be a few minutes of quiet time, self-reflection, or meditation. Maybe today you have extra time, and you go out for a hike, join your friends for yoga, or begin something you wanted to do for years.

What if, starting right now, you dedicate one thing to do each day just for you? One small act of self-care leads to the next small act and then suddenly you realize that you have created a beautiful practice of self-love.

# August 3

## The Gift of Listening
## By Bonnie Larson

One of the greatest gifts we offer is being present to *listen* to others. Earlier, conversations were often either about me or topics I would be interested in learning more. Having matured, I find great pleasure in listening to others. Their ideas are stimulating, and their innermost thoughts are quite personal and engaging.

Conversations, generally relevant, can lead to remarkable breakthroughs at just the right time. Have you noticed how often we listen, nod, and support, and then solutions flow right to the surface? The magic of synergy gives birth to brand new ideas and concepts. There is a reason you've come together at this moment.

One of the casualties of recent social distancing is the ability to converse one on one. Instead, we see a surge in the old technique, trolling. In our tiny community, everybody has a locked mailbox at the post office. It's a convenience. But, oh my goodness, DO NOT stop by the post office! Trollers lurk behind every bush! Like a nightmare, someone is stepping from behind, taking your sleeve, holding you tightly.

"I want to talk to you." Their eyes dart desperately between my eyes.

How can we turn down a friend in need of an audience?

Expediency goes right out the window at most retail businesses, and certainly at drive-through lanes. They want a conversation, anyway they can get it!

A sign of the times, a lovely retail store owner recently posted a notice on her store's window, "Please keep your opinions to yourself!"

Ouch!

If they cannot capture our attention any other way, they are willing to drive ten miles per hour—sure to pick up an engaging exchange!

But all kidding aside, we all want to be heard. We are social beings, best when warmly embraced by people caring enough to listen to our thoughts and concerns.

Have you sat back and been uplifted by a roomful of laughter or moved by the echoing silence of an audience in total reverie? During these moments, only goodwill exists. The key is connectivity. Being present and engaging is caring. Once we connect with our families, tribes, and communities, the gifts are ours.

# August 4

## The Power of Spirit Animals
## By Carolan Dickinson

Our own intuitive abilities have a way of making themselves known. We all have these abilities. Listening to Spirit and your own soul will guide and connect you to what you need most. This is also an act of self-love. In the Native American tradition, animals have a unique ability to be able to communicate and share with us what we need the most. Your animal totems just like guardian angels are with you from birth and will stay with you throughout your life. They are already sharing with you the attributes of your soul as part of your spiritual team, just like a guardian angel, ascended master, or the archangel. For this exercise, you will need a pen and paper and some quiet time. Get somewhere quiet and then go within through mediation or just sit quietly with your eyes closed.

1. With your eyes closed, imagine that you are sitting quietly, and you have asked your animal totems to be with you and share with you their knowledge and wisdom. Then see before you three different sizes of containers (all cruelty-free, of course) that are covered. At this point, you cannot see within.

2. Take the cover off the first container and see the spirit animal within. Write down every aspect of that animal that you are aware of. For example, maybe that animal is an eagle, and you are aware of that they are majestic, can soar highest to heaven, and mate for life. You may also notice the color of the eagle and if it lands on a nest and what the nest looks like and where it is.

3. Take the cover off the next container and repeat the instructions above.

4. Follow the instructions again for the third container.

After you have written everything down and only then, consider that the first animal is how you personally operate in the world, the second animal is how others see you. The third animal's attributes are what can most serve you today. This is a fun exercise that you can do any time, and you will be surprised at how accurate it is.

# August 5

## Stepping Into My Purpose
## By Gloria Dawn Kapeller

For the last ten years or so, I have been busy taking courses such as theta healing, Reiki and Reiki masters and access consciousness. Shortly, I will be taking my karuna masters. I have always believed that I needed to heal me before I can even think to help heal others.

We are all capable of healing as we are all sparks of the creator. Often it is our belief systems or the ego that holds us back and stands in the way of doing what we are divinely called to do. Mediation and gratitude have become very important in my journey. It is a good practice to go inward and listen to what spirit has to say. I too often second guess myself or do not listen to my intuition. That gut feeling you get has actually saved my life on a few occasions. There are so many tools available now that you can use. YouTube and other recorded guided meditations are a very great way to start this practice.

Have you been ignoring or not listening to what spirit is trying to tell you? I also love the practice of reading angel cards as you can set the intention of calling in your angels and getting the messages that you need to hear. I also notice number sequences, and I get a lot of messages in nature, seeing animals, cloud formations. I see a lot of angels in the clouds. I often Google the dream meaning of what see and I always get a message that resonates with me.

What have you been noticing? Anything repetitive is usually a message trying to come through. Dreams are a way that messages get through when you are more open during that time. Write down what you remember then Google or ask what message you are intended to get and see what resonates with you. You will never go wrong just use your intuition.

# August 6

## Take Out the Brushes and the Paint
### By Marsha Johnson

Do you have a closet full of crafting supplies, paints, brushes, markers, paper, scissors, sewing machine, fabric, almost a mini arts and crafts store, but you rarely get to use them? I am an example of a "someday" artist. I always joke that I'm ready for anything. I'm ready, willing and able, but just not doing.

Life can get so busy with work, family obligations, and then just general feelings of overwhelm. We can go weeks and sometimes months without doing anything creative for ourselves. When we get into a feeling of overwhelm, it's as if our minds can think of nothing else except the problem at hand. Maybe we had an argument, and we are thinking about all the things we should have said or done differently. We wake up each day with a to-do list that may not have anything that really nourishes our souls on that list. Perhaps we are just doing, doing, doing and not being present at the moment, feeling like our wheels are just spinning on the hamster wheel of life.

I would encourage you that when you are at a feeling of, *I don't have time for anything*, go to your crafting center, either in your own home or out to the local store and get out the paper, pens, paint, you name it, and spend some time creating. Make time for you.

For me, when I am painting, I can't think of anything else. The world around me fades away as I am looking at colors and brushes. Which shade of blue should I use or no blue at all? What needs to go into this open space over here? I am lost in what is coming to life right in front of me. After a while, when I am done, I feel like I can face all that I need to do. My mind becomes clear and answers I may have been struggling with become available. Afterwards, not only is your mind at rest, but you will have something beautiful to look at and be proud of. You can say that you did it with joy in your heart.

# *August 7*

## Emotional Purging
## By Dee Dee Rebitt

*I* have been packing up memories. I have been processing the garbage I let invade me for more than thirty years. I was tossing away photo albums in my mind, giving away memories of my soul to the winds, memories that were locked up. My collection of thoughts was tossed around like a cyclone. At times I would run away and cry, not sure of even how to process any of it. Tears were more frequent and at times I could not even explain to anyone my silence. I knew I was not happy with things that had taken place in my life. All the shit that happened in my life held me captive to my very core of who I was. I was letting life defeat me and at what cost?

My health had taken a beating. I was hiding everything from everyone because I felt utter shame for the events that took place decades ago. But occasionally, they would pop back into my life, terrifying me. I always say, once you open Pandora's box, there is no turning back.

I can still to this day see an image clearly of me as I laid on the floor, weeping uncontrollably. This time there was only me. I had to save myself. The memories flew around my very soul. I felt darkness around me. What I was seeing was frightening, but I was being shown my past.

I had to release and move forward.

I had always hidden my emotions and my pain very well. It was time to move on and let go, time to heal and move forward, which is easier now today since I spend a lot of my time writing. I write about my experiences in my life, and I will go as far as writing those letters to others that may have hurt me as a young child or a teenager or as a young woman, as a wife and as a mother. I let it all go. Bottling up those emotions nearly cost my own life. Now I am incredibly happy to say health is improved a weight has literally been lifted. My soul feels freedom. I still get those memories or others that come up, but I allow them to flow and deal with them the best way I see fit and it is usually in my writing.

# August 8

## Love's Embrace
## By Lisa Seyring

*Grace, grace, grace, would someone please tell me what is this thing called grace?*

I giggle inwardly now when I remember my plight with grace. Everyone around me seemed to understand it, have a handle on it, and I was left in the stupor of not knowing from which language they were speaking.

It is no wonder I did not "get it." I was too busy being perfect, being a task master and being unrelenting in self-judgment. The tension inside my body did not lend itself to the spaciousness of grace. Here comes another giggle. I was actually put out and mad that I could not figure out this thing called grace!

It was a message I received in an unconventional way that made a great impact on me and showed me the way. I was at a spiritual expo having an intuitive reading some time after my dad died. I was forty-one and the message that came through the reading was from him. His message was the game changer that helped me to more fully understand grace and what grace actually feels like, and I invite you to receive this message as well.

I was told to imagine holding a newborn baby or a puppy and to imagine how it would feel. That was easy. Instantly, I remembered holding each of my newborn children in my arms. I immediately felt the swell of my heart and the undeniable love and adoration I had for them.

I was then directed to regard *myself* in the same way. Wait, what? I resisted at first but my desire to experience something different was greater, so I imagined my adult Lisa holding an infant Lisa with adoration and love. Suddenly, I understood! As I *allowed* that unconditional love to embrace me and hold me, I discovered that loving without conditions is, in fact, grace. The tension within me eased and I knew what it felt like to love myself. I felt like I had been given the greatest gift in the world for I now had a knowing of grace.

Go ahead, give it a try. Hold yourself in love's embrace and allow any tension to fall away.

# *August 9*

## Authentic Beauty
## By Marie Martin

Beauty is not just an aesthetic; it is a way you live. You are most likely familiar with the expression "Beauty is in the eye of the beholder." I cannot entirely agree with that. To me, beauty is within the body of the creator. As it is in you, the living breathing person reading this. Beauty is something that we achieve when we express ourselves in an authentic way or a thing we experience when we are attracted to something; that attraction is a form of self-recognition.

When you live a life for yourself, expressing the wonders of your uniqueness and enjoy all your many layers, this is beauty. When you have an appreciation and are touched by the blooming flowers and the green trees, this is beauty. When in your busy day you bring a person back to peace emotionally, this is beauty. Beauty is a way of existing, learning, feeling, and living. It is your relationship to the world and in the interactions of your everyday life. Having this understanding of beauty is living purposefully, choosing to cultivate what is in your world with the best version of you.

Beauty brings joy first to the one who is making it, then to those who view the making of it. This is not how we usually think about the idea of beauty. It often is something that we see as a physical thing, achieved by striving for conditioned ideals. But when I think about my relationship with the idea of beauty, the normal feels so incomplete. Yes, beauty can be a physical thing, but it is not solely physical.

We, as humans, want to grab on and try out what we are attracted to. This is such an excellent way of knowing what is authentic to you. We recognize what is right for who we are on a soul level, and again this is beauty.

Having this understanding of beauty is powerful because it removes the pressure of having to fit in. The beauty ideals of society simply do not seem to matter as much when you are being deliberate about the way you are living your life. By feeling your way through your expression, you will know what is right for you and what no longer fits. This is a beautiful thing.

# August 10

## Hear Beyond The Song
## By JoAnne Eisen

Addictions and attachments are distractions to avoid acting and living from your pure soul's desires. They are not your inner truths but merely an internal dialogue you have with yourself, a conversation of non-truths that are hidden deep within you. They are real and deep wounds you are fearful of facing. They don't control you and will be released as you trust and step into allowing your soul to soar. Every addiction slowly leaves your life as you surrender to your inner guidance to follow your heart and soul's desire. You are allowing your soul's beauty to be expressed. Living from your soul's need, not from a fearful self-limiting reality.

Life can bring challenges, causing you to become doubtful of yourself and overburdened. You lose sight of your purpose at moments. It is essential to stop, breathe, and take some time to listen deeply. You are in the exact place you should be right now at this very moment. You may not trust or know it yet.

Listen to nature around you. It is speaking always. There is where you find your truth, grounding you to Mother Earth. Nature has much to say, guiding you back into balance. Watch how birds, without worry or fear, freely sing their songs of life and joy, knowing they are taken care of every day without having to do anything but be themselves. Be still and deeply listen, allowing their songs to soak into every cell of your body, bringing you comfort and healing. Listen beyond their song; listen to the joy that is alive in your world. Listen to the music of life, washing away old clutter within your mind, the judgment of yourself. Hold onto your inner strength that is alive and well deep within you. Birds will teach you where to place your focus, helping to lift your spirit, realizing the world will be good and balanced once again.

Breathe! What if you completely and fully trust that you are right where you need to be right now? In this space, at this time? You earnestly listen to your heart's requests. The home to your soul as it calls you. Trusting the path it leads you on. You walk that path with complete acceptance and surrender.

I have complete love and acceptance for myself. I trust my inner guidance entirely with no judgment.

# August 11

## Move Your Body towards Self-Love
### By Grace Redman

*Y*ou are fat! You are short. Your nose is too big. Your butt is too wide! These are the messages I heard as a young girl about my body. I internalized the messages and believed them as the absolute *truth*. Even though I abused her, my body has been loyal to me because it wakes me up every morning to a new day. My body has carried me through the most challenging of days. She kept me moving forward when I wanted to lay down and tap the f- out.

Would we ever treat anyone the way we treat our body? Abso-f-ing-lutely not! Yet we treat our bodies so badly and they continue to carry us through another day.

As resilient and miraculous as our bodies are, our bodies will begin to crash and cry for help if we continue to abuse and berate them.

Taking care of our bodies is critical for our overall health. The mind, spirit, and body are all connected. There is no separation. What the mind and spirit think is felt through the body. Our bodies are one of the vessels that speaks to us when we are off track. Those headaches, neckaches, stomach aches, and other aches are signals from our bodies that we need to look closer to making changes.

Movement is as important to the body as food and water. Exercise is one of the best anti-depressants. When you get your body moving for just ten minutes, you are activating endorphins and changing your emotional state and yes, it only takes ten minutes.

I can hear you moaning about how you don't have time to exercise. My dear sweet friend, you can't *not* make the time to get moving. I will tell you why. Consistent exercise increases your energy and when your energy is increased and your endorphins have kicked in, you will be more productive and focused!

You do not need a gym membership to get your body moving. Nature is one of the most amazing gyms there is. Plus, you kill two birds with one stone by getting your vitamin D while you are outside moving your body. The main thing is movement. You can walk, dance, jog, run, climb stairs, do jumping jacks. There are hundreds of ways to move your body.

One of the greatest acts of self-love is loving your body by moving your body!

# August 12

## The Gift I Give Myself Today
### By Bernadette Rodebaugh

- I will love myself unconditionally because nobody will love me or treat me better than I treat myself.
- I will forgive myself for *not* being perfect *because nobody is perfect.*
- I will focus only on myself and how I can make my life more fulfilling.
- I will not distract myself from my own life by worrying or trying to fix other people or the dramas in their life.
- I will only think and talk about positive aspects of my life and my world.
- I will think positive thoughts about others because I know what I give out will come back to me.
- I will remind myself that *I love myself* every day by tearing out this page and hanging it up so as I get ready every morning, I will read this again to start every morning knowing *I truly love myself no matter what the day might bring!*

# August 13

## I am a Survivor
## By Mindy Lipton

Whatever I do and wherever I go, I always try to have a Plan B. It is just what seems to work for me. Another strategy I found to help me was to create lists of pros and cons. Decisions can be tough at times.

Self-love did not come easy or at an early age. I was one to strive for perfection until I realized that nothing is perfect. Who says what is *perfect* or *normal*? And who is *who*? That has always been a big question. Will you have to answer to 'them?' Probably not. You are in charge of you and yourself only.

I sure love the woman I turned out to be. I do not mind being alone so much. Although it would be nice to share the love. In the meantime. I will follow the lyrics of Gloria Gaynor, "I Will Survive."

Think about your Plan B. Spend fifteen minutes creating your list of pros and cons for the decisions you are facing and on top of that list write, *whatever happens, I will survive and thrive.*

# August 14

## What You Think of Me...Is None of My Business
## By Charel Morris

*W*hile working on Hill Street Blues, I discovered an amazing powerful and positive woman minister doing a TV church show. Her name is Terry Cole-Whittaker, and when I met her, I got woke.

She wrote *What You Think of Me Is None of My Business*. The title spun my head and then it changed my world.

How many of your life choices and decisions are based on the thoughts of others your parents or someone you don't know. Young or old too often we fall into this trap.

I have had times when *comments* from years back float into my mind and haunt me, causing me to question my choices and decisions influencing my life, my emotions, and how I felt about my own value.

When I realized that their thoughts about me...where *theirs* and not *mine*. In fact, it was truly "none of my business" and with that awakening my life, moved into flow.

So how do you breakthrough these old rather crusty and annoying wounds?

### Claim your Mantra

To change your reaction to these random thoughts, make a decision. Stop giving anyone power over you. Let *What You Think of Me... Is None of My Business* become your Mantra. And use it regularly.

## Forgiveness

Practice Forgiveness. It can be individual or cast a wide net forgiving them all at once. You may want to repeat this but there is healing at the end this tunnel. Journal, meditate or go outside and shout it to the universe. Do whatever feels best for you!

## Celebrate

Acknowledge your own strength, your creative skills, celebrate YOU! Spends some time really looking at what you have done in life. Recall what it felt like when you knew you had the answer and during those times when you intuitively made the right choice. Write your story about your successes and your mistakes. Mistakes are where you really learn and grow so do not hide them. Claim them. They are yours.

## Gratitude

Be grateful for being you! Write about your gratitude for the gifts you have received. Love those bumps in the road. And celebrate when you were in the flow. Look in the mirror and tell yourself, "I AM Enough." I AM Loved." "I AM Respected." Welcome to your self-love!

# August 15

## Putting Me First
## By Janice Story

*N*ot taking care of myself has been a continuous pattern throughout my life. I never seemed to be able to make myself a priority, always putting my own needs on the "back burner." I'd become a master of excuses. "I don't have time. I will start tomorrow. I have to do this first." Tomorrow inevitably turned into next week, next month, and unfortunately next year. Do you know that feeling or have you had similar thoughts?

A few years back, I made some major shifts in my life and started implementing some self-care practices. *Wow,* has it been life changing! As I started making a commitment to loving myself and taking care of me, everything around me shifted. I became happier, healthier, and my personal business started thriving. I started to reach my goals and was able to achieve my desires that I had thought would never be anything other than far-fetched dreams.

Sure, I still get off track sometimes, but I've learned to be more compassionate and forgiving with myself, which has allowed me to be able to move forward again instead of becoming stuck like I had always done in the past. I have learned to write things down and have a better plan helping me be more committed.

A few of my most important daily practices include mediation, exercise, and journaling. I just feel better if I am least doing those three things. I'm always looking for things I can read, or classes I can take to gain wisdom and increase my knowledge. I schedule time for the things that bring my joy.

Here are a few ideas to help encourage and assist you in starting your own self-care routine.

- First, and most importantly, make a commitment to yourself to begin a consistent daily routine.
- Invest in or create a planner or notebook to help keep you on track.
- Sit down and create some daily, weekly, monthly, and yearly goals and organize them in your newly purchased planner.
- Decide what your self-care routine is going to look like, and how much time it will take you, and start adding it to your daily agenda. Block out times on your calendar, making appointments with yourself. You would always keep your appointments with others, right?
- What are you going to do today to begin putting you first?

# *August 16*

## Mirror Mirror
## By Ann Marie Asp

*Mirror, mirror on the wall, who is the fairest one of all.*

How do these enchanting words speak to you? They always seemed magical when I said them aloud as a young girl. It was then I looked at life through brilliant-colored lenses. These lenses sent visions and tiny glimpses of the dreams and hopes held so dearly by my inner child. They were inspirational reflections that would be played out through many different times in my life.

Through memorable moments in life, we witness mirrored reflections of ourselves thru the distinctive experiences that define the essence of who we are. As creative individuals, we look at the world in our own unique style. We slowly start developing that unique style of our own self beginning with those formative years during childhood. It is a time of such innocence, a time where we watch with bright and wide-open eyes the miracles of life unfolding around us. Through these early reflections, we begin to sense where we want to journey with our own precious gifts that we have been given.

I look back and recall visions of a treasure chest. Each time I opened the chest's door, a wonderful opportunity found its way to me. These opportunities served as pathways to new adventures. There were many times I could barely wait to open the magical chest and find that next special treasure. These adventures began to serve as stepping-stones in reaching the desired dreams that had always been within my reach. These stones helped form and serve as a solid foundation. Each stone had a resonance that spoke and helped me believe that when you trust that every moment in life is fully complete in its own way, you can then embrace the joy of what unfolds during each day in your life.

Take time out of your busy schedule today, if only a few minutes to look back and reflect on those defining moments. Begin with that adventurous young child, then travel up thru the amazing person you are today.

Make a list of those life changing stepping-stones. Write a short story on how they have shaped your life. Share these unique and magical stories with yourself often. You will find yourself smiling and your heart laughing.

Now, take a look in the mirror. I trust you will be in awe of the amazing individual looking back at you.

# August 17

## A Complete Surrendering
### By Nanette Gogan-Edwards

*S*elf-love begins with complete surrender. Self-sacrifice is not depriving yourself of resources, energy, or time to yourself. It is more about sacrificing the selfish desires and "addictions" that fuel our self-centered ways.

We all hold on to destructive feelings and habits such as anger, negativity, control over self or others, animosity, and fear. All of these stem from our past experiences and circumstances and serve as a self-preservation mechanism. Self-sacrifice requires a complete surrender of what you hold in your heart.

After my divorce, I was hell-bent on rebuilding my life the way I wanted it and no body, and no thing was going to stop me! I busted my hump by attending culinary school, acquiring a specific set of skills as a foundation for my new life. This education led me to a career in the grocery industry that has been extremely satisfying and challenging in many ways.

I also did my share of dating during this time. I dated control freaks and I also was the occasional control freak. I spent much of my emotional energy maintaining walls I had built during my first marriage to protect my heart. I desperately wanted to trust my partners with my fragile heart but just could not let my vulnerabilities be revealed. I actually verbally threatened my partners that if they did anything to hurt me, I would drop them like a bad habit and leave them with nothing. I would walk away the winner every time. I was always "a step ahead," watching and waiting ready to pounce like a cat waiting quietly and patiently with its tail twitching!

After suffering many disappointments, I finally decided I'd had enough. I began to realize that the common denominator in all my failed relationships was me! This was the beginning of my journey to discovering and releasing what I had held in my heart. This was the beginning of a complete surrender, a surrendering that continues to this day.

Self-love is a constant process that we must work on every day for the rest of our lives. We must always be aware of what's in our hearts and develop discernment to know what to keep and what to surrender.

"I've learned that nothing is lost in surrender. Hear that again: NOTHING is lost in surrender"! -*Reclaiming Your Heart: A Journey to Living Fully Alive* – Denise Hildreth Jones, 2013.

# *August 18*

## Look Up
## By Carrie Newsom

*I* grew up looking down.

I was one of a handful of white missionary kids in the middle of Africa. Many Africans had never seen a girl with long, sleek hair and pale skin. Strangers often reached out to feel my hair as I walked past them, and I felt violated and freakish.

I developed the habit of looking down because I was afraid of the reflection of myself, I would see in other people's eyes.

I loved taking hikes through our forest preserve, but when I began walking, I directed all my attention to the path. I ignored the beauty around me and focused on the struggles.

One particularly hot day, as I wrestled my body up a rocky hill, I happened to look up into the trees swaying in the breeze high above my head. My struggle melted away. The obstacle in front of me no longer held me in its grip. Instead, the beauty of where I was enveloped me and lifted me through the challenge.

Paying attention to the dense, quiet beauty surrounding me made the steep path less difficult.

When we focus solely on the challenges right in front of us, we get lost in the anxiety of the moment. We forget to look up. We miss the beauty of life passing right in front of us. The *beauty* is the point, not the challenge.

When I spent my life looking down at the challenge right in front of me, I got lost in stress and fear. I didn't see the moments of tranquility, beauty and support. It's easier to get through a challenge if I focus on where I want to end up, rather than on how hard it is to get there.

I spent so many years looking down, trying to build a wall around my heart so I would not be hurt. But looking down forces me to miss all the beauty that makes the challenge more tolerable. I encourage you to look up in your life. Do not get trapped by fear about the next step. Focus on where you want to be and take note of the beauty that surrounds you on your way to that place. Don't miss out on the gifts life puts in your path because you're too afraid to look up.

# *August 19*

## Forgiveness
## By Kim Richardson

*"Holding onto anger is like grasping a hot coal with the intent of throwing it at someone else; you are the one*
*who gets burned."*
~ Buddha.

*H*ave you been burned? I know I have. I spent many years holding onto anger and waiting to see justice served. Then one day, I was tired—tired of being burned. I realized this anger I was holding onto was manifesting in my physical body, affecting my mental wellbeing, and no longer served me. As I was trying to let it go, it was quite painful. I could not figure out how to forgive. Forgiveness felt to me like saying, *it's okay you did this horrible thing.* It was as if I was absolving them of their sin.

One day while watching Oprah, she stated a definition of forgiveness that I had never heard before. She said, "Forgiveness is giving up the hope the past could have been any different." I was stunned; a huge light bulb went off in my head. I thought, *I can do that.* I can '*Give up the hope the past could have been any different.*' I cannot change the past, *but* I can change my future.

I started to create a list of those I needed to forgive and through the process, I realized I needed to put myself on that list as well. I wrote letters to them all. Most were not so nice, however, I made sure to thank them in the end for the lessons they provided and the stronger person I became as a result. I did not mail the letters; instead, I burned them. Burning them felt so amazing. As I watched them go up in smoke, I felt a release as I was letting all that energy leave my body.

Take an inventory of all those that hurt you. Create a list. Don't forget to include yourself on that list. Write them a letter then have a little burning ceremony of your own. Take note of how you feel as you release the hold each one has on you.

As time goes by, some feelings of anger may start to reappear. Do the exercise again and again until you have completely released the attachment to the anger and let go of the control they or the situation has over you.

# August 20

## Compassion In Pain
## By Dominique Trier

*D*uring hardship (enduring a pandemic, childhood trauma, romantic heartbreak, caring for family ailments, or your own illness) you can falter and fire a litany of questions aimed at yourself, but giving ourselves love is invaluable. I have often asked myself "Why do I deserve this?" I have set out questions to the universe like "How do I even begin to handle this?" Of course, these questions came to me while I felt defeated and out of energy for the most minuscule of tasks. I did not understand how to help myself due to various variables that were far outside of my control.

The only control I was used to was a forced containment of my emotions. It would lead me to bottling all of my emotions up until I found myself crying in the shower while listening to Amy Winehouses crone about the existential crisis that is love and life in general. These moments of self-indulgence were not always productive, but they were necessary in trusting myself. I gave myself permission and validation to feel the way I felt. I needed to truly process hardships at my own pace.

When I started taking self-love seriously, I was not as gentle in handling situations at my own pace like I would be with a close friend or family member. I wanted to find a shortcut to expedite feeling better when I encountered harmful external variables outside of my control. At some points I would put on cringe-inducing positive affirmation videos before I slept. Sometimes it worked, but the times it did not, I was sent to a harmful place. I was thrown into a tornado of panic and an increased self-awareness that I was incapable of handling my circumstances.

Not only did this shortcut not help … it made me feel worse. If I would have been self-indulgent, I would have given myself the compassion to process. It is easy to grow impatient, as we rely so heavily on technology that can instantaneously change because we demand it to, but we cannot expect the same for ourselves. We are not robots! We are deserving of the compassion we easily give to others. Giving ourselves compassion and telling others of our needs can create a support system enabling healthy and productive resolutions to our pain.

# August 21

## Connect to Your Wise Counsel of Power for Clarity
### By Paula Marie Rennie

*Y*our soul has what I call a "wise counsel" that are higher conscious parts of yourself and specific guides that support you through your life experiences. The counsel knows your soul's life purpose and is a powerful guiding force that can help you make decisions to grow and fulfil your greatest yearnings and potentials. We communicate with our wise counsel through our thoughts and intuition. It is important we take time to center within ourselves each day so we can listen to our guidance and our body's wisdom.

Let this exercise build your connection with your wise counsel of power and grow your intuitive abilities.

- Sit in a quiet place and be mindful of your breath. With every breath, imagine being filled with a golden healing light.

- Feel your feet grounding down into the Earth. Now draw the Earth's energy up through the centre of your body, all the way up and out the top of your head. Feel your entire being connecting to the divine universal energy.

- Place your attention on your heart space. Start to feel your energy flowing in rhythm with the universe. Expand it now out to the edges of the room.

- Observe your body, where are there feelings of discomfort? Place a hand on this area and ask this part of you, "What do I feel?" Breathe and listen.

- Invite your higher self to step forward in front of you. Feel and sense their energy or see what they look like. Ask the wisdom of your higher self to embrace your body and reveal what you need to know right now.

- Now become aware of any guides that are present. See or sense their energy and what they look like. Allow any images or messages to come. Ask your guides questions to help you with clarity. You may not receive answers straight away, so be aware of signs and synchronicities as you go about your day.

- Ask your higher self to show you your future potential in any area of life two years from now. Use all of your senses to fully imagine yourself there. What are you doing? Who is with you? What do you look like? How are you different? How do you feel?

- Journal about any guidance and actions you can take, reflect on the divine wisdom you received.

# August 22

## Questioning Your Worth
## By Karen Cowperthwaite

*D*o you have a little critic in your head that chatters away? This not-so-nice voice likes to remind you where you do not measure up. That inner judge wants you to know that you messed up or that you do not know what you're talking about. It creates all kinds of critiques such as too fat, too quiet, too anxious, too serious, too stupid or the biggie—no one cares about you. I know that inner meanie seems like it is spouting off facts. I promise you that you are not the only one with a saboteur voice that chatters away creating lies.

What can you do to stop the thoughts that run wild and out of control? First things first, make a choice to be the observer who is in charge of noticing your reactions. The quickest way to change what you believe about yourself is to notice when you think you are broken or when you beat yourself up about something that happened. This kind of stinking thinking consists of thoughts about the past, replaying your mistakes, worrying about the future or my former favorite, blaming others for why you feel this way.

There is one tool that can truly shift a mind that is critical of self or others. It is a very small shift in your beliefs. You and you alone are responsible for your feelings. Self-love has two parts: how you show up for yourself, and how you think about yourself. In every moment you get to choose. When the judge comes knocking at your mind's door, you can open the door all the way and say, "Come on in!" or you can pull up a comfy chair, sit down, and observe your thoughts like you are watching a movie.

When the mind comes up with all kinds of reasons why you are not good enough, imagine the most comfortable chair or love seat available and sit down. It is time to watch a mind movie and just watch the drama playing in front of you. This is not your story, but a frightened part triggering your survival brain. It is not the true you. When you are finished with that story, change the channel.

# August 23

## A Recipe for Self-Love
### By Amy I. King

My mother taught me how to bake when I was in preschool. I remember coming home from kindergarten, dropping my lunchbox on the kitchen table, and asking my mom, "What kind of cake are we baking for Grandma's birthday?"

I would sit, perched on the counter in the kitchen, pouring each ingredient carefully, blending and mixing my sweet masterpieces or so I thought of them! I reveled in the appreciative joy of recipients.

Somewhere it says "love thy neighbor as thyself." Giving has always been something that has boosted my spirits. It creates a feeling inside, not unlike the warmth that a hearth provides for a home. Baking a batch of cookies and distributing them amongst the neighbors, who I adore, is how I take care of myself. When I am feeling blue, sharing makes me feel more connected, improving my mood. I to live on a street filled with some pretty amazing and helpful neighbors for whom I am incredibly grateful. One lovely neighbor describes it as living on Sesame Street.

Chocolate pixies always give my mood a lift. I have had the recipe for about forty years. They never fail to satiate the sweet tooth. These cookies, with their ooey-gooey (if you bake them just right) chocolatey goodness topped with powdered sugar, are hard to match.

Here's the recipe should you decide that you could use a little self-love in the form of baking. A staple at Christmas, I have started making them a few times a year for my neighbors and friends.

# CHOCOLATE PIXIES

## INGREDIENTS:

One 4-oz box Baker's unsweetened chocolate
2.5 cups flour
2 tsp. baking powder
1/2 tsp. salt
1/2 cup vegetable oil
2 cups sugar
4 eggs
2 tsp. vanilla
Powdered sugar for rolling

## DIRECTIONS:

Melt chocolate in double boiler or microwave

In a separate bowl, sift together flour, baking powder, and salt.

Combine oil, sugar, and chocolate. Mix well. Add eggs, one at a time, beating well after each. Add vanilla. Add sifted dry ingredients a little at a time and blend thoroughly. Cover and chill the dough for a couple of hours or overnight.

Preheat oven to 350.

Roll the dough into small 3/4 to 1-inch balls, dip in powdered sugar.

Bake at 350 on a greased cookie sheet for 10-12 minutes. Let cool, remove.

# August 24

## Un-plant the Seeds
### By Kim Richardson

*W*e are all born a blank slate and as we grow, we are taught about the world around us. There are many teachers with our parents being the obvious ones. What about our friends, family, co-workers, and general society or most importantly, ourselves? Starting with our parents, they plant the seeds in our minds of the things they think we should know. Then more seeds are planted from all those around us and the inner dialogue we created based on those beliefs we have learned. As we grow, maybe some of those seeds that were planted no longer hold a truth for us.

Time to weed the garden my friend, what seeds have been planted that you need to weed to make room for the new ones? What inner dialogue do you have that can be changed? Which of these beliefs are no longer serving you in a positive way?

# *August 25*

## Nature's Nourishment
### By Ashlie Bradley

*The sunshine warming your shoulders, a gentle breeze.*

*A delicious fragrance emanating from flowers, the earth under your feet.*

*The cleansing of a rainfall, the rejoicing in a rainbow.*

*A beaming blue sky, a striking cloud contrast.*

Is there anything so magnificent as a sunset's canvas, rich in vibrant colors? Or the majesty of the moon, illuminating all it touches?

There is nothing quite like the healing hands of mother nature, effortlessly available to us at any moment we choose to hold her hand. She provides a calm and subtle stillness in which we can allow ourselves to be opened up, so divinity can penetrate our hearts.

Sit under a tree, bask in its glory. Submerge in a body of water, a cleanse to the aura. Hike a mountain, regain perspective. Simply listen to the sweet song of the birds. Give yourself permission to be held, supported, nurtured, and loved by nature. Here you will find presence. With presence, love becomes our essence. When love is our essence, life becomes grand.

What can you do today to be nourished by nature?

# *August 26*

## How Do You See Yourself?
## By Debra Moore Ewing

*D*ebbi was a young lady in her twenties who lacked self-esteem. To look at her you would never think she struggled with that. She was beautiful, dressed well, and had a lot of friends, but something was missing, and she felt unworthy.

She never seemed to attract the right man and she was desperate to have a healthy relationship so she could marry and have children. She was unaware of the law of attraction (as you are you will naturally attract to you) until she was thirty. Before that she attracted those who were desperate and lonely ... and broken, exactly like her. It seemed she would grovel at the crumbs they would throw her way in hopes that the next guy may be *the one*. She would even joke that she must have *doormat* tattooed on her forehead. It was easier to laugh at herself, so she did not have to feel the pain.

Things changed one day when her therapist asked her to write down all her good qualities and read them twice a day.

"It takes twenty-one days to change a habit or belief," she said.

Debbi was concerned she would never be able to think of any, so the therapist suggested she ask her friends to share what they felt was special about her. Debbi created a list of what I call "I statements." She taped the paper to her bathroom mirror and read it every morning and evening while brushing her teeth. She wrote statements as if she already had them or believed them to be true. I remember when she grappled with the notion of writing "I am beautiful" or "I am financially secure," but she did it anyway.

Ironically, after one month of planting these words of wisdom into her conscious and subconscious mind, it raised her vibration and she started to believe them! Over time Debbi grew into the type of woman she always wanted to be. She finally met the man of her dreams, got married, and had a daughter who she adores. When her daughter was having trouble in elementary school with bullies, she had her do the affirmation process, so she did not endure years of low self-esteem. She broke the pattern.

How do I know so much about her? Debbi was me.

# August 27

## The Power of Your "ASK"
## By Marilyn Miller

*L*earning how to *ASK* for what you want with a clear expectation of getting a *YES* answer is so important. Here is a way to do it. First, summon the clear realization that you deserve to have what you want. I know I have failed miserably in getting what I want in relationships simply because I did not ask with an expectation that I truly deserved what I was asking for.

Rehearse your *ASK* by saying it clearly to yourself. Be organized, be precise, and be hopeful. Say, "I have an idea". State what you want. (For example, it could be a new product or program.) Next, without pausing add, "What do you want and need from me to consider my idea?" This allows the other person to participate with your idea before dismissing it. If they have conditions, listen carefully. Then decide if you are prepared to accept the conditions. This method can produce miracles. Remember, you deserve it!

# August 28

## The Art of Self-Love
## By Nancy Toffanin

*I* believed that if I could look in a mirror and said, "I love you," it meant I do love myself! It did not! The process of self-love I learned was much deeper.

Every relationship taught me I did not love or value myself. All the illusions of self-love got scraped away because I settled for less than I deserved. Still, please look in the mirror every day and say, "I love you!" This is a great start to self-love.

After healing from a breakup, while working through my lessons, the greatest gift I received was deep self-love, value, respect, trust, worth, and expansion. The process was not easy. It was figuring out what traumas I still had to heal from my childhood. Just like peeling an onion, just when we thought we had it figured out, a deeper layer showed up.

In discovering self-love, I learned that it was about choosing myself every day, being consistent and keeping my word. It was about making me priority every day, putting myself first, having boundaries, and doing self-care. I needed to create a life I did not have to escape from while living from my internal yes or no and listening to my internal yes or no. Each time someone asked a question, I would listen to my first thought—that gut feeling.

Truly honoring ourselves is the best gift we can give ourselves.

Self-love is about filling our cup, doing things we love, practicing self-care, and taking "me" time every day. When our cup is empty, we feel tired, drained, and frustrated, etc. Taking fifteen minutes or longer each day helps us feel the benefit of putting ourselves first. Though the journey is challenging at times, it is truly magical and rewarding!

### Self-reflection!

What lessons did you learn from your relationships?
What are your preconceived thoughts about self-love?
What emotions still have another layer to heal?
How many times have you said yes out of guilt or obligation?
Do you listen to your internal yes or no?
Does it light you up?
Does it make you happy?
Do you feel tension in your body?
Write a self-care list!

# August 29

## How Would You Treat a Friend?
## By Paula Obeid

*I* am a reformed people-pleaser! It is often said that God will not give us more than we can handle. We all know sometimes it does not feel like that. A good friend is necessary to get through difficult moments. I have experienced so much in my life. That included the sudden death of my husband when I found myself wondering if my young children will ever smile again.

My best friend from high school was my rock. I believe all my life trauma and experiences have helped me show compassion and be a rock to all my friends and even complete strangers. Now, looking back, I see that I have had great friends who were lifelines in the many storms of my life. However, I can also see where I was throwing out all my lifelines to others, depleting my energy.

I am a sensitive person who absorbs the emotional energy of people. I had friendships in my life that were reciprocal with each taking turns to be the rock. I also had friendships that left only me emotionally drained. I felt good friends were supposed to allow themselves to be emotionally depleted while offering support. I thought this was being the loving friend. Now, I do not feel like it was the most loving thing for myself. I was able to take responsibility for the energy I also brought to the relationship. I did not feel like I was enough, so I over gave! I created co-dependent relationships trying to rescue others which made me feel better about myself. I was constantly throwing out lifelines to friends and being an emotional dumping ground. I was always putting other's needs before my own. I was disappointed, expecting others to respond to me as I responded to their suffering. Finally, I started to think how things might change in my life if I gave myself the same treatment and love that I gave to my friends.

If I were asked the question "How would you treat a friend?", my advice would be that friendships are energy exchanges of giving and receiving compassion. I would treat myself the same as I would my friend. I would listen to the same advice that I lovingly give my friend. I am ready to love myself. I deserve a friend like me! How would you answer the question? How would you treat a friend?

# August 30

## Survival Mode
## By Selena Urbanovitch

*T*rauma or loss takes its toll on a soul. I know this as I lived with a trauma that rocked my world. I did not know how to move past it. I was all about "This happened to me!" and what I did not realize is that it happened to us!

Fight or flight kicks in here. And I went into flight mode. I did not want to face this trauma like a lesson! I was mad, and I did not cope well at all. Panic attacks happened. Anger happened, and loss happened. It took what felt like a very long time before I was able to take steps to heal from this. It took doctors' appointments and physiotherapy. It took meetings about the trauma that happened to me.

I am sharing this with you to say that I get it. It is almost easier to not eat, to not get out of my pajamas and to just have a few drinks! As time went on, I knew I had to face me. I was fortunate in that I was surrounded by beautiful souls that never gave up on me. I would go to meetings on aneurysms, as I had a right frontal lobe one in 2015 that almost took my life. I remember going to them thinking, "Wow my experience is not as bad as that person's." I would say, "I don't need this as I am doing ok!" This in actual fact was not true, so I went back and I cried and I asked the questions that I couldn't stop thinking about and I started to heal, which meant my family started to as well.

Is it survival mode for you? Do you want to fight? Take a deep breath and trust your answer. Here are some steps that helped me.

1. Seeing my family doctor helped me talk about the things that scared me, which in turn he suggested therapy.

2. Going to a meetup group of people going through what I was going through helped so much.

3. Be gentle with yourself, know time heals. There is no time limit on healing.

4. Reach out.

5. Forgive yourself. You deserve the kindness that you give others ... Forgive you!

# August 31

### Connection
### By Crystal Cockerham

You can connect with your deepest knowing and set yourself up for a most excellent day with these simple steps:

- Schedule sacred time for yourself. Start with ten minutes if that is all you can spare. It's just the time between hitting the snooze button! Believe it or not, for most, the best time for this communication is upon waking.

- Mindfully breath in the light of the new day and exhale the remnants of slumber and stretch your body as you do so. Feel into the physical spaces of yourself and put a smile on your face.

- Continue your breath and ask yourself, "How do I wish to *be* and feel as I move through the day?"

- Once you have connected with this state of *be*-ing or feeling, take it to the next level and envision yourself moving through the day's planned activities and remaining firm in this state of *be*-ing, your power zone. Do not lose track of your breath and keep that smile on your face all the way through the end of your day and settling into a great restful night of restorative sleep.

- Somewhere in this space, a word or phrase is going to come to you. Turn this into an affirmation or mantra to help you re-align with your power zone as you go through the day.

- At the end of the day, it would be a good idea to note if you were taken out of your power zone. What triggered it? How did that make you feel? Was there something you would like to do differently to re-direct your energy should this happen again? Also note if you weren't taken out of your power zone. How does this make you feel? What can you do to ensure this success every day?

- After trying this for a period of time, go back and review your entries of the days you found yourself straying from your power zone and see if you uncover a pattern or a recurring theme. If so, what is it? What have you discovered about yourself? What are you ready to let go of?

- Reach out for support when you need it. You are not alone. You are not the only one who has ever come face to face with their own shadow in some form or another. We all have shadow, and we all have the light to move through it.

# September 1

## The Stretch
## By Susan Hoyle

*H*ave you ever been *stuck?* Been in a place so long you can't even remember the dream you had for yourself? Well, me too! Sometimes we get so caught up in *adulting* that we forget that little spark of passion we came here with. That spark of pure possibility for the purpose that lies within each of us. Do you remember?

Juggling my life became who I was. Running from one thing to the next, running an office, taking kids to practices, play dates, parent meetings, P.T.A. Until one day I realized, my name was never on the calendar! There was no time for *ME*. Self-care of any kind was nonexistent. Maybe you can relate?

I began to slowly look at my life and what needed to change. I understood the power of self-care, even taught it in my classes, but when I began to put myself on the calendar, I struggled. This comfort zone I had become so comfortable with, made it so hard to leave it. I thought my keeping this *flow* in our family was what others found comfort in. But was this true?

I started with one simple step. Putting myself on the calendar! Simple, right? Whether it was quiet time for myself, self-reflection, meditation, a massage, lunch with a friend, it went on the calendar. Not going to lie. This made me very uncomfortable, I wasn't sure why?

But this is where the change came in. Change I was not sure I was ready for until I learned about *the stretch*. *The stretch* is that place where we find ourselves as we move out of our own comfort zone. It is uncomfortable, yet empowering. Scary, yet exciting. The more we move into this space, feel it, trust ourselves in it, the more we begin to fan those inner sparks of pure possibility.

If you have felt yourself stuck in your own comfort zone, I invite you to just begin. Put yourself on your calendar every day even if it is just a quiet sacred time you schedule. Put it on the calendar. Write it in! Trust your inner knowing! Your time is valuable. You are worthy. Your voice matters. It is time to be seen in all your glory. Start fanning those inner sparks of possibility and before long they will be flames of achievement.

# September 2

## Happy Cheesecake
## By Delores Garcia

Several years ago, I made a decision about cheesecake. I had just finished a frustrating conversation and thought, "Cheesecake would sure make me feel better right now." It was quite silly when I said it aloud. How was cheesecake going to help me feel better? I decided at that moment, I would only eat "happy cheesecake,' when I felt happy and when I could fully focus on the experience of eating cheesecake. I decided to not desecrate the experience by being distracted or agitated. I loved cheesecake too much!

Self-care creates mindful eating experiences. Benefits include learning self-trust with any food and enhancing gratitude for food and our bodies.

Ready? Create a peaceful place. Select a food you adore. Relax and breathe into the experience. Close your eyes and become present in the room by noticing sounds, smells, feeling of your space. Bring your attention to your breath and notice any feelings or thoughts. Peacefully notice them and let them be. They may have a message, or they may just be old corrupt messages trying to dissuade you from being mindful and trusting yourself around food. Using your senses, bring awareness to your food.

SIGHT: Notice its color, shape, texture.

SOUND: Notice what sounds it makes when you open the package or when you cut/bite into it.

SMELL: Take a whiff of your food. Does the smell remind you of your childhood?

TOUCH: Close your eyes as you deliver the food to your mouth. How does it feel in your mouth?

TASTE: Hold the food in your mouth without chewing or swallowing. Savor it without hurry. Notice its flavors and mouthfeel. Think how you would explain this experience to someone who had never eaten it.

Take another bite. Continue to bring awareness to the experience. How does the second bite compare to the first? Check in with yourself. Are you feeling satisfied, or do you desire more? If you want another bite, continue with focused intention on pure enjoyment. Once you are *satisfied*, do not eat anymore. You want to experience pure enjoyment of this food. Once you are *satisfied*, if you continue to eat more, you are not coming from a place of pure enjoyment. Stop when you are satisfied. There is no need to eat any more. Keep it pure. This is where the self-care, self-honor, and self-trust are found.

# September 3

## Divine Meditation
## By Tabitha Weigel

*M*y path as the Spiritual Warrior Mama began when I gave birth to my baby boy and at the same time was diagnosed with cancer. My life became a battlefield, fighting for breath while also trying to be present for my family. To fuel my heart and drive, I needed connection, love, and spiritual support that was true to me. It was through my newfound and growing appreciation for tarot/oracle cards, the Bible and working with angels (as well as source energy) that I began to understand my unique connection with God.

It is through these relationships and the evolving practice of self-love, reflection, and awareness that I learned to communicate with God, my source, my team divine. The absolute beauty in this message being, that we all hold this sacred ability, to pray too, sit with and communicate with *our* team divine. Too reflect, manifest and co create as a powerful force of will, love and light.

So how do we start this practice of receiving and noting divine guidance this very day? This depends on you. You may feel comfortable with simply developing a habit of stillness, of prayer, gratitude, and self-reflection. I call this a divine meditation. With this devoted time to quiet, we can focus on being, breathing, and envisioning a healing and loving energy comprised of beautiful shades of purple and indigo.

This energy travels throughout our bodies and stimulates the energetic sources of our higher consciousness, opening these chakras to the healing light that is source energy. It connects you to your higher, intuitive self, or sense of knowing. Moments of revelation and messages from your guides may flow through your mind.

Take time to journal, reflect, set some intentions, and share your gratitude for such blessings of guidance. Or simply begin here with this divine mediation, and then further your practice by working with a set of oracle cards. Doing so is easy. Be still and feel your energy, as well as the light of the divine, move through you and into the cards, then pull a card or two. Read and take note of the card(s) pulled and from here write out a more detailed and reflective journal entry, exploring the advice or theme of the card(s) pulled. Track your evolving relationship with your team divine and sense of self in a loving yet constructive way.

# September 4

## Color Therapy
### By Nancy Meikle-Mousseau

When I was growing up, my first bedroom was painted yellow with yellow print drapes and I remember it to be very soothing and happy. When I turned eleven, all my presents were red. I loved that color and it made me feel safe and confident. When we moved homes during my early teens, I chose my bedroom colors to be purple and white. Those teenage years when we spend a lot of time in our rooms, the purple color seemed to ignite my creativity, from writing poetry, lip syncing to all my favourite folk songs, to rehearsing for the current play I was in at school.

Having a mom who was an interior designer, we were introduced to color while growing up and we learned it affected our feelings and emotions and were taught to not be afraid of color. Looking back, I loved all the chakra colors and looking in my closet today, the chakra colors are prevalent; red, orange, yellow, green, blue, purple and lilac. Color makes me happy when it is in my clothes, my home, my cars, my gardens, my surroundings.

Color affects mood, whether consciously or subconsciously. Color uplifts your spirit, making you feel happy, calm, relaxed, energized, refreshed, stimulated, or can weaken your spirit by making you feel sad, depressed, subdued, serious, reserved.

What do you see when you look in your closet?

Try wearing a dark color for a day. Be mindful of your mood and any feelings the color evokes.

The next day, choose a brighter color to wear. Color is subjective, but you will be able to tell how it makes you feel. From your wardrobe to buying fresh flowers for yourself, painting a wall in your home, bedsheets, bathroom towels or home décor, choose colors that make you happy. Be mindful of the role that color plays in your life.

# *September 5*

## The Ebb and Flow of Life
### By Florence Acosta

*T*he contrast between the ebb and flow of our own life is necessary to learn when we need to implement self-care and compassion. We cannot always be in a state of flow, nor can we always be in a state of ebb. We need them both for balance. In my experience, the ebb is a signal for self-care and a time to reset. It allows me to consider what things are good for me and what things are draining me so I may make changes that are for my highest good. It allows me to hear the whispers I have been ignoring because something did not "fit in" with the life I envisioned for myself.

Embracing the ebb is not easy because it challenges me to examine what is working and what is not. It is a necessary state of allowing me to know what I truly desire for myself. I allow myself grace during an ebb—allowing my *ebb* to *flow* so to speak. I release the need to control and surrender into where the ebb takes me. The time of ebb is letting go of how my life has been and prepares me for changes that are in my near future. I embrace it because I am doing things that are opening me up in new ways.

As you navigate the ebb and flow of your own life, remember to have self-compassion and trust that the ebb happens for a reason. Remember, it alerts your attention to something in your life that you may need to examine more deeply. It is a wake-up call that something may need to change in your life in order for it to properly flow again for your highest good.

The best part about the ebb is that it is a period of transition between what was and what is to come. You can decide what feels right and good to you. You make the choice in how you move forward with your life. That is not to say that the decisions will always be easy. Some may be easy. Others may be difficult, but necessary. The act of embracing the ebb will lead you into the flow of your life.

I invite you to journal on this prompt: What ebb in your life are you currently resisting and why?

# September 6

## Declutter
## By Danielle Fierro

*Y*es, you read correctly, decluttering your space is an act of self-care. How you feel in a room makes a huge difference in your mood and productivity. There are so many times that we keep things because we "think" we might need/use them, but we rarely do. They take up the space for things that could be of more use or bring us more joy.

Let's do a quick exercise.

Close your eyes and visualize you are in your kitchen. Imagine that your countertops are covered with appliances, utensils, and other miscellaneous items. Next, imagine your cabinets bursting with cookware, food containers, plates, glasses, and more coffee cups than you can use. You get so frustrated because you never find the proper lid for anything. Now move to the refrigerator. You open the door and a funky smell hits you. You are not sure where it is coming from and your kind of scared to see what you will find. You are not quite sure what is in there, which always makes cooking dinner interesting. You take a look at the condiments on the refrigerator door and realize that you don't recall the last time you used most of them. Finally, you go to the pantry. UGH! It takes you twenty minutes to find the spices you need for your favorite recipe because it is so disorganized. It feels like a black hole for all the pantry items that you buy because it is on sale but then forgotten about.

After visualizing all of that, how do you feel? Do you feel anxious, uninspired, annoyed, irritated, or not wanting to be in that room?

Let's do it again. Close your eyes and this time you will imagine a kitchen that has empty countertops except for a few essential appliances. The cabinets are neat and organized. There is not as much stuff in them, but you have exactly what you need. The refrigerator smells fresh, and you know exactly what is in there. You are most excited about the pantry because you know exactly where everything is, including your spices. You can get what you need for your favorite recipe in a few seconds. Now, how do you feel? Do you feel relieved, relaxed, calm, and excited to be there?

Decluttering the space you are in can keep you organized, ease anxiety, and it allows you to release what no longer serves you and makes room for the new.

# September 7

## Procrastination
## By Margaret-Maggie Honnold

*H*ere is a limerick to focus on today's topic, procrastination.

There once was a woman named Maggie,

Who found it so very handy,

To put off today,

Those things in her way,

Cause tomorrow to her seemed just dandy.

One of the biggest stumbling blocks in putting yourself first is procrastination. Everything but you get precedence. When procrastination becomes a comfort measure, it is probably not in your best interest, and self-interest and self-discipline are forms of self-love.

Procrastination has always been my specialty. I convinced myself years ago that I do my best work under pressure. You can stop laughing. This manuscript your reading is due in four days from when I am writing it. That is a good example, isn't it?

Procrastination became a defense mechanism over the years, and it did not serve me well. Whenever I was truly stressed, I shut down, put off, or ignored. It was not until I aged into the seventies with nobody around to help me that I decided that to stop procrastinating was in my self-interest.

Intermittently I tried not procrastinating. I even bought a little charm for my bracelet that said, "Just do it." But platitudes are easy to speak and hard to live—until I found a system.

All the credit for this goes to my sister, Angie Fenimore. Angie is a writing coach and *New York Times* bestselling author. She was lecturing her clients about organizing their thoughts. One thing she said changed my procrastination life and after today, I think it will change yours. It is this little phrase, "if it is only going to take five minutes and it is important, just do it."

I began the five-minute approach to everything. Five minutes to load the dishwasher, five minutes to sweep up the spilled dog food. Five minutes to put the recycling at the curb. After several days of five-minute chores, I looked around the house and wow, it was cleaned up, laundry was put away, some other little things I had been putting off were finished. I had just done them not realizing how much I was accomplishing. Now I say to myself when I start to procrastinate, "Will this take five-minutes?"

Today, pick a five-minute chore and just do it. Even though you might still be a procrastinator, by spending five minutes on a little thing just for you, you are loving yourself.

# September 8

## Life and Letting Go
## By Dee Dee Rebitt

*L*ife is all about releasing and letting go and setting yourself free from being a prisoner of your thoughts and emotions. If someone has brought harm in any way to you, release and let go, let go of the pain and toxic feelings. Are their words sharp and painful? Sometimes it can be a mirror or it's just them dumping their hurt all over you.

You will know when letting go feels right and when it does not. For me it has been a long road of letting go,

I have been walking silently in my words of forgiveness to them, sending them love, and then moving forward.

It is a choice to move forward or to stay stuck. I have spent a lot of my younger years holding on to my emotions, pain, and grief. Where it exactly got me, I have no clue, I have been learning more about myself and healing with ease and grace and moving on, learning gentleness and creating a better understanding of who needs me in my life and who I need to let go and what actions or thoughts are toxic and that does not resonate with me anymore.

We make better choices for ourselves when we become more aware of what resonates with our lives. I know my past is doing much more than healing me. I am openly and honestly sharing so that others may do the same. No matter how life played out from the beginning till now, the players, the scenes, the acts in the play called our path or our journey, you need to trust those elements no longer matter. The time is now, and I choose myself and love over any pain.

I choose forgiveness over regret. I will walk away and leave the table when I feel I need to do so if I am not being respected and boundaries need to be placed. I do it because I love my soul enough. It's unconditional love not only for me but for you as well. I do so from afar, but I do what is necessary as I let go. I do so without guilt or arguments and animosity. Let go of chains that held you a prisoner in your thoughts and emotions. Your wings lift you. Set your soul free.

# September 9

## The Blame Game
### By Judith Manganiello

*Y*ou can blame, judge, hate and be angry at everyone who plays a negative role in your life, or you can take your power back and *free* yourself …. It is all up to you.

I did not blame anyone growing up because I was comfortable in my martyrdom role. I thought it was normal to be treated like that because I just wanted to be loved. The more I healed, the more I was able to love *myself*. The more I loved myself, the more people showed up to love me.

When someone throws dirt on your Divine Radiant Light, Spirit told me that you just brush it off and Shine your Light even Brighter! When you genuinely love the Divine Radiant Love and Light within you, you then take your power back and own yourself again. You become your awakened self and then there is nothing you cannot do, have, or be. I now live-in gratitude for all my lessons. I now know who I am because I cleared it so I can finally see *me*.

I was telling a friend on the phone, "It is fortunate that God does not judge, hate or resent all of the people out here for our choices," Then out of my mouth flew "Spirit holds the space for us that we are supposed to get back to! Which is Divine Radiant Love and Light." I am going to try to do my best to do the same as God, live my life by example, which is Divine Radiant Love and Light. Living in God's Light taught me the necessity to cut the cords from all my hatred, resentments, anger, judgements, and to live my life by God's example. Everyone has the freedom to choose this path. Make a list and write down anyone who has hurt you or made you angry or hurt someone you love. Anyone or situation that you cannot free yourself from the hurt, anger, or judgement. Anyone that you cannot forgive for any reason. Take your power back by sending them Divine Radiant Love and Light and cut the cords they have tied to you. Send them the Divine Radiant Love and Light from your soul to their soul.

# September 10

## Source Self-Love
### By Lisa A. Clayton

*Y*our soul is a spiral of light energy that is eternal, complete, whole and perfect. However, with societal norms of competition, comparison, and dual consciousness, we are constantly striving to feel the connection of loving ourselves unconditionally. The good news is humanity is shifting towards more wide-spread collaboration and cooperation with each other in which love will flow more easily.

Your heart is the generator for your soul's light power and unconditional love flow. As you connect with your heart through breath, focus, and intention, your Source self-love becomes fully engaged. Source self-love is the most powerful love because it is a direct reflection of the universal creator's unconditional love that connects us all.

When you activate your soul spiral of light, you feel unconditional love that dissolves any conditional love you have been taught, experienced, or activated through competition or comparison.

Practice this ritual or create one similar to fully engage your Source self-love.

1. Breathe in and out of your heart area much slower and deeper than normal, focusing your breath into the sacred space of your heart, the area between each heart chamber, your heart's core.

2. Visualize each breath as light energy streaming from your above resources: angels, spirit guides, ancestors and ascended masters which represents your Divine Team.

3. As you inhale these beautiful light frequencies, visualize a golden spiral taking form in your heart area. Its spiral shape is sparkling and radiating with a powerful illumination of light. With each inhale feel your golden spiral growing and expanding inside and outside your heart chakra area.

4. On each exhale, radiate your beautiful golden light to every cell of your body. Start by sending rays upward to your crown chakra and downward to your root chakra all the way to the soles of your feet.

5. Feel the sensation of every vein carrying golden light to each cell in your body. Sense the luminosity of your entire being radiating Source-self's golden light.

6. Breathe deeply into your golden spiral of light in the heart area for another minute, feeling its power to dissolve negativity and non-love conditions in your life.

7. Place your hands over your heart and repeat an affirmation of Source self-love to yourself. One example is "I am Source love. I am Source light. I am committed to love my Source-self each day I am gifted on this earth."

# September 11

## Love Letter
## By Sheryl Goodwin Magiera

*I* have been blogging for several years and a few years ago I decided for Valentine's Day I would write and publish a love letter to myself. It is not often we think about writing to ourselves; if you are anything like me, probably next to never. I will be the first to admit, I felt somewhat selfish at the thought since I would be publishing it in my weekly blog post. Would people think I was self-serving and self-centered? However, the more I thought about it, the more I liked the idea of finding and celebrating the things I loved about myself and recognizing them. It was easy to name strengths about others but even more important we need to recognize and believe them about ourselves.

*Dear Precious Self:*

> *You are an amazing woman that should take time to remind yourself daily. You have raised two beautiful children, both inside and out, that are kindhearted, generous, and thoughtful. Both are independent and strong enough to stand on their own. You have provided a home filled with love and laughter.*

> *You are a loving mother, daughter, sister, aunt, and friend. You are witty, playful, dependable, and much stronger than you know. You have an adventurous spirit, love to laugh and have a tender heart. Your laugh is contagious and you're not afraid to poke fun at your wacky antics.*

> *You try hard at most things you do, and your word means everything. Even though things may not always work out as planned, you keep your commitments. You make every effort to be giving, generous,*

*kind, and polite. You are not without fault, but that makes you imperfectly perfect.*

*You are my best friend and the one that can inspire me to be better than I was yesterday. I promise to try and remember all the wonderful things I adore about you.*

*Love always,*

*Me*

Writing a letter to yourself may seem odd, even self-serving, but we owe it to ourselves to realize just how incredible we are. Even though it was challenging to write myself a love letter, it was a gift of self-love to me, from me. Give it a try; you deserve to be celebrated.

# September 12

## Endless Energy
## By Judith Manganiello

*I* used to be drained just like everyone else. My logical mind would say to me, of course you are tired. Look at all the work you did today. That happened until I received a message from Spirit.

Spirit said, "You can choose to be drained and tired, or you can use your Endless Energy." I asked Spirit what that was?

Spirit said, "It's using the energy from within. It is your Divine Light inside of you."

Since I already met my Inner Light at the age of thirty-eight, I understood what I was being told even though it was the first time I heard how to work with my Light. Now it is the only Energy I choose to use.

Exercise: I start by saying "Spirit or God (whichever one is the most comfortable for you), I am using Your Energy today."

Believe it or not it is really that simple. The hardest part of this whole exercise is to trust that you totally deserve it. Then all you have to do is ask and believe. I know how hard it is for a giver to ask for help. We are usually the ones only helping others. I used to be just like that myself. I was always only the giver and constantly being drained by my own choice of how I chose to give.

In the beginning I had to say it quite a few times a day. Then occasionally I jumped ahead of Spirit to do the work with my human energy self. Now I rarely have to say it. Because why would I want to get drained or tired anymore? Plus, I realized the best energy for me to use and the best energy to help others with would be my Divine Light Energy from within me. That is the energy that not only can help me the most, but it is never ending with sharing the best for us all.

Now I am finally a true believer! It is a gift of Love from God to you when you are open and ready to embrace it and use it

# September 13

**Lightful Seeing Eyes**
**By Charlie Fenimore**

*A*ngels love with lightful eyes for our brightest truth. It is peaceful to live in the soul of joyness and shine for freeing our hearts. Faith means living in light for our beautiful spirits from Godness so we are happy angels of love.

# September 14

## Finding the Silver Lining
## By Stephanie Fontaine

There were only four days before the final deadline for this project. I had written five of six exercises with total ease. Now here I was, a week out of the hospital after another bipolar episode, feeling broken and lost, my brain foggy and I had a severe case of imposter syndrome.

If you have never heard of or experienced imposter syndrome, it is probably one of the biggest tricks our ego plays on us. The nasty, ugly voice, deep within telling us we are not good enough, and asks, "Who do you think you are?"

In my case it asked, "Who do you think you are writing about self-love?"

I had gone days barely remembering to do the basic things we need to do to function: eat, sleep, take my medication, brush my teeth and shower. Truth be told, I am not an imposter. I have practiced self-love and self-acceptance many times over the past several years and this time my body and brain were just not on that train. The train had come off the track and there I was, trying to put it back on the track all by myself.

Sometimes in life, we need to admit that we need other people and that we need help. As a woman, I truly believe, this is the one area we dig our heels in the deepest, especially the moms of this world, and it is usually never for our highest good. Please know if you are feeling this way or have ever felt this way, you are *not* alone.

I encourage you to ask for help, even for the simplest of things so you do not end up where I did. I am very fortunate to have the most loving partner, friends and family. They all rallied around me, supported me, acted as an advocate for me when I was not capable of doing so myself. I had to surrender. I accepted the help being offered to me and for me.

One of my self-love, self-care practices during this time that helped get me back on track was to colour. It was calming, helped me focus my attention, and was a form of meditation for me. The pictures were fun. The colours were pretty and uplifting. So, give yourself permission, go colour and find the beauty and brightness within the practice. Find your silver lining of self-love.

# September 15

## Moon Meditation
## By Tonia Browne

*I am part of the rhythm of life.*

Looking at the moon and stars helps to calm me. Taking time to quieten my mind and soothe my nervous system restores my balance at the end of the day. A walk in nature, a swim in gentle waters, listening to music or taking time for a few slow, deep breaths are great ways to calm a gentle soul.

Using the energy and mystery of moonlight is something I've enjoyed over the years, although it's only recently that I've used it as part of my meditation practice to reclaim serenity, balance, and clarity. I hope the script below helps you to start or return to your own practice.

Use the atmosphere of the night's sky, either outside or near a window. Record and listen to this meditation and then sit in solitude—all offer the desired outcome.

Either with eyes open or closed, take a deep breath in. As you breathe out, place your attention on your breath and let your thoughts disperse. Anything of importance can be visited again, later. This is your time. As you breathe in, notice how this replenishes you. As you breathe out, allow the air to escape slowly. With each breath become aware that your world is slowing down and that you are merging with the space and energy around you. This state feels good. Notice the stillness. You do not need to do or think about anything, just be in this space of receptivity. Give yourself this time to relax and to receive. Allow yourself time to recharge. There are times to be active and times to let things be. The moon has its phases and so do you. Breathe in again, deeper now, filling your being with the moon's positive energy of possibilities. Feel your vibration rising and as you do notice it radiate from you. Let it ease your body, your mind, and your spirit, and beam out into your world. Then, when you feel it is time, bring your attention back to your breath and slowly back to your physical plane. When you are ready, open your eyes if they are closed and smile because you have chosen to give yourself time to be open to the mysteries offered by the moonlight.

# September 16

## Creative Balance of Earth
### By Virginia Adams

I was recently energetically shoved away from what I had known as my life's career, and I hurt physically and emotionally down to a soul's level. I was lost, confused, and deeply worried about my future. I knew I was heading in the right direction, but it felt intensely foreign to be without an earthly job.

"Ohhh, that feels glorious!"

How long had it been since I allowed myself to feel the "gooshy" feeling of mud squishing through my toes? I loved the experience, but how was this going to make me feel any better?

During the time of gooshy mud, I had been led to the concept of balancing my energy through earthing. Earthing (also known as grounding) refers to contact with the Earth's surface electrons by walking barefoot outside, sitting, or lying on the ground. I was a few days into a thirty-day grounding process, and the assignment was to create a puddle in dirt and step into it with bare feet. It was early spring, so I had to use hot water to soften the frozen ground in my garden. I still wonder what my neighbors thought of me during those days of exploration.

That was several years ago, and still to this day, I walk barefoot outside to touch, feel, and experience Mother Earth, no matter the weather outside, as Gladys Kravitz, the neighbor from *Bewitched*, looks on. During those thirty days of exploration with the healing effects of our Mother Earth, I learned that allowing five minutes a day to connect and absorb her energy in the form of electrons is life-altering. When the effects of worry plague me, showing up in my body as aches and pains or anxiety, I now know that I can take a blanket and go outside, lie flat on my tummy or my back, and receive the most amazing energetic alignment.

Ok, I hear you. What do you do if you are unable to go outside?

- Walk barefoot or lie on the concrete basement floor.
- Take a bath.
- Create an indoor garden or replant indoor plants.
- Take a "cat nap" in the sunshine.
- Step barefoot or sit on the hearth of a fireplace.
- Eat earthy root foods, or drink earthy teas.
- Lie on the floor and imagine you can feel the ground below you, even if you live in a high-rise apartment.

The creative energy of Mother Earth is transformative.

# September 17

## Releasing Guilt and Shame as Useless Emotions
### By Vonnie L. Hawkins, LCSW

*T*here is a growing body of behavioral thought that guilt and shame are truly useless, unproductive, and profoundly harmful emotions that rob us of joy and surrender to others an unearned influence over our lives. With the best intentions to drive children to behave better, good parents have been inflicting these negative emotions for generations. It is how they were raised, and so on it goes.

Research has illuminated that the residual programming and vulnerabilities produced by the emotions of shame and guilt may work in the short term to produce compliance, but in the long term they can reduce a child's, and then the adult's, motivation and capacity to excel. These negative admonitions send a message of unworthiness, and oftentimes set the goal as perfection, which is beyond human capacity to achieve.

Raise your hand if you have ever heard a parent say to a child, "Shame on you, you should know better."

In studying and teaching human behavior, I have learned that neither guilt nor shame achieves what people intend it to achieve. In fact, Brené Brown has made a career out of teaching that shame is much more likely to be responsible for the most painful, self-defeating, and outwardly projected emotions that drive harmful behavior and impair relationships of all kinds. This happens between partners, parents and children, siblings, friends, and strangers on the street. We have all done it to ourselves and to others. However, within our power lies the ability to become mindful of when this occurs, and even when we are not, we can heal and forgive ourselves, and heal and forgive others.

In your journal, can you make note of a time in the past when someone made you feel guilt or shame? Then can you write a statement of forgiving them, for doing it in the state of not knowing that they were hurting you? Then can you forgive yourself for receiving it and feeling it?

Can you make note of a time in the past when perhaps you made someone else feel guilt or shame? Then can you write a statement of forgiving yourself for doing it?

And if it is possible, can you speak or write to the person and ask for their forgiveness for conveying these negative emotions onto them? In setting this example, you become the ripple in the pond to undo this myth and bring healing to yourself and others.

# September 18

## Easing into Growth
## By Yumie Zein

A big part of having a human experience is experiencing what it is like to fully expand and live out our full potentials in whatever way that looks like. Having said that, the process of expanding and shedding those tight, limiting layers can sometimes be quite uncomfortable, to say the least.

The metaphor of a caterpillar turning into a butterfly is frequently used to describe the process of growth, but there is little said about the actual biological process that the caterpillar undergoes in this transition. There is a complete dissolving of the caterpillar's outer body, a full letting go of any semblance of what it was like to be a caterpillar. An entire restructuring, disassembly and reassembly. There is a death and rebirth that is required to accommodate this level of expansion that allows you to be someone you never were. And you do this without even knowing what you will look like or become.

As I pondered this process and how it reflected my own journey of growth, it occurred to me that the amount of love, faith, and trust required to do this was beyond anything I had ever perceived. I began to imagine the tender state of that cocooned caterpillar. How fragile and vulnerable a place it is to be. I would recall that state every time I was faced with the opportunity to expand and shed yet another layer as feelings of overwhelm, fear, distrust, judgement, and doubt would wash over me.

At times I would even enact the self-talk that that caterpillar must have been having with itself as it went through this intense journey.

In my mind I would hear, "It is all working out perfectly. Allow the process to unfold. Even though you do not know exactly what lies on the other side, you know you were born for this and that it is going to be beyond anything you have imagined. Get ready to meet your new self. Rest and ease into this growth. What you think you are losing are actually those parts of you that you no longer need, and they will be replaced with the most magnificent pieces. Just let go and breathe. Trust the process."

# September 19

## Transform Your Goals, Transform Your Life
### By Ewa Blaszczak

There is a saying that "man makes plans and God laughs." How many of the plans you made for the past year went down the drain? I know. I feel you.

Well, we need to set our goals in a totally different way. Instead of planning external achievements, let's turn inward and make our plans around our feelings which are internal and not subject to the volatility of the world. That way we are going to regain control over our lives.

Instead of thinking "what do I want to achieve this year/this month/today," ask yourself, "how do I want to feel this year/this month/today."

At the end of the day, it is not so important how many items on the to-do list you will cross off during your life. What matter is how you are going to feel about your life and what kind of a person you become.

I urge you to apply this change in mindset to things other than yourself, too. It may well be applied to people around you, your family, and your business teams. For people may forget what you said, people will forget what you did, but people will never forget how you made them feel. Therefore, when you get up from bed in the morning, think of the people you care about and ask yourself this important question, "how do I want to make them feel?"

It is not that I want you to dump all your important plans. It is just that before you make those plans, it is crucial for you to set the emotional direction first and you will see how your life is going to transform.

It is time for your exercise.

Focus your attention in the area of your heart. You may even want to touch your heart. Imagine your breath is flowing in and out of your heart. Now ask yourself the following questions:

1. How do I want to feel today, this month, this year?
2. How do I want to make others feel?

# September 20

## Creative Balance of Metal
## By Virginia Adams

*"Grief is not a disorder, a disease or a sign of weakness. It is an emotional, physical, and spiritual necessity, the price you pay for love. The only cure for grief is to grieve."*
Dr. Earl A. Grollman

*A*s I began to write about this element, I realized that I had not explored this element's creative effects as extensively as I have the other four elements. It made me wonder if I had subliminally done this on purpose as a means to hold on to the energy of grief. Now that leads me to the question, how does my grief serve me, good or bad? Throughout my life, I have experienced many levels of loss. Have I unknowingly taken that loss on as a coat of armor? Had I created my identity around what I have lost instead of what I have gained?

According to Chinese medicine, the element of metal represents structure and boundaries. Balanced metal allows for healthy boundaries, a manageable routine, and inspiring rituals; on the other hand, too little metal will lead to sloppiness and numbness. When metal becomes overbearing, which I believe is the case in my life, we will have difficulty expressing ourselves with intimacy and spontaneity.

To keep metal balanced, we need structure and routine complemented with an ability to let go and allow ourselves to be supported. We find balance when we soften our boundaries to connect with others, be social and spontaneous, and give ourselves the time to follow our passion.

When I hold myself back, disallowing spontaneity, silliness, and authentic, intimate interaction, I am wearing my grief as a coat of armor. Grief is not a destructive emotion; it is a catalyst to live life to its fullest with no regrets.

Stop right here, right now, put down this book and get up and do a super silly, unencumbered dance. Let go and engage in the creative force of metal. I support you right now, right here in the silly expression and life-giving energy of the dance of life.

Allowing ourselves to be spontaneous, silly, and accepting the support of others is a means of self-love and self-care. Do you have any silly voices or faces you would like to add to your dance of life? Go ahead. I won't tell anyone.

# September 21

## Love Yourself Juice
## By Jamie Rudolph

*T*ry an exercise in self-love with the addition of a daily juice or an extended juice cleanse. Raw, organic, fresh-pressed juices are full of nutrients to support and nourish your body. Fresh juices are a natural way to boost energy, detoxify the body, and boost your immune system. Flood the body with vitamins and minerals and feel lasting benefits of juicy- love.

### *Love Yourself Juice*

*Makes approximately 32 ounces*
2-3 granny smith apples
1-2 lemons, skin removed
1 thumb size piece of ginger root
1 large or 2 small cucumbers
½ bunch of celery
½ bunch of parsley
½ bunch of kale

Chop ingredients into smaller pieces if needed. Process ingredients in a juicer. Pour into your favorite glass. Enjoy!

Have fun and experiment with your favorite fruits and veggies and find your perfect juicy mix.

# September 22

## Inner Wisdom
## By Sheryl Goodwin Magiera

*I*nner wisdom, also known as intuition, is something we all possess. It knows our truths, our authentic selves and hearts. We had no trouble following our inner wisdom as children; it was natural, easy, and felt good, but as adults we think too logically and somehow manage to creep out of our heart space and into our head. Letting the head take over will wreak havoc on our minds, bodies, and spirits.

The head space is the ego and is cloaked in fear, anger, chaos, the past, the future, and pride; the list goes on. It keeps a hold on us and tells us lies about ourselves that cause fear and self-doubt to take over. Ultimately, it keeps us stuck and holds us in the past of should haves and could haves.

I have been working on developing my intuition skills and listening to what I need. I have been consciously getting out of my head space and opening my heart. The heart is connected to our higher self, knows exactly what our soul desires. It's drama-free and is seated in love. Along with love, it baths us in joy, forgiveness, being present, humility, peace, acceptance, and understanding. The heart is where our intuition resides and if you listen, it is the little voice that guides us.

Sometimes our inner guidance speaks to us in a soft whisper. Other times, it practically bops us over the head desperately trying to get our attention. If you have not been hearing any messages from your heart, it's most likely you have been ignoring it again and again. The good news is that it will always return when we decide to listen. And it will be patient and faithful when it does.

It is time to reconnect with your heart again. Commit to rediscovering who you truly are and what you are meant to do. Each time you listen to your intuition, acknowledge, and respect it and do what it is asking. It will always be truthful. Stay curious, open, and wise like the owl. Inner wisdom will come.

# September 23

## Five Steps to Level up Your Look
## By Melanie Morrison

*H*ave you ever thought of changing yourself or completely reinventing your look? We change so much inside. Why not allow ourselves to change on the outside? What if we looked at our body as a canvas of expression? What if we empowered ourselves to unapologetically be the artist? Let's work through this process together in steps:

- Reflect and journal on how you have changed. Your beliefs, values, age, hobbies, relationships, career, and /or ideas about things.

- Now sit in front of a full-length mirror look at yourself lovingly and ask what you would like to upgrade, update, reinvent, and/or level up? Take a moment to journal your thoughts and feelings. Be gentle. This is not a self- bashing session. This is an act of love and an opportunity to let go, free yourself from the past, wipe the slate clean and step into a whole new you created solely out of self-love. Let go of any past labels and allow yourself the freedom to reinvent your-self however you wish.

- Send love and gratitude to everything that you are ready to let go of. Thank them for serving you for the time. If it is a style, thank it for making you feel good at the time. If it is a body change, thank those parts of your body for doing the best it could under the conditions it had. Appreciate what is, put your hand on it and send it love. Now lovingly let it know it's time for a new and exciting change. Think of it as an adventure.

- Now it is time to research everything you decided to level up. This part is especially important with both style and body changes. With style, you will want to search different types of current styles to not only find new ones but to also rediscover your taste. The exciting thing about researching health and fitness is that there are so many new methods, updated research, ideas, and information on the internet. Take full advantage of all the online tools at your fingertips.

- Lastly, let go of anyone's desire to keep you the same. Reclaim your right to change. If you feel reluctant still, sometimes it is helpful to go a bit M.I.A. while you are "under construction." Enjoy the change and embrace the new you! This is your life. Allow yourself to shine!

# September 24

## Personal Enrichment
## By Tanya Thompson

*I*n his book *Outliers*, Malcolm Gladwell explains that it takes about ten thousand hours to become an expert in most fields. Ten thousand hours is about five years of work, considering an average forty-hour work week. However, there are a few exceptions.

During the first half of the year 2020, I found myself with a bar of more than twenty bottles of Kentucky bourbon, mostly unopened. After a bit of online research, I decided to taste them all and work to identify their nuanced and unique flavors. After all, we were in the middle of a pandemic and quarantined at home.

The Stave and Thief Society, through Moonshine University, offers an online program to become a certified bourbon steward. The course is around $60 and includes a small book on the history of bourbon, how it's made, the various requirements for bourbon and how to assemble and present a bourbon tasting flight. I've started and finished larger books on an airline flight or waiting to be called at the dentist's office. The self-paced course includes an online test to complete your certification. All of this can be accomplished in just a few hours over the course of a couple of weeks.

Personally, this first step opened an entire world for me that had previously been unknown. I completed "100 Days of Bourbon" on Instagram, entered a World's Top Whiskey Taster contest, started a private neighborhood bourbon society, and met hundreds of new people that I would have otherwise never met, locally and internationally. Additionally, learning more about bourbon and being able to discuss it more intelligently has opened up other conversations and relationships for me, both personally and professionally.

What area of your life could you devote a little more time and effort to enrich your personal experience? What topics would you like to discuss with others that have similar interests? Is there a club in your community or online that you can join? If not, can you create one? What small step can you take today that will get you one hour closer to being an expert in an area of personal interest?

The importance of one hour a week or month, spent on a subject that interest you, cannot be understated. Dare I say it can be life altering? What is your next step?

# September 25

## Movement for the Soul
### By Delores Garcia

*O*ur physical bodies were designed to move and work. When we neglect this aspect of well-being, our bodies show the effects. A fond memory from my childhood is of my mom telling my brother, sister, and I to "Just go outside and play." She knew it was what we *needed*. Today as you ask your High Self what you need, you might be told the same! What kind of movement appeals to your soul right now? You can make any activity truly self-caring when you set the intention to reconnect to Source and honor your soul's desires. Movement also has a profound impact on raising our vibrational frequency. Not only are our bodies made to move, but our souls are also! It is a win-win for the whole of us! Please consider the following examples and make them your own.

When I desire an enhanced sense of empowerment and strength, I might go to the gym and do a conscious and intentional weightlifting workout.

When I desire an enhanced flow of pure energy and vitality, I might go for a brisk walk outside or use cardio equipment in the gym, setting the intention to have my blood course vigorously through my body with its renewing and refreshing energy.

When I desire centering and grounding, I might do a yoga flow, setting the intention to slow down and be present with myself. I am in complete solitude within myself even if I am in the middle of a packed studio.

When I am feeling in need of clarity and perspective, I might get in the pool or creek, floating or swimming or paddling around, setting the intention to have my perspective cleansed and endowed with clarity.

Do you need to feel love? Safety? Connectedness? Gratitude? Divinity? Self-honor? Courage? How can you consciously and intentionally move your body to receive those today?

Movement for the soul does not have the same intention as a regular workout/exercise program, although you might do the same activity. The intention is different. The intention is based on answering the question: "What does my soul need today?" This is where self-care begins and your transformation into a healed soul blossoms! Welcome to your new life of happiness!

# September 26

## Accepting Change is a Form of Self-Love
## By Talia Renzo

*I*f I were to ask you, how would you describe yourself? Would you say, "I work full time. I am a parent. I am a son or daughter. I am a brother or a sister. I am a friend. I am a husband, or wife. I am a student."

In any of those answers, would you say that you struggle filling the roles of any of those positions? Do you work full time at a job you hate? Do you struggle in relationships and feel like you cannot be your true authentic self? If you struggle with filling these positions in your life, and you feel like you cannot do it to your best ability, please know you are not alone.

Everyone has struggled in each and every one of those departments. Please take this crucial feedback with you when I say do not hide yourself in self-doubt and drown in low self-esteem because of your insecurities. If you struggle trying to be a good parent, child, teenager, employee, friend, family member, or lover, don't be too hard on yourself for not being the best. Do not hold a higher expectation of yourself through the eyes of what you think everyone else sees. Do not juggle more than what you can handle. Believe it or not, this is a serious act of self-love. Part of self-love is radically accepting that you cannot please everybody.

Whenever you accept a role in your life, do not lose yourself and the other parts of you that make you who you are in the process. Do not primarily focus on one role that doesn't nurture your soul. If it brings you more pain, distress, and takes away from who you are, it is not meant for you. That might be investing in a job that has no opportunity for growth or you have a toxic relationship in your life that is taking more than it is giving. Sometimes it hurts more to hold on, than it does to let go. Let go of anything that no longer serves you.

What others think of you is none of your business. Do not stay stuck somewhere just because your insecurities, anxiety, or flaws tell you to "stay put" because it's "convenient" or it's "comfortable." Take a step into who you deserve to become. Follow your heart, and your dreams will pave the way for you.

# September 27

## Spiritual Batteries
## By Ashlie Bradley

*D*o you feel disconnected or out of sorts? Or maybe you feel like you are just existing and drifting. If so, it sounds like you need to recharge your spiritual batteries!

There are a multitude of ways to start firing up that soul of yours! Since we are all on our own paths, each exercise will benefit each of us differently. The goal is to find what works best for you. So, let us explore.

Yoga: Movement of the body, connection to our inner world, and breathe. A cocoon of stillness to the chattering mind. The aim isn't to stress over the postures, but to rest in presence. With a closing of the eyes, a releasing of the judgments, and a cleansing breathe, we can let it go.

Reading: The most significant role in this from my experience, is finding an author you connect too. Not only are books a great way to gain spiritual connection and awareness, but reading is a simple way to just slow down. Go to your local bookstore and see what calls to you. Maybe ask your angels for guidance upon entering the store. Audiobooks are also available right at your fingertips. Find a book that becomes a friend. You want to look forward to your time spent. Nestle in and allow a re-charge.

Journal: Pen to paper is just magical, folks! Write. It. Out. Write the lessons, the grief, the repetitive thoughts, the disappointments, whatever needs to be out of your brilliant being! All the excess jargon is sure to drain the batteries. Write it out and be done! If you're up for it, have a mini full moon ritual. After jotting it all down, go out into the moonlight, and SAFELY burn it to ash. Allow the moon to fill the dark with light.

The more you make spiritual practice a routine in your life, the more you will experience the wonderous benefits. Consistency is key in keeping the batteries charged! Now allow the Universe to conspire in your favor!

# September 28

## Joy
### By Symone Desirae

What brings you joy? When you take note of this, how does this make you feel? Where in your body do you feel this sensation? There are many times that we lose our own inner joy due to daily life such as work, relationships, and even just being burned out. Remember when we were kids and the simplest things like skipping rocks on the water, or going outside and getting our hands dirty in the soil brought us so much delight? Our inner child wants to play!

I can think of a time when I took life way to seriously. I had these expectations and demands on myself to always strive for the best, and to put all of my effort into my work and career. This made me feel sluggish, tired, and unmotivated.

I started to take notice of a pattern when I would go out to my family cabin and feel such great joy and happiness out there, but the minute I was back I would start to slowly feel the same tired way. After continuing this cycle for far too long I asked *Why don't I bring joy into my daily life?*

There comes a time when your inner child is screaming to play. Allow yourself to do just that. I love being out in nature, closing my eyes and smelling the fresh air, hearing the birds chirping, and the sound of the wind rustling. My family cabin is a place where I can connect with my inner child by going down to the river and splashing around in the water, or just running through the woods with my dog, occasionally stopping to look at the beauty of nature around me. When I am not at my cabin, I am going for walks in parks, doing baking at home, or even singing in the shower at the top of my lungs.

When was the last time you felt joy? What are some things you do to connect with your inner child? Write at least three things that bring you joy and start incorporating them into your life. Here are some things that can spark your joy and bring out your inner child;

- Singing
- Dancing
- Skipping rope
- Skating
- Gardening
- Being in nature
- Going to the beach

# September 29

## Writing Your Own Headlines
## By Ellen Elizabeth Jones

*T*he written word is one of the most powerful and influential tools humanity has created. Writing is how you can communicate with others and is also a way you can communicate with yourself, tapping into your thoughts, becoming aware and releasing yourself from fears, and creating your dreams. It is a way to release and express your thoughts, feelings, and emotions. When you take time to put your thoughts on paper, you're providing space to understand yourself more fully so that you can live a more authentic life. It can be a life-changing habit.

Setting aside five minutes each morning to connect with yourself is one of the most beneficial things you can do to create your day. Many benefit from setting their alarm a few minutes earlier to create space for this sacred practice.

Commitment and consistency create results. If you make it a daily habit, the following practice can reduce anxiety, increase clarity, and help direct intention. Your morning journaling lets you acknowledge and let go of discomfort. It provides clear, objectives for the day, helps set your mood, and shifts you to a space of gratitude, creativity, and hope. This practice can shift and expand your experiences.

Here is one way to begin. As always, listen to your own inner guidance and tweak it however your spirit guides you.

You will need a pen you love to write with and a journal of your choice.

- You will want to write the date at the beginning of each day.
- Write freely. Write stream-of-consciousness. You may find that you wake up and have anxious thoughts about the day

ahead or perhaps you feel excitement about opportunities that may be created. You may feel tired. Whatever the thought or emotion, write it out. You may find that they do not make much sense. Put anything and everything you are thinking on paper. Get it out of your head. This helps you clear space for the thoughts that you want to consciously put in your mind.

Start by doing this for a single day. Then do it the next. Before you know it, it will become a new habit.

# September 30

## Cultivating Self-Love
## By Carolan Dickinson

*I*t always seems to be easier to develop a relationship with others than it does with ourselves. Why do you think that is? I tend to believe it is because most of us will be more judgmental and harder on ourselves than we are with other people. With other people, we have dialogues and communications. And we also have constant inner discussions and conversations with ourselves. This can be where most of us get into trouble. When we have harsh or judgmental thoughts about ourselves, we are internalizing that communication. What we focus on we believe and internalize. And if we internalize something, then we believe that negativity must be true. At least that is what our spirit hears, and our mind, body, and spirit respond to that belief. What if you could reframe every negative thought you had into something positive? What if you believed that you are as amazing as I know you to be?

For a day, try to write down every negative thought that you have. It can be anything including the simple stuff like "I don't know why I'm cleaning the house, no one appreciates it anyway" or "That was really dumb. I don't know why I said that." For today just list every one of those negative thoughts. On the next day, I like you to go back to what you wrote and challenge those ideas, turning them into positive statements. For example, "I do not know why I'm cleaning the house, no one appreciates it anyway" can be reframed as "I clean house because I'm grateful for my home and it makes me feel good." The thought "That was dumb, I don't know why I said that" could be reframed into "I always speak in loving and kind ways."

Affirmations and reframing, our inner dialogue keeps us focused on the positive, and according to the law of attraction will create more positivity. Have fun creating your own reframes. I am happy to share some of my favorites.

"My soul shines as bright as a million stars on a moonlit night."

"I support and love the people around me."

"I am loved and supported by the people around me."

"Every day and in every way, I am divinely guided and protected."

# October 1

## Fear as Fuel
## By Nanette Gogan-Edwards

*L*ove yourself enough to be honest with others about your fears.

This morning I listened to a short interview between Brendon Burchard and the late Larry King. Mr. King told the story of his first day on live radio. His fears, doubts, and anxieties all came to a head the moment he went on the air. For the first two minutes he said nothing until the producer gave him a scolding and told him to "say something!" He then proceeded to tell his audience about his fear and doubts. This vulnerability gave him the confidence he needed to continue, and the rest is history. He became one of the most well-known and respected reporters ever to hit the airwaves.

Love yourself enough to be confident in your vulnerabilities, knowing that we all have fears and doubts. Your ability to push through these feelings results in an amazing breakthrough and a huge confidence boost!

"Vulnerability is the birthplace of innovation, creativity and change." ~ Brené Brown.

Many times, we feel guilty and/or unworthy of true joy and fulfillment. Love yourself enough to allow joy to enter and stay in your life and love others enough to share it.

Remember, fear is not from God. Fear is the enemy whispering lies in your ear, filling you full of doubt. The things you fear the most are the things that will catapult you into the next level of spiritual growth and happiness. You are not only worthy, but you have the privilege and the obligation to move forward!

# October 2

### I am a Producer
### By Mindy Lipton

*A*fter a week of driving from New Haven, Connecticut to Los Angeles, California I felt pretty self-assured. I found a fabulous job as a secretary working for a cardiologist on Camden Drive, parallel to the infamous Rodeo Drive.

I stayed at that job for ten years, working eight to five, Monday through Friday. The doctor was a pleasure to work for. I am still in contact with him and his wife to this day. He was always like father figure to me.

I decided to get married and leave the eight to five and work behind the scenes in the entertainment industry. Tri-Star Pictures hired me as an assistant in a production company in Century City. This was the holiday season and all that was ever on my desk the short time that I was employed there were issues of the trade papers. Oh yes, and a poinsettia plant. "Bored to tears" was an expression I had often heard but now the tears were really flowing down my cheeks nightly. I would get home from work and cry to my newly-wed husband because I was so bored. I told my boss that I would have to look elsewhere for work if she was not going to keep me busy. She brought in a script for me to retype. It was disgusting. Filthy language and it was not what I meant by busy work.

After a doctor's appointment, I walked back into the office and said, "Well, I'm going to produce! Yes, I'm going to have a baby!"

Weeks passed and my boss informed me that they needed to let me go. I was so taken back that I asked, "Go where?"

I thought for a moment and asked, "Can you fire me if I'm pregnant?"

She asked me if I was going to sue? That was not my intention, but we had to pursue.

After three months of pregnancy, I looked more like five months. I went to have an ultrasound and it showed three babies on the screen. I was expecting triplets. I was so shocked that I remember the first words out of my mouth were, "Do I move back to Connecticut?"

My husband and I raised them in Northern California. I never was the performer, but I sure made one helluva producer!!! No fertility. Manifestation is what brought us our miracles.

You deserve to get your goals and to not settle in life. Set a list of five things you want to manifest in your life. The first step to manifest them is by writing them down each day, first thing in the morning, every morning, allowing yourself to focus and center on them during your day.

# October 3

## Put Your Oxygen Mask On
## By Carrie Newsom

*M*any women, myself included, are people pleasers. I have four kids who have special needs, and for eighteen years, all I did was take care of them. I devoted myself to them. I sacrificed almost everything about myself in order to make sure my children lived as healthy and happy lives as I could possibly provide for them. Ultimately, this enormous sacrifice led to my body and soul feeling depleted, frazzled, and dried up.

Throughout my parenting years, I was told that the most important person to care for was myself. After all, if you do not put your own oxygen mask on first, you won't be able to help anyone else. My brain understood this message, but my heart and soul fought it. I ate, breathed, and slept my children. I moved Heaven and Earth so they would have each of their needs met. I am the ultimate mama bear. Nothing and no one got in the way of me finding resources and support for my kids. No one got in the way except for myself.

Because I spent almost two decades neglecting myself and my needs, my body, heart, and soul started to revolt. I became very ill. I had debilitating anxiety, insomnia, and a multitude of diagnoses. I had not put the oxygen mask on myself for twenty years, and it began to catch up with me.

I realized I needed to figure out what I want, who I am, what I want to do. For the first time in decades, I allowed myself time to think about me. I began to care for myself. I realized that I love to create. When I create it is like my heart glows brighter and more intensely. On a whim, I enrolled in an art class, which was something I had always adored but had not participated in since I was in high school. I began to write more frequently. I immersed myself in *creating*, and my soul began to bloom. I found space and light and inspiration inside of me.

I encourage you to find a way to create. Let a piece of your soul out into the world; express yourself and see what happens. You are the most important person to care for. You deserve to be cared for, comforted, and feel safe in expressing yourself. Creating brings risk, but also great satisfaction.

# October 4

## Maintaining Boundaries
## By Denise Kirkconnell

If you have ever dealt with a difficult person, which I know we all have at different times in our lives, the importance of setting and maintaining boundaries is absolutely paramount. When we allow others to make decisions for us, or when we go along with things to keep the peace, we are only violating our personal boundaries. Doing so can cause intense internal turmoil.

In order to set and maintain your personal boundaries, you must first stop constantly explaining yourself. Your boundaries only need to be briefly explained. Do not offer explanations to people who try to ignore the boundaries. They will try over and over until they tire of your reinforcing with gentle reminders. In my experience most people will push back against any changes from what they are used to.

Some will become angry, and most will say you are being difficult. Stand firm in your new power. Only you can make boundaries stick. Ignore all the name calling and know they too are going through a change. As with all changes, they will take time to adapt to them.

When the day comes and you realize you are now being taken seriously, there is a feeling of personal empowerment that comes with that.

Enjoy.

# October 5

## Being a Super Mom
## By Karen Cowperthwaite

*I* do not exactly remember when I changed into my Super Mom costume. It was not like in the movies, where the unassuming news reporter with glasses sneaks into the phone booth and emerges as a buff flying hero. But somewhere along the way, I morphed into the role of mother, and the woman I was before kids faded away. My interests and passions began to disappear along with the awareness to even care. I had the faulty belief that it was easier to succumb to everyone else's wants and needs than it was to assert my own.

The chipping away at my identity did not really hit me until much later in my motherhood journey. One night my oldest shared an essay she had written. The first sentence read, "My mom is the most selfless person I know." Listening to my daughter describe this woman with the big heart, who taught her life lessons and had significantly impacted her thoughts and actions brought tears to my eyes. It also caused a certain word to rattle around in my head.

*Selfless.*

Without a self? Forgetting myself? Less of herself? The realization hit me hard that I had been avoiding my own self-care and I was modeling an expectation that a mother's role is to put everyone's needs before her own.

Self-care is what you decide you need; it is what you enjoy and what makes you feel inspired. It is how you speak to yourself and that is one of the easiest places to start. I started with reading inspiring passages each morning, following positive social media accounts, and discovering affirmations to say out loud as I looked into the mirror.

Making an "I feel good" list is one way to let your family know what inspires and delights you. So often as the family giver, mothers inherently know what their kids like and exactly how they like it. It's also important that you share what brings *you* joy and puts a smile on *your* face. You may not know exactly what you want, but you can experiment and figure it out. Create a doable self-care list of activities that signifies that self-care is your responsibility. Remember caring for yourself does not mean that someone else is not being cared for. Self-love is knowing you are deserving of your own love as well as the love of others.

# October 6

## My Journey to Self Love
## By Gloria Dawn Kapeller

*M*y weight issues started when I was six years old. I arrived at my foster family that later adopted me. The sexual abuse started immediately and in trying to deal with this, eating and stuffing my feelings became a way to cope. I gained forty pounds that first year and so began my lifelong struggle with weight, body image, and self esteem. After my first son was born, I began to eat and purge, so I became bulimic. I lost over one hundred pounds that way and was pleased with myself, but then started throwing up blood, so I really wrecked my stomach. I then decided that my son was more important than this so stopped. I gained weight again and tried every weight loss fad out there, and over the next many years I joined TOPS and Weight Watchers in hopes that they could help me. I continued to gain and lose the same weight over and over. Needless to say, I'm sure that my metabolism was totally wrecked. Surprisingly, my health remained pretty good, but I was considered obese, and I did develop high blood pressure.

At the age of fifty-five when I began dealing with my past. I also approached my doctor about bariatric surgery. After a year of appointments and showing that I was ready for this surgery, I had my surgery. Some may think that this was an easy way out, but it absolutely is not the case. I now am again at the point where I am healthy. I also had a breast reduction and a pandectomy (fat removal from the stomach area). I am feeling that this was also part of my journey as a part of the healing process for me. I feel that I match the inside with what is on the outside.

How can you make yourself feel good each and every day? I write down affirmations:

I am beautiful just the way I am.

I am enough.

I am safe to be me.

# October 7

## Boundaries
## By Crystal Cockerham

*I*t is okay to say no.

Especially if you do not have the desire to or the time. Neither party is going to benefit from you trying to cram in one more thing.

Think of your energy pool as an investment account. Even though it is your money, you cannot touch it because it is tied up in investments. So do not overcommit and run your energy account into the red; you will come out ahead in the end.

In practicing saying yes to yourself and no to others, you fortify your energetic and spiritual boundaries. This allows you (and you alone) that direct access to your personal power, your energy account.

Formulating and practicing setting, maintaining, and fortifying your boundaries can seem like a daunting task. It does not have to be. Here are a few simple tips to help you get started with mindfully setting and honoring your boundaries.

1. Start visualizing what it could look like if you only said yes to that which you truly want to invest your time and energy in rather than playing into what you feel is expected of you.

2. Write down on a sticky note something that kindly says no such as "Thank you for thinking of me, but this is not something I can commit to or say yes to at this time." Practice saying it! You do not need to justify or explain your no to anyone.

3. Visualize someone asking something of you and this being your response. By practicing saying it before there is a commitment to say no, you help yourself set boundaries and strengthen your personal power.

4. Write out multiple sticky notes with varying responses and/ or reminding yourself to say yes to yourself and place them where they are in your sightline. Put them on the bathroom mirror, in your wallet, on the dashboard of your car, in your office space, on the refrigerator, on a kitchen cupboard. Take a picture and make it a screensaver on your electronic devices, etc. At first this may seem like overkill, but the constant reminder will help your mindfulness kick in sooner!

Commit consciously by asking yourself: Do I really have the time and energy for this? Is this something that I truly want to do?

# October 8

## The Truth of Love
## By Courtney Parreira

We are taught to love one another, to turn the other cheek, to do to others as we would have done to us. We are taught to honor our parents, to be truthful, and to respect our elders.

What if we were also taught to love ourselves, to give ourselves another chance, to be kind to ourselves especially after we make a mistake? What if we were taught to honor our intuitive knowing of who we really are, to be true to our soul, and to respect the innate wisdom passed on to us by our ancestors?

It is not too late. It is perfect timing to offer these gifts to yourself. Tap into the great mothering energy offered by Gaia and allow her to guide you through these truths. She is the perfect mother from which to learn.

Offer this prayer to Gaia as you look to learn from her:

*Blessed Gaia,*

> *I am grateful for all that you offer me, and I ask for your guidance and support in teaching me of the love, forgiveness, and trust that I can offer myself, just as a masterful mother offers to her child.*

> *Thank you, thank you, thank you.*

# October 9

## JOY
### By Giuliana Melo

*J*oy is the highest expression of love, yet it is an energy that is not tapped into on a daily basis. Joy seems to be something that we humans tap into sporadically. Well, that is up until now because I am going to share how I learned how to do it.

A beautiful way to tap into joy is to ask in the archangel Jophiel. She is the archangel whose name means "beauty of God." Her colour is brilliant yellow like the sun. I learned to invoke her energy by saying out loud or in my head: *I now invoke the beautiful bright yellow light of archangel Jophiel. Please help me infuse more joy into my life. Please help me experience joy. Amen and so it is.* It really is this easy. I sometimes like to wear the colour yellow to remind me that she is with me. I may also wear yellow gemstones, such as citrine to help me elevate my vibration to connect with hers.

Once I have invited her in, I follow my intuition and take action with people, places, and things that bring me joy. Three ways of inviting more joy in are:

1. tune into your intuitive guidance
2. trust the signs that you are getting
3. take action

The way to do this is to become present. Presence is the awareness of being in this current moment. The way I do it is STOPPING what I am doing. BREATHING into this moment, breathing in deeply and exhaling slowly, I ASK for what I need and then OPEN myself up to receive.

Another way is by placing your feet flat on the floor. Connect with the white light of the divine through your crown area on the top of your head and then place a hand on your heart. Then breathe in happy energy and exhale any yucky energy you are holding onto.

I do that a few times until I feel a shift. Go ahead. Try it.

**How will you bring JOY in today?**

These are a few of my favourite ways:

- pet cuddles
- random acts of kindness
- music
- nature
- sunshine
- swimming
- playing games
- watching a funny movie
- colouring
- dancing

In your journal, write down ways that bring you great joy and be sure to tap in every day. That is the secret.

# October 10

## Body Lovin'
## By Lisa Seyring

*H*ow often do any of us stop and take the time to marvel at what a miraculous body we reside in? It is through our magnificent body that our soul can experience life. One day through a guided meditation, I was directed to relax my scalp. I could hear my brain clicking, trying to grasp and process this command. Never had I once considered there were muscles in my scalp to *be* relaxed! It was actually quite eye opening. The act of relaxing these muscles in my scalp allowed me to I realize just how much tension I had been holding in my head and ultimately my entire body. Go head, relax your scalp. It feels marvelous!

This experience alerted me to the need of giving my body much more of my attention. I made a conscious choice to relax different parts of my body with regularity. Reiki enhanced this practice by teaching me to love and appreciate my organs. I reveled in the new way I was being present and actively loving my body. I experimented with relaxing my jaw and loving my kidneys! I became deeply aware and appreciative of each of my organs and the roles they played to keep me alive. Ultimately, I expanded my inward care to include extending love and gratitude to the systems of my body. I no longer took the actual wonder of my human body for granted.

The following practice is to simply start a rhythm of being present and lovingly grateful for all parts of your body.

Taking three deep breaths will get you settled and then you can move your attention inward. Allow yourself to "look" inside your body, taking your time to focus on and acknowledge each of your organs individually—heart, lungs, kidneys, liver, etc. It may feel awkward at first, but your body will be ecstatic that you are talking to it! Tell each organ how much you appreciate it and its function in your body. Tell it "thank you" and "I have so much love and gratitude for you."

Do not rush this process. Pause and allow each organ to receive your love and gratitude. I invite you to include the systems of the body (nervous, skeletal, endocrine, respiratory, circulatory, etc.) in your repertoire as well. May your journey inward be all that your body had ever hoped for!

# October 11

## Vibrational Eating
## By Bonnie Larson

*E*ating is a daily activity we all have in common. Food is a multi-billion-dollar industry. Everywhere we look, we can see, touch, taste, smell, or sense the allure of its temptation.

Unlike other addictive behavior, there is no quitting *cold turkey*! Like a great romance, my relationship with food may ebb and flow, unfortunately, measured by inches and pounds.

"Less is good," I would convince myself, or perhaps "Hungry is a good feeling." Abstinence is not the answer. As we push away from it, we create an attraction.

It is all about the relationship. Food is not our friend nor our opponent. Some food, in moderation, is necessary. The key, for me, is to understand the vibration of food. First, is the *charge* positive? If we listen, our bodies will tell us what it needs. Tune in.

Our bodies may shout about cookies, but rest assured, this is not a food group.

Universal mysteries pique my curiosity. The electromagnetic spectrum reveals everything has a vibration, including food. Weight, volume, molecules, stored energy, and proportions—it sounds like science. Have you ever noticed the *weight* of food takeout? So often, it is *heavy*. Not on my rump! Seriously, though, that is our sign. An interesting concept from ministerial training is the ancient Essene restricted the *weight* of their daily consumption. Honestly! Three pounds of maximum intake, no exception. One take out can easily exceed the maxim. Next, never more than three food types at one sitting as some food combinations combust. Finally, food is to be seeded, grown, and cultivated with love in our local environment. All the vitamins and minerals we require for maximum health and immunity exist within a twenty-mile radius of home. Thank you, Graham Kerr, The Galloping Gourmet, for bringing this to our attention! Officially, this is called *cuisine*.

Ancient grains, seeds, and nuts provide nutrition for added health and wellness. Until the twenty-first century, glucose intolerance was relatively unknown. If we listen to our bodies, they speak loudly.

My body responds quickly to the clear, clean vibration of a good salad, vegetables, and fruits, yet is soothed with the comfort of a nutritionally made homemade soup. Remember to include vibrantly radiating rainbow colors, building blocks of a healthy body.

Lastly, *feel* into the expression *well water*. Vibrationally, it is far more appealing than plastic bottled water. Like all food, fresh is best!

# October 12

## Self-Love Check List
## By JoAnne Eisen

*T*angible ways to practice self-love and self-care.

I unconditionally love myself and share that with others.

I honor and respect myself.

I believe I am enough. I have enough. I do enough.

I make time to care for my needs without guilt.

I buy myself flowers because I am valuable.

I understand the importance of practicing deep breathing.

I write myself heartfelt love letters.

I make time to sit with my higher self in quiet time or meditation.

I light an aromatic candle and set my intentions.

I trust my desires and needs will be taken care of.

I love and care for my body, making it whole, healthy, and balanced.

I solely focus my attention on what I eat as it nourishes my body.

I make wise and loving choices to put foods with nutritional value in my body.

I go out into nature to breathe, move, and release all things unwanted.

I allow and trust myself to try new things to expand my mind.

I am not afraid to do my inner work. It brings me peace and calm.

I listen to beautiful, uplifting music, and I may even dance and laugh.

I make time for my friends that uplift and encourage me in love and truth.

I keep a gratitude journal, knowing the importance of remembering how blessed I am, and I am grateful for it.

# October 13

## How Your Body Talks to You
## By Bernadette Rodebaugh

- Extra weight gain or loss of weight unexpectedly.
- Easily irritable.
- Health issues that keep recurring or are not able to be resolved.
- Thinning hair or turning gray rapidly.
- Sleep issues. This can mean *not* sleeping through the night or waking up at inconvenient times or that your body is tired, and you are wanting to take naps during the day.
- Wanting overindulgence with food or liquor.

Since I have primarily been working with women for more than twenty years, I have noticed women are very good at lying to themselves about their lack or need of self-love! Then they wonder why their husband doesn't treat them better or why they keep attracting men who don't treat them "right" or why their children don't respect them more. *Remember nobody is going to treat you better than you treat yourself. This also means nobody is going to love you more than you love yourself!*

We teach people how to treat us by how we treat ourselves, which is self-love.

To me this means that *in my life I make myself a priority and then everyone else*. This often has a stigma of selfishness, but I beg to differ! Airlines show this example best. Have you ever seen the video on the airlines when they explain what to do if the airplane starts losing oxygen? These directions distinctly show *the mother* putting the mask on herself and then putting it on her child. This is because in reality of the airplane, you really help no one if you pass out. But the bigger picture in life is that if you do not take care of yourself, then you're not going be around for your family for as long as you possibly could. That is because you will wear yourself out.

Today, right now, let's reclaim your self-love as you read out loud the following.

*"Starting today I will no longer put myself last on my priority list, because I know when I do this it shows up as extra weight, sleeplessness, aging my body faster than it should, extra glasses of wine that I regret in the morning or being irritable with others when I'm really angry at myself!*

*I promise to make myself a priority and by doing this I will teach everyone around me how to respect me and love me on a deeper level because I am worth loving!"*

# October 14

## Reconnecting
## By Janice Story

*I* love being outside in nature, listening to sounds around me, feeling the warm sun on my face, and a slight breeze brushing against my skin. Spending time with my horses or dogs always brings me joy and gets me out of my busy mind. I feel as human beings we've become so disconnected, and task oriented that we forget to make time for simple things in life. We desire materialistic items that our children will one day stress over having to sift through as they are mumbling under their breaths about all the crazy stuff we have gathered through the years.

We have forgotten how to just be present, how to be comfortable with ourselves enjoying our own company. When was the last time you simply went for a walk and really noticed all of the things around you? The birds singing, an ant crawling on the ground, the shapes in the clouds, or the incredible sound the wind makes while blowing through a saguaro cactus? When did you last sit outside with your cup of coffee and allow yourself to just be without any agenda or thoughts?

Do you listen to or take care of the needs of your body? What about what fuels your mind, heart and soul? Are you ignoring them, not creating the time that you need to lift your spirit?

Do you spend hours in front of the television set or on social media? When was the last time you made a date with yourself? Have you noticed the little signs, symbols, or messages that surround you trying to support you?

When you start to slow down a bit and allow yourself to reconnect with who you are, you gain clarity into what you desire to achieve in life. By taking care of and loving yourself, you create the space for joy and happiness to come into your life. By allowing yourself to become still and quiet your mind, you start to receive the messages that are meant for you to hear. You begin to deepen your connection not only with yourself, but with everyone, and everything around you.

Start by taking a few moments daily for some quiet time. Go for a short walk and find a quiet place to sit down for a little while. Set your thoughts aside, reconnect with yourself, and you'll begin to feel your own peace within.

# October 15

## Nourish You for More Energy!
### By Grace Redman

*H*ey Hey, Beautiful Soul!
Do you find yourself running around trying to do it all *and* please everyone in the process? If so, what was the result? I bet you felt spent and exhausted. And when you are feeling that way, there's no room to feel enthusiastic or passionate about life. All you feel is pissed and drained.

Nourishing our minds, bodies, and souls is vital in maintaining our energy. But we often work in ways completely contrary to this. For example, we

1. **Constantly try to meet insane expectations** just because society expects us to.

2. **Beat ourselves up** for things we should have done - things that really are not a big deal.

3. **Bend over to please others** and do so even at the risk of our own sanity.

These things are all draining your energy, mind, body, and soul. If you do them consistently, it is inevitable that you will burn out. And believe me, it takes much more time and energy to recover from burn out then it does to make time to maintain your energy and nourish yourself just a little bit each day.

Today, I invite you to set the intention to honor your own needs and to focus on you. It is not selfish to take care of you; in fact, it is necessary so that you can take care of others. We cannot give from an empty cup. When we take care of ourselves and fill ourselves up, we have more to give, and we are happy to give because we have the energy! You would not drive your car on an empty tank or let your phone battery run out!

The beauty in taking care of ourselves is that we inspire other to take care of themselves. When we are all taking care of ourselves, there is also much less tension, stress, and anger in the world. I know that sounds silly but it is so *true*!

## Some Energy Boosting Ideas

- Spend ten minutes sitting in silence, just breathing or bringing to mind a joyful memory.
- Put on your favorite song and dance for five minutes. I promise, you will feel amazing, and you will elevate your mood and increase your energy in just five minutes.
- Call a friend and have a chat or go out for a coffee. Reconnecting with those you love is a wonderful energy boost.

# October 16

## Empowerment
## By Carolan Dickinson

*W*hat exactly does empowerment look like? Well, that entirely depends on who is defining it. We do talk about it a lot and discuss giving our power away or having someone else trample on it. Yet, it just isn't that easy to define. I think that by knowing ourselves, we can decide what empowerment means individually, not collectively. My definition of empowerment is when I act with personal integrity and authentically, that I voice where I need to without drowning out someone else's, and that I remain kind in the process. It isn't always perfect, and the threshold of empowerment wavers from day to day.

I do believe in the law of averages, though, when it comes to empowerment. On most days, I feel empowered and grateful that I have that freedom. Some days are better than others. I do believe that one area of self-love that can be toppled quickly is when we do not feel empowered. It's when we feel oppressed and stifled that we can begin to fold in on ourselves. We begin to feel less gracious and loving towards ourselves and listen to and accept the less than loving stories others want to tell us. I ultimately believe that if you can be compassionate with yourself, you can be compassionate with anyone and it will cultivate that self-love because you are being the best version of yourself that you can be.

When you are feeling less than perfect empowerment on some days, what do you do? Instead of folding in, try making your energy bigger. It's an exciting experience. Just imagine your spiritual energy getting bigger and bigger until it's larger than the outline of your body. Then larger than the shape of your house. Then write down what you experience. You are not blocking anything; you are just expanding your own energy.

You can also ask Archangel, Michael to help you shore up your power when you are feeling vulnerable. By making your energy bigger when you feel that you want to fold in or retreat, it will help you feel more empowered. A good question to ask may also be "Is this an important issue, or can I let it go?" Empowerment is an essential step in self-love, especially if you can define that empowerment.

# October 17

## Throw Away a Gift
## By Marsha Johnson

*M*emories are held in all things. We may have a ripped and torn T-shirt that we wore to our favorite concert when we were eighteen that we just cannot get rid of. We look at that and all the memories come back in a flood, the friends, the laughter, the excitement. We hold that t-shirt in a special place, and just holding it can bring us right back to that time.

We may have a special afghan that belonged to our grandmother who passed away, and when we pick it up, it has a certain smell, a softness to it that reminds us of our family. We are brought back to a time when we may have sat at her feet as she was crocheting that afghan, and when we wrap ourselves in it we can literally feel her love coming from the fibers.

What happens when we have something that someone gave us as a gift? Perhaps it is a special piece of jewelry or a pillow that matches our room's décor oh so perfectly, but that item brings with it memories of a lost love, or a betrayal by a close friend. I do not know about you, but I have a hard time throwing things away that still have a lot of life left in them or are an expensive item.

I had a beautiful glass figurine that was given to me by an old friend. It really fit so perfectly in my reading room, but after the relationship ended, every time I looked at that figurine, the memories came in a flurry—hurt, sadness and heartache. I kept that statue because it was beautiful and looked so nice where it was.

One day after looking at it and feeling all the feels, I decided to throw that beautiful statue into the trash, and throw it I did, with a vengeance, an over-the-head smash right into the trash. Like magic, all the hurt feelings went with the broken pieces. That one good smash took with it all the hurt that had been hanging around for years.

# October 18

## Breaking Points
## By Dominique Trier

*I*n all of my breaking points, I discovered the most valuable action of self-love is to trust the process your body wants to take you on. To be clear, I am not condoning self-harm, but I am suggesting giving ourselves grace to feel what our bodies are telling us to feel. Without feeling those moments of hurt, sometimes we are unable to find the grace to gently move ourselves beyond it. The best way I can describe gently moving ourselves past breaking points is imagining we are moving a friend, pet, or family member to a more secure, or comfortable position. We are so gentle with the ones we love, but we are not gentle enough with ourselves. Loving ourselves means trusting, being gentle, and practicing gratitude.

It is effortless for us to give those around us special pieces of ourselves because we love them, but giving ourselves the love we crave and deserve can become difficult. The world can make us crave validation from people surrounding us, but the craving for validation suggests we are not giving ourselves enough attention.

My call to action to those who read this is to refocus energy to make sure your needs are met. As adults, we forget that we are the parents we never had and we can give ourselves the love we have always craved, because no one else knows how to love ourselves better than us. In any other situation, you must teach other people what you like, but intrinsically, we automatically know how to love ourselves best. Self-love is a continuous action we cultivate. No one deserves our trust and love more than ourselves during breaking points in our lives.

# October 19

## Choose You!
## By Nancy Toffanin

*G*rowing up in an Italian family, I learned to put everyone else first. For years I was people pleasing. I am learning that if I choose me every day and make myself a priority, then the message I give myself is that I am important too. There are different ways to choose "you." Keeping your word, being consistent with your goals, and listening to your inner child is how you can make yourself a priority every day. Make only the promises you can keep.

Relationships taught me that when I didn't choose myself, I attracted men that didn't choose me. A part of being consistent with yourself is doing the mirror work so that people in turn will show you consistency.

In choosing ourselves every day, it helps fill our cups and helps us give to others from a better place. There are a lot of layers with self-love; some are easier than others.

When we truly let go of our hurt, expectations, attachment, pain, and bitterness, it allows a deep expansion inside of us. It took a long time for me to put myself first, listen to my internal yes or no, and not do things from obligation.

It is not selfish to choose yourself. Make a commitment to love and trust yourself.

If you're true to yourself that is the only thing that matters. Practice listening to your intuition and listening to what is right for you.

I use oracle cards; I use my body as a pendulum, and I ask for signs. These tools help me decide what's right for me. I've decided that I am not aligned with anyone who doesn't choose me. When I reflect back on the times I didn't choose myself, I realize that I had low self-esteem, no confidence, and I didn't love myself. On my journey I discovered that every day we make a choice; we make a decision about situations and people. Life is about choices, and not every day is easy. We have a lot of programming in our minds that run on guilt, shame, fear, not being good enough, etc. The key is to realize how we self-sabotage. Changing our mindset changes our focus, thoughts, and beliefs. Choosing "you" expands all the energy around us to the infinite energy of the universe!

**Self-reflection**

What thought patterns stop you?
How can you choose you every day?

# October 20

## Circle of Friends
## By Amy I. King

*Y*ou know how sometimes you meet someone and you click? You understand each other in a way that exists in few friendships. Those are the keepers. The people who listen to you, hear you, and have your back no matter what.

Having a circle of people who are supportive, and loving is essential to one's happiness. It is like wrapping yourself up in the softest, warmest blanket you can find. Self-love involves not just taking care of our inner body and outer appearance. It is also essential to take stock of our circle of friendships. Those with who we spend the most time should always have our best interests at heart. At times, I have found myself spending far too much time with people who are not supportive and loving but who just wanted to use me.

That no longer happens because I have done a lot of inner work. Learning that I was holding onto relationships for the sake of having said relationships was eye-opening. That makes no sense to me anymore.

Recently, I took stock of all of my relationships. It was not something I did in one day; it was a process. It is something that you can start today. I evaluated every relationship that I was putting my energy into and realized that some of those people were not putting the same energy into the relationship. Instead, they were there when there was something to take. I removed those people from my life and found an inner peace that I had never felt.

Remember, you do not have to let people go harshly. It is not easy, but you can be honest and kind, still ending the relationship.

Today, I feel the warmth and love of every friendship that I gave my energy. I have room only for healthy, reciprocal, supportive, loving relationships. The relationships that made the cut were primarily those that I have had for over twenty years. They are the people who have been there as I waged health wars and lost my family members, one after the other. Self-love is all about how you love yourself, and one sure-fire way to love yourself is by surrounding yourself with a circle of love. Make sure your circle is strong, loving, supportive, and that you have relationships based on honesty.

# October 21

## Create the Space you Choose to Be in
## By Paula Marie Rennie

*W*hen feelings and emotions are high or weighing you down, it's hard to remain calm and positive or to have faith and trust in your situations. In moments like these, I turn to my badass magical self and call the energy to me that I want to experience by creating clear intentions. I also use this tool to cleanse the energy in my situations or any future events I'll be going to. This helps me feel safe and empowered and curious to see what happens.

Find a quiet space where you can sit or stand. Be bold, playful, and creative.

- Place a hand on your heart space and allow your gentle breath to relax your body. Feel your feet now ground into the Earth.

- Set your intention and create a powerful space within you or a situation that will fulfill the highest needs of all involved. You can also repeat this process and set your intention for a future event.

- Focus your attention on your heart space and imagine a golden energy flowing in that's full of love, light, and wisdom. Imagine it filling every cell of your being, releasing anything that does not serve you.

- Imagine this golden energy expanding out into the space around you, cleansing and clearing all old energy in the entire space. Imagine this golden energy also cleansing any situation, person, or event connected to your intention.

- Call forth now to you the energy of love, strength, courage, and vitality. Feel these energies fill your body systems.
- What else do you want to call forth within you or this situation? Be specific and bold! Draw this to you now and feel, sense, see, and know it is being created.
- How do you want this new energy to serve you? How are you going to show up differently? How can you be committed to yourself or your situation?
- What do you need to let go of?
- How can your strengths serve you or this situation right now?
- Take a deep breath in and say to yourself as your energy expands, "I manifest my love, power, and my value here right now." As you exhale feel your energy radiate out of your entire being into your space and situation or future event.
- Feel complete by saying aloud, "And so it is and so it shall be."

# October 22

## Looking in the Mirror
## By Selena Urbanovitch

When I used to look at myself in the mirror, I did not like what I saw. It took a life-changing moment and a few courses to finally look at what I needed to heal. I have come to find that life is all about lessons and that people are put in our path to help with the lessons on my journey. I figured out that some are here for a short time and some a long time. And that all have something I need to learn from, and I have something to teach them! Self-love was a process of really liking me to loving me!

Each course took me to a new level of self-awareness to another part of me that wants to be-come and for light to heal through. Here are some tips on how to be the best version of you:

1. It is okay to say no. This establishes a boundary, and boundaries are healthy to have.

2. It is okay to have a me day. This fills up your cup.

3. Ask for help when you need it. It isn't a sign of weakness to ask for help. It actually shows strength.

4. *No* is a complete sentence. No need to say anything more.

5. Say *yes* to the things that make you light up.

6. Face your fears, one fear at a time!

7. Look in the mirror and say, "I like you," and move to "I love you."

8. When in doubt take a deep breath and ask, "Does this serve me for the best or do I walk away?"

9. Surround yourself with the people who bring light to your journey.

10. Believe in you. You are magnificent.

Self-love is possible. It is possible to have healthy boundaries. And it is possible to be happy. How possible it can be by how much you believe you are worthy of it. Do the work on healing. You find the courses that call to you. Find your light and believe it is there even if it is just a spark for now! Healing and growing! Sharing your pillar of light is beautiful.

# October 23

## Love is Forgiving
## By Jannirose Fenimore

*I*t is an immeasurable blessing to share life with someone like Charlie, who sees through the eyes of love.

I think back to a time during his fifth-grade year when he was bullied by another child. I was called by the principal to meet with Charlie and the other young man in her office. Once I arrived at the school, I was ushered into the conference room where I saw my son seated near a boy who hung his head in fear and shame.

I quietly sat down across from the kids and made eye contact with the principal. But before she could utter a word, Charlie moved next to the frightened child and stretched an arm around his shoulder. Then he leaned toward the boy's ear and softly said, *"Are you sad today?"*

That was all it took for the floodgates in his classmate's heart to open in a deluge of tears. Through sobs, the child released the pain he tried so desperately to hide beneath a well-worn façade of toughness.

As his tears slowed, the principal and I were moved to hear my sweet son say, *"It's okay. I will be your friend."*

The young man turned and looked at Charlie—shocked at what he had heard.

Then in a halting voice, he asked, "You mean…you…forgive me?"

Wrapping the boy in a bear hug, Charlie answered, *"Yes! Love is forgiving!"*

Not long after receiving this unexpected lesson in grace, I was given a powerful exercise in forgiveness that was surely inspired by

Charlie's loving example. Sitting alone in silence one day, I was shown an image of a person whose words and actions had hurt me deeply.

As the vision unfolded, I watched in awe as this man became a young version of himself. Then I witnessed myself transforming into the precious little girl from my past. As our child-selves stood face to face with playful curiosity, I was reminded of the innocent, loving essence of our true natures. In one holy instant—through the lens of love that heals all things—I saw there was nothing to forgive. In the blink of an eye, I freed two people and received the most extraordinary loving gift.

As one fellow traveler to another, I offer you this consideration. Is there space in your heart *forgiving love* to your beautiful self?

# October 24

## Bright and Kindful Loving
## By Charlie Fenimore

*F orgiving will heal our relationships and make us bright of light. Hurting souls feel our love when we think to understand them. We must feel our own hearts, too. With joyful souls of forgiveness, we shine our lives with brightful kindness of love for our hopeful human heartness.*

# October 25

## Goddess Eyes
## By Marie Martin

Beauty is a power of personality that is ignited by the soul. For each woman, this is different, but her beauty is in the fiber of how she lives her life. She is a direct reflection of the beauty of the divine feminine.

When you look into a mirror, you may find that the first thing you see is your imperfection, if you will, the things that make you feel ugly. But you can never be ugly because you are one of the faces of the divine feminine. Even when you are heavy, old, wrinkled, and have no makeup on, you are still the reflection of one of the faces of the divine feminine.

She is looking through your eyes and feeling through your heart! What you think, she thinks, and what you love, she loves. That is the way of the divine; it lives within each and every one of us.

To help you with a gentle reminder, I would like to instruct you in one of my favorite mirror tools to grow your connection to this part of yourself.

The first thing is first; your thoughts are food for the mind. Start shaping your mental image of yourself by standing in front of a mirror and studying the reflection that looks back at you. Eliminate the negative thoughts about your body, face, and hair.

Ask yourself these questions. Who is this person? Are they a person of worth and integrity? Am I helping to make them a person who I would like to be? Looking a little deeper into the mirror, find at least one thing about your physical body that you like. I chant to myself, "See the beauty. See the beauty." on the days I am having a rough time.

Sometimes you must look, and sometimes we see the goddess reflection straight away. But once you have it, study her for a length of time and enjoy your connection. See her as the divine being she is as she peeks at you from behind your eyes. The more you practice this mindset tool, the easier it is to connect with that part of the divine feminine that lives within you.

# October 26

## Who's Running the Show
## By Sheryl Goodwin Magiera

*A*re you running the show in your life or are others? Do you find yourself doing what other people are telling you to do rather than following your own heart-centered guidance? Setting boundaries on what you allow or do not allow in your life can feel overwhelming at times and may feel like a circus balancing act.

Boundaries are limits you set around what you will or will not tolerate. You have the right to your feelings. If you haven't set boundaries in the past, it could be for fear of conflict, being a people pleaser, making sure everyone else is okay, or doing things out of obligation. However, setting healthy boundaries is taking back the power in your life, and instead of abandoning your needs, depleting yourself and holding back; put yourself first and what's best for you.

If you do not set boundaries, you can become a sponge for other people's problems or allow yourself to be the doormat for their dirty shoes. Setting boundaries will be uncomfortable at first, but if you communicate your needs with kindness and honesty, most will be open to your wishes. Some may not accept them at first, but if communicated in a loving way, it should help them to understand or at least think about your needs.

Start off by creating your boundaries. What are your desires and needs? Because, if you don't decide, others will decide for you. Then speak your truth, communicate, and express your desires with honesty and kindness. People won't know unless you tell them. Compromise within your relationships to make things work or at least respect each other's limits. Finally, maintain the boundaries you set.

Try creating some boundaries with honesty, kindness and respect, and say, "No" with grace and gratitude. The next time you're feeling like someone has crossed your boundary lines, ask yourself "Who's running the show?" and then course correct. Remember, you're not responsible for other people's feelings, but you are responsible for yours. Be your own best friend.

Three steps to setting boundaries: **Create, Communicate, Cultivate.**

## Affirmations for setting boundaries:

- My boundaries are sacred and I honor them.
- I am a spark of the divine and my boundaries matter.
- I am worthy of creating, communicating, and cultivating my boundaries.
- Every day I'm becoming clearer on the boundaries that serve me best.
- I honor myself by honoring my boundaries.

# October 27

## Replace Stress with Self-love
## By Paula Obeid

*I*t is no secret that stress is known as the silent killer affecting our physical bodies. Long term exposure to stress can contribute to serious health problems, such as heart disease, high blood pressure, and diabetes. However, stress affects our emotional wellbeing via mental disorders such as depression and anxiety. The great news is that by utilizing self-love practices, we can combat stress in our life. Although the concept of self-love does not readily seem to be a cure for physical health, many psychology studies show that compassion and self-love are key for physical and mental wellbeing. When you take responsibility for your wellbeing, managing your stress is a form of self-love. Please look at your life and decide where changes could be made to help reduce stressors in your life. Exercise is known to be one of the most important stress reducers, so be loving to yourself and create time for daily movement in your life. Take time to create action plans to reduce stress in your life.

Replace stress with self-love by asking yourself, "What causes stress in my life?" Common causes of stress are constant worry or racing thoughts, being under lots of financial pressure, facing big life changes, and having too many responsibilities that feel overwhelming or sometimes a situation that you do not have control over the outcome. This practice can be used anytime of the day when you are feeling stressed. At this moment, think of one specific situation in your life that is causing you stress. When you think of the situation, notice where you feel emotional discomfort in your body. Without judging the discomfort as good or bad, simply notice what you are feeling and acknowledge the discomfort using any statement like "This is stress."

Now place your hand on your heart, you can for a moment be mindful of your hand on your heart while breathing into the discomfort. Then choose a phrase that expresses self-love to your discomfort. Compassionate phrases that are gentle and loving to yourself might be "I accept myself;" "I love myself just as I am;" "I am not alone and other people feel stress also;" and "All is well!"

Remember you can use this practice in your daily life not just when experiencing stress to expand into more love. Practice self-compassion which is self-love in action!!

# October 28

## Source and Self-Love
## By Sarah Berkett

Source, God, or a higher power, whatever you like to call it, wants more for us than for our thoughts to be consumed with picking apart parts of ourselves that we are insecure about. After all, we are created perfectly. We are pure spirit that is encased in our bodies. It pains the universe to see us putting ourselves down time after time. So, how can we help ourselves let go of this obsession of being not good enough?

Let go of the idea that you have to be perfect, you already are.

Live in the moment, every day.

Practice gratitude. Come on now, you can do it!

# October 29

## Beauty Royale
## By Salli Sebastian Walker

Close your eyes now and take a walk down your memory lane. See if you can remember an incident that made you smile. Now write that thought down. I did this very exercise and here is my story of what churned a grin for me.

The year was 1970; I was ten. It was summer break, and I was bored. My dad suggested I take a typing class at the school where he taught. This idea sounded like a fun summer-time activity and after a few weeks of schooling, I got pretty good at this new hobby. I was also, super lucky because I could go home and practice what I learned on my dad's old typewriter in the basement. The name brand of this old typewriter was a Royal. I would regularly conjure up games of make-believe on this machine. What fun it was to let my imagination run free pretending to be a teacher or a secretary or just a kid in a classroom goofing around on a typewriter.

Forty years later, it was that memory that made me smile and follow a hunch I had. Searching eBay, I spotted a 1949 Royal Quiet Deluxe typewriter and bought it. When the box arrived, I giggled and slowly unpacked it. It was a surprise to see that the typewriter even came with its own carrying case. Locating a fresh roll of inked ribbon and wiping down the keys, I was ready to roll. What came next came was a tip from a friend who told me that one sure way to clear writer's block was to type a letter to the typewriter asking it for help, and then giving it its own name.

Finding a comfy spot, I placed my fingers on the keyboard and began.

Hello Beauty Royale,

My name is Salli Walker. I cannot wait to see where our journey together goes. I will bet you have had quite a few amazing stories pass over your keys over all these years. I would love to hear them sometime when you feel like sharing. Is there a way we can work together to relieve some of the tension between us?

I waited for a bit and my fingers moved over the keys typing, "just type."

Whenever you feel a bit blue, how about taking a walk down memory lane? Beauty Royale would love a new friend.

# October 30

## Forgiveness
## By Dee Dee Rebitt

*W*hen you think of that word forgiveness, how does it make you feel? What are you thinking of or whom? Is it someone else perhaps its you?

The greatest thing we can do for someone or ourselves is to just forgive.

And by forgiving them, it sets us free and unclenches the chains that kept us a prisoner in our thoughts and in our emotions.

This is the greatest and selfless thing we can do in unconditional love.

The person we feel that hurt us is truly standing before us asking for love.

Their behaviour is not where they are bad, but where they carry their own deep-seated wounds, and the only way out of our pain is to bless them and appreciate them for what they did, whether it was wrong or right.

They stood before you naked in their pain and truth, and the mirror's reflection is our own painful truth staring back at us. When we understand fully the reason, we can move past it.

When you realize what it means to forgive you give yourself emotional freedom. It is a part of your soul on this journey.

It will bring all sorts of emotions like joy and love, and it will raise your vibration. When we are at the start of this journey called forgiveness, we will feel so many emotions. You may even feel sadness and anger. Whatever it is, be okay with it as its presenting itself to you. You have the choice to let it control you or to take your power back and control how you react. Let everything come to the forefront. Just know the harm may not have been intentionally done. Hold your hand over your heart as you process the images and feelings that surface. Just be totally present. Let it all flow, no matter what. Your very soul knows what needs to be.

When you are ready, just let it all go, release it, and forgive. Release from the scenario the energy that bound you for so long. Heal from it. This is all part of our journey back to unconditional love. It is a recognition that none of are perfect and that is okay. We are all a little fucked up and we are in no means perfect.

Be kind and loving.

# *October 31*

## Saying No Could be More Powerful than Saying Yes
### By Grace Redman

*H*ey Hey, Beautiful Soul!
Do you have a hard time saying no? Does your chest tighten and you feel a dread when you need to say no? That was me! I used to have such a hard time saying no. On my journey of self-love, I learned that saying no is a complete sentence and a form of self-care. I also learned that saying no could be more powerful than saying yes!

We have a hard time saying no for many reasons. Here are a few. We do not want to appear to be a bad person. We want to be loved. We want to look "good." We want to be accepted.

As a result of having a hard time saying no, we take on too much, get stretched too thin, and end up getting overwhelmed and frustrated. We also tend to get resentful when we say yes to things we really wanted to say no to. If you say yes and you really wanted to say no, the energy behind your yes is not sincere and the person will be able to pick up on that resentful energy and that does not feel good to either person involved.

When you begin practicing saying no, there are going to be people who get bent out of shape. Those people do not mean harm. they are coming from their own ego and taking it personally when it has nothing to do with them. It's about you taking care of you. If you tell a true and sincere friend no, they may feel hurt initially, but they will get over it and you are setting the example. This is where saying no is more powerful than saying yes. You are setting an example for them to learn to say no.

One way we can begin to practice saying no is visualizing the scenario in your mind with the best possible outcome. Imagine yourself communicating with the person that you want to say no to. Be loving. You can choose to provide an explanation or not. Next imagine their ideal response back to you. Go over the scenario in your mind several times. Visualization is very powerful. When you visualize you are setting the intention for the outcome. Often, the way the situation unfolds in reality after your visualization will unfold even better than you had imagined possible.

# November 1

## Where Attention Goes Energy Flows
## By Susan Hoyle

*W*here attention goes, energy flows. Have you ever had one of those days when things just are not going your way? Maybe it is as simple as hitting every red light, so you are late for work. Maybe it is a fight with your partner. It is in these moments we have a choice to make. We can focus on the problem at hand, discussing it with peers, friends, our partner, explaining every detail of our *awful* day. Or we can choose to look through the negative experience and find the positive in it. For every day holds its own little miracles, waiting for us to learn from. But so many of us are so focused on the little negative experiences that we are incapable of seeing these little miracles unfolding right in front of us.

Let's take a closer look at what this means. If we are constantly focusing on what is wrong in our world, our energy will flow to what is wrong in the world. Complaining, listening to the news and shows supports the angst we feel inside as we continue to focus on the doubt and fear that is perpetuated in our society, especially through the media. Then we take this doubt and fear, allowing it to become part of the energy we carry around. We begin to project it onto our families, coworkers, friends, and even strangers! We begin to surround ourselves with people who share our opinions, beliefs, and purpose, which is to continue to complain, gossip, and generally be unhappy with our current situation, life and society as a whole. Sound familiar? You know these people, right?

The next time you feel yourself annoyed at a situation and you reach for your phone to call someone to share with, stop, and remember, what you focus on expands. What we focus on, we get more of. If we can teach ourselves to search for the positive in each negative situation, be grateful for it, we will begin to see more things show up in our lives to be grateful for. Because *where attention goes, energy flows*.

What are you choosing to focus your attention on today? What is expanding? The negative situations or the positive lessons in the circumstances? Awareness is key. Once you have awareness around this concept, watch the energy flow.

# November 2

## Three Simple Words
## By Sheryl Goodwin Magiera

*S*everal years ago, in my capstone and final college class, the students were given an assignment that made me shudder at the thought of completion, and frankly felt beyond my mental scope. The class was instructed to reach out to a handful of friends and family and ask them individually to provide a list of three words that came to mind when they thought of the student. At first, I was mortified then embarrassed about asking people since it seemed self-serving and narcissistic but knew I needed to complete the assignment.

So, I put my big girl pants on, committed to the assignment, took a deep breath, and sent the individual messages. Each time the send button was pressed, I cringed for the people on the other end receiving my request. What happened next took me by surprise; every single person but one replied within an hour. No one asked for any further explanation; they just replied with three simple words.

I made a list of names, along with their three words, circled and highlighted all the duplicates, and I spent the remainder of the day in tears of joy and gratitude for the lovely words they used to describe me. My heart was bursting. I took bright pink and orange Post-it notes and wrote a single word on each paper, then placed them on my bathroom mirror to remind me each day.

Why is it so hard to believe the words about ourselves when we say and believe them about others? The assignment had such a profound impact I knew I wanted to do something more permanent with my words to get them off my mirror, and created a framed piece of artwork that hangs on my wall as a daily reminder of words that describe me. Reading them always makes me smile and I often find myself standing a little taller.

I am betting if you commit to the same project, you will be touched but the results. Even though it was only three simple words each person provided, they lifted me up beyond what I imagined. I am humbled and filled with gratitude of love and joy for the friendships and family in my life that saw something special in me. Be courageous, reach out, then believe and claim who you are.

# November 3

## You Become Whatever You Tell Yourself
## By Kim Richardson

When we are young there are seeds planted in our brains by our parents and those around us. The problem is not all those seeds are flowers; many of them are weeds that become deeply rooted and become part of our beliefs.

The truth is ... we are love. We all came from love and the world around us has maybe hurt us or caused us to be judgmental of ourselves and others. Once you begin weeding your garden, getting rid of the old belief system that is no longer serving you, miraculous things start to happen.

We have the power to be and feel whatever we want. You have to re-train your brain. You have so much power in your thoughts; if you are telling yourself that you are not good enough, then you become not good enough. If you tell yourself you are magnificent, beautiful, and successful ... you *become magnificent, beautiful, and successful.*

Louise Hay was an innovator in the world of using positive affirmations to heal your physical body. Her book, *You Can Heal Your Life,* was very life changing for me and so many others. When I started implementing her practice of using positive affirmations to re-wire my brain, I wasn't totally convinced. I was overweight, depressed, and really broken at that time in my life. I was learning to heal and love myself unconditionally. I started looking in the mirror at my naked body. Feeling disgusted and ashamed, I whispered the words out loud, "You are beautiful in every way."

The truth is that I did not feel that way. I felt like I was lying to myself. Part of this affirmation thing was I had to *feel* it and *believe* it. I didn't give up. Every day I stood in front of that mirror saying a little louder each time, "You are beautiful in every way."

It was not long before I started to believe it. A trickle effect of positive things started happening. I was losing weight with no changes to my diet or exercise. I was becoming more confident and (most importantly) feeling happier.

You play a role in the seeds that you plant in your own mind. It's time to weed the garden, my friend. Let go of those old beliefs and inner dialogue so you can allow room for the new seeds to blossom. Tell yourself you are beautiful today!

# November 4

## Finding Maggie
## By Margaret-Maggie Honnold

ave you ever had everything change? One day you are chugging along leading a normal life, the life you had been expected to live and had cultivated for a lifetime and then … oh dear.

Suddenly, your husband has Alzheimer's; your house burns to the ground; you lose three dogs, a kitty, and all possessions in a fire; you retire from a lifelong career; move back to your hometown after forty-three years away; you become a widow and turn sixty-five. It is a lot to process, especially when you are not sure who you are because all the markers that defined you are gone.

All those events happened to me. Afterward, it took five years for me to discover who I was when alone. In raising kids, caring for elderly parents, school, marriage, and divorce, I had been too busy to even think about myself. I had just gone forward. I identified through what I did in society and lost who I was as a person. Now, I had all the time in the world I did not know what to do next. The question became "who is Maggie and where is she?"

What do people do when they do not know who they are anymore?

First, do not rush it, that is when bad decisions are made. Permit yourself to grieve the old while you search for the new you. Love yourself enough to go easy on your decision-making process.

Second, set aside one day a week to have a "Finding (insert your name here) Day." I chose Friday. Then pick an activity for that day which you have not enjoyed, perhaps since childhood. Can you remember what's fun? Starting simple, I began to color and investigate my favorite medium (gel pens) and the type of coloring books I liked best. Could you color one picture today?

Third, trust that the Lord, your God, has a plan for you. After the fire, I held on to a Bible verse, in the last chapter of the book of Job that I paraphrase as God blessed Job even greater in the later years.

I am seventy-two. These are my later years, and I am blessed. In the past seven years, I have found Maggie and learned to love her for who she is, not what she does. You can too. I will be cheering for you.

# November 5

## Embracing My Body's Way
## By Ann Marie Asp

How often have you found yourself looking at pictures in a fitness magazine and asking what would take for you to get your body to look like the ones scattered throughout the pages? I have spent years engaging in many styles of exercise and movement and hoping to get that beautiful sculpted and toned athletic body. There was always the latest exercise or yoga class that I could not wait to sign up for. After just a few classes, the search was back on. What I was truly looking for was that unique experience that would bring joy to my life.

We spend so much time in our lives searching for ways to feel good about ourselves, especially our physical selves, yet we overlook the amazing vehicle that guides us every day. This vehicle is our connection to truth, and it allows us to go after our dreams and helps us to live our lives with purpose. It was my wondrous vehicle that led me to finding the Nia dance technique. After only one class, I knew my life would be forever changed. My heart was overflowing with joy. This is a sensation we all love to feel. This powerful practice began a transformation not only in my physical body but also in my mental and spiritual bodies as well.

The Nia dance technique was founded by Debbie and Carlos Rosas. It is a system that offers anyone the ability to find healing, wellness, and self-joy thru what they refer to as the medicine of movement. Movement holds the key to unlocking of the healing of our own body. It is so important for each of us to tap into the wisdom the body wants to share.

Find time today to listen closely to your body when it speaks to you. It is revealing a powerful life force. Begin by writing a daily log of the different sensations that you are feeling in certain areas. This is referred to as body awareness and is a very important tool used in Nia.

As you begin to deepen your experience with this practice, you will begin trusting the body to signal when it needs to adjust and then what was needed to help you stay aligned with the truth of what your own body already knows. Take the needed time to honor your amazing vehicle daily.

# November 6

## Connection and Communication
### By Tabitha Weigel

*W*hen reflecting on the beauty and power that is connection and communication, my heart swells with love and gratitude for the potency of using my voice. I think of how I gained such capability, such confidence, in the use of my voice. Much thanks goes to the magic that is sharing circles, a true blessing of self-connection through the honor of sitting with, communicating with, and as a loving collective, holding space for each other also known as collective therapy.

A sharing circle is created by a host or circle facilitator. They are responsible for holding sacred space for participants to vocalize and share their truths. A safe space where you are encouraged to remove the social masks—the masks we are trained to wear, the masks of adherence to social norms and expectations. This allows a sense of belonging and acceptance to form with each passing share. It creates the opportunity to use our words with wonder and confidence, highlighting a simple truth: that the power of the voice is mighty, but there is something even more influential, more healing, when using your voice to engage with, learn from, and give (as well as receive) support from your fellow human.

Through gathering, reflecting, and sharing, we can learn how to speak from our heart *and* without the fear of judgement. We can remove that heavy mask energy we grip onto by expressing ourselves with honesty, stimulating our senses of self-worth and pride, opening our energetic fields and abilities to not only express, but to also act on our desires.

I encourage you to strengthen your love of self by finding your support group. Your circle. Your therapeutic outlet of connection and communication.

Take time to sit with yourself. Place your hands around your throat and breathe in a sky blue. Think of your voice, and how and where and who you would like to express it with. Channel that breath through your heart, activating your heart chakra, and asking for its guidance in where your heart and voice is needed. From here, you begin the search. Your circle, your form of communal support is out there, now you simply need to find it. I myself am a circle facilitator and if you are interested in learning more about the variety of circles I host, both in person and virtually, you're welcome to connect with me at mothermoonsharingcircles@gmail.com.

# November 7

## Marine Magic
## By Tonia Browne

*I am an empath with a gentle soul, but I have the strength of the ocean supporting me.*

I have always enjoyed being in, on, or near water and although I felt intuitively this was good for my soul, it's only recently that I have learnt how much water can benefit the body and the mind, especially cold water.

As a self-declared mermaid, I have an infinity with water. Having lived in temperate climates with warm seas, regular swimming was both possible and a joy. It was only after moving to Scotland, Covid-19, and the various restrictions on our usual way of life, that I began to explore the possibilities of cold-water swimming and its health benefits more seriously.

I did my research and read everything I could on cold water swimming. I joined wild water swimming Facebook groups that inspired me, and I did a Wim Hof Challenge that started the process of turning theory to practice. I exposed my body, slowly and safely, to colder water in the shower and then finally, after a particularly stressful day, I went to a safe beach with my partner, and I dunked in the refreshingly cool waters whilst he looked on in disbelief! Since then, I've become a regular cold-water dunker. Not as cold as many, but cold enough to feel the numerous benefits. The high I get from it is unbelievable, the rush of energy I achieve lasts most of the day and is greatly appreciated, and my new ability to feel the cold so much less when I am out of the water is a great blessing.

It is over six months since I started my cold-water forays and I'm proud to say I'm now dunking in the North Sea monthly. Although this may seem like an extreme self-care exercise routine I invite you, if the idea calls you, to be curious enough to read more about the benefits of cold water and who knows, you may just decide to turn the hot shower a little colder once in a while and before you know it, you might start experiencing some marine magic of your own.

## Consider

- Am I interested to learn more about the advantages of cold water exposure?
- Would I be up for trying a cold shower for a few seconds?
- How could I safely include cold water into my self-care routine?

# November 8

## Won't Look Back
## By Bonnie Larson

*M*any reading *365 Days of Self-Love* desire a moment of relaxation, hope, or perhaps, inspiration. Rather than a single nugget, I would like to share the story of my success. Assuredly, it will work for you.

Determine what it is that truly brings you joy. Then step boldly forward doing precisely that. Be the person you most desire to be. Do not hold back!

If you desire to be an author, pick up your pen or keyboard. Write the things that inspire you. What makes you happy, joyful— the best you? Then, do so! Follow your passion! Be prepared to see yourself blossom into all that you can be.

My secret to connecting to the *source* is listening to excellent music and attuning to it—particularly authors, songwriters, and singers of exceptional talent. For me those are Shakespeare, Hemingway, Josh Groban, Jimmy Webb, and Micky Newbury. To quiet my mind, I use a song by Steve Winwood and Eric Clapton, *"Can't Find My Way Back Home."*

I've never experienced writer's block. I tune in to that which inspires me. Meditations and prayers are excellent tools. My favorites are Cathleen L. Balfour, Peter Woodbury, Sunny Dawn Johnston's *Arch Angel Michael Meditation*, and Gregg Braden.

With songs and lyrics, observe the rhythm and vibration. Today, it is as if music is playing in the background, Josh Groban's song, *"Won't Look Back."* These are sure to catch my attention. What is the message of the song? *Knowing the days left to come, are the best yet. And I wanna be there, wherever you lead me, for better or worse, for the rest of my life. Won't look, won't look back.*

The message is to love unconditionally with all our hearts! Live and love with faith, inspiring all those around you. Never look back!

When writing there is a pivotal moment. That moment is when rather than writing, the story writes itself. When *the story has me*, I know I have it! The story becomes the driving force; we become the instrument.

Search for your true passion—that which brings you joy. People often ask, *what is my purpose*? When you discover your passion, you embark upon the journey. The best days are yet to come!

# November 9

## Appreciating Your Physical Vessel
## By Vonnie L. Hawkins, LCSW

Thanks to childhood and adult trauma, like many of us, I have always had a complicated relationship with my body. For most of my life, my body was a recalcitrant, rebellious source of shame and guilt, and I detested, resented, and punished it accordingly. As a lifelong comfort-eater, I struggled to maintain a desirable weight, and even when it was achieved, often by less than healthy means, I always lost control, and gained the weight back. My body became a shield to unwanted emotional connection and a constant confirmation that I was not perfect and therefore unworthy of love.

Recently, I was doing some yoga to a video. The instructor told me to feel my body and thank it for moving me through the world. I burst into gut wrenching tears because I had an epiphany. I had never given myself permission to love my body. It had always been this "thing" separate from who "I" was. It was far less valuable than my sharp mind that made me a living. My body was this burdensome thing that I had to manage. It constantly failed to meet my expectations, frustrated me, and always fell short. I cannot adequately express how much this realization caused me to weep tears of sorrow, pain, regret, apology, and finally forgiveness for myself, at having walked through life for nearly five decades with such an unhealthy, unloving relationship with my physical vessel. I resolved to practice loving my physical body from that day forward, celebrating my efforts and forgiving myself when I did not quite get there.

In your journal, rate your relationship with your physical body on a scale of 1 to 10, one being "needs work" and ten being "I'm totally in love with my physical self and take excellent care of my vessel!"

If needed, express forgiveness to yourself and acknowledge you are where you should be. Next, list actions you could take to increase your score by one point. Drink more water. Take a daily walk. Add more vegetables to your diet. Add small, incremental, mindful choices that say "thank you, body, for moving me through the world."

Set a loving intention to add what you feel called to add to be in a more loving relationship with your physical body and revisit this daily to move closer and closer to a ten, a loving relationship with your physical body!

# November 10

## Being In-Bodied
## By Yumie Zein

*T*he body is a highly intelligent vessel. You can say it is like a spaceship navigating you through this world.

For a long time, I tried navigating my spaceship from the outside. Not fully connecting with it. Peering through the windows from time to time. Perhaps catching a glimpse of something floating inside, only to look away quickly, scared of what I might find. What I did not realize was that this vessel was constantly recording every moment, every emotion, every experience that I was going through. The more I avoided going inside, the more stuck, heavy, and uncomfortable it got for me, no matter how detached I thought I was. Coming back in my body was a big breakthrough for me. It happened when I allowed myself to ask myself what this emotion feels like in my body.

The first time I tried it, it was like flood gates opening. I started to feel sensations in my body that I had not felt before. The emotions felt like they were electrical pulses finding their way through a new circuit. Waves of memories filled with emotions would wash over me frequently; almost like buttons being triggered by my re-entrance into my body. I began to experiment with different ways of easing myself back into my body every time I would feel myself detaching because of an overwhelming emotion or experience. It was challenging at first. I was so used to jumping ship because it was my default coping mechanism. As I found ways that felt very enjoyable to me (dancing, singing, stretching, jumping around, screaming even), it started to become more familiar territory. I began to understand that because emotions are an energy, an electrical pulse, they require a clear and open pathway to move and shift.

That allowed me to let go of any judgement I had towards feeling any emotion. It is ok to feel all of it. It is all just part of navigating this vessel through this experience and the more that I can allow myself to fully be present in-body, the richer and more fulfilling the journey becomes.

# November 11

### Be Your Own Cheerleader
### By Nancy Meikle-Mousseau

*I*n the early nineties, I was in a career where I needed a strong backbone to exist in a male dominated field. I was reading Louise Hay and Wayne Dyer books at the time and they introduced me to affirmations. Louise Hay wrote, *"Every word you speak is an affirmation. The subconscious is always listening."*

I wrote out ten affirmations on a recipe card, starting with *I am*, included my name, saying them aloud every morning. I felt proud of myself for having my back. Years later, I attended a *Heal Your Life* workshop in Toronto. One of the speakers was Patricia J. Crane, Ph.D., who had worked with Louise Hay. Patricia's book, *Ordering from the Cosmic Kitchen*, propelled my affirmations to the next level. Patricia gave many examples of affirmations for all areas of your life. I chose affirmations that I resonated with, since I continually redesigned my life. Affirmations are the way we talk to ourselves, and self-talk is critical in how we handle things in life. As I practiced better self-talk, I became calmer and through the years began to release some of my affirmations, sending them off with love for their empowering service.

My affirmations provide love and strength to my authentic self, *cheering me on* every day. Saying them in the shower each morning, as I cleanse my physical body, my affirmations prepare me emotionally, mentally, and spiritually, for the day ahead.

*Wouldn't you enjoy being your own cheerleader?*

Begin this exercise by creating a list of *I AM* affirmations. Empower your affirmations by including your name. Start small and then become as specific as you wish, as you grow along. One of my very first affirmations was, *I, Nancy, am enjoying the moment,* reminding me to be *present*. Today, I have sixteen daily affirmations and I cherish each one of them. *I AM* are the two most important words in the universe. They can either make you or break you depending on the words that follow them. My hope is that this exercise inspires you to begin a new vision for yourself.

# November 12

## Dance: A Moving Prayer
## By Florence Acosta

*M*any live inside their heads and beat themselves up about the past or worry about the how of the future. We tend to spend a lot of time in our heads—overthinking, overanalyzing and detaching from our physical existence. When we live only in our head, we are disconnected from our body. The result can be anxiety, irritability, frustration, low energy, and a general feeling of uneasiness. We can become less trusting of the process, less connected to intuition and experience feelings of more stress and overwhelm.

When we are not connected to our body, we do not hear the whispers for help until they become screams. We are not feeling in tune with the wisdom or guidance that our body is constantly sharing with us. This disembodied way of living can lead to unhealthy coping mechanisms, a lack or loss of confidence and an overall feeling of numbness. For some people, it can feel unsafe to be in the body. To be truly embodied can feel intimidating because it forces us to drop out of the thoughts in our head and into our body to really feel into what is present. Some may have not been taught to express emotions in a healthy manner or that expressing them is not safe.

There is a certain freedom that comes in learning how to balance our thoughts and live in the present moment.

Music can raise our vibration to the highest frequency, whether we want to increase our energy level, shift our mood, lift ourselves out of sadness, or help us have an amazing breakthrough. Music can open our heart, lift our spirit and be a conduit for dropping out of the head and into the body. It is a catalyst that helps us release what no longer serves us and achieve profound states thus creating space for our dreams. Music allows movement—movement of feelings through us and creative expression through dance. Dance allows us to be in our bodies. It ignites the fire in our belly and leaves us feeling excited. It drives us to connect even deeper within and can break down walls of our silence. Dance is a moving prayer that allows us to be in our body. I invite you to turn on the music and dance it out!

# November 13

## Take a Leap of Faith
### By Selena Urbanovitch

*I* took a leap of faith in 2019. For as long as I could remember, I wanted to swim with wild dolphins. The fear of swimming in the wide-open sea was daunting, but I just knew I wanted it. I actually used to swim in the ocean when I was a kid. I am not sure why am I so scared to do it now as an adult.

What I found in me was the courage to just go for it, and I believe that we all have the ability to look fear in the face and say, *Not today. I am not letting this control me.*

I knew this was a life changing moment. I did not know why I had to do it, but I had that gut feeling it needed to be now. It is just like writing in this beautiful book. I do not know why the call is so strong. I am just trusting my gut feeling.

Before, more often than not, I would let fear win. What I found was that I had lots of regrets. I finally got to the point where I was not settling. If I was supposed to do something, I asked the universe to help me get to it. I say now, "If I am supposed to do this, I need help in getting there." And more often than not, the universe shows me a way.

Swimming with wild dolphins woke something in me—an ability to go with the flow and to be more fluid in my life! This meant I could dream bigger, manifest faster, and be more in my now. So, what I am saying is, if your heart and soul are crying out for something, if your gut is saying, "I have to do this," then take a leap of faith and go for it!

# November 14

## Cacao-Cherry Love
### By Jamie Rudolph

One of my all-time favorite smoothies is cacao-cherry love. Nourishing foods are an excellent way to show yourself some self-love. This recipe is filled with superfood ingredients to nourish your body and feed your soul.

*Raw cacao.* Raw, un-altered chocolate. Raw cacao has many wonderful benefits as it is full of antioxidants, minerals, and healthy fats. It helps boost serotonin levels in the brain, which supports a healthy, happy mood due to its heart opening properties. Cacao also supports cardiovascular health and glowing skin.

*Cherries.* A lower-glycemic fruit full of vitamin A, C, and manganese. It contains anti-inflammatory properties with the potential to reduce gout and arthritic conditions. My favorite is the tart or Montmorency cherries.

*Hemp seeds.* Slightly nutty and full of healthy, essential fatty acids. They are excellent protein sources with the added benefit of fiber. Hemp seeds contain omega-3 and omega-6, vitamin E, iron, and much more while providing cardiovascular, skin, and brain support.

*Maca root.* A root from the Andes, maca root is considered an adaptogenic herb. Maca root helps to support the body in times of stress and assists in bringing the body back into homeostasis. It supports energy levels and mood, balances hormones, and supports our overall health and wellbeing.

*Bananas.* A yummy fruit that is full of energy. They are a great source of prebiotics, which help to promote a healthy digestive system. Also, it's a precursor of melatonin to help with creating a more restful sleep.

*Coconut water.* Nature's electrolyte drink. Full of minerals and lower in sugar than your conventional packaged energy drinks, coconut water is the perfect hydration drink to prevent dehydration and nourish the body.

## Cacao-Cherry Love Smoothie

*Makes one healthy serving.*

1 large, frozen banana

1.5- 2 tablespoons of cacao powder

1 cup of frozen, pitted cherries

3 tablespoons of hemp seeds

1.5 cups of coconut water

1 tablespoon of maca root (or use your favorite apoptogenic herb) *

*\*This ingredient can be omitted. Please follow the manufacturer's recommended serving or your health care professional's recommendation.*

Directions: Place all ingredients in a high-speed blender. Blend until smooth.

For an additional nutritional boost, sprinkle the top of your smoothie with hemp seeds, raw cacao nibs, dried cherries, or bee pollen.

Enjoy the love!

# November 15

## Four Steps to Tough Self-Love
### By Melanie Morrison

*I*t is not uncommon for us to talk about tough love when we are talking about other people, but what about when we are incorporating self-love? Self-love is not always baths and pedicures. Sometimes self-love involves making ourselves uncomfortable and letting go of things to make room for healing and growth. It can be tough to walk away from habits that have been bringing us short-term comfort and long-term sabotage. The key is to be strong, tough, and committed while still holding yourself with love.

As parents we might say to our children, "I love you, but you cannot have another candy." While we realize that denying a want may cause temporary distress, we know that is best for the child's health. There are times when the walk you committed to doing may be tough and cause a few sore muscles, but if it can be done while honoring your body, the long-term result is worth it. When we talk about tough love, we often refer to setting healthy boundaries with the person in question.

1. Take a moment today to write down what commitments to yourself you would like to honor.
2. Identify triggers that cause you to break those commitments.
3. Create boundaries for yourself going forward.
4. Forgive yourself for breaking previous commitments and send love to any feelings of guilt.
5. Recommit yourself to letting go of unhealthy habits and setting boundaries to encourage and enforce healthy habits with love.

Steps 2-4 may need to be repeated. Remember to give yourself grace as you push yourself though growth. Let your self -love be unconditional even when you are enforcing boundaries.

# November 16

## Observer
## By Kim Richardson

 *T*here are a lot of things that happen in us, around us, and to us in this world. With the media, and the ever-growing social media we are bombarded with opinions that do not match ours and people find it easy to be hurtful as well as people in and around our lives that can also deplete our energy if we allow it.

Years ago, in one of my therapy sessions when my life was in total chaos and turmoil, my counselor said, "what can you control?" I proceed to list of the millions of things I was trying to control only to realize that the only thing I could control was myself and my reaction to the things happening around me. I learned everyone has lessons to learn and if I keep jumping in to save the day, they may miss out on learning their own lessons.

You see, at one time I was an absorber. I absorbed the energy of everyone and everything around me. I took all their stuff on as if it were my own to fix. I often would be depleted and out of energy in many ways. I started to realize; I was possibly hindering them more than helping as I was talking away their chance to learn what they needed to so they could expand into their own greatness.

I flipped the switch. I became the observer the one who was here to be of support when I was able to, however I stopped taking over and started letting them figure it out. When I was unable to give support in the way they wanted it, I would simply hold a loving space and send prayers to them for them to learn whatever they needed to for their highest good. I realized I could be the light for others without having to dim mine.

What areas in your life can you become the observer?

# November 17

## Receive
## By Kim Richardson

*M*ost of us are much better givers than receivers, we simply feel better giving than receiving. There are many reasons we may not be good receivers as many of us are taught that we need to work hard for what we have, that there may be an expectation of something in return if we are given something, that it is selfish to receive, and so much more.

The truth is, the better you are at receiving the more you will receive! As you learn to be open and truly feel good when things come your way, the universe will continue to provide amazing things in your life.

Here is how I am working to be a better receiver;

1. Every day, I open my arms during my morning meditation practice and state, I am open to receive.
2. I have learned when someone offers me something to just say 'thank you' and just feel the gratitude in my heart of the gift or gesture.
3. Stop feeling like I must return the favor. Only give when my heart wants to but never out of obligation. When I do give, I do it without expecting anything in return.

Today, take notice of all the small gifts given to you throughout the day and try to be a better receiver. It could be a smile, a compliment, or a tangible gift. Take the time to notice in your body how it feels to receive these beautiful gifts. If you are like me and are a much better giver than receiver, maybe practice receiving up to five times before you give.

We are all entitled to abundance in every way and while I certainly think there is so much beauty in giving, we must learn that it is just as beautiful to receive as well.

# November 18

## The Beauty In Our Perceptions
## By Dominique Trier

"Though we travel the world over to find the beautiful, we must
carry it with us or we find it not."
~ Ralph Waldo Emerson.

After a long and tumultuous relationship ended, I was left
feeling disillusioned by love, as many do when experiencing
heartbreak. I put a lot of weight on the beauty others brought into
my life through love. As it does hold value to appreciate what others
bring into our lives, we cannot forget the reason we see how beautiful things are—us. We are in complete control of our perception.
We are the reason why we find certain things beautiful and love so
magical. There is an immense amount of power in knowing we can
experience beauty and magic because of our perceptions, not just
because of what others provide. We are able to provide the magic
and beauty in life ourselves.

Knowing we can create a life full of love for ourselves makes
it easier to take action in things that are good for us, rather than
focusing on external validation. We spend so much time attempting
to learn how to please and accommodate others, but what about
ourselves? How can we create beauty and magic for ourselves? I
know several of my friends have taken the time to go above and
beyond to make relationships work. It is common among my
friends to read books like *The Five Love Languages: How to Express
Heartfelt Commitment to Your Mate*, and even I have read it. Yet we
often do not think of expressing our commitment to ourselves in
our preferred love language. Why are we not taking those moments
where we learn about ourselves to better provide support for how

to feel loved by ourselves? Life is not always about what others can provide for us, but what we can provide for ourselves and others. Expectations of others are outside of our control, but what we can control is ourselves, our perceptions, the magical moments we create, and how we begin to care for ourselves. The relationship we have with ourselves will never end, and that is why it's so important we understand how we manifest the beauty in our lives.

# November 19

## Connect with Your Higher Self
## and Unconditional Love
## By Lisa A. Clayton

*Y*our higher self is an extension of your soul in light. Your higher self is always with you reflecting a higher consciousness frequency.

Your higher self is the universal source of cosmic energy and helps access the universal wisdom and knowledge within you. The higher self's greatest gift to you is unconditional love.

Being open to receive and exchange unconditional love with your higher self reframes self-love. It provides a different perspective of self-love as an unconditional love that is always available to you.

Use this protocol to connect with your higher self. Have pen and journal ready to capture key messages.

1. Find a quiet place to sit.

2. Focus your breath into your heart area, breathing slower and deeply for seven seconds. Exhale slowly seven seconds. Keep this breathing rhythm going for at least three minutes.

3. Now, imagine your breath filling up a special space between your heart's chambers called your heart's sacred space or heart's core. Your heart's sacred space is where your higher self is able to connect fully with you.

4. Sense or visualize rays of golden light beaming from your higher self through your crown chakra to your heart's sacred space. Feel its warmth filling your heart like the sun's rays.

5. Breathe in your higher self's unconditional love-light rays and hold for five seconds in your heart's sacred space. Then

exhale your unconditional love-light rays to your higher self. Complete this exchange twelve times as you are alchemizing your unconditional love-light rays together.

6. After this exchange feel the difference in how light your body feels. Radiate like the sun from your heart's sacred space. Visualize your energy field outside your body forming a powerful orb of unconditional love-light.

7. Visualize your higher self's orb of unconditional love-light coming close to yours until it becomes one with your orb of light. Feel its powerful presence and union with your orb.

8. Listen closely to what your higher self says to you. Write these powerful, light filled love messages in your journal.

9. Next, write twelve attributes you love and respect about yourself. Say these out loud to your higher self, giving gratitude for this exchange of unconditional love with each other.

This powerful exchange of unconditional love with your higher self brings forth the true essence of loving yourself.

# November 20

## Creative Balance of Water
## By Virginia Adams

*"Nothing is softer or more flexible than water, yet nothing can resist it."*
~ Lao Tzu, Tao Te Ching

*Rub a dub dub, an achy body in a tub.* Oh, the divine attributes of a good, old detox soak. When we approach bath time as a sacred holy ceremony, the outcome is soul cleansing. This sacred ceremony can be done as a bath, shower, a foot soak, a dip in a river, ocean or lake, a playful encounter with a hose, a baby pool, or a thoughtful drink of cool water. It does not matter what; this is all about the how.

When I think of sacramental waters, it brings to mind spiritual baptism, new life, cleansing, and rejuvenation. Interaction with Earth's life-sustaining waters can always be a holy moment if we understand it to be so.

When we wrap our minds around the fact that sixty percent of the human adult body is water, we begin to comprehend that water is an aspect of Source's life force energy. In the United States Geological Survey's article "The Water in You: Water in the Human Body," it states, "According to H.H. Mitchell, *Journal of Biological Chemistry*, 158, the brain and heart are composed of seventy-three percent water, and the lungs are about eighty-three percent water." Our brain, our heart, our lungs are basically fluid or water. What makes us tick, think, and breathe is water. Are you getting this?

In honor of your magical body of water, create a "ceremony of life" using water. Light a candle, some incense, and take a bath with Dead Sea salts and essential oils, soak your feet in Epsom salts and then anoint them with frankincense and myrrh. Stand under the shower and with intent feel the water wash over your body as you immerse yourself in gratitude for all that is. Each time you take a sip of water, give thanks to the water and feel it in your mouth, throat ,and all the way down to your stomach. Be creative; the sky is the limit on how we can celebrate water's energy.

The energy of fear cannot share the space of love. It is impossible. When we immerse ourselves in the power of self-love and self-care through the creative energy of water, we release the physical, mental, emotional, and spiritual effects of fear—creating a storehouse of love to support us through the darkest night.

# November 21

## Worthiness Points
## By Delores Garcia

*I* used to keep a *score card* on myself: performance, productivity, overall human value. When I wanted something better in my life, my brain would offer up my *score-to-date.* Had I earned enough points to deserve the dream item, be it a new relationship, more money, a fit body? Did I really *deserve* it? Unfortunately, I rarely seemed to accumulate enough *worthiness points,* based on all I tried to accomplish in life. I just was not doing enough to deserve my dreams. Return to the grind. Try harder to earn *worthiness points* to prove I deserved the goodness I desired.

I was also reminded of point deductions, like when I judged someone, or raised my voice at my teenagers, or ate donuts for breakfast instead of egg whites. *Worthiness points* seem to be disappearing at an alarming rate with every imperfect step I took!

Then I learned something brilliant. Worthiness is *not* based on what we do or do not do in this life. Worthiness is based on who we *are* at our true center. We were created inherently worthy of all goodness. We do not deserve good because we *do* good. We deserve good because we *are* good. Our true essence is worthy. This resonated truth with my soul. Abundant goodness flowed into my life. My human behaviors became vibrationally higher, not to prove my worth, but, indeed, to show my worthiness.

Thoughtfully read this list of affirmations. Notice which ones create strong resonance within you … ones that you wished you believed. These are affirmations your soul desires for you to embody.

I am worthy.

I am deserving.

I am worthy of love.

I deserve to live my best life.

I am deeply connected to Source/God.

I know who I am.

I am always winning.

Close eyes. Cross arms at wrist. Place at heart center.

Breathe deeply three times while silently repeating chosen affirmation several times.

Uncross arms. Place hands on thighs, palms upward.

Using fingertips of left hand, tap on palm of right hand while silently repeating affirmation several times.

Then switch and use fingers on right hand to tap on palm of left hand while silently repeating the affirmation several times.

Do this back and forth several times.

Lastly, interlace fingers. Place hands in lap.

Continue to silently repeat affirmation several more times, while taking three more cleansing deep breaths.

# November 22

## What Have You Done for You Lately
## By Sheryl Goodwin Magiera

There is a little-known secret that women think it's selfish to do for themselves before doing things for others. Where did that come from anyway? Even on a plane, they instruct us to administer oxygen to ourselves before helping others. Thinking about that when I flew with my children at a young age somehow felt self-serving since a mother's nature is to take care of other's first.

Over the last several years, I have been learning and practicing to the contrary, and frankly have discovered this is not true or even good for us. It's not selfish or self-serving, or narcissistic. It's the opposite. It is about loving ourselves enough and knowing we are worth it. Of course we want to take care of others, which is fabulous, but doing and giving to ourselves is the greatest and best thing we can do not only for our souls, but for our family and friends.

Loving yourself can be as simple as taking a relaxing bubble bath, reading a book, exercising, or a simple five-minute meditation. It does not have to cost any money at all, just dedicated, precious time to connect with your mind, body, and spirit. This year I have committed to seeking new things just for me to help me connect with whom I am at my core.

Find time to pamper and love yourself as you continue to give to others. Make a conscious choice to do something just for you. Whether it is a planned outing with friends or tucked at home in a favorite spot, do something you love. Ask what have you done for yourself lately, and what is the thing that sets your soul on fire, or one thing you can do for yourself that connects your mind, body, and spirit? You are worth it. I am worth it. We all are deserving of our own love.

# November 23

## Miracles
### By Bernadette Rodebaugh

*I* have heard it said that miracles do not come to those that do not believe in them. That is simply because miracles cannot find you, if you are not looking for them.

So during this uncertain time when many are living in fear and feel unloved, forgotten, and are worrying about tomorrow I choose to believe that the power of love and all that is good is stronger than hate, fear, and worry!

I choose to remind myself that in this world there are miraculous, endless possibilities and miracles happen every day to somebody somewhere. So why can't I, my family, and the world I live in be the next miracle?

Since the best thing for me to do to help allow miracles into my life is to believe in them, I will do the following:

- Today I choose to believe in the best outcome possible for everyone everywhere.
- Today I choose to think about only the things that make me feel good, healthy, and happy.
- Today I choose to only spend my time and energy being positive: giving instead of taking, loving instead of worrying.
- Today I choose to look for opportunities where I can be somebody's miracle with just a smile, a kind word, or anything else I am guided to do for others.
- Today I choose to be thankful for the things that I *do* have as I look at my life and the world I love.

- Today I choose that wherever I may go, no matter who I am with, that I will be looking for the endless possibilities of miracles so that they can find us.

*That is because I choose miracles!*

# November 24

## The Heart of Stillness
## By Courtney Parreira

Stillness calls us back to our own hearts, our own natural rhythm. It can take many forms, but the constant throughout all forms is the space for which we allow our souls to speak. The simple act of allowing for that space creates a direct connection to our truest self, the partnership of soul and heart which together weave our personal connection to the divine. The more time we spend in stillness, the more we will know ourselves. The more we genuinely know ourselves, the more fully we accept and love ourselves. And that is when we will know the divine.

Look at the forms of stillness below. Identify which you already practice and which you want to practice in the future. There may be only one or two that call to you or there may be more.

- Sitting in nature.
- Playing calm music.
- Snuggling with your pet and allowing nature's animals to show you stillness (They are experts!).
- Meditation or prayer.
- Energetic body scan.
- Sound bath.
- Singing bowls.
- Heart breaths.
- Connected walk in nature.

- Lighting a candle and sitting in its glow.
- Sitting on the bed and connecting to the comfort around you.

Can you think of another form of stillness not listed above? Which form of stillness will you practice today?

# November 25

## Redefining Superwoman (Superman)
## and Perfectionism
## By Carolan Dickinson

*S*omewhere along the line, most of us have gotten the message that we are supposed to do all things, be all things, and do it without error, perfectly and with a God-like presence. We do all of these things to be lovable as a mom, dad, spouse, or friend. We also do this to verify our own self-worth. When we cannot live up to those self-imposed standards, then what happens? We feel small, less than, and that we are not good enough, worthy enough, and therefore damaged in some way. When you think about it, it is sort of ridiculous that any human being should have God-like qualities and the ability to be omniscient. And, yet . . . we persist in striving for perfection. I believe it is admirable to always be striving to be better and do better. However, that does not encompass physical acts of inhuman abilities. It is more compassionate to strive to live a fulfilling life with purpose and meaning. As a fellow human, you already are everything you need to be. You are an incredibly valuable person worthy of all the joy and abundance the universe can manifest for you.

What does perfectionism cost you? I think that striving to be perfect cost us many things, including our connection to other people. It robs us of our genuineness, self-worth, and ultimately self-love. The negative self-talk that happens when we discover that we cannot walk on water is a great place to begin unraveling unkind messages to ourselves. Those negative messages remind me of the sneaky Dementors from Harry Potter that slide into our minds to steal our joy. I am wondering what you tell yourself in those moments where you feel defeated for not being Superwoman or Superman?

For the next week, just notice when you are in Superwoman or Superman mode. When you notice that you have donned your cape:

1. When you recognize a feeling, what is the thought that goes along with that? For example, *when I have donned my cape, I feel anxious and stressed.*

2. Next, notice the thought that goes along with that feeling. It could be, *there is not enough time in the day; I'm a terrible parent, spouse, worker.*

3. Challenge that thought with a positive affirmation. I have all the time in the world to do everything I need and want to do. I am a great parent. I am doing the best I can. I am worthy of self-care. I am worthy. I am perfectly imperfect. I do not want Superwoman's job (just kidding, positive affirmation should always state what you want versus what you do not want).

4. When you first start to use positive affirmations, you may feel awkward when saying them, even internally, and your believability level might not be 100%. That is okay. Say them anyway. At some point, a shift will happen, and you can annihilate the Dementors.

# November 26

## Being Intentional
## By Lisa Seyring

*H*aving a purpose for doing something can change the whole experience. I turned my everyday living into purposeful living by learning to create intention for my day, for an experience, or for a task.

Let's take cleaning my living quarters. Drudgery comes to mind when I feel I *have* to clean. However, if I create an intention behind the cleaning, I can change the whole experience. I can intend to be joyful while cleaning so that I can create a comfortable, clean environment for me and my loved ones. Creating an intention gives a completely new energetic purpose to the task. The former drudgery simply slips away.

I put this notion to the test when we took a family vacation which included a four hour canoe trip. Admittedly, I was slightly uptight and a little hesitant about maneuvering a canoe. I decided to have a different experience by creating a specific intention for my trip. What I truly desired was to be carefree and just have fun. I made my intention to be childlike in my approach so that I could experience joy. Once I was in the canoe with my daughter, I reminded myself of my intention and we pushed off. All was well until we hit a shallow part and had to get around rocks protruding from the river. My thoughts instantly seized up with fear and simultaneously the canoe started turning perpendicularly towards the rocks. The more panic I felt, the more the canoe turned.

In my tizzy, my daughter reminded me to remember my purpose. Quickly, I redirected my thoughts to be curious of *how* we will get around the rocks, not *if* we will. The canoe changed direction and was in flow with the river. I lined up with my intention a few more times going down the river. Had I not known where to direct my thoughts as established in my intention, our experience would have been tense and fretful rather than the joyful one we experienced!

We do, indeed, create our experiences and learning opportunities with our thoughts, so why not be intentional and create more loving experiences? Experiment and use the following formula to create an intention for your day.

- I intend to be _____, so that I may experience _____.

What is your desired state of mind and what is it you wish to experience?

# November 27

## Crystals and Chakras
## By Gloria Dawn Kapeller

Crystals are something that I have always loved but am only now just learning about their meanings and how to use them. They can enhance our lives and here are a few ideas to help. Here are some things that I have learned.

1. Crown chakra—moonstone—encourages personal growth, protective especially for travelers and balances female hormones.

2. Third eye chakra—lapris lazuli—strengthens confidence in our abilities, gives reassurance—flurite—balances emotions, wards off negativity and protects against stress.

3. Throat chakra—angelite—brings calm and peace in times of stress and protects against negativity. Aqua aura—deflects harmful energy and promotes self expression in a calm loving way.

4. Heart chakra—rose quartz—soothes emotions and raises self esteem and promotes self love. Malachite—protection from low vibrational energy and alleviates anxiety.

5. Solar plexus chakra—amber—helps balance emotions and promotes patience and helps shield against negativity. Tiger eye—used for grounding and protects from negative emotions and boosts confidence.

6. Sacral chakra—carnelian—boosts energy and promotes courage and is motivating. Red jasper—balances emotions and gives emotional security and encourages strength and is grounding.

7. Root chakra—black tourmaline—cleanses energy block-
   ages and helps protect against negativity and electromagnetic energy. Hematite stabilizes and increases mental
   clarity and repels negative energy.

How can you benefit from using crystals and learning about
their powers and energies to enhance your life?

# November 28

## I Found Joy
## By Mindy Lipton

*I*t was Christmas, 2013, and I was working two seasonal jobs at Macy's and World Market. I was going through a divorce after sixteen years of marriage. You might say the marriage was fifty/fifty. The first eight years were fabulous. He was thrilled we were expecting triplets in our first year of marriage.

The stress of it all led to major stomach problems. Being on prednisone for five years straight made him a new man. A man I did not marry.

After years of counseling, he confessed that he just was not attracted to me anymore. I moved on.

Being that it was the Christmas season I found joy everywhere. Ornaments, signs, cards, even cookies spelled out joy. It was that word that gave me strength and that will be the way for many years to come. My living room is decorated with joy.

So, what brings me joy? Walking in nature, finding flowers and heart-shaped leaves. Breathing the beautiful fresh air, we often take for granted. Here in California, we have that extra season, the fire season, so we do appreciate the fresh air.

For two years I worked as a part-time nanny to several families. Joy beams out of you as the infant rests on your chest. We would play bubbles for her first time and that was so thrilling to her. Oh yes, tickled with joy. She would giggle and giggle as I would tickle and tickle. Her parents asked me what was "dickle dickle?" It was their child's first set of words. If I should feel down these days, I remember "dickle dickle."

Many will not admit to it, but I do love Facebook. Living alone with just my sweet cat, Willow. Facebook is my only outlet right now. Music fills my apartment all day long with Alexa playing all my requests from Carol King, Pharrell Williams's *Happy*, Cher, Bette Midler, and Barbra Streisand. Facebook also provided me with a new community of people from all over this country as well as out of the country. I began very interesting classes online and that brings me a lot of newfound joy. Imagine my surprise to see the December, 2020 special edition cover of *Time Magazine* was *JOY*.

It all depends on where you put your focus. I chose joy. Meditation, affirmations and keeping a journal with a separate notebook for writing & burning helps immensely and I encourage you to use those tools to help you choose joy.

# November 29

## Self-Love for the Highly Sensitive
## By Amy I. King

Since I was a little girl, I have been a highly sensitive person. I grew up thinking that something was wrong with me. Nothing *was* wrong with me; I had a gift that others lacked. I can feel the energy of every person, shifts in energy, how people feel toward me, and when that feeling changes. It wasn't always roses and sunshine. I felt weird, and my family did not understand me.

When I was growing up, there was a tradition on your birthday to sing "Happy Birthday" as many times as your age. So, if you were eight, they would sing it eight times. I remember covering my ears because the noise overwhelmed me. Crazy right? That is what I grew up thinking.

I heard more than a few times from my family, "What's wrong with you?"

Wishing I had the words, I felt like responding with "I feel things so intensely that at times I go into overwhelm. I need a quiet place to recharge." But, not having those words, I just shrugged and internalized that there was something wrong with me.

Self-care for the highly sensitive may look the same as it does for other people. A highly sensitive person must do it regularly to maintain good health. My routine looks something like this.

I make sure that I exercise daily. Exercise rids the body of excess energy and helps to maintain your body's function.

Meditating is beneficial to the life of a highly sensitive person. As little as twenty minutes a day will make an enormous difference.

Eat healthy, whole foods, including plenty of fruits and vegetables. Nutrition is essential to self-care.

Sleep between seven and nine hours per night. Trust me. It will make an impact on your life and your day. You will feel less irritable and more able to focus on the day ahead.

Connect with people who understand you. Feeling connections with people who support and love us is vital to our good health.

Get out in nature. Touch the plants and enjoy the songs of the birds. You will feel more connected to everything when you connect with the natural world.

Honor yourself and your needs. Say yes to the things that feed your soul and no to those that do not.

Happy Self Care!

# November 30

## Mother Mary and Self-Love
## By Giuliana Melo

One of the most loving ways to heal is to connect to the energy of the dear mother, Mary. She is the mother of Jesus, queen of Heaven and the holy angels and a beautiful goddess. Her healing quality is self-love. She encourages us to love our own hearts first. She wants us to fill up our golden chalice to overflowing and then give from the overflow. She says to never give in obligation, but to give when you want to and with an open heart. She also helps those of us who are adopted, feeling abandoned, and who do not have great mothers in our life. She is our beloved divine mother and loves us so very much. She wants the best for us.

She says to see yourself through the eyes of love. One of the tools to do that is by looking in a mirror and saying, "I love and accept myself exactly as I am!" Say it each and every day and until you truly believe it and receive it into your heart.

Mother Mary also wants us to welcome miracles into our lives. Miracles happen for those who believe in them. Right now, take the time to be open to miracles. You will experience miracles when you decide to let life love you completely and freely.

To affirm say, "I am open to miracles and I am ready to receive."

To invoke her into your life just say, "Dear Mary, mother of Jesus, please help me. Amen and so it is."

You may feel a warmness envelope you. You may smell roses or feel drops of water or see ladybugs.

Now, write a list of five things you love about yourself.

1. _____

2. _____

3. _____

4. _____

5. _____

Next list what activities do you do in your life to fill up your cup?

1. _____

2. _____

3. _____

4. _____

5. _____

# December 1

## Accept and Believe
## By Nanette Gogan-Edwards

Believe in who you are and in who you will become. This begins with a solid acceptance of your current abilities as well as your shortcomings. So often we focus on what *could be* or what *will be* instead of being in the present moment and expressing gratitude for what *is*. There is no way we can genuinely appreciate who we are today if we are constantly dreaming of a different life.

Every morning I spend a few quiet moments in gratitude for wat I have and who I am. Somedays I write these down in a notebook. Other days I sit outside with my eyes closed and feel my blessings: the sun on my face, the birds chirping, the neighbor children laughing, the airplane flying over. It is fascinating how your thoughts begin to change toward more positive vibrations. The more you focus on these things, the more you will notice them!

Let yourself feel the joy, peace, sadness, anger, contentment, confusion—whatever is a part of you at that very moment. Accept it and embrace it as a part of your existence. Every feeling you have and every action you take is based on one of two things—love or fear. Once you can discern which it is, it will be easier to let go of what is no longer serving you and your purpose.

In the same way you wash your outside body, you must also cleanse the inside daily of the "dirt" both seen and unseen. Every day presents new challenges and often unrecognized spiritual burdens. Pretending they do not exist leads to a thick buildup of this *dirt* that eventually cannot by ignored by us or by others.

Believe in your ability to shift your focus and in turn shift your life in the direction of your soul. Have the courage to accept everything about you as part of that wonderful and glorious journey!

# *December 2*

## Self-Soothing
## By Denise Kirkconnnell

From as far back as I can remember I was a natural self-soother. I was a childhood rocker. Yes, I literally was. I would go into a zone and rock back and forth and hum some gibberish endlessly. I did not realize it for a while what I was doing. And somewhere along the way, I stopped doing it and the things I chose to self sooth with were not the healthiest or in my best interest.

After years of being uncomfortable hearing my own voice, by learning about self-care I became more familiar with my voice again and especially humming.

Self-love in any form is a huge win-win.

Begin to play with your voice by humming or singing. No judgment.

In most situations I find it is best to hum it to yourself then let it pass through your lips.

# December 3

## Self-Love through Friendships
### By Vonnie L. Hawkins, LCSW

As I sat down to write, resistance overcame me in the form of imposter syndrome. Who was I to be writing about self-love? What about my experience could be meaningful to others?

Most of my life, I sought redemption through over-giving. I have not always been the best friend and I am terrible at remembering birthdays. When I do remember, my gifts are functional because I see myself as a serious person with little time for frivolous things. Fortunately, the universe has been teasing this part of me out of its rigid patterns.

You see, the universe has recently gifted me with two beautiful, amazing, women friends who had difficult lives like mine, but also found their way to fun, laughter, self-love, and embarked on journeys of inspiration and uplifting others.

In a moment of questioning my gifts and my journey, I only had to reach out for a loving, powerful reminder that all is as it should be, that we are all just walking each other home, and even though we are at different points in that journey, that we are all one, all here to love, lift up, and support each other.

In her beautiful words and actions, my friend held up a mirror so I could see a version of myself that I forgot, the version of myself who I always long to be, but because I listen to the voices in my head, I sometimes forget I already and always am. And because I have been practicing my own self-love, I was ready to ask for, and receive her gift.

Self-love is believing we deserve amazing, beautiful friendships to help us along the way! Self-love is connecting to friends who see the most divine and enlightened versions of ourselves. When that happens, we can remind each other we are beautiful and always worthy, and that all of experience is part of the journey. That includes even the squishy dark parts. Even those parts are to be loved and embraced because they make us who we truly are.

Today write down the names of the friends who lift you up, who hold in their hearts that version of you that you sometimes forget you already are. What actions could you take to bring these precious gifts from the universe closer to you, to remind you more often, of the amazing, brilliant, loving, eternal, divine soul that you are?

# December 4

## Half Full or Half Empty
## By Karen Cowperthwaite

Self-love is more than a feeling. It is how you show up for yourself and how you think about yourself. As human beings, we have about 60,000 thoughts a day and it is a pretty even split between positive and negative ones. Some of us see the glass as half empty; some of us see the glass as half full. Whichever way you naturally lean, it is important to acknowledge a phenomenon called the negativity bias. What this means is that human beings tend to give more weight to negative emotions than to positive ones. In fact, we may hear three positive reactions from someone about our performance and then there is the one comment we feel is more critical. That is the one we take to heart. The same judgment also comes straight from our own minds when we dwell on one mistake rather than the big picture of many forward moving action steps we have taken.

When I was learning how to trust my intuitive skills, there were many approaches I tried to help me to quiet my fears so I could open up to the inner guidance that was waiting for me. The most important piece of advice I give now is that when your desires are being choked out by your fears, shift into play mode, explore, and be curious. You have goals and passions still inside of you. And yes, you also have fears. You may be rejected. You may fail. You may face difficulty. But here are three easy tricks to help you reach for the life you want and still enjoy the process of getting there:

- Play Dress-up
  Imagine you are the bravest person on earth who is invincible. Don the outfit. See the "Super You"

leading the way for the "Small You" to experience success.

- Picture Your Party
  How will you feel when you succeed? Envision the celebration and the atmosphere that you will be a part of when you reach your goal.

- Listen for Your Cheerleaders
  There will always be doubters, discouragers, and naysayers. Remind yourself that those voices are not the only ones and send in the cheerleaders! Imagine a whole section of cartwheeling tumblers with megaphones and uniforms bearing your initials. See them smiling and cheering for you from the stands.

# December 5

## Note to Self
### By Marsha Johnson

Who does not like to receive a handwritten letter in the mail? Isn't it exciting to go to the mailbox and see an envelope, handwritten, and addressed to you? What a pick-me-up that is. And another thing that is especially nice is to hear words of praise about yourself. Today is a good day to write a note to yourself, to let yourself know just how spectacular you are.

First thing is to set the mood. Maybe go to your favorite coffee shop, sit outdoors while having a picnic or find your favorite spot in your home, grab a favorite drink, get comfortable and get started. I like to pick up a sentimental card to write in or get some beautiful stationery. A personal touch I like is to use a special and fancy pen. Make this as special a time as you can to honor yourself.

I invite you to become the observer of your life—with no attachments. Write a letter to you, as if you are writing a recommendation letter for you. Another way to do this would be to write the letter as if you were writing about a great friend or loved one. You can start it off "Dear (your name), I want to let you know just how wonderful you are, or I love how you care about (fill in the blank)." Here is where the fun begins. The following is a list of areas that you can write about:

1. Accomplishments, awards, and recognition you've received in all areas of your life, your work, home, health, hobbies, dreams and ambitions.

2. Your appearance.

3. What is unique about you?

4. A time you were brave.

5. How you are a good friend.

6. Things that make you happy.

7. An experience where you were kind and helpful.

After you have written the letter, I would suggest putting it in the mail to yourself, and then once you receive it and open it, keep it in a special place, a drawer in your desk, or in your nightstand. If you ever start to experience any kind of self-doubt, unworthiness, or the like, take that letter out and read it to yourself to be reminded of just how special you are. It is guaranteed to bring a smile to your face and a bounce in your step.

# December 6

## Lose Yourself
### By Carrie Newsom

*I* have never been good at meditating. I have tried countless times, in so many ways, to turn off my brain chatter and find inner peace, but it just feels so difficult. The instant I am *not* supposed to be thinking about something, it is all I can think about. I used to feel like I was a failure because I cannot figure out what everyone loves about traditional meditation. If you are one of those who finds peace in meditation, I am in awe of you, and quite envious! But then I stumbled upon a different way to meditate that works for me, and it may work for you too.

I found my way of meditating by accident. I found a way to turn off the endless, exhausting mental chatter by losing myself in activities I love. It feels like "losing myself" because I can turn down the meaningless brain noise and focus on just being.

We live in a super stressful, challenging, ever-changing world. Sometimes I feel like there is no way to escape from the stress- to decompress, to let go, even for a moment. But then I realized that I can lose myself. We have all heard the phrase "lose yourself in thought." I have found it is an excellent way of coping with stress.

When I walk through the forest preserve near my home, I lose myself. I plug in my earbuds, tune out the world, and soak up nature. The miles just tick by as I put one foot in front of the other and just walk, walk, walk. The same thing happens to me when I paint- hours can go by and it feels like the blink of a second. I lose myself in the act of putting brush to canvas, my mental chatter is silenced, and I have inner peace. Soul peace.

You will be better able to handle the Crazy that life throws at you if you can locate that sanctuary of inner stillness. It is important to lose yourself for a little while, whether it is in thought, in the meditative actions of painting or walking, or something completely different. Sink into your soul and get to know it better. Humans were made with talkative minds, but sometimes we need to turn off that noise just for a little while and rest in deep silence.

# December 7

### Love
### By Giuliana Melo

*L*ove is a high vibration. It is also the greatest healing quality there is. When I was sick and healing from stage three cancer, I had to tap into love in a big way. All the love I had given to others, I had to give to myself. I learned that love is who we are and where we came from and to where we return. Love is the great I AM presence. I learned how what you put after your I AM is what we become.

Let's do some together now. Grab a journal and write them down or say them out loud or silently in your head. For Example:

I AM Love. I AM kind. I AM generous. I AM beautiful. I AM worthy. I AM holy. I AM happy. I AM a child of God.

Now you can add whatever words you would like after your I AM.

Love is the answer to all our questions. When you are in pain or judgement, place your hand on your heart and ask yourself "What would love do, be, or say in this situation?" Then take action from there.

Feeling loved is our truest heart's desire. It is up to us to be love in order to attract more love into our life. Love is available to us in abundance, and it is offered to us freely by the divine. To tap into it, imagine your heart attached to the love of the divine. Imagine a pink energy cord from your heart to the God of your understanding. Allow that pink energy to flow to you and through you and then go out and surround everything and everyone you know in love. Sometimes I like envisioning my loved ones in pink blankies of love. What a beautiful visualization.

Another way to ensure you are loving is to be mindful of your words, actions and deeds. Always choose to be loving and kind. Begin with your own heart. You are worth it.

# December 8

## The Art of Joyness
## By Jannirose Fenimore

One of the defining characteristics that my son Charlie possesses is a naturally joyful heart. I am certain he was created this way—even as a baby, he exhibited an undeniable lightness of being. For him, joy is the signature of his *Charlie-ness*. When he 6Ab was a teenager, I once asked him playfully, "Why did God make Down syndrome?" I wanted to know how he perceived the purpose of his unique chromosomal make-up (which he believes to be a superpower.)

Charlie considered my question for a moment and answered in a clear, confident voice, *"For the spirit of joyness!"* \

I thought about his response, and it made perfect sense from my perspective. I realize that the Down syndrome community works hard to eliminate stereotypes, but in my sixty-plus years of living and observing life, this has definitely been my experience. And what a brilliant idea for God to design some people with an extra-large capacity for joy. I am sure He knows the world can use it!

In my understanding, *joyness* encompasses a keen ability to find joy in nearly everything. I am grateful to have been mentored well in this art by my own resident joy master. This becomes more obvious to me during times like the one I am facing now. After an arduous two years as my father's sole caregiver, I am tired. And yet, my heart overflows with joy and gratitude for the gift and blessing of this life.

For many of us, *joyness* is hard to find in the midst of life's challenges. There can be so much happening in our little corners of the world that joy does not even appear on our radars. Through my everyday lessons from an earth angel, I am learning that living in *joyness* requires us to keep our hearts as finely tuned as possible.

I have found this is most easily accomplished when I see my heart as a team mate with whom I journey through life. As with any team, communication is imperative for the success of its intended mission.

Today, I encourage you to check in with your heart partner throughout the day to hear what it has to express. Then, be sure to honor what it needs. You will be delighted to discover that your *joyness* becomes more expansive as you clear the way for its unimpeded flow.

# December 9

## Graceful Giving Joyful
## By Charlie Fenimore

*S*ometimes we forget our life of graceful souls in light with God around us. We must remember our goodness and our joyness. Remember God loves us, and we are all love. We can live in loving hope and change our sadness to a joyful shining life.

# December 10

## How Do You Treat Yourself?
## By Debra Moore Ewing

*W*hen is the last time you did something just for *you*? As women it is so easy to get caught up in the *game of life* and put our needs and desires on the back burner. We typically do not make ourselves a priority.

You may be a mother, so it is only natural that your children come first. You may be married or a housewife and we typically look to the matriarchs in our own lives as role models. I was told that I would get married, be a mom, have a white picket fence, and take care of the children and my husband. I laugh as I write this because none of that happened!

Your career may be your focus. You may not know when to put the brakes on at the end of the day. You are too exhausted to do anything but come home, possibly pour yourself a glass of wine, relax on the couch with your feet up, only to repeat the process all over again.

I know I am guilty of not putting *me* first. I have a gift certificate for a massage and another for a facial that I have not used in two years. I ask myself why that is. I know I am worth it. I am worth taking time for myself. It is not being selfish. It is putting myself *first* because at the end of the day who will be there for me?

So, if you are reading this, and you are on the *hamster wheel of life*, I encourage you to ask yourself, "When was the last time I treated myself to something special?"

Maybe take the day and go to a movie by yourself or with a girlfriend. Possibly it is lunch at your favorite spot. It can be inexpensive. I remember when money was tight. I found beauty schools where I could feel pampered without breaking the budget. Students who are practicing need clients, so they can hone their skills for facials and special treatments, massage therapy, and even hypnosis! When I was a student, I needed clients to practice on and it was free! If you are on a limited income, think outside the box. Do something for yourself *today* and see if you can find one online in an area near you! You *are* worth it!

# December 11

## The Gift of Getting Curious
## By Grace Redman

*H*ey Hey, Beautiful Soul!

We have all been there. You are at a party and you approach someone, but they give you the cold shoulder. It hurts, doesn't it? It leaves you wondering what you did wrong to deserve such disrespect. It's happened to me and it used to bother me so much that it ruined my day. Sometimes I even stewed on it bitterly for the whole week, creating stories in my mind about what I did wrong. What an utter waste of energy and time!

I have learned an important lesson about taking things personally. Namely, I should not because more often than not, the other person's behavior has nothing to do with me. Maybe they are having a bad day, or their dog just died. Maybe they were spaced out and did not even see me. Whatever it is, it is all about them, not *you*.

One of my friends who wanted to go away with me and was excited about it all of the sudden felt cold with me and told me she wasn't sure that she could go. I felt hurt because she always made time for other friends and going away was her idea. I felt that I was not a priority to her. I felt hurt for a while and then I flipped the script and got curious. I thought maybe she was having a hard time finding someone to watch her kids. Well, a week later she gave me some crazy news. During the time that I felt she was being cold and putting me off, the doctors had given her husband a cancer diagnosis. Luckily, it was a false diagnosis, and all ended fine, but in those days, she was going through hell and her coldness to me had nothing to do with me but with her own fear and confusion.

The next time you are in a situation where something happens and you take it personally and you feel that ache in your heart, flip the script. Instead of taking it personally, get curious about the other person …. What could they be going through in that moment, that day, or in their own life? Also, if you create a story in your head about the interaction, ask yourself is that really true? How do I know it is true?

This, my sweet friend, is one of the greatest gifts of self-love you can give yourself. Take nothing personally.

# December 12

## You Are Enough
## By Kim Richardson

There are many days that can be overwhelming. Life can take over and we can easily lose a sense of who we are. We can get caught up in the opinions of others and what they think we should be doing or who we should be. I find that most of the time we are our worse enemy, placing judgments or simply feeling the guilt and shame that we are not doing enough or have feelings of inadequacy in so many areas of our lives.

Today, I would like to remind you that YOU are enough, that everything is perfect inside of you in every way. Remember to quiet the negative chatter in your own mind and block out the negative chatter from the outside world. Throughout the day, tell yourself, "I am enough."

## "If you have to disappoint someone don't let it be you!"
## ~ author unknown

The reality is, we cannot please everyone all the time. The most important thing is to put your emotional, physical, and spiritual needs first. Know that you will disappoint some people, just try not to disappoint yourself!

You need to know that you are doing the best you can. Everything we move through in this life serves as a lesson and some lessons may be harder than others. With each lesson there is an opportunity to grow and expand into the best version of yourself. As you move through these lessons, heal the past, and work on discovering the true essence of who you want to be, you will break the cycle. Those lessons will no longer repeat. Now, new lessons will arise, and we are always growing and learning. Head into each lesson with excitement for the opportunity to grow.

You can do your best every day and each day your best may look different depending on what you are going through. *Your best in that moment is enough.*

Always keep your chin up, my friend. You got this! You are enough!

# December 13

## Love's Call
## By Lisa Seyring

*I* gave myself the opportunity to be able to listen more deeply to my heart.

I asked myself, "What if love was calling me? What would love say?"

I allowed the narrative of my mind to rest and I focused on the voice of my heart. You see, my mind can get tangled in thoughts, frozen in fear, and stuck in old stories. The truth, however, is that love is always calling to me. I just have to slow down, put my attention into my heart and listen. The act of intentional listening and giving your heart—your higher knowing—a chance to be heard is the real essence of this exercise. It is in the free flow of writing where the nuggets of love and wisdom we are not expecting come forth.

The invitation for you is to practice listening to your heart through stream of consciousness writing. There is no pressure; there are no expectations in this exercise. Just set the intention to listen to the voice of your heart and write.

What does your heart have to say? Experiment with the following guidelines.

1. Get pen and paper and set a timer for ten minutes.

2. Pick one of the following prompts and write it down:

   a. Self-Love

   b. Loving the self

   c. What if love were calling me? What would love say?

   d. My heart speaks

3. Take your attention and place it into the area of your heart. To get you into your heart space, take a breath and exhale as if you are exhaling right into your heart.

4. Revisit your writing prompt, start the timer, and begin writing. Write whatever comes into your mind; do not filter it. Keep writing non-stop until the timer rings. When thoughts stall, simply write, *I do not know what to write*, until a new thought stream comes.

5. Read and receive your rich wisdom.

The message will be meaningful to *you*! It does not have to make sense to another person. Approach this with curiosity and a willingness to be a good *listener*. Receive the love within you that is beyond the limitations of your mind. If you like this exercise, try extending the time to thirty minutes or experiment with other topics such as "Who am I?" or "Compassion toward the self." Have fun exploring your heart's perspective!

# December 14

## Love Leads the Way
## By Crystal Cockerham

*A*re you, and those you love, going through a rough time? I know you want to be there and help them, but here is the thing - You cannot be there for anyone when you have got nothing in the tank to keep *you* going. This is also known as serving from an empty cup. Truly, it helps no one to serve from an empty cup including you.

So how do you fill yourself up so that you can do and be who and what you want in support of your loved ones?

Love yourself through it. Loving yourself through it means slowing down and taking care of yourself by:

- Hydrating. Drink plenty of water
- Eat. Even if you are not hungry. It can be something small and healthy at least. Remember the rainbow rule.
- Rest. You need your sleep. Even if you can't sleep, resting is *very* beneficial.
- Unplug. Take the time you need to stay away from your normal routine to allow yourself the space to grieve and take care of whatever you need to take care of *including* yourself.
- Do not try to tackle your everyday to-do list. Re-prioritize and/or ask for help.
- Write or journal. Write letters. Write to honor the person/situation you are grieving, even if that person is a version of you. Writing is sooo healing and you do not have to hang yourself up on grammar. No one else ever even has to read it.

- Connect with nature. Its healing properties are beyond measure and the resources it has are endless. Sit outside and soak up the sun, play a yard game, take a walk, play fetch with your dog and laugh at the shenanigans, etc.
- Laughter is another healer with boundless reach. Laughter heals.
- Be gentle with yourself as you re-enter your 'normal' daily activities. It may take some time to get back into the swing of things.
- Live. Laugh. Love. Not necessarily in that order and not a cliché. If I have learned anything, it is savor every moment. Live. Laugh. Love.

Not only does this help fill you up so you have the strength and energy to support your loved ones, it also shows them how they can take care of themselves and love themselves through it, too.

Nature heals. Laughter heals. And love leads the way!

# December 15

## What Is It You Need?
## By Marie Martin

*A* lesson of love: express your needs and voice them for your-self. Learn to let the world adjust to what you need.

Speaking up for yourself is a skill, and like most skills, my love, you may find other people who are better at voicing what they need than yourself. Even years after finding this act of self-love and iden-tifying it as a skill, I can still struggle with my truth from time to time. And, like a skill, you need to practice this ability to grow it.

Imagine for a moment that you can share without guilt or other negatively aligned emotions what you need but have been afraid to voice. What would that mean for you? How would voicing your needs let you shape your world into a focused extension of your will? Words are powerful. They can cut, and they can heal.

In a world that does not hear your truth, you are the one left adjusting. When, however, you share what you need, the world can adjust to you. The problem that many people fall in to is when they feel that sharing their needs may make the other person feel bad or speaking up may draw unwanted attention. Do not dim your light simply to make someone else comfortable; this never feels good. I have found in my life that it is the times that I did not speak up that I regret the most.

At first, as you may suspect, you will find this difficult and maybe even a little scary as time moves on; however, you will find yourself becoming happier as you speak your thoughts. This practice will also help you become less sensitive emotionally.

To grow the skill of speaking up, begin with taking small steps and start in areas where you will have simple successes. Simple suc-cess is the building block to growing confidence.

# December 16

## Personal Power!
## By Nancy Toffanin

When I reflect on my life, I realize how I constantly gave my power away. I did not stand up for myself, speak my truth, or listen to my intuition. I put other people's wants before mine. The list goes on. Eight years ago, I lost power in my house. I was in a relationship where my partner's anger controlled my voice and power. My dad's friend was an electrician, but he could not find the problem.

I sat on the couch, saying over and over, "I have no power." Then I realized the problem was not just electrical! It was me. Anger really scared me! That day I started affirmations on personal power. Ironically, I fixed the electrical problem by resetting an outlet.

I realized I had to get my power back. I left that relationship, and I started working on my confidence, self-esteem, value, and respect. I started putting myself first, speaking authentically, and not holding back just to make someone else feel comfortable.

I worked on speaking my truth with grace, kindness, and transparency. I noticed where I lost my voice in relationships.

I expanded my throat chakra. I loved myself enough to realize I had the power to change, the power to work though my traumas, and the power to heal myself.

Learning to listen to my intuition and trusting myself allowed me to be open and to speak my truth. Personal power really helps us open up to self-love. When we expand our power center, we stop putting up with less than we deserve. Helping women find their personal power is really rewarding.

There are different crystals can be used to help ignite our personal power. Citrine, oro verde, and sunstone are good examples. For the throat chakra use blue lace agate, amazonite, and aquamarine, lapis lazuli. For the heart chakra use pink rose quartz, garnet, alexandrite, or morganite. Crystals can help with self-esteem, self-worth, confidence, value, self-love, balance, and grounding, etc. We can carry crystals in our bra or pocket; we can keep them beside our bed. It is fun to make an altar with crystals. Finding our personal power will help expand our self-love, confidence, esteem, value.

**Questions to ask yourself:**

Do you speak your truth with everyone?
Do you hold back in certain relationships?
Do you have trouble swallowing?
Do you clear you throat lots?
Do you get throat infections?

# December 17

## Healing with Crystals
## By Selena Urbanovitch

For as long as I can remember, I have been fascinated with crystals, wanting to know their healing qualities, and working with them on myself. There are so many books out there that have so much information on crystals. I definitely have a few I love to go to when wanting to know more about a crystal. When finding one for yourself, you just need to trust that the right one will show up when you are looking for it. I am a strong believer that the crystal calls to you when you need it the most. I also believe they leave you.

The power of rose quartz helps the wearer to be more open to love, starting with one's self. Citrine brings in abundance in all aspects that the wearer is needing. Abundance of love, money, acceptance, abundance of anything.

Which crystals can you work with today?

# December 18

## Speaking Your Truth
## By Salli Sebastian Walker

*"Someone once asked me how I hold my head up so high after all I have been through. I said, it is because no matter what I am a survivor, not a victim,"* ~ *Patricia Buckley (1).*

No one should have to know what the inside of a courtroom looks like, but I do. For over thirty years, I have been a licensed massage therapist helping hundreds of individuals achieve wellness by delivering caring and ethical, therapeutic massages. This was my life path. Then one sunny day in July, my profession was turned upside down! An individual stepped into my protective bubble without permission.

Licensed massage therapists know there are standards and protocols that exist when working professionally on clients. It is one of the reasons we are required by law to be licensed. So, wouldn't you think it makes sense that when receiving bodywork on yourself, ethical care should be given to you, too? My massage was to be given to me on a beautiful afternoon. I booked this session from a trusted professional, so I thought. That day this person decided to cross into my protective space. I lay frozen on the table unable to move! I fled as soon as I was able. I was in shock!

I lay awake all night, frightened and in disbelief? The next morning, I chose to speak my truth by reporting this incident to the police. An investigation began and the case continued for nearly a year. Every few months, I was ordered by the state to show up in the courtroom. Had I not been present in the courtroom, the case would have been dismissed. I was present each time a new date was set. The date of the trial finally arrived. I was placed on the stand

and cross-examined for over thirty minutes by the lawyer. Then the moment of truth arrived as the judge spoke. She found his "behavior egregious." He was guilty and she sentenced him.

No person should be victimized during a massage session or ever for that matter. Find the survivor in you and speak. I hope this story helps you see that no matter what, *you* matter.

# December 19

## Light Up your Energetic Boundaries
## By Paula Marie Rennie

*B*efore we can create authentic connections with others in our day, it is vital to our energy and wellbeing that we check in first with our body's wisdom. This way we can be responsible for our own energy needs and happiness, creating healthy boundaries in our relationships.

We can create clear heartfelt intentions for our desires that draw to us the energy, people, and situations that are uplifting, supportive, and fulfilling. We also can hold a strong space and container for our energy that does not let outside negativity or others unwelcome energy in.

Start your day authentically glowing with this empowering exercise.

- Sitting or standing ground your feet into the Earth, become aware of your body and allow your cleansing breath to gently flow.

- Imagine expanding your energy out around you and create a golden energy bubble. This is your safe and powerful energy container.

- Breathe in through the top of your head a cleansing magical white energy. Feel it filling up your entire body and out to the edges of your energy bubble. Fully exhale clearing away any heaviness or negativity, let it all go.

- Notice your energy. Have parts of it been left with others or in a situation? Bring it all back to you and fill up your energy bubble.

- How is your body feeling? What support do you need to feel good?
- What does your heart desire? What do you want to experience? What actions do you want to create? How can you show up as your best self today?
- Imagine calling to you all of the qualities that you desire. Call forth strength, love, courage, peace, and joy …. Keep that list going with all your own qualities that you desire.
- Feel all of these qualities ignite your energy and light up the boundaries of your bubble. Let your entire being expand out and be in awe of this powerful and divine energy.
- Imagine placing mirrors on the outside of your energy bubble. These reflect away any negativity.
- Take a moment to appreciate how good it feels to be you, and how much being your best self is needed by others in this world.

# December 20

## Be Kind to Yourself
## By Danielle Fierro

*T*here was a time when I was not very nice to myself. In fact, I was downright mean. What made it worse was that I could not get away from myself. I said things to myself that I would never say to a family member or friend. Have you ever done that? Have you beat yourself down because you made a mistake or did not get things perfect? Thankfully, through a lot of self-work, I realized what I was doing. Awareness is key. I learned that the ultimate form of self-care was to be kind to myself. No matter what is going on externally, it is important to be your own best friend. Things do not get any better by pushing, prodding, or bullying yourself. You can get just as far, and further, by being kind to yourself.

I used to get so upset with myself when I made a mistake. I learned that mistakes and failures are okay, especially when I used those same mistakes to learn the lesson and make different decisions.

Another act of kindness is to forgive yourself. There is absolutely nothing that you can do to change the past. Holding on only brings the past forward, keeping you in what feels like a prison cell of shame, blame, and guilt. None of those emotions feel good or help you in growing as a person. They are toxic and only create more toxicity. Forgiving yourself allows you to release those emotions, learn from the situation, and be able to move forward with the wisdom that you gained.

Give yourself time and space to grow. There are so many times that we want immediate change, but that does not always happen. I have done that quite often, especially when it comes to my health. Sometimes it is not about pushing yourself through something that may not even be meant for you but about giving yourself time and the space to figure out what *is* best for you. Maybe what you were doing really did not fit your lifestyle or maybe you are in a new stage in your life.

These are just a couple of examples. There are so many ways that you can be kind to yourself. You are deserving of the very best. You are worthy of the very best. If you cannot be kind to yourself, who will?!

# December 21

## Affirm Self-Love
## By Paula Obeid

*I*magine walking through your day even after your cup of coffee and only using 5% of your brain to tend to your daily tasks. Most tend to think only teenagers are not fully present, however neuroscience has shown that most of our behavior and emotions depend on 95% of our subconscious brain.

The brain is like a computer hard drive; all the trauma, thoughts, and experiences since birth are filed in your subconscious brain. Many of the thoughts and experiences have built up beliefs like "I am not enough," "I am not loveable," or "I cannot accomplish my goals."

Our thoughts create our beliefs that create our reality. We can change our life experiences by changing our beliefs. The bulk of our brain activity is beyond our conscious awareness and has stored many limiting beliefs.

Science shows that we can reprogram limiting beliefs using intentional effort. The twenty-eight-day rule states that it generally takes twenty-eight days to create a new habit. The first weeks are often the hardest to shift a perspective in our life, but it gets easier.

Below is a method for tapping into the subconscious mind that can be utilized to identify areas we want to shift our subconscious beliefs and create a different perspective in life.

- First use automatic writing to identify an area in your life that may need a different perspective. I suggest starting with the area of self-love asking, "What area of my life can I love myself more?"

- Spend a few moments with your journal doing automatic writing and contemplating the question.
- Writing in a journal allows you to tap into your subconscious emotions and beliefs. Without judging whatever you wrote in your stream of thought, identify any negative self-talk or an area loaded with emotions.
- Create a positive affirmation addressing the negative self-talk. Complete the statement, "I am ___."
- During the next month, whenever the negative self-talk shows up, be gentle and patient and use your affirmation. Preferably do this aloud but silently works since we are changing a belief and reprogramming the subconscious brain.
- Reinforce the new belief you are creating during the day by saying your affirmation at any time, writing it down daily, and using Post-it notes at locations you can see throughout the day. Ignore any thoughts that you are not doing it correctly or that the affirmation is not working. You are reprogramming your subconscious beliefs!

# December 22

## You Have the Music in You
## By Ellen Elizabeth Jones

*M*usic has the power to evoke memory, capture a moment, and shift a mood. It is a powerful tool to raise your vibration. When you hear music you enjoy, your brain releases dopamine, a chemical that positively shifts your mood. Studies show that listening to music can benefit overall wellbeing, help regulate emotions, and create happiness and relaxation in everyday life. The benefits include:

- Lessens stress and decreases anxiety.
- Improves memory and cognitive function.
- Eases physical and emotional pain.
- Increases feelings of comfort and connection.

You can bring music into your life by attending live shows, making your own music, or creating a playlist of music that brings you joy!

Music has the ability to inspire us to dance like no one is watching.

Dancing is one way to connect your spirit, instinct, and intuition with the physical movements of your body. So often we view our mind, body, and spirit as separate entities. When you add music and movement, the three converge and integrate. In allowing yourself to connect fully, you are showing yourself love and care. Dancing can free you from the ego's controlling grip so that spirit within you can quickly *move* you to follow intuitive nudges that protect, guide, heal, and support in the present moment. Dancing is about freedom, expression, and allowing your instincts to move through your physicality. In removing inhibitions or self-criticism while you dance, you can perform an act of self-acceptance and self-expression, which are both forms of self-love. The most important aspects of dance are connecting your spirit, instinct, and intuition with the physical movements of your body. In allowing yourself to connect fully, you are showing yourself love and care on multiple levels at once.

So today, find some music that resonates and dance like no one is watching. The ability to have an impromptu "dance party" creates an uplifting release and connection with your soul. I hope you dance!

# December 23

## Manifesting
## By Symone Desirae

Ever wonder why some people are able to manifest their reality regardless of the obstacles that have come their way? They always have a smile on their face and are capable of creating their actuality despite being in need of something. Somehow, the thing they needed the most comes into their life almost seamlessly. I remember observing people with these 'blessings' and thinking "How are they manifesting this? Where am I going wrong with my manifesting?"

It did not click until I had heard a spiritual teacher say, "You must feel it to receive it!" You can write it down, and say it all you want, but if you cannot truly feel the emotions of it, then you will not acquire it.

What are some things you want to manifest in your life at this moment? How would this make you feel when it is in your reality? Get specific about what you want to attract into your life and write down a minimum of thirty qualities that pertain to this.

An example would be manifesting a romantic relationship; the specifics could be a loyal person, good communication in the relationship, someone who is family oriented, and trustworthy. Remember to get particular with your list as the universe gives us exactly what we ask for and believe our reality to be.

When you are done writing down your list, reflect back every day, reading it to yourself or saying it aloud while being aware of how it makes you feel to have this in your life. Do this over the course of thirty days making sure to do it at least once a day if not more. Taking the time to not only write down and say these words out aloud, but also feeling the emotion with each one will bring it to fruition.

# December 24

## Dress Your Future Self
## By Tanya Thompson

*H*ow you feel in your own skin significantly impacts how you present yourself to the world. We have all heard the saying, "look good, feel good." Scientific research has found that the way you dress can impact how you think and impact other activities like physical performance, attitude, and behavior.

We all get stuck in a rut, wearing some of our favorite clothes well past their fashion periods. There is nothing wrong with your favorite sweatshirt, complete with paint stains and holes. However, many occasions require us to dig deep and present our best self. For these times, it is important to have seasonal go-to clothing in your closet that allows you to feel your absolute best. Look for clothing that makes you feel strong, confident, powerful, and smart.

One of the best activities I have done for myself in recent years is engage with a personal shopper at my local department store. They may also be called a professional stylist. At most large department stores, like Nordstrom or Macy's, this service is free, and you get to set your budget ahead of your dressing room consultation. Based on the information you have shared, the personal shopper will scour the department store for you, including items on sale, and have everything ready for you in a private dressing room. This saves you hours of time and frustration. It also gives you an opportunity to try clothing suited for your body style, allowing you to accentuate your best features.

Here are a few tips to make the most of your experience with the self-love of looking and feeling your absolute best:

- Plan your budget in advance. It can be as low as $100 for a new top or bottom that you can mix and match with clothing you already own.
- Decide if you want to dress for a specific type of occasion or to add a few new pieces to extend a season.
- Let the professional do their job. They will pick clothing and sizes ideal for your body type. Let them help you try different styles so that you can decide what feels best on your skin and most importantly, how it makes you feel emotionally.

Ask yourself if you can conquer the day in this outfit? Yes, you can.

# December 25

## Flowing with Life
## By Yumie Zein

Perhaps the biggest grace we can give ourselves is to allow ourselves to be taken into the flow of life. So many of my previous years were spent in the desire to control or forcefully navigate the events of my life. There were times when it felt like I was thrashing around and having a tantrum against the Universe because things were not going "my" way. That is because in my mind there was no possibility that any other outcome could possibly be better than my way's outcome.

As with many things in life, lessons keep coming back to teach you if you do not get it the first, second, third, fourth or however many times it takes. After being faced with the reality that my desire to force an outcome was coming from an extremely limited perspective of what really is possible in this expansive universe, I allowed myself to try what I called "experiments with the universe." During times and situations where a wave of overwhelm would pass over me because things were not working out the way I was expecting, I would take a moment and visualize myself stepping back from the entire situation. I would then visualize a river with many branches flowing in front of me, which represented the infinite possibilities and outcomes available. I would then ask to flow with the one branch that has the strongest, clearest energy and see myself being taken with it, trusting that this is indeed the path of least resistance. There were times when I was consciously aware of what the energy in that river branch meant i.e., the decision or direction I should take, and then there were other times when surrendering the need to know was a big part of it.

The magical part was observing what unfolded after that process. As my own desire to feel "in control" eased off, I realized I was giving myself the grace and gift of flowing with an energy that is beyond space and time. The same energy that creates magical waterfalls, powerful volcanoes, stars, and galaxies can create unlimited ease and abundance in my life if I would only allow it to.

# December 26

## Thou Shalt Not Should Thy Self!
## (With Love to Louise Hay)
## By Charel Morris

*Y*ears ago, as I began my spiritual training at a new church in West Hollywood serving people facing a brand new 'epidemic' AIDs. I wanted to study with this minister and began years of training. And had the wonderful opportunity to watch Louise Hay at her *HayRide*.

Louise became famous for her book *You Can Heal Yourself* and many more. But one night at the *HayRide* she said something I have never forgotten. She introduced 'The Eleventh Commandment' and to this day I follow this commandment as it is chiseled in my heart and my mind. Here is her Commandment: *Thou Shalt Not Should Thy Self!*

Very simple, yet so powerful!

Think for a moment, how often do you *should* yourself or others? In your mind or out loud. I am sure you have experienced someone lovingly or otherwise telling you what you *should* be doing or *should* have done. And you just let it in. Then you realize that word – that judgement is stuck within you. It has left you feeling wrong, doubting yourself or maybe frustrated with yourself that you did not stand up to that person judging you.

And maybe you realize that this is not the only time someone "Should-ed all over you!" Yes, Louise had a great way to drive this healing home! When did you "Should-ed on Yourself?"

It is time to step out and let the universe know you are not willing to "should" on yourself or one else from now on. Not your partner, parents, friends, strangers, or people at work. Now you cannot control how others talk but you can choose if you are going to accept it into your heart or your mind. This is a very important decision for you to make to allow you to practice self-love.

Here are a couple of ways to clear the should wounds and step into self-love.

Forgive yourself and know you are perfect. Forgive others and know they like you are perfect.

Realize that most are not aware of the effect their words have on others.

Stand up and honor your Eleventh Commandment and experience the self-love that comes from your decision to make this change. Actually, following her commandment is the only thing I suggest your 'should do'! And please do it with love.

# *December 27*

## Through the Eyes of Self-Love
## By Talia Renzo

I look in the mirror.
I see you for who you are/
Your reflection couldn't be clearer.
In my eyes you are a superstar.

You are truly beautiful, inside and out.
I know you've had your heart shattered,
But here we stand, confident and proud.
We finally realize that we do matter.

I embrace you for all that you are.
I accept you for all that you are yet to be.
Together, we have come so far.
The deeper I look, the more I see me for me.

Your smile glows and radiates.
Your eyes are deep with compassion.
Your heart is pure and holds no hate.
You are beautiful, kind, and passionate.

I will continue to love you.
I will continue to support you,
No matter how many times people try and devalue.
I will always see and love you from this point of view.

This poem was written from my own personal experience of self-love and self-sabotage. I wanted to include this poem to demonstrate that if you want to live in the light, you must reveal your shadows. No matter how dark your shadows are, they are a part of you, but they do not identify your identity.

# December 28

## Through the Eyes of Self-Sabotage (upside down)
### By Talia Renzo

This poem was written from my own personal experience of self-love and self-sabotage. I wanted to include this poem to demonstrate that if you want to live in the light, you must reveal your shadows. No matter how dark your shadows are, they are a part of you, but they do not identify your identity.

I physically wrote this poem to mirror my interpretation of self-sabotage. I wanted you, the reader, to experience this poem from a different point of view. It's not easy to live in a world that feels upside down. But I want to illustrate that it is possible to revert your image, and interpretation of how you see yourself and your situation.

By Talia Renzo

# December 29

## Define Self-Love
## By Kim Richardson

Self-love can mean different things to different people. When you think of self-love what comes up for you? I challenge you today to journal about your definition of self-love.

What does it look like?

What does it feel like?

What practices do you need to put in place?

Now, let's take things a bit deeper. For the next questions, I want you to be truly honest with yourself. Once you answer the questions, decide if you may need to make some changes in yourself, your routine, your relationships, or your life in general.

Do you need outside validation?

Do you have a gratitude practice?

Am I playing small?

Do you have feelings of unworthiness?

What habits do I have that make me unhappy?

Do I judge myself?

Can I graciously accept compliments from others?

Take some time with these questions, journal your answers. I like to write the date when I journal. Then as time passes, answer the questions again. You will find it interesting how your answers change as time passes. As you re-do the questions and see the growth you have had, celebrate and honor all that you have accomplished.

# December 30

## Say What? Love Myself?
## By Sarah Berkett

I look in the mirror,
and I see a stranger looking back.
Your impurities couldn't be nearer.
Your flaws reflect and the glass begins to crack.

I see your pain.
I see you hiding behind your mask.
You are who you are with nobody to blame.
I see your wounds from when you were under attack.

I don't love what I am seeing.
I see your smile on the outside.
On the inside I can hear you screaming,
trying to break through the glass and be alive.

I wish I could love you,
but people have proven you to be unworthy.
I know you just want somebody to love you.
I hear you crying for mercy.

When the glass shatters,
I cannot put you back together.
a whole life, permanently scattered.
We will be unloved forever.

My mother always said, "You are so selfish." She would say this whenever I did something for myself instead of others. My mother defined others as my sister, my brother, my father, herself, my neighbors, my cousins, on and on and on. It is no wonder that I grew up with that sick feeling in the pit of my stomach whenever I did the smallest gesture for myself. I felt like I was bad if I did not put the needs of others before my own. Every single time I did something for myself, my mother's voice would haunt me and again I would feel that same sick feeling and I was tired of it.

If you find yourself in this state of mind, I highly recommend that you try the following simple exercises daily.

Become Mindful—People who have more self-love tend to know what they think, feel, and want. They are mindful of who they are and act on *this* knowledge, instead of acting according to what others want for them.

Practice Good Selfcare—You will love yourself more when you take better care of you and your basic needs. Practice exercise, good nutrition, proper sleep, and healthy social interactions.

Concentrate On What *You* Need First—By staying focused on what you need, you turn away from those old behavior problems or patterns that get you into trouble and keep you stuck in the past.

# December 31

## Free Movement and Energy Play
## By Tabitha Weigel

hen was the last time you let your body move without boundaries, rules, or fears? When you simply allowed your body to flow, dancing and releasing energy in a natural rhythm that brings you joy, pride, and the love of self as if you were a child with no worries. It may have been just yesterday or years ago. Either way today is the day to move. To play. To dance and let that inner child of yours move freely. Yet, as the loving adult, it is also on you to recognize the opportunity within this play, the opportunity to nourish the body with movement, nature, breath, energy clearance, and overall health. This is your time to play, yet also give love to that perfectly imperfect body of yours.

First, you must give yourself the permission to be—to be silly, wondrous, sensual, daring, and true to you—to not hold judgement over yourself and to be thankful for the body you are so blessed to inhabit here on mother earth. Put some music on or embrace the quiet. Set your space in a way that calls to you and your heart. I come alive when I am outdoors in my backyard amongst the trees and fresh air with a playlist that matches my mood. The air fills my lungs, sun warms my skin and the sounds of home fill my heart with gratitude. When ready, I start with a few deep cleansing breaths and then … I just vibe.

Yes, I incorporate some common and basic stretches, exercises, dance, yoga, or shakti moves within my flow, but none of it is planned. There is no counting. There is no remembering. There are only intentions of stimulating and opening my chakra centers, getting my blood pumping and my mind free of stress. Allowing the energy within and around me to move through me and my auric field with ease, I circle my hips, shake out energy with a solid shimmy, swing my arms around my torso, stretch to the skies, throw in a few leg kicks and lunges, and then slow down and roll my neck, breathing through any tension my body may hold. I give love to my body, nourishing it physically and energetically, creating a moving mediation if you will. It is a meditation of play, of acceptance and love, of free movement and of gratitude for the life our body holds.

# Reference/Bibliography

Debbie Rosas and Carlos Rosas. The Nia Technique, Harmony Books

Heart Math Institute, Heartmath.org

Hay, Louise. *You Can Heal Your Life*, California, Hay House Inc, 1999

Hay, Louise. *You Can Heal Your Life*, California, Hay House Inc, 1984

Sparrow Christy, Lynn. Evolutionary Spirituality and the Edgar Cayce Readings. Venture      Inward. October-December, 2011.

Williams, Paul and Ascher, Kenneth. "The Rainbow Connection." 1979. The Muppets.

Cole-Whittaker, Terry. *What You Think of Me Is None of My Business*, New York, Berkley an imprint of Penguin Group. 1988.

Holmes, Ernest Shurtleff, The *Science of Mind*. New York, Dodd Mead & Company. 1938

"Reclaiming Your Heart: A Journey to Living Fully Alive". – Denise Hildreth Jones, 2013

"Can We Gain Strength From Shame". "TED Radio Hour" with Guy Raz, www.npr.org. March 11, 2013

"Why Pain and Suffering are Necessary if You Want to Feel Happy by N.A. Turner" – www.medium.com/the-ascent. July 31, 2019

Hay, Louise. *You Can Heal Your Life*, California, Hay House Inc, 1999

Rumi. "A Quote by Rumi." Goodreads, Goodreads, 2021, www.goodreads.com/quotes/9726your-task-is-not-to-seek-for-love-but-merely.

https://www.quotespedia.org/authors/p/patricia-buckley

Bryne, Rhonda. *The Secret*, Oregon. Atria Books, Beyond Words Publishing, 2006

https://www.intensivejournal.org/

www.waitbutwhy.com

Beth Johnson, SilentPlaceWithin.blogspot.com, "First You Sigh, Toning in Meditation, Creating the Vibrational Gateway to Wonders of the Universal Mind.")

# Show us some love!

We are so excited you picked up our book! By doing so you are sharing in our mission to change the world, one person at a time as it starts with *you*.

Now, you can show us some love! If you liked the book, please go to Amazon.com and post a review letting others know how much you loved it.

Reviews are extremely important on helping this book reach as many people that may need it. All the royalties earned from the sales of this book are donated to two different charities of which both are a 501c3;

**The Time Out Shelter**, a women's shelter to aid women to leave an abusive relationship and get back on their feet. This amazing organization offers many classes and programs to help these women heal and learn to love themselves. The Time Out offers: Emergency shelter to women and their children, including basic essentials and a broad range of supportive services as well as Transitional housing for families leaving the emergency shelter.

If you feel guided, you can also support their organization by visiting their website:

timeoutshelter.org

**The Sunlight Alliance Foundation (SLAF)** was created by Sunny Dawn Johnston who is the leader in teaching those to love themselves. The mission of Sunlight Alliance is to assist humanity whether that's emotionally, physically, spiritually or mentally. brings hope and support to people in the Arizona community who are battling diseases either emotionally, mentally, physically, or those who have been burdened with catastrophic circumstances in their lives and thus cannot cope alone in day-to-day living. The SLAF continues to express the importance of self-development and self-reliance while providing this transitional assistance that individuals and families need to grow and develop.

If you feel guided, you can also support their organization by visiting their website;

https://sunnydawnjohnston.com/sunlight-alliance-foundation

# Meet the Authors

We encourage you to connect with the authors that contributed to this beautiful project. Feel free to visit their websites and/or drop them a message if their exercises had an impact on you in some way. Authors are listed alphabetically by first name to find them easier.

If you are looking for more support, be sure to join our Facebook community to connect with the authors and others who are on their journey to loving themselves more.

facebook.com/groups/134307215508450

**AMY I KING**, is a certified life coach and international best-selling contributing author of *Inspirations: 101 Uplifting Stories for Daily Happiness, Manifestations: True Stories of Bringing the Imagined into Reality, The Grateful Soul: The Art and Practice of Gratitude, and The Courageous Heart: Finding Strength in Difficult Times.*

Amy has overcome a plethora of life challenges. Her greatest joy is in helping others move past personal blocks and old beliefs to transform their lives. She welcomes the opportunity to work with you to help you create your phenomenal life.

**Connect with Amy:**
Email: yourphenomenallife585@gmail.com
Phone: (916) 718-0914 text/call.

**ANN MARIE ASP** is a spiritual intuitive who focuses upon healing modalities and wellbeing practices. She is a gifted Reiki and shamanic Reiki master. She has completed her master certifications for both healing modalities. She uses her love and knowledge of crystals and aromatherapy in her practice. Her true passion for dance and music has led her to certifications in Ageless Grace and the Nia white belt training. Ageless Grace is referred to as "Timeless fitness for the body and brain." Nia is a "sensory-based movement practice that draws from martial arts, dance arts and the healing arts."

**Connect with Ann Marie:**
Email: anniem0410@hotmail.com

**ASHLIE BRADLEY** is a self-love motivator, yoga and crystal practitioner, modern day mystic, and creator of *Soul Sprinkles*—a crystal infused, full-moon-charged facial toner/aura mist. Her services include chakra alignment, personalized yoga guidance, crystal healing, and self-love support.

**Connect with Ashlie:**
Facebook: Ashlie Denice Bradley
Instagram: Soulrenity_love
Website: Soulrenitylove.com
Email: Soulrenitylove@gmail.com

**BERNADETTE RODEBAUGH** is the author of *Believe IT to Receive IT* and is a "miracle-ologist" with a mission to guide and remind you that you are the miracle magnet in your own life. Through her personal experience, Bernadette has learned that miracles are an inside job; however, people must first believe and see their miracles as they call them into their lives, which she teaches in her professional and personal coaching, workshops and mastermind groups. Bernadette resides in Grand Junction, Colorado, with her husband, son, and rescued pit bull.

**Connect with Bernadette;**
Website: themiracle-ologist.com
Facebook: miracleologist
Instagram: The Miracle-ologist
Email: miracles@bernadetterodebaugh.com

**BONNIE LARSON** is a spiritual mentor and healing minister, also teacher of HeartMath's Coherence—the alignment of the heart and mind to the subconscious, where the healing begins. Her passion is empowering others to reach their highest possible potential while living a joy-filled life.

Bonnie is a certified past life regression hypnotherapist, gateway dreamer, ordained minister, and life-long student of religion, spirituality, science, and history. Her inspiring book, *Flying So High*, was an Amazon #1 bestseller in the category, world aviation history.

A published author and accomplished business executive, she serves local government, public schools, holistic health, and wellness activities.

### Connect with Bonnie:
Visit her website to claim your free gift; flyingsohigh.com
Facebook: <u>bonnielarson</u>
Email: bonnie@flyingsohigh.com & bonnie@bonnielarson.net

**CAROLAN DICKINSON** is a psychic medium, angel communicator, bestselling author, and soon-to-be licensed counselor. As a psychic medium, she will get to the heart of the matter quickly and uncover the most urgent needs of your spirit or that of your deceased loved ones. Carolan believes that one of the most critical missions she has in this life is helping others learn how to connect and communicate with their own spiritual teams.

Most recently, she published her first fiction novel and Amazon bestseller, *Three Full Moons.*

**Connect with Carolan:**

Website: carolandickinson.com
Facebook: carolandickinson
Email: carolan903@gmail.com
Instagram: carolandickinson

**CARRIE NEWSOM** is an author, entrepreneur, missionary pastor's kid, Reiki master, MSW, and mama to four incredible children who have special needs. She has organized support groups, advocated for people with special needs, and currently serves as the Illinois chapter leader for The Foundation for Children with Neuroimmune Disorders. Carrie believes that learning to love her authentic self has invited magic and peace into her life, and she would love to share that gift with you!

**Connect with Carrie:**

You can follow Carrie's blog at carrienewsom.com, on Facebook at Carrie Newsom, and her business, Nonah & Bean, at NonahAndBean.com.

**CHAREL MORRIS** is a minister, practitioner, energy healer, writer, ceremonialist and shaman. She loves to work with quantum energy as it supports moving into higher vibrations or frequencies that cannot be accomplished within our traditional time and space world. With over forty years of experience, she moves seamlessly between various healing modalities. Often combining ancient knowledge with state-of-the-art thinking and scientific research, Charel weaves decades of skills, knowledge and experience to fast track you into breakthroughs to understand and heal your issues and challenges. She is comfortable working with individuals, business owners and large groups of people.

### Connect with Charel:

Be sure to visit Charel's website and request your free gift;
StoneCirclepro.com
Email: Charel@CharelMorris.com
Speak with Charel: calendly.com/charelm/what-s-next

**COURTNEY PARREIRA** is a holistic educator and family partner. Her mission is simple: invite connection, balance, and abundance into homes and communities one heart at a time. She is passionate about ushering in a new parenting and educational paradigm rooted in harmony and compassion. With both her holistic education and collaborative family coaching, she helps to transform roadblocks and limitations at home and in the classroom into freedoms and opportunities. She does so using her background in alternative education, emotional intelligence, heart coherence techniques, restorative practices, basic astrology, and her own intuitive nature.

**Connect with Courtney:**

Website: courtneyparreira.com

Email: courtneywparreira@gmail.com

**CRYSTAL COCKERHAM** is a Spiritual Mentor, Certified Red Tent Facilitator, International Best-Selling Author, & founder of Wisdom Awakens, LLC, Crystal Cockerham works with awakened, empathic women to unlock the shackles of pain, shame and self-condemnation so they can reclaim their sovereignty and liberate themselves from the world's perceptions. Discover her other published works at: crystalcockerham.com/published-works.

**Connect with Crystal:**

Website: crystalcockerham.com

Facebook, Instagram, Pinterest & Twitter: WisdomAwakens

Email: Support@CrystalCockerham.com

**DANIELLE FIERRO** is a transformational coach, motivational speaker, energy worker and Reiki master providing a space of safety and encouragement to allow her clients to work through their challenges and move into the life they want. Her services include individual and group transformational coaching, Reiki healing sessions, motivational speaking engagements, and engaging workshops and classes.

### Connect with Danielle:

Facebook: DaniFierroLifeofLotus
Instagram: dani_fierro_lol
Email: DaniFierro@lifeoflotus.com

**DEE DEE REBITT** is a proud mom of two amazing daughters, who are twenty and twenty-six. She is an independent business owner and a mind, body and spirt practitioner, a third-degree Reiki master and teacher, certified crystal healer and psychic medium. She also creates natural healing products for friends and family. After embarking on her own personal healing journey, Dee Dee was drawn to create a healing circle for women to safely share their voice and feel supported. Recently after healing the divine masculine within, she noticed that men were beginning to reach out for her guidance and support.

**DEBRA MOORE EWING** is a certified hypnotherapist with specific training in past life regression. She is here in this incarnation to be of service to others whether in the realms of spirituality, helping those transition, or to comfort those grieving. She also has a vast knowledge of codependency with a passion for helping others live their happiest and best life. She is studying for her bachelor's degree in metaphysical science in conjunction with becoming an ordained minister. She is working on finishing her two books *Recovered, from a Woman Who Loved Too Much* and *Faith … When I Met Jesus.*

### Connect with Debra:

Website: YourSpiritualConnection.net
Facebook: Debra Moore Ewing
Email: YourSpiritualConnection@mail.com

**DELORES GARCIA, MS, CPT, CLC** is a personal success coach who guides her clients to reprogram their mind for unprecedented personal success. Do you feel stuck?! Delores finds that most goal-setters have personal drive, yet are restricted by negative mind chatter: old, recycled, habitual thoughts that actually block their path to abundant health, wealth, and happiness. She helps them rewire their operating system (their subconscious mind) to accomplish more work in the flow, while enjoying incredible work/life satisfaction.

Visit Delores' website to schedule a complimentary thirty-minute "Success Session."

**Connect with Delores:**

Website: DeloresGarciaCoaching.now.site/home
Facebook: DeloresGarciaCoaching
Instagram: FLYGirl.Nation
Email: DeloresGarciaCoaching@gmail.com

**DENISE KIRKCONNELL** is a mother to two teenage children. She has spent the past ten years studying and learning self-love practices. She is a mind, body, spirit practitioner, sister, daughter, aunt, friend, and mother. Her life's mission is to share with others what she discovered has helped to guide her in her own personal journey.

**Connect with Denise:**

Email: denisekirkconnell@yahoo.com

**DOMINIQUE TRIER** is a bilingual consultant with experience in finance, social media, marketing management, public speaking, event management, website design, sale generation, and data and market analysis. After her father's late-stage cancer diagnosis in July of 2018, she has devoted herself to empowering others to improve their lives and businesses.

**Connect with Dominique:**

Email: dominiquetrier@gmail.com

Facebook: dominique.trier.5

Instagram: dom_emma

Website: dominiquetrier.com

Additional Business Coming Soon: dandylyn.com

 **ELLEN ELIZABETH JONES** is a spiritual teacher, soul oracle, mystic messenger, speaker and author. Are you feeling the call? Are you ready to experience your own divinity with greater awareness, love, grace and peace? Ellen is passionate about empowering others to experience their personal mind-body-spirit connection, activating and claiming their own natural healing gifts as they listen to the wisdom of their own inner truth. Ellen is available for private sessions, workshops, and retreats.

**Connect with Ellen:**

Website: ellenelizabethjones.com, sacred-journeys.org

Email: ellen@ellenelizabethjones.com

Facebook- Group- GoldenKeyMessages

Instagram: ellenejones444

Amazon Author central: https://www.amazon.com/Ellen-Elizabeth-Jones/e/B06XZM8H4Q%3Fref=dbs_a_mng_rwt_scns_share

**EWA BLASZCZAK** is an intuitive, a medium, a spiritual guide a power speaker, and a mentor for leaders and teams. She will help you figure out who you are, what your purpose in this life is, what are your unique gifts and talents, and how you can create a life you are passionate about. If you are ready for a deep dive, Ewa will help you to reconnect with your spirituality, discover your higher self and provide you with guidance available to you in your Akashic Records. She is the author of *Colors, User's Guide to Human Interactions* and *Agile Management. Simple, Brief and to the Point.*

**Connect with Ewa:**

Spirituality: akashicreadings.eu
Mentoring: ewablaszczak.com
Email: info@ewablaszczak.com
Facebook: Ewa Blaszczak

**FLORENCE ACOSTA** is a Certified Registered Nurse Anesthetist, Reiki master, Women's circle facilitator and an Abundance mindset mentor. Outside of her twenty-five year career in health care, Florence's life experiences inspired her work with women in circle and guiding women to attract abundance in multiple areas of life. Her purpose is to inspire and empower women to live the highest vision of their life. She believes in continuing her personal development and learning for her constant evolution. She enjoys all things metaphysical, traveling, hiking, being in nature, writing, and meditation.

**Connect with Florence:**

Emails: abundanceflows888@gmail.com
Facebook: abundanceflows888
Instagram: _abundanceflows_

**GIULIANA MELO** is an international spiritual teacher, certified angel intuitive, best-selling author of Love Yourself to Health and eighteen multi-author compilations, a speaker and prayer facilitator. She is also the CEO of KindnessCrewCalgary Society LTD.

**Connect with Giuliana:**

Be sure to visit Giuliana's website to claim your free gift.
Website: GiulianaMelo.com
Facebook:HealWithGiulianaMelo
Email: healwithgiulianamelo@gmail.com

**GLORIA DAWN KAPELLER** specializes in coaching people to heal from the past. A Reiki master, Theta healer and access consciousness practitioner, she currently lives in Stettler, Alberta, Canada with her husband Jon, and two sons, working as a healthcare aide for Alberta Health Services. She is a bestselling author of two books: *Behind The Eyes: A Story of Perseverance*, a story about her life, and *Walking Through The Storm Weathering Life After A Stroke*, a story about her son Byron, who had a stroke at seven, and their journey together dealing with life's ups and down and life's challenges and lessons.

**Connect with Gloria:**
Email: glow_kapeller@hotmail.com

**GRACE REDMAN** has owned and managed one of the most successful employment agencies in the S.F. Bay Area for the last twenty-two years. She is also a success and transformation coach who helps guide others to diminish their negative mental chatter and create a fun and fabulous life that they love. Grace has a passion for guiding others to step into their authentic selves to own their power and as a result they inspire others and raise he collective vibration. Her services include: one-on-one sessions, mentoring packages and VIP days.

**Connect with Grace:**
Website: daretoachieve.com
Facebook: grace.s.redman
Email: grace@graceredman.com

**JAMIE RUDOLPH** is a licensed esthetician, certified laser technician, and yoga teacher. The realization of "true health and beauty starts from the inside out" led her to pursue an education in holistic nutrition, aesthetics, and yoga.

As a skincare specialist, she integrates advanced aesthetics with a holistic approach focused on natural beauty, plant-based nutrition, and lifestyle wellness. Her services include skin wellness consultations and treatments, holistic lifestyle coaching, and private yoga sessions. Jamie is currently attending nursing school.

**Connect with Jamie:**

Website: Wholebeautyaesthetics.com

Email: Wholebeautywellness@gmail.com

Instagram: wholebeautyaesthetics

Facebook: wholebeauty.aesthetics.wellness

 **JANICE STORY** brings over thirty years of expert horsemanship into her work as an equine assisted coach. She is co-founder of The Freedom Way Equine Assisted Coaching Certification Course, a certified Reiki master/teacher, mind, body, spirit practitioner and a published author and speaker.

Janice's compassionate and gentle spirit provides safety for others. She has a strong connection with her eight horses who have been a big part of her own healing. With the presence and unspoken language of her horses, she helps create an opening for healing and transformation to occur in ways beyond that of human contact alone.

**Connect with Janice:**

Website: janicestory.com

Email: janice.story@me.com

**JANNIROSE FENIMORE** is a bearer of light and a weaver of words. As a seasoned healer, she assists students and clients in tapping into the rich wellspring of personal power that awaits their discovery. Author of *Loving Outside the Lines— Lessons from an Earth Angel*, Jannirose is a messenger for one of God's special angels—her son Charlie who is blessed with Down syndrome. Together, they share his inspiring words of hope and healing with the world. The pair lives near magnificent Mount Shasta outside of Weed, California.

### Connect with Jannirose:

Website: LessonsfromanEarthAngel.com

Facebook: Lessons from an Earth Angel

**JOANNE EISEN** is an inquisitive talk show host, inspiring others to embrace their potential. Using her gifts as a evidential medium and truthsayer, she opens ways for profound healing. The same hidden treasures JoAnne spent years running from helped others become conscious of their connection back to self, seeing the multitude of life options, ultimately bringing freedom and peace.

JoAnne provides psychic and mediumship readings to groups and individuals, teaches classes, launched an online community center to coach, train, and mentor others. She is a certified tarot card reader and studied with many internationally known mentors in the metaphysical field.

**Connect with JoAnne:**

Email to: joanne@reachtheunlimited.com
website at: reachtheunlimited.com
Facebook: reachtheunlimited.
YouTube: Reach the unlimited with Joanne Eisen
Join the Reach The Unlimited community at:
reach-the-unlimited.mn.co/share/REVdmq8L5GTr_6lL?
utm_source=manual

**JUDITH MANGANIELLO**, founder of A Peace of the Universe Spiritual Bookstore in Scottsdale, Arizona, a New Jersey native. Judith is an Author, Teacher, Open Channel with Spirit and the Angelic Realm since childhood as well as a Numero-logist, Transformational Healing, Ordained Minister, Reiki Master and Spiritual Advisor.

Judith will help you discover your own self-love, soul purpose and define your Light. One of Judith's special gifts is energy elevation the transfer of negative thought energy into results that are positive. People who have been fortunate to meet her know that she offers the most powerful, healing, and loving hugs.

**Connect with Judith:**

Website: JudithAndSpirit.com
Email: judith999apotu@gmail.com,
Phone:480-338-9815.

**KAREN COWPERTHWAITE**, also known as "Souly Sister," is an intuitive, soul nurturing, transformational life coach. She supports women to reset their mentality to a healthy and positive one so they can stop getting stuck in negative self-talk and manifest the life they want to live.

She facilitates vibrational energy shifts and is a messenger for the angels and spirit. Through intuitive readings and life coaching, Karen is a teacher and a guide who is here to inspire and provide a soulful toolbox that individuals can use to move forward—strong and confident in all areas of their lives. Claim your free training *Free Yourself from Self-Sabotage* on her website.

**Connect with Karen:**

Website: soulysister.com
Facebook- Join Karen's Community: livinglifesoulfully
Email: karen@soulysister.com

**LISA A. CLAYTON** is the Founder of Source Potential, Inc and a successful business entrepreneur, author and spiritual leader who offers more than thirty-five years of experience in corporate consulting and professional transformational coaching.

Lisa combined Source Potential's proven leadership learning process with her intuitive abilities to establish the *Inner Leader Movement*, aligning individual's spiritual gifts with their life service. As an ordained angel minister, Lisa is known for her lifechanging intuitive transmissions. Lisa is a HeartMathâ master trainer-coach, teaching renowned stress-reduction and resiliency techniques.

Author credits include *365 Days of Angel Prayers, 111 Morning Meditations, 52 Weeks of Gratitude Journal and Heaven Sent.*

**Connect with Lisa:**
Website: lisaaclayton.com or subscribe to patreon.com/lisaaclayton to receive a free gift.
Facebook: lisa.clayton.9
Instagram: lisaanneclayton
Email: lisa@sourcepotential.com

**LISA SEYRING** is an emotional energy healing practitioner, poet, and founder of Healing FreeQuencies, Inc. Finding great joy in discovering the wisdom held in her heart, it is Lisa's passion to help others listen for the guidance of love and wisdom in their own hearts. Through both a conversational approach and Reconnective Healing®, Lisa helps individuals identify and release unproductive thought constructs and resulting emotional pain. Alleviating this unease opens a path of deep healing. The resonance of the heart wisdom captured through her channeled poems heals and soothes.

**Connect with Lisa:**
Website: HealingFreeQuencies.com
Facebook: healingfreequencies
Email: Lisa@HealingFreeQuencies.com
Instagram: lisaseyring

**MARGARET (MAGGIE) HONNOLD** writes based on her experiences as a registered nurse, health educator, widow, mother, grandmother, former Alzheimer's caregiver, and animal lover. A graduate of Kankakee Community College and Eastern Illinois University with degrees in Nursing and Health Education, she has worked in both the hospital and community health settings, enabling her to write insightfully of life's circumstances. Her first book, *The Cloisonné Heart: A Memoir of Love*, was a #1 Amazon bestseller and a finalist in the International Book Awards for 2018. She has contributed to several compilation books, all of which are available on Amazon.

**Connect with Margaret:**
Email: machonnold@yahoo.com

**MARIE MARTIN,** of Candid and Classy, is an inner beauty cultivator, who helps women cultivate their inside beauty and deliberately shape their perceptions of themselves. Marie uses beauty and fashion as tools to heal those parts that have been hurt and mistreated. With a women's relationship to fashion being a representation of how she views herself, clothing is a powerful change maker. Marie's journey to a better-loved reflection has given her the kind of firsthand experience that lets her relate to other people's struggles.

**Connect with Marie:**
Website: candidandclassy.com

**MARILYN MILLER** helps women in business who want to embrace self-care while making the money they deserve. She provides simple tools for reducing the juggling act many women face. Forced to resign her dream job due to illness, she learned how to regain health and create a six-figure income. Marilyn is Founder/Director of the Women's Health and Wealth Academy, which provides private and group programs to support women who want to "be well and well paid." She is an award winning author of *America's Holidays & Heroes: Roots & Stories of All Faiths*

### Connect with Marilyn:

Website: MarilynMillermentor.com
Email: revmarilynmiller@yahoo.com
Facebook: Marilyn.miller

**MARSHA JOHNSON** is an intuitive psychic and physical medium as well as certified tarot card reader. Marsha believes anything is possible when co-creating with spirit and is a master manifester, well versed in the law of attraction. She is one who always looks to find joy in any situation. She hosts classes and workshops as well as private sessions providing guidance and encouragement to those in search of spiritual fortitude and personal empowerment. Marsha is also an artist who combines her artistic ability and spiritual connection to create auragraph readings as a way of presenting a psychic or mediumship reading.

**Connect with Marsha:**

Website: joyful-soul.com
Email: Marsha@joyful-soul.com
Facebook: Marsha.JoyfulSoul

**MELANIE MORRISON** of Sacred Shifts LLC is a Let Your Yoga Dance teacher, author, professional angel card reader, public speaker, women's circles facilitator, and psychic development teacher. She is passionate about helping people shift their energies and mindsets by connecting to nature's cycles through music and movement. Using cards, she guides clients through the deepest waters of the heart and helps them clear blocks to reach their highest potentials! Her sacred circles and classes empower everyone to connect to their inner guidance, leading to lives full of freedom, purpose, and joy!

**Connect with Melanie:**

Email:Contact@melaniemorrison.info
Website:MelanieMorrison.info
Facebook: SacredShifts1
Youtube: Melanie Morrison
Instagram: MelanieMorrison.info

**MINDY LIPTION** has had a visit from Archangel Michael twice. She is a believer of miracles after giving birth to triplets. Mindy was married for sixteen years until they felt the need to go on to different paths. Self-love became a part of life she needed to grasp a hold on. Another miracle appeared when she was hired to the president's office at a university. Mindy is now a Joy Facilitator and you can connect with her on her Facebook where she is spreading joy.

**NANCY MEIKLE-MOUSSEAU** is a certified Usui/Holy® Fire III Reiki master teacher, practitioner, author, and vision board workshop coach. Her services include; reiki sessions, classes and educational talks on the benefits of reiki for seniors. Nancy hosts vision board workshops using law of attraction and affirmation techniques, all infused with Reiki energy. Nancy helps clients connect to their spirit through reiki, where she has created a safe, nurturing environment in her home for you to relax, receive and rejuvenate. Holy Fire® is the registered service mark of William Lee Rand.

### Connect with Nancy:

Website: relaxreceiverejuvenatewithreiki.com
Email: nancymousseau3@gmail.com
Facebook: Relax, Receive, Rejuvenate with Reiki by Nancy

**NANCY TOFFANIN** is a higher priestess practitioner, and a Goddess Master. She is currently taking the "Living the Goddess Master Life, Certified Instructor Course." She is certified in crystal healing and is a Reiki master. Her mission is to use her incarnate wisdom to heal and empower people. In her healing practice, she helps people work through traumas. She teaches classes to develop self-love. In her practice she has a variety of techniques to release the deep trauma that is stored in the chakras. She has been an esthetician for thirty years, and she owns Bella Luna Esthetics.

### Connect with Nancy:

Email nancydvall@shaw.ca
Facebook: Nancy Toffanin or Bella Luna Spa
Website: bellalunathunderbay.com
Instagram: nancydvall (Fancy Nancy)

**NANETTE GOGAN-EDWARDS** is a wife, mother, mother-in-law, grandmother, home cook, customer service expert, aspiring author, and believer. Nanette appreciates all feedback, questions, comments, and ideas.

### Connect with Nanette:

Email: nangogans@gmail.com
Facebook: nangogan

**PAULA OBEID** shares love with the world as a master hypnotherapist & National Association of Trans-personal Hypnotherapy trainer, Reiki master, intuitive life & business coach, and author while serving on several nonprofit boards. She motivates individuals that are ready to create an extraordinary life! Utilizing proven effective strategies and modalities, she supports achieving your business and personal goals with a compassionate approach, intuition, reflective listening skills, storytelling, and knowledge gained from her life experiences. Paula's passions are reflected in her heart-centered endeavors that provide services, education and products that allow individuals to lovingly move through life with joy and ease. Be sure to visit Paula's website to claim your gift.

### Connect with Paula:

Website: PureBlissAlways.com
YOUTUBE: PureBlissAlways
Facebook: Pure Bliss Always
Email: love@pureblissalways.com

**PAULA MARIE RENNIE** is a medium, life coach and EFT Practitioner. With compassion, humour and inspirational wisdom, she shares heartfelt messages from loved ones in spirit and guides powerful shifts in awareness and emotional breakthroughs. Her passion is to empower and teach people how to believe in themselves and their greatest potentials, transform relationships, health conditions and limiting beliefs by developing their intuition and confidence to trust and express themselves authentically. She offers readings, personalized coaching, EFT sessions and transformational self-development programs.

Co-author of *The Last Breath, True Stories of the Afterlife & Messages from Heaven, an Amazon top seller.*

**Connect with Paula Marie:**

Learn more about Paula Marie by visiting her website.
Website: paulamarie.com
Facebook: paulamarierennie
Email: paula@paulamarie.com
Amazon: Paula-Marie/e/B08JFYR7YN

**SALLI SEBASTIAN WALKER** is a licensed massage therapist with over thirty years of experience and a member of the America Massage Therapy Association. As an independent contractor, her jobs included working with the Chicago Bears, the Chicago Bulls, PGA golfers and movie directors. She enjoys working-out, exploring alternative methods of self-help, photography, painting, crocheting, and cooking. When Salli is not traveling the states in her Cricket camper, she can be found hanging out with her husband, her daughters or her amazing extended family.

**Connect with Salli:**

Website: SalliWalker.amtamembers.com
Email: salliwalker@mac.com

**SARAH BERKETT** is an animal intuitive, Reiki master, professional spiritual teacher, Angelic Life Coach, and author. Her unique brilliance will awaken your intuition with grace and ease and ignite magical possibilities within your soul. She teaches infinite spiritual connections with your animals by shaping, nurturing, and revealing that magical spark within all of you.

**Connect with Sarah:**
Website: beamerslight.com

**SELENA URBANOVITCH** is an Angel Empowerment Practitioner ™ and a Goddess Master ™ She has also been a hair stylist for over thirty years. Selena is an author, as well as a Reiki practitioner. Selena uses her gifts not only to heal and empower herself on a deeper level, but to assist in creating a world where everyone can realize their interconnectedness with each other, see their value in their dreams, and reach for the stars. Selena lives with her husband and two beautiful children in White Rock, British Columbia.

**Connect with Selena:**

Email: Selena.urbanovitch73@gmail.com
Facebook: selena.urbanovitch73
Instagram: selena_angel_intuitive

**SHERYL GOODWIN-MAGIERA,** founder of Wellness Within, is a certified life coach and hypnotherapist, bestselling author, writer, facilitator of women's retreats/workshops, and international trainer. She connects women to their hearts to uncover who they were created to be. Sheryl provides heart-centered guidance, filled with humor and love to support their journeys, and uncovers blocks and barriers to help move them forward. She loves yoga, the outdoors, writing, reading, adventure, traveling and spending time with family and friends. She's honored to support your path of discovery and wellness within; it's time to step into your light and shine. Connect with your heart and Sheryl's to schedule a complimentary discovery session.

Coauthor of *Kindness Crusader* and *Spiritual Leader Top Picks*

### Connect with Sheryl:

Website and Weekly Blog: SherylBeth.com
Email: magierasheryl@gmail.com
Facebook: sheryl.magiera
Instagram: sheryl_goodwin_magiera

**STEPHANIE FONTAINE** is a certified Usui/Holy Fire® III and Holy Fire® III Karuna® Reiki master teacher, reflexologist, Access Bars® practitioner and author. She is also the creative force and founder of an eight-week program, The Fierce Warrior. Stephanie's services include: online classes, Reiki, reflexology and Access Bars® sessions. She is an empathic, intuitive energy practitioner with the ability to recognize and illuminate synchronicity in everyday life. Holy Fire® and Karuna Reiki® are registered service marks of William Lee Rand. More information on the The Fierce Warrior program can be obtained by contacting Stephanie.

### Connect with Stephanie:
Email: infinityenergetics8@gmail.com

**SUSAN HOYLE** is a writer, blogger, speaker, spiritual coach, Reiki master, NRT practitioner, business manager at Hoyle Chiropractic, wife of twenty-five years and proud mother of Brittany (21) and Dylan Hoyle (17). Her passion is assisting women in coming home to themselves through spiritual coaching, intuitive energy healing, emotional release and workshops. Be sure to visit Susan's website for your free gift.

**Connect with Susan:**
Website: susanhoyle.com
Facebook: showmewellness
Instagram: ShowMeWellness
e-mail:susanhoyle4@gmail.com

**SYMONE DESIRAE** is a higher priestess practitioner ™, Reiki practitioner, and an intuitive oracle card reader. She has learned and used these modalities to help herself and others to heal from their trauma in life. Symone was born and raised in Calgary, Alberta where she still resides with her boyfriend and their two fur babies, Zahara and Chloe. She loves being outside in nature, especially at her family's cabin in B.C., collecting crystals, and spending her free time with her cats.

**Connect with Symone:**
Facebook: Symone Desirae- Divine Intuitive
Email: Symone.hg@hotmail.com

**TABITHA WEIGEL** is one tough warrior mama and energy worker. She is a cancer survivor who has devoted her life to healing, accepting, and (with compassion) transforming her emotional and physical body. Her focus is on shedding the energy of victimhood while embracing her survivor-hood with power, hope, and faith. She is a certified

Reiki practitioner, and tarot spiritualist, who works one-on-one with clients, but also holds communal space as a circle facilitator and workshop host, encouraging those she works with to reclaim their power, their health, and their sense of self, through holistic and spiritual practices.

**Connect with Tabitha:**

Website: linktr.ee/spiritualwarriormama
Instagram: spiritualwarriormama
Email: sunnysidetarotbyTabitha@gmail.com

**TALIA RENZO** was tremendously bullied at a young age in school and her dad passed away unexpectedly all in the same year. Shortly after her dad's passing, Talia was abandoned and grew into adulthood rather quickly. As she experienced great loss, it brought her to a higher appreciation for wisdom. Talia decided not to fall the same way as everyone else did through life's greatest trials. Instead, she took all of her pain and channeled it into passionate writing and pearls of wisdom.

Coauthor of *52 Weeks of Gratitude Journal, Life Coach,* and *Kindness Crusader.*

**Connect with Talia:**

Website: taliarenzo.com
Facebook: taliarenzo

**TONIA BROWNE** is a bestselling author, teacher, and coach. She is a strong advocate of inviting fun into our lives and encouraging people to see their world from a new perspective. Her writing includes coaching strategies interspersed with spiritual insights and personal anecdotes.

Enjoy Tonia's books *Spiritual Seas Diving into Life: 12 Strategies for Riding the Waves of Life* and *Mermaids: An Empath and Introvert's Guide to Riding the Waves of Life*. Dive into her website and enjoy her beautiful mermaid cards and apparel, part of her Diving into Life Series.

**Connect with Tonia:**

Website: ToniaBrowne.com
Amazon: amazon.co.uk/-/e/B00ZATHS4M
amazon.com/Tonia-Browne/e/B00ZATHS4M
Facebook: Time4Tonia

**TANYA THOMPSON** lives in Charlotte, NC with Andy, the love of her life, and their English bulldog, Mayberry. She is a leader in the financial services industry, where she has worked for over twenty years. Her lifelong mission is to help others lead a better life. Tanya holds a BS in financial management and an MBA from Clemson University. She is a fellow in the Life Management Institute (FLMI), an associate in the Academy of Life Underwriting (AALU) and a certified bourbon steward. Tanya and Andy enjoy live music, Kentucky bourbon, and sharing time with friends and family.

**Connect with Tanya:**

Instagram: thompsontanya

**VIRGINIA ADAMS** is a master energy healer, artist, intuitive mentor, and business development mentor. Creating a legacy of love, she has positively impacted many individuals with her writing, workshops, personal, and professional mentoring and website design.

Virginia is the author of the award winning, bestselling book, *The Universal Gravity Code – A Guide to Personal and Global Enlightenment,* Co-author of *52 Weeks of Gratitude Journal, Healer – 22 Expert Healers Share Their Wisdom to Help You Transform, Owning Our Truth – Stories Our Souls Came Here to Tell and 365 Days of Self Love.* Be sure to subscribe to Virginia's website to receive a free guided meditation download.

**Connect with Virginia:**

Websites: vadamsenterprises.com, linktr.ee/VirginiaAdams
Facebook: gingersreconnection333
Instagram: virginia_adams_inspirations
Email: Virginia@VAdamsEnterprises.com

**VONNIE L. HAWKINS, LCSW** discovered her healer's journey in 2014 after an extended work drought led her to finally commit to a consistent meditation practice. She founded and leads a nonprofit that promotes trauma-informed social change projects, and teaches about family violence in a graduate social work program, helping to build an army of trauma-informed, well-trained social workers. She is a Reiki practitioner, essential oils dabbler, and breaker of old stories that no longer serve her. She is muse and harmony vocalist to her singer-songwriter husband of twenty-four years, Shawn, with two rescue pup fur-children, Luna and Rosa, in Louisiana.

**Connect with Vonnie:**
Websites: vonniehawkins.com, SocialWorx.org
Facebook: VLHawkinsInc
Twitter: VonnieCo
Instagram: IAmVonnieH
Email: Vonnie@VLHawkins.com

**YUMIE ZEIN** is an Egyptian creatrix, akashic alchemist, hypnotist and divine feminine circle holder. Through the twists and turns of her own awakening journey, she unknowingly stumbled across her greatest passion—empowering women to explore and embody their authentic selves. Her purpose is to assist in awakening and raising the divine feminine, whether it be through offering alchemy tools for transformation, Soul Coaching, Healing Hypnosis, Akashic records facilitations or sacred women's circles and events. Through her Egyptian ancestry, she incorporates ancient wisdom with new Earth teachings to bring about unique transformation and self-empowerment.

**Connect with Yumie:**

Facebook: Yumie1111
Instagram: yumie1111
Website: OfHeavenOnEarth.Com
Email: Yomna@OfHeavenOnEarth.Com

Made in the USA
Columbia, SC
02 November 2021

48014039R00396